The In
Hostel

England
Wales
Scotland

**Edited by
Sam Dalley and Alice Lockett**

 Independent Hostels UK

ISBN 978-0-9565058-5-9

Independent Hostel Guide 2016: England, Wales and Scotland
25th Edition, Editors: Sam Dalley and Alice Lockett
British Library Cataloguing in Publication Data. A catalogue record for this book is available at the British Library ISBN 978-0-9565058-5-9
Published by: The Backpackers Press, Speedwell House, Upperwood, Matlock Bath, Derbyshire, DE4 3PE. Tel: +44 (0) 1629 580427.
© Independent Hostels UK, 2016

Printed by: Sterling Solutions, www.sterlingsolutions.co.uk
Cover Photos by Robert Morris Images www.robertmorrisimages.co.uk

Front Cover Photograph: Alnwick Town Centre, Alnwick Hostel (pg 282).
Back Cover Photographs: Alnwick Hostel (pg 282), The Hides (pg 284).
Internal Photographs: Photo on page 1 taken at The Hides (pg 284). Photo page 4 taken at Palace Farm (pg 86). Photo on page 8 taken at Spring Hill Bunkhouse (pg 286). Photo of people on page 18 taken at Morags Lodge (pg 494). Photos on page 401 credited to Tony Jones. Photo on page 507 credited to Brain Sutherland. Photo on page 308 credited to stayinwales.com. Photo on page 514 credited to Ike Gibson. Other pages contain photos provided by the bunkhouses and hostels.

Distributed in the UK by Cordee Books and Maps,
3a De Montfort Street, Leicester, LE1 7HD. Tel: (0116) 2543579

ISBN 978-0-9565058-5-9

9 780956 505859

CONTENTS

INDEPENDENT HOSTELS UK

Independent Hostels UK is a network
of 350 bunkhouses, hostels and group
accommodation centres. These provide a
unique form of accommodation ideal for
groups, individuals and families who enjoy
good company, travel and the outdoors.

GREEN TOURISM

The IHUK office and many of our hostels are members of the Green Tourism Business Scheme. We are audited by their assessors to ensure we are using the most environmentally friendly practices. Green Tourism is the largest sustainable certification body of its kind. Look out for the Green Tourism symbols on the hostel pages to see who has achieved the grading. The IHUK office has been awarded GOLD.

to find your perfect place to stay

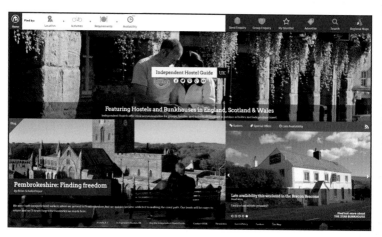

Wouldn't it be great to send an enquiry to all the hostels and bunkhouses that would be ideal for your next holiday, then sit back and wait for them to contact you with details and availability?

You can do this using the 'Send Enquiry' button on our website. Simply select your requirements, including facilities and location. Then view the list of hostels that has been selected for you and write a message to send to them all.

KEY

Dormitories

Private rooms

Family rooms

Blankets or duvets provided

Sheets required

Sleeping bags required

Hostel fully heated

Some areas heated

Drying room available

Showers available

Cooking facilities available

Shop at hostel

Meals provided at hostel (with notice)

Breakfast only at hostel (with notice)

Meals available locally

Clothes washing facilities available

Facilities for less-able people

Computer with internet facilities

WiFi available

Within 1 mile, 3 miles, 5 miles of a NCN cycle route

Bike shed

Affiliated to Hostelling International

Simple accommodation. Clean, friendly and basic

Best Price Guarantee

	Accommodation for groups only
	Dog friendly
	VisitScotland Quality Assured
	VisitWales Quality Assured
	VisitEngland Quality Assured
	Bronze, Silver or Gold Green Tourism Business Award
pp	**per person**
GR	**Ordnance Survey grid reference**

BEST PRICE GUARANTEE

The hostels and bunkhouses displaying the Best Price symbol promise that you will get their accommodation at the lowest price available if you contact them direct. Contact them by phone, email, via the hostel's own website or via www.independenthostels.co.uk and you can be rest assured that you will get the best rates.

Why do we offer a Best Price Guarantee? Booking engines such as Hostelworld and Booking.com take a commission of between 12-20 % from your money before they pass payments on the bunkhouse or hostel. This increases the price you pay and means the hostel / bunkhouse has less money to spend on your stay. Four European hostel networks have joined forces to encourage guests to book direct. Founded by Independent Hostels of Germany, the Best Price Guarantee scheme is co funded by Swiss Hostels, Europe's Famous Hostels and Independent Hostels UK. To find out more about Best Price Guarantee and to see a list of all the European hostels offering it take a look at:

www.bestprice-hostels.com

WHAT ARE
INDEPENDENT HOSTELS ?

Independent hostels have shared areas, such as self-catering kitchens, and they often have sleeping accommodation in bunks. Bunkhouses, camping barns, backpackers hostels and outdoor centres are all types of independent hostels.

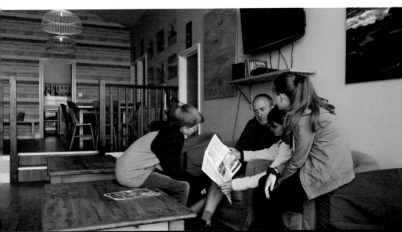

Unique Qualities of Independent Hostels:-

▲ Self-catering facilities available

▲ You can stay for just one night

▲ There are private bedrooms, en suite rooms and dorms

▲ Wild locations for outdoor activities

▲ City centre locations for independent travellers

▲ Families, individuals and groups are all welcome

▲ Hostels can be booked 'sole-use' for get-togethers

▲ No membership required

▲ Independent Hostels are all privately owned. Around 5% are also affiliated to YHA or SYHA marketing schemes.

The holiday ideas on the following pages are extracts from our website blog. Every week a new holiday idea is added. You can read the full articles on www.independenthostels.co.uk/blog

News and and special offers are added to our website every day. Follow our social media to be keep informed.

fb.com/independenthostelguide

@indiehostelsuk

@Indiehostelsuk

IndependentHostels

HOLY ISLAND

By Dave Mowle

We were staying at The Hides in Seahouses (p284) and had taken a short drive to Holy Island, leaving our car on the mainland and taking our bikes across the causeway. We intended to cycle back to The Hides but the romance of the island was luring us to stay longer.

We had to decide quickly, there were only 30 minutes left before the tide cut Holy Island from the mainland. To stay and see it all or cycle NCN Route 1 back to the hostel .

We stayed and it was absolutely the right decision. You can read about it all on www.IndependentHostels.co.uk/blog

By Sam Dalley

Our group of families stayed at Snowdon Lodge (p398) in the centre of the village of Tremadog, well known for its wide variety of climbing and gentle micro climate. It was fantastic to have the solid old house all to ourselves! Blessed with glorious weather, on our three day trip we climbed Snowdon, visited the intriguing village of Portmerion and swam in the sea off the Llyn Penninsula. All topped off with a Haloween party to remember! Read more about it on www.IndependentHostels.co.uk/blog.

Independent Hostels are perfect for group holidays. Use the group enquiries service on independenthostels.co.uk to find your perfect holiday with friends and family!

By Brian Sutherland

My family and I spent five wonderful days on Mull and surrounding islands based at The Shielings in Craignure (p468).

As we explored the site we came upon the communal bonfire which was dancing in the breeze and brightening up the families gathered around. We made friends with folk from Liverpool, Brighton and Dundee; and Shaggy the seventeen year old dog wrapped in a blanket, all enjoying the fire. A few big pans of fresh mussels from the Mussel Farm were cooked in a white wine and onion sauce. Scottish sea food is amazing! Why don't we eat more? Read more about our holiday on www.IndependentHostelGuide/blog

WATERFALL WALK

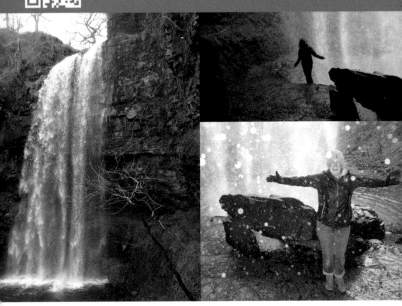

I have always half-dreamed of walking behind a waterfall, deafened by thundering water as I hide behind the curtain of sound. My dream came true in an unexpected place in the Brecon Beacons. Staying with a group of friends in a bunkhouse at the extraordinary Craig Y Nos Castle (p316), the receptionist told us about Henrhyd Falls.

By Rachel Sharratt

A steep but easy path leads from the Coelbren car park to a big noisy waterfall cascading into a perfect pool, set in a valley of trees. Here a path leads around the back of the waterfall to a cave where you can shelter as the water tumbles around you.

But why is the Craig Y Nos Castle extraordinary? A celebrity palace, a sanitorium and now said to be haunted. Find out more on www.IndependentHostels.co.uk/blog

By Owen Peters

Any physical problems I had along the way, were all of my own making; no excuses, just daft decisions. The Great Glen Way has some of the most exhilarating scenery and views you are ever likely to see. The hostels along the way have been well run with supportive and attentive staff. I would have hooked up with a lot more people if I hadn't been so tired at the end of my self inflicted route marches. Everyone seems to be supporting each other. If you have boots a backpack or waterproof, you're in the club. No registration required.

Find out more about Owen's adventures and the hostels he stayed in on www.IndependentHostels.co.uk/blog

By Sam Dalley

The Gower Peninsular pokes out of the south Wales coastline, westwards from Swansea. It was the very first Area of Outstanding Natural Beauty and is well known for the many varied beaches along its coastline. I discovered some glorious castles, un-promoted but brilliantly adapted for visitors. The combination of good facilities and emptiness made these castles feel like a personal discovery, set as they are in such atmospheric locations. To find out more about holidaying on The Gower have a look at www.IndependentHostels.co.uk/blog

MONKTON WYLD

GOTHIC MANSION

By Sam Dalley

What a privilege it felt to spend a night in this simply furnished ornate Gothic building. A peaceful atmosphere imbibes the building from the community's separate accommodation. There they live sustainable lives working the land, using compost toilets and the minimum of fossil fuels. Caring for Monkton Wyld Court (p70) is a role handed down to the community from its history as one of the first schools teaching how to live closely with the land and share decision making. Caring for us and other hostel and B&B guests provides the income the community needs to sustain the building. Again I felt privileged, this time to have the use of flushing loos and electricity!

To find out more about Monkton Wyld Court see www.IndependentHostels.co.uk/blog

NORTHUMBERLAND

For the first 3 nights of our Northumberland holiday we stayed at the wonderful Alnwick Youth Hostel. Cosily nestled in the midst of the historic town of Alnwick, we enjoyed all the comforts and surprises the hostel had to offer. A games room, complete with pool table, air hockey, football table, free WiFi, Nintendo Wii, TV and even a piano, kept us entertained in the evenings, while in the daytime we set out to explore the towns, castles and beaches around Northumberland.

You can read about Hetty's holiday on the Independent Hostel Guide Blog. www.IndependentHostels.co.uk/blog

Sheffield
160
153
158 164 156 46
148
166 154 162
152 150 136
142 138
134
167
144
Derby
Nottingham
124
Birmingham
122
Coventry
Leicester
132
Lincoln
Skegness
King's Lynn
126, 127, 128
125
130
Norwich
Peterborough
Northampton
Cambridge
Ipswich
100 102
Colchester
Luton
91
Oxford
82
London
92 to 99
Reading
90
86 88
Canterbury
Dover
80
Guildford
Salisbury
78
77
79
84
Hastings
Portsmouth
Brighton
76
Bournemouth
74
72

South England

KEY

45 - Hostel page number

45 - Page number of group
only accommodation

Berwick Upon Tweed

288

290
Wooler 291

A697

280

A68
292

276

274

A696

A68

270 272
A69 Haltwhistle
273

257 261
Carlisle

Hexham
266

265

264
263 262
Alston

268
A689

M6

258
260 Penrith

251
250
Keswick 249 247
253 246
252 244 242 Patterdale
254 255 240 210
238
232 236 231
233 234 248 230
224 217 218
228 205
Windermere
220 Kendal
222 226

216
Ulverston 214

A66

212

A66
Barnard
Castle
Brough

208
204
203

206 A684
Aysgarth

198
Ingleton
197

195

190
192
196

188

Workington

Wasdale Head
Coniston

199 200

201

B6160

A65

M6
A59
Skipton

ISLE of
MAN

Ramsey

293

Douglas

Castletown

Blackpool

Preston

Hebden Bridge
186

SCOTLAND

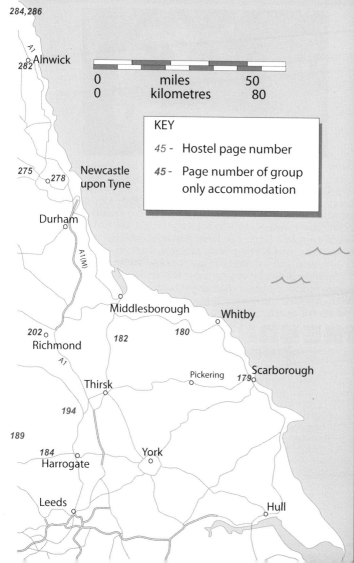

284,286

A1

282 Alnwick

0   miles   50
0   kilometres   80

KEY

45 - Hostel page number

45 - Page number of group only accommodation

275   278

Newcastle upon Tyne

Durham

A1(M)

Middlesborough   Whitby

202   *182*   *180*
Richmond

A1

Pickering   *179* Scarborough

Thirsk

194

189

184   York
Harrogate

Leeds   Hull

North England

JERSEY ACCOMMODATION
AND ACTIVITY CENTRE

ENGLAND

A 5 minutes' walk from the pretty fishing port of Gorey in St Martin (restaurants, bars and a regular bus to St Helier), the JAAC has a wide range of rooms including private en suites and dorms with shared showers. Facilities include 60 seat dining room, sauna, 2 large lounges, laundry, drying room, cycle storage and extensive outside space. Ball and board games are available as well as a TV and DVD player. Ideal for families and large groups who can often be in the same area of the hostel. Single sex dorms available. Breakfast included, packed lunches and a 2 course evening meals available. Camping with electric hook-up, running water and a shower and toilet block available. On-site activities include climbing wall and zip wire for under 12s, archery, bush craft and an all ages obstacle course. Off-site: a wide range of outdoor pursuits or "Escape from a Castle" by completing a range of physical and problem solving tasks. Beds, food, transport & activity packages available. Walkers and cyclists welcome.

DETAILS

- **Open** - All year, 8.30 - 20.00,
- **Number of beds** - 110 (Bunk 1x10 6x8 1x6 4x4) (En suite 1x6 2x4 2x3 4x2 2x1)
- **Booking** - First night deposit required. Full payment if less than 10 days before arrival. 20% deposit for group bookings.
- **Price per night** - Breakfast inc. Bunks £25-£30pp. Singles and en suite bunk £27-£32pp. Twin en suites £54-£64. Family 3, 4 & 6 en suites please enquire.
- **Public Transport** - No1 bus from Liberty Station, St Hellier to Gorey Pier (8 min uphill walk to JAAC) or No13 bus to Ramsons Garden centre. (5 min walk to hostel).
- **Directions** - Follow directions to The East and then Gorey. From Gorey Pier continue up the hill past the church take the next right, JAAC is 200m on your right.

CONTACT: Anna Stammers
Tel: 01534 498636
info@jerseyhostel.co.uk www.jerseyhostel.co.uk
La Rue de La Pouclee et Des Quatre Chemins, Faldouet, St Martins, Jersey, Channel Islands JE3 6DU

Cohort is a newly renovated hostel housed in an old Wesleyan chapel and schoolrooms in the centre of St Ives. It has spectacular original features and comfortable, contemporary rooms with custom built pod beds.

Facilities include free superfast WiFi, an in-house bar, lounge, courtyard, movie/TV room and a fully equipped kitchen with a small supermarket open 7 days a week next door. Sleeping accommodation is in private rooms and shared dorms. Storage for (surf) boards, bikes & bags is available. Helpful staff will be delighted to share with you all the delights that South West Cornwall and St Ives have to offer. Situated just 5 minutes from train/bus stations and lots of parking nearby. Less than a minute's walk to over 50 cafes, bars and galleries and seconds from St Ives' 5 spectacular beaches and the coastal path.

DETAILS

- **Open** - All year. All day,
- **Number of beds** - 64: 2x8, 6x6, 1x4, 2x dbl/triple, 1 x twin
- **Booking** - Book via website. Groups should email or phone
- **Price per night** - Beds from £20
- **Public Transport** - From Penzance Train get off at St Erth take branch line to St Ives, also National Express Bus from London and Newquay.
- **Directions** - From A30 take A3074 (St Ives), follow the road for about 2 miles into St Ives. At St Ives Harbour Hotel turn right into the main town and follow the road until it turns sharply to the right and goes downhill. At Nat West bank turn left. Cohort is past Co-op on Right. NO PARKING use local car parks.

CONTACT: Reception
Tel: 01736 791664
hello@stayatcohort.co.uk www.stayatcohort.co.uk
The Stennack, St Ives, Cornwall, TR26 1FF

PENZANCE
BACKPACKERS

Penzance, with its mild climate, its wonderful location looking across to spectacular St Michael's Mount, with all the coach and rail services terminating here, is the ideal base for exploring the far SW of England and the Scilly Isles.

Whether you are looking for sandy beaches and sheltered coves, the storm lashed cliffs of Land's End, sub-tropical gardens, internationally acclaimed artists, the remains of ancient cultures, or simply somewhere to relax and take time out, Penzance Backpackers is for you. Situated in a lovely tree-lined road close to the sea front, with the town centre, bus station and railway station only a short walk away. Accommodation is mostly in small bunk-bedded rooms with bed linen. Fully equipped self-catering kitchen, hot showers, comfortable lounge, lots of local information and a warm welcome all included.

DETAILS

- **Open** - All year, 10.00-12.00, 17.00-22.00,
- **Number of beds** - 30: 2 double, 1x 4 (double + 2 bunks), 3x6, 1x7.
- **Booking** - We require a deposit equivalent to the first night of your stay.
- **Price per night** - From £16 per person.
- **Public Transport** - Penzance has a train station and National Express service. 15 mins' walk from train/bus station or catch buses 1, 1a, 5a or 6a from Tourist Information/bus/train station. Ask for top of Alexandra Road.
- **Directions** - From Tourist Information/bus/train station either follow quay and promenade to mini-roundabout, turn right up Alexandra Rd, we are a short way up on the left; or follow main road through town centre until second mini-roundabout, turn left down Alexandra Rd; we are on right.

CONTACT: Mathew
Tel: 01736 363836
info@pzbackpack.com www.pzbackpack.com
The Blue Dolphin, Alexandra Road, Penzance, TR18 4LZ

Just three miles from St Ives' beaches and 5 miles from Penzance, Lower Penderleath Farm Hostel near St Ives provides self-catering accommodation in four twin rooms, one room with an alpine dormitory for 12 (large room with mattresses) and a family maisonette. All rooms are private and lockable, three rooms have twin beds and the fourth has a bunk bed. No bedding is provided. The hostel has a fully equipped kitchen. A dining room adjoins the kitchen and there are plenty of showers and toilets. Heating is by oil filled towel radiators and drying racks are provided. The self contained family maisonette has a small kitchen and private shower and toilet. The water on site is natural mineral water sold as bottled mineral water in 1989 and now visitors can cook, drink and shower in it. A picturesque footpath leads to the village of Cripples Ease just ten minutes' walk away where there is a pub that serves meals. The village of Halsetown, with its own pub, is also in walking distance.

DETAILS

■ **Open** - Easter to Oct incl. Open all day. Leave by 11am arrive between 2pm-8pm.
■ **Number of beds** - 24: 4x2, alpine platform of 12, 1x4 self contained maisonette
■ **Booking** - Please PHONE before arriving. Office hours 8.30am to 9pm
■ **Price per night** - £17pp. £34 twin room. £80 maisonette. Children full price, bring your own cot. 1 person per bed. Bring your sleeping bag and pillow.
■ **Public Transport** - Local buses pass the road end three quarters of a mile from the hostel. Service runs four times a day between St Ives and Penzance.
■ **Directions** - Pass Penderleath camping park on left and 300m further on right hand side you will find Lower Penderleath Farm and Hostel.

CONTACT: Russell Rogers
Tel: 07723 014567
rusrogers60@gmail.com www.stivescampingandhostel.com
Lower Penderleath Farm, Towednack, St.Ives, Cornwall, TR26 3AF

Tregedna Lodge offers comfortable, spacious accommodation. The Lodge has been converted to a high standard, yet keeping much of its originial charm and character. There are 24 bedspaces in a range of five bedrooms - single occupancy or shared. You can book a little space or the whole lot. All the facilities have disabled access and include; a shared, fully equipped kitchen and open dining area, a relaxing lounge with comfy chairs, laundry room with coin operated washer/dryer, separate showers and toilets. Bed linen is provided and towels are available to hire. There is ample parking for cars and boats and a secure area for bikes etc. The South West Coastal footpath is adjacent for walks with spectacular views and Maenporth beach, only half a mile away, offers a safe, clean, sandy beach. Nearby Falmouth has a wide range of restaurants, pubs, places of interest. Ideally located to explore the many delights of Cornwall, Tregedna Lodge has a 4-star grading by VisitEngland.

DETAILS

- **Open** - All year, all day (please phone between 9am-8pm).
- **Number of beds** - 24: 1x8,1x6,1x2, 2x4 / family (double bed and bunk bed)
- **Booking** - Booking essential. 25% deposit.
- **Price per night** - £20pp in dormitory style rooms, Family rooms £60. Enquire for group rates.
- **Public Transport** - Trains at Falmouth (1.5 miles). Buses run past Tregedna hourly during summer months, less frequently during winter months.
- **Directions** - By car from Truro take the A39 to Falmouth. At the ASDA roundabout go straight across. At the Hillhead roundabout turn right, go straight over the next two roundabouts and continue on this road for approx 2 miles.Tregedna is on your right.

CONTACT: Liz
Tel: 01209 200757 / 07979645946
tregednafarm@btinternet.com www.tregednafarmholidays.co.uk/
Tregedna Farm, Maenporth, Falmouth, Cornwall, TR11 5HL

FALMOUTH LODGE
BACKPACKERS

Falmouth's beautiful natural harbour provides a picturesque background to the main street of charming shops, restaurants, cafés and pubs. Voted the 2nd best coastal town, Falmouth is renowned for its sandy beaches, Pendennis Castle, exotic gardens, Arts Centre and the Princess Pavilion. Go sightseeing on ferries to St Mawes, Truro, Flushing and the Helford Passage. On a rainy day visit National Maritime Museum and the Ships and Castle leisure pool. Take advantage of watersports, fishing trips, sailing, diving, with tuition and equipment hire. Judi has moved back from Grenada in the West Indies to be your host at Falmouth Lodge. Judi welcomes guests to enjoy all Cornwall has to offer and has added her own character and flavour to the hostel. Relaxed, friendly and clean, Falmouth Lodge Backpackers is just two minutes' walk from the Blue Flag beach of Gyllyngvase and the South West Coast Path and eight minutes' walk into town and the harbour. Free WiFi and internet facilities. Free parking. No curfew. Complimentary tea, coffee and breakfast. Well-equipped kitchen and cosy lounge with TV/DVD and games.

             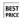 **BEST PRICE**

DETAILS

- **Open** - All year. 9am-12 noon and 5-10pm. Reception open from 5pm.
- **Number of beds** - 28: 2x2/3, 3x4/5, 1x6/7, 1 double en suite (some sea views)
- **Booking** - Telephone or email in advance. Walk-ins also welcomed.
- **Price per night** - From £19 per person
- **Public Transport** -   Train - change at Truro for Falmouth town station 250 mtrs. National Express to Falmouth. By air - London Stansted/Gatwick to Newquay
- **Directions** - On A39 look for Gyllyngvase Rd on right, then left to Gyllyngvase Ter.

CONTACT: Judi
Tel: 01326 319996, mobile 07525 722808
judi@falmouthlodge.co.uk www.falmouthbackpackers.co.uk
9 Gyllyngvase Terrace, Falmouth, Cornwall, TR11 4DL

EDENS YARD
BACKPACKERS

Welcome to this quirky, Camino inspired new hostel, just a short leafy lane from the world-class Eden Project. Keep things simple in spirit and pocket as you rest up or explore from this comfortably converted stable yard. Facilities include mixed bunk rooms, communal lounge and self-catering BBQ with courtyard kitchen. Free WiFi, and a simple toasty breakfast are also included. Full breakfast and evening meals are available on request.

Situated in Garker Hamlet near bustling St Austell, 2 miles from the Northwest Coast Path at Carlyon Bay and a little beyond enigmatic Charlestown, Eden's Yard is five miles off the Saints Way and nestled in the award winning Clay Trails. National Cycle routes 2 and 3 converge at the gate. Par and St. Austell mainline railway stations are both nearby providing easy access to Newquay, Truro and onwards to Falmouth.

Edens Yard can accommodate cars but only by prior arrangement.

DETAILS

- **Open** - April to September (inclusive). Arrive between 4pm and 10pm.
- **Number of beds** - 1x6, 1x8
- **Booking** - Book by phone or enquire by email.
- **Price per night** - £15
- **Public Transport** - Trains to St Austel or Par. Take bus from St Austal to Eden Project and short walk to hostel. Pickup from train station available for £5.
- **Directions** - Cars only by prior arrangement please phone for directions

CONTACT: Neal or Julia
Tel: 01726 814907
info@edensyard.uk www.edensyard.uk
17 Tregrehan Mills, St. Austell, Cornwall, PL25 3TL

Globe Backpackers Plymouth is located just five minutes' walk from the ferry port where boats leave for Roscoff and Santander. The hostel is close to all amenities and a short stroll to the famous Barbican waterfront, Mayflower Steps and city centre. Also near to the bus and railway stations. Excursions to Dartmoor, canoeing on the Tamar River, local boat trips, sailing and walking the coastal paths can be arranged from Plymouth. The theatre, sports/leisure centre, ice-skating rink and National Aquarium are a short walk from the hostel. Globe Backpackers Plymouth has 4, 6 and 8 bed dorms, plus 2 double rooms. Bedding and linen are included in the price. Fully equipped self-catering kitchen, TV lounge, separate social room and courtyard garden. Free WiFi. Free tea and coffee. Brits and overseas visitors all need to produce valid ID.

DETAILS

- **Open** - All year (phone for Xmas). Daily check in from 3.30-11pm only. No curfew.
- **Number of beds** - 38
- **Booking** - Please phone ahead to make a secure booking.
- **Price per night** - Dorms: From £16.50pppn. Weekly rates available. Private rooms from £38. There is a 50p surcharge for debit/credit card payments.
- **Public Transport** - National Express, local buses and various rail networks. Parking tickets available from hostel, which are cheaper than local metered parking.
- **Directions** - From train station walk up Saltash Road to North Croft roundabout, turn right along Western Approach to Pavilions on your left. From bus station walk up Exeter Street, across roundabout to Royal Parade, cross road to Union Street, Pavilions on your left. From Plymouth Pavilions walk towards the Hoe, turn left up Citadel Road, the hostel is in 100 metres on the right hand side.

CONTACT: Duty Manager
Tel: 01752 225158
info@plymouthbackpackers.co.uk www.exeterbackpackers.co.uk/plymouth/
172 Citadel Road, The Hoe, Plymouth, PL1 3BD

Harford Bunkhouse & Camping offers comfortable budget accommodation on the edge of South Dartmoor. An ideal choice if you are planning to start the Two Moors Way walk from south to north.

Run alongside a working Dartmoor farm, the bunkhouse offers dormitory style accommodation with bunk beds in each of the rooms. A kitchen, large seating area, toilets and showers are all within the bunkhouse.

The camp site is divided between two of the farms meadows. Campers can use the toilets and showers located within the bunkhouse buildings. Facilities include a wash up area, drying room, laundry facilities and disabled access. There are also two camping pods and a cabin in the meadows. These sleep up to 6 people each and have the same facilities as camping. Small campfires and BBQs are allowed at the farm's discretion. Children and dogs welcome.

DETAILS

- **Open** - All year. Open all hours.
- **Number of beds** - 40-50 beds
- **Booking** - Phone or email.
- **Price per night** - From £15pp. Camping pods and cabin £50 each. Camping £7.50pp.
- **Public Transport** - Yes, train or bus nearby
- **Directions** - From Ivybridge take Harford Road. Bunkhouse is 1.5 miles from Ivybridge in The Dartmoor National Park.

CONTACT: Julie Cole
Tel: 01752 691883 or 07968566218
julie.cole6@btinternet.com www.harfordbunkhouse.com
West Combeshead, Harford, Ivybridge, Devon, PL21 0JG

Powdermills Bunkhouse located right in the centre of Dartmoor National Park, is ideal for groups who wish to walk on Dartmoor or for kayaking groups wishing to tackle the white water rivers over the winter.

The Bunkhouse is run by Spirit of Adventure outdoor activity centre and many of their course participants elect to stay in the bunkhouse. All you need to bring is towels, your sleeping bag (or duvet and sheets) plus a pillow.

There are beautiful views across the North and South Moors and there is an excellent choice of local inns and restaurants within 5 miles. Powdermills Bunkhouse is an ideal venue for individuals or groups. Spirit of Adventure also run Dewerstone Cottage in the heart of the Dewerstone National Trust Estate.

DETAILS

- **Open** - All year.
- **Number of beds** - 26: 2x4, 1x8, 1x10
- **Booking** - By telephone or email
- **Price per night** - £15 per person per night. £12 for under 18's and students. Exclusive use £250 per night with a deposit of £100.
- **Public Transport** - Trains at Plymouth bus no 83 towards Tavistock to Yelverton Roundabout then take bus no 98 to end of road to bunkhouse (short walk)
- **Directions** - Follow brown signs to Powdermills pottery off the B3212 Princetown to Morehampsted road. Bunkhouse is first left turn after the pottery (there is a small sign on the road)

CONTACT: Martin
Tel: 01822 880277
martin@spirit-of-adventure.com. www.spirit-of-adventure.com
Powdermills Bunkhouse, Powdermills, Princetown, Yelverton, Devon, PL20 6SP

DARTMOOR
EXPEDITION CENTRE

Great for walking, climbing, canoeing, caving, archaeology, painting or visiting places of interest nearby, Dartmoor Expedition Centre has two 300-year-old barn bunkhouses with cobbled floors and thick granite walls. Simple but comfortable accommodation for groups, with bunk beds and a wood burning stove, radiant heaters (two in each area) and night storage heating (one in each barn). Kitchen area equipped with 2 fridges, water heater, electric stoves and kettles. All crockery and pans provided, and there is freezer space available. Electric appliances are coin operated (£1 coins). Solar hot water system for free showers in wash rooms. House Barn has the living area downstairs and upstairs sleeps 8 plus 5 in an inner cubicle. Gate Barn sleeps 11 downstairs and 10 upstairs. There are three upgraded rooms (2 double, 1 twin). Beds provided with sheet/pillow/pillowcase, sleeping bags needed.

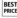

DETAILS

- **Open** - All year. 7.30 am to 10.30 pm,
- **Number of beds** - 39: 1 x 1, 2 x 2, 1 x 8, 1 x 5, 1 x 11, 1 x 10
- **Booking** - Book in advance with 25% deposit.
- **Price per night** - £14.50 pp (£16.50 in upgraded room). £350 exclusive use, £700 for two nights exclusive use. Discounts for longer lets depending on numbers.
- **Public Transport** - Nearest train station Newton Abbot. Summer buses to Widecombe (1.5 miles from hostel). Taxi fare from station £30.
- **Directions** - GR 700 764. Come down Widecombe Hill into the village. Turn right 200yds after school and travel up a steep hill past Southcombe onto the open moor. Continue for one mile until you reach crossroads. Turn right and take first left after 400yds. Hostel is 200yds on left.

CONTACT: Pauline
Tel: 01364 621249
pauline@dartmoorbase.co.uk www.dartmoorbase.co.uk
Widecombe-in-the-Moor, Newton Abbot, Devon, TQ13 7TX

FOX TOR
CAFÉ AND BUNKHOUSE

Princetown in Dartmoor is an ideal base for anyone wishing to spend time on Dartmoor whether it is to walk, climb, cycle, kayak or just relax and enjoy the spectacular scenery. Fox Tor Café Bunkhouse is situated near the centre of the village and offers self-catering accommodation for up to 12, in 3 rooms of 4. It is newly decorated, has central heating and a kitchen equipped with microwave, fridge, kettle, toaster and sink. There are separate male and female showers and toilets with under-floor heating. Bunkhouse guests have the option to use the drying room / store room (big enough for bicycles) and can book packed lunches and breakfasts for an early start. The café has a wood burning stove and hosts seasonal events and activities such as Christmas wreath making. Guided walks and off-road mountain biking are available and outdoor adventure holidays can be arranged to your requirements. WiFi and cycle hire now available. Contact Abbi or Dave for more details

DETAILS

- **Open** - All year. All day. Arrive from 4.30pm, leave by 10.30am.
- **Number of beds** - 12: 3 x 4
- **Booking** - Advisable with 50% deposit.
- **Price per night** - From £10.50 pp. £32.00 for 1 person in a private room. £35.00 for 2 in a private room. £38.50 for 3 in a private room. £42.00 for 4 in a private room.
- **Public Transport** - Trains at Exeter and Plymouth. Devon Bus 98 Tavistock-Princetown. Devon Bus 82 Exeter-Plymouth. First 272 Gunnislake-Newton Abbot.
- **Directions** - GR 591 735. Just off the mini roundabout in the centre of Princetown on the Two Bridges road (B3212). 20 mins' drive from Tavistock, 15 mins Yelverton, 35 mins Ashburton.

CONTACT: Abbi or Dave
Tel: 01822 890238
enquiries@foxtorcafe.com www.foxtorcafe.co.uk
Two Bridges Road, Princetown, Dartmoor, Devon, PL20 6QS

GALFORD SPRINGS
HOLIDAY FARM
ENGLAND

Galford Springs Holiday Accommodation is situated in rural Devon on a 300 acre farm nestled in the Lew Valley, overlooking some of England's most stunning scenery. It is ideal for families, groups, schools and clubs. Situated next to a 17th century Devon longhouse, the hostel is a recent conversion and contained within the same building is a free-to-use 15m indoor swimming pool and sauna. The main area is large and ideal for holding meetings and events as the furniture can be moved into a variety of configurations. This area also contains bunkbeds for 10 people and two single beds. In addition there are three en suite double bedrooms two of which also have a single bed in them. The hostel has all modern conveniences including pool table, table tennis and skittle alley. Outside there is barbeque area. It is recommended that a maximum group size of 15 people is ideal for the facilities in the hostel. Farmhouse B&B is also available with double en suite rooms. Dogs by arrangement.

DETAILS

- **Open** - All year.
- **Number of beds** - 22:1x13,1x4 (family),1x3 (family en-suite),1x2(double en-suite).
- **Booking** - Recommended
- **Price per night** - £25pp. Min £500,10 people or 5 for a two night stay. B&B £30pp.
- **Public Transport** - Bus route to Lewdown village, 1.5 miles from hostel
- **Directions** - Turn left off A30 at Sourton Services. Turn right at end of slip road then immediately left towards Lewdown. Follow for 6 miles then turn left, signposted Chillaton. After reaching Lewtrenchard Manor, turn left and further down the road take the right turn to Lew Mill. Turn left at T junction, Galford Springs is on the right.

CONTACT: Mr F. Harding
Tel: 01566 783264
claire_taylor1@btconnect.com www.galfordsprings.co.uk
Galford Farm, Lewdown, Okehampton, Devon, EX20 4PL

SPARROWHAWK
BACKPACKERS

Sparrowhawk is a small, friendly eco-hostel in the centre of Moretonhampstead, popular with cyclists, hikers, bikers, artists and photographers, located within the breathtaking Dartmoor National Park. Moretonhampstead is 14 miles west of Exeter and can be reached easily by frequent direct bus. Accommodation is in a beautifully converted, fully equipped stable, with solar-heated showers and a secure bike shed. High open moorland is close by for great hiking, cycling and off-road mountain biking, while the rocky tors rising up on the hilltops offer climbers a challenge. Wild swims in the rivers amongst woodlands or out on the moor are a must for the adventurous traveller. Magnificent stone circles, dwellings and burial sites of ancient civilizations together with wild ponies, buzzards, flora and fauna are all here to be explored. Moretonhampstead has shops, cafés, art gallery/studios and pubs serving good food/ beer. CTC/ Cicerone LeJoG cycle routes are on the doorstep.

DETAILS

- **Open** - All year, all day.
- **Number of beds** - 18: 1 x 14 plus double / family room
- **Booking** - Book ahead if possible by phone or email.
- **Price per night** - Adults £17. Under 14 £8. Double/family room £38/ £8 per child.
- **Public Transport** - Direct from Exeter Bus 359, indirect 178. From Okehampton or Newton Abbot Bus 173 or 179. Enquires Tel 0870 6082608.
- **Directions** - From Exeter, take the B3212 signposted on the one-way system at Exe Bridges. From Plymouth head towards Yelverton and then B3212. The hostel is on Ford Street (A382) 100 metres from tourist office.

CONTACT: Alison
Tel: 01647 440318 - 07870 513570
ali@sparrowhawkbackpackers.co.uk www.sparrowhawkbackpackers.co.uk
45 Ford Street, Moretonhampstead, Dartmoor, Devon, TQ13 8LN

Blytheswood Hostel is a detached wooden chalet in secluded woodland overlooking the Teign Valley on the eastern edge of Dartmoor. It is an ideal base for exploring rugged high Dartmoor and the delightful lower slopes rich in wild flowers, butterflies and birds. The surrounding native woodland and nature reserve are home to badgers, deer and otters. There are walks straight from the door (come and see the daffodils in spring) and fishing, golf and cycling nearby.

Local attractions include Castle Drogo, The Miniature Pony Centre, Canonteign Falls and picturesque thatched villages. The cathedral city of Exeter is 8 miles away and the beaches of South Devon are 40 minutes' drive. Blytheswood Hostel provides flexible accommodation in cosy rooms sleeping between 2 and 8 people in bunks. It is ideal for use by families and groups who can book sole use of the whole hostel. There is a fully equipped self-catering kitchen, lounge/dining room, drying room and picnic areas. Duvets and linen provided.

            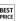

DETAILS

- **Open** - All year.
- **Number of beds** - 20: 1x8, 1x6, 1x2, + family room (1x double + 1x bunk)
- **Booking** - Booking is essential. Deposit required.
- **Price per night** - £14pp. Children under 16 £8. Whole hostel £200 per night.
- **Public Transport** - Trains Exeter. Bus 359 from Exeter + 82 on summer wknds
- **Directions** - On the B3212 between Exeter and Moretonhampstead, 1 mile outside Dunsford. Approx 100m from Steps Bridge, opposite car park. Please use car park when staying at the hostel.

CONTACT: Lewis and Sarah
Tel: 01647 252435
hello@blytheswood.co.uk www.blytheswood.co.uk
Steps Bridge, Dunsford, Exeter, Devon, EX6 7EQ

EXETER GLOBE
BACKPACKERS

A city centre hostel within easy walk of the beautiful old port, cathedral, shopping district and a wonderful mix of pubs, clubs, live music, restaurants and café scene. Great for the young and "young at heart" who enjoy a vibrant city centre. Twenty minutes' drive to Exmouth with its 2 mile sandy beach for all sail sports and start of the Jurassic Coastline, and the same to Dartmoor National Park for walking, climbing, cycling and horse riding. Exeter is an excellent place to find work and is just 2½ hours by train to London. In addition to male, female and mixed dorms there are private rooms and three large double rooms with additional bunks, sitting area, tea/coffee making facilities, hair dryer and towels. The new 5 star wet rooms are going down a treat! Free WiFi. Not suitable for hen and stag groups, DSS, unaccompanied under 18s and families. ID required.

DETAILS

- **Open** - All year (phone for Xmas). Check in / Check out. Mon-Fri: 8.30 to 12noon and 3.30pm to 11pm. Sat,Sun: 8.30am-11pm. Earlier checkout by arrangement only.
- **Number of beds** - 46-52: 1x10, 3x8, 1x6, 3x2/4 (dbl/twin plus bunk bed)
- **Booking** - To secure booking please phone ahead.
- **Price per night** - Dorms from £17.50pp or £75pp per week. Private rooms from £45 for two people, £75 for four people. 50p for card payments. £5 key deposit.
- **Public Transport** - National Express, local bus companies and rail networks. 24 hour parking ticket available from hostel which is cheaper then local car parks.
- **Directions** - Bus station: over main road, take first turning on left "Southernhay East". Stay on LHS walk until you reach the Southgate Hotel. Hostel is diagonally opposite. From Central Station: take Queen St to High St, turn right then, at 1st lights turn left South St. Continue to large junction at bottom of hill. Cross at lights.

CONTACT: Duty Manager
Tel: 01392 215521
info@exeterbackpackers.co.uk www.exeterbackpackers.co.uk
71 Holloway Street, Exeter, EX2 4JD

ELMSCOTT
HOSTEL

Elmscott, a former Victorian school, offers a next-to-nature retreat, surrounded by unspoilt coastline with sea views of Lundy Island. Great for walking, cycling, surfing and bird watching, there are amazing rock formations and quiet lanes to explore. The famous fishing village of Clovelly is a few miles away with its cobbled streets and pretty harbour. Elmscott is a few minutes' walk from the South West Coast Path which passes spectacular coves and river mouths. The accommodation is in one unit of 20 beds and another of 12 with mixed dorms, single sex dorms and private rooms. Access is available from 5pm in the afternoon to 10am in the morning (unless by prior arrangement). In winter accommodation is only available for groups. There is a new spacious large kitchen and dining area which is a great addition to the school room and the original well equipped kitchen in the school house. Games room and shop.

DETAILS

■ **Open** - All year (winter for groups only), hostel opens each afternoon at 5pm.
■ **Number of beds** - 32 (35 in winter): 1 unit of 20: 2x6, 2x4; 1 unit of 12: 1x6, 1x4, 1x2. Extra 3 bed room available for sole use bookings in winter.
■ **Booking** - In summer book direct with the hostel by phone or email. In winter book via the YHA website, or for last minute sole use bookings call the owners.
■ **Price per night** - Adult £17 to £22, under 18s £15 to £17(discounts for YHA members). Enquire for special prices for groups or longer stays.
■ **Public Transport** - Nearest trains Barnstaple (25 miles). Buses from Barnstaple to Hartland (4 miles from hostel). Phone hostel for taxi service.
■ **Directions** - The hostel is in the small hamlet of Elmscott 4 miles from the village of Hartland. Grid Ref 231 217.

CONTACT: John, Thirza and Kate
Tel: Hostel 01237 441367/ House 01237 441276/ Kate 01237 441637
john.goa@virgin.net www.elmscott.org.uk
Elmscott, Hartland, Bideford, Devon, EX39 6ES

NORTHSHOREBUDE

ENGLAND

A relaxed place with a variety of bedrooms and large garden.

Close to town, beaches and South West Coastal Path.

No stag groups please. An ideal base to see the South West's attractions: The Eden Project, Tintagel Castle, The Tamar Lakes, Dartmoor and Bodmin Moor. There are competition standard surfing beaches nearby. Families with children aged over 5 welcome. Meet old friends or make new ones, on the deck, in the lounge or around the dining room table after cooking up a storm in the fully fitted kitchen. You can make your stay whatever you want it to be.

DETAILS

- **Open** - All year except Christmas week, 8.30am to 1pm and 4.30pm to 10.30pm.
- **Number of beds** - 39: 2x6, 4x4, 1x3, 1x2, 3xdbl
- **Booking** - Advisable, credit card secures booking. Photo ID at check in. (Groups 6 or more by prior booking) No stag groups. At least one adult (18+) per booking.
- **Price per night** - From £18pp dorm rooms (single night supplement)
- **Public Transport** - To Bude: From Exeter via Okehampton buses X9, 599. From Newquay X10 (changing at Okehampton). From Bideford 85. All buses First Bus Company. There are train and bus links from London to Exeter.
- **Directions** - From A39, head into Bude down Stratton Rd past Morrisons on your right, follow the road down past Esso garage. Take the second road on the right, Killerton Road (before the Bencollen Pub). Continue up to the top of the road and Northshorebude is on the corner on your left. Turn into Redwood Grove and parking is the first on the left.

CONTACT: Sean or Janine
Tel: 01288 354256 or 07970 149486
northshorebude@uk2.net www.northshorebude.com
57 Killerton Road, Bude, Cornwall, EX23 8EW

Set in 30 acres on the coastal preservation area of North Devon, the farm boasts sea views overlooking Woolacombe, Lundy Island, Lee Bay, Ilfracombe, and the Welsh coast on a clear day. The camping barn is a former stable block with all accommodation on ground level with raised sleeping areas. Each platform has mattresses at no extra charge, bring your own sleeping bag or bedding as well as warm clothing. There are air curtain heaters throughout the barn. Accommodation includes a dining area and well-fitted kitchen with electric full-size oven, hob, fridge-freezer, microwave, toaster, kettle, sinks with hot water from a water heater (all coin-operated) and basic cooking equipment and cutlery. A tumble dryer has also recently been added. Candles are NOT allowed, as they are a fire risk. A picnic and BBQ area are adjacent and a toilet block with ladies and gents toilets and electric shower (coin-operated) is a few steps away; as is a covered storage area for rucksacks, cycles, surfboards etc. Sorry no stag/hen parties. Mullacott Farm also provides B&B, camping and static caravan accommodation.

DETAILS

- **Open** - All year, all day.
- **Number of beds** - 20
- **Booking** - By phone or email
- **Price per night** - £7.50 per person per night. Sole use: by arrangement
- **Public Transport** - Train to Barnstable, No 21 bus to Mullacott Cross 300m walk
- **Directions** - A361 towards Ilfracombe. 300m from Mullacott Cross turn left into Mullacott Farm drive. Follow the signs, up to the farmhouse on the rhs.

CONTACT: Alison and Adrian Homa
Tel: 01271 866877
relax@mullacottfarm.co.uk www.mullacottfarm.co.uk
Ilfracombe, Devon, EX34 8NA

OCEAN
BACKPACKERS

Ocean Backpackers is situated close to Ilfracombe's picturesque harbour. This cool, clean and friendly hostel offers excellent facilities for walkers, cyclists, surfers, divers as well as families, schools and activity groups. Facilities include a self-catering kitchen, dining area, communal lounge with free internet/WiFi, large storage basement, patio area and free car park. Nestled in an area of Outstanding Natural Beauty, Ilfracombe has many shops, galleries, pubs and restaurants.The harbour became home to Damien Hirst's statue "Verity" in 2012 and is fastly becoming an "arts destination." Ilfracombe is the start of the Route 27 Coast-to-coast ride to Plymouth and the South West Coast Path provides wonderful walks with stunning scenery that take your breath away! It is just a short drive to the sandy surf beaches of Woolacombe, Croyde and Saunton and the spectacular Exmoor National Park. We welcome groups of all sizes that enjoy the buzz of a Backpackers and have a love of the great outdoors! Weekly discounts are available and the whole hostel can be hired for exclusive use.

DETAILS

- **Open** - All year, reception 9-12pm and 4pm-10pm No curfew.
- **Number of beds** - 56:- 1x8, 5x6, 1x4, 1x twin, 2 x double, 2 x double & bunk.
- **Booking** - Booking advised but not essential.
- **Price per night** - Dorm Beds £13.00-£19.00. Double rooms £45-£50 per room.
- **Public Transport** -   Direct coaches from London Victoria/Heathrow/Plymouth/ Exeter. By train take the Tarka line to Barnstaple then bus to Ilfracombe.
- **Directions** - Ocean Backpackers is by the harbour opposite the bus station. For more detailed directions go to the website and click on directions.

CONTACT: Chris and Abby
Tel: 01271 867835
info@oceanbackpackers.co.uk www.oceanbackpackers.co.uk
29 St James Place, Ilfracombe, Devon, EX34 9BJ

ROCK AND RAPID
BUNKHOUSE

An ideal place to come for an adventurous or relaxing break. The Rock and Rapid Adventure Centre is an AALA registered centre that offers activities such as climbing, coasteering, canoeing and surfing. The bunkhouse can be rented out for sole use, for an activity package or a full programme, including food, can be put together for your group.

The North Devon coastline is only 15 minutes away from the centre, and surfing lessons and other water sports are on offer. On-site there is an indoor climbing and bouldering wall where climbing lessons are available for the beginner or climbers can register and use the wall themselves. The bunkhouse lends itself to groups wanting good quality but cheap accommodation. Being in a rural setting there are no neighbours; therefore it is ideal for groups such as hen and stags, as well as family or school groups wanting a quiet escape.

DETAILS

■ **Open** - All year, 24 Hours.
■ **Number of beds** - 40: 2 x 18, 2 x 2
■ **Booking** - Email or phone us for any more information and for a booking form.
■ **Price per night** - £225 per night sole use
■ **Public Transport** - Railway station in either Tiverton or Barnstaple with buses or taxis easily available to South Molton.
■ **Directions** - Rock and Rapid Bunkhouse is based at the Rock and Rapid Adventures Ltd centre in North Devon. Only 15 minutes from the North Devon coastline and minutes from the Exmoor National Park.

CONTACT: Keith Crockford
Tel: 0333 600 6001
info@rockandrapid.co.uk www.rockandrapidadventures.co.uk
Hacche Mill, South Molton, EX36 3NA

BLINDWELL
BUNKHOUSE

Bunkhouse on traditional Exmoor hill farm, with far reaching views of Devon and Dartmoor with high quality comfortable bunks and mattresses, including drying/laundry room and secure cycle/equipment lockup. The bunkhouse has hot water and underfloor heating from biomass boiler, solar panels supplementing electricity all included. Half a mile from Sustrans cycle route 3, off-road mountain bike trails nearby and many beautiful walking trails. Set at the top of a secluded valley with lots of wildlife including red deer, buzzards, Exmoor ponies. Many Exmoor beauty spots within easy reach. 16 beds in three rooms The Mole x 6 ,The Danesbrook x 4 and ground floor The Barle x 6 with disabled access. Shared toilets and showers with underfloor heating and disabled facilities. Outside toilet facilities. Traditional local pubs near by, groceries can be ordered through local shop or supermarkets with prior notice.

DETAILS

- **Open** - All year,
- **Number of beds** - 16 1x6,1x6,1x4
- **Booking** - Booking via website or telephone 01598740246
- **Price per night** - £15 pp inc bedding. any week night whole bunkhouse £220, Weekend Fri/Sat £480, Christmas and New Year by arrangement.
- **Public Transport** - Trains to Taunton, Tiverton or Barnstaple. Buses to South Molton and Dulverton. Local Taxis service see website
- **Directions** - From A361 at South Molton turn right and go through North Molton towards Withypool after 4miles at the top of the hill turn right towards Twichen Cross the next cross roads then take sharp back right immediately before cattle grid Blindwell Farm is half a mile on right hand side

CONTACT: Carol Delbridge
Tel: 01598 740246
delbridge.carol@googlemail.com www.blindwellbunkhouse.co.uk
Blindwell Farm, Twitchen, Sandyway, South Molton, EX36 3LT

Set beside the pretty meandering river Exe in the moorland village of Exford, Exford Hostel is in the middle of the Exmoor National Park. The perfect base for mountain biking, horse riding, walking and lots of other outdoor activities and fantastic for school trips and field visits. This former Victorian hunting lodge, with private en suite rooms as well as dorms, is perfect for individuals, couples, families or larger groups. Catering is available for parties and schools requiring sole use. Facilities include a fully equipped self-catering kitchen, dining room, lounge, conference & classroom provision and ample parking. The tranquil wooded garden is surrounded by the river Exe and is perfect for camping (8 pitches) and viewing the stars in the Exmoor Dark Skies Reserve. Close the South West Coastal Path, the Coleridge Way & the Doone Valley. Exford Hostel provides a unique taste of Exmoor for those on a quest for adventure, looking for a moorland break, celebrating with family & friends or simply enjoying life at a slower pace.

DETAILS

- **Open** - All year, all day.
- **Number of beds** - 49
- **Booking** - via email or phone
- **Price per night** - from £19 per person.
- **Public Transport** - nearest train & bus stations at Taunton. 1hr by taxi/minibus.
- **Directions** - A358 from Taunton toward Minehead for approx 3 miles, turn left onto the B3224. Keep on B3224 for approx 16 miles eventually signed Exford. Go through Exford, over the bridge and turn left, then immediately left into the hostel car park.

CONTACT: Reception
Tel: 01643 831229
info@exfordhostel.co.uk www.exfordhostel.co.uk/
Exford Hostel, Exe Mead, Exford, Somerset TA24 7PU

BASE
LODGE

Base Lodge is ideally situated for exploring Exmoor, the Quantocks and the North Devon coast by mountain bike or foot. Excellent off and on road mountain biking for all levels. Guided mountain biking and secure lock up facilities. Exmoor affords excellent scenic moor and coastal views and the 600+ mile long South West Coastal Path starts here in Minehead. Other activities can be arranged including mountain biking, navigational training, climbing, surfing, pony-trekking and natural history walks and talks.

Base Lodge is clean, comfortable and friendly, providing a shared, fully equipped kitchen and dining room. Local pubs and restaurants are all within walking distance.

DETAILS

- **Open** - All year, all day access once booked (reception open from 3pm).
- **Number of beds** - 22: 2x2, 1x7, 1x6, 1x5
- **Booking** - Booking advisable, bookings taken by phone or email or take a chance and call in. Deposit required for groups or exclusive use.
- **Price per night** - Dorms £17.50, private single £7.50 supplement, twin/ double £40. Exclusive use of Base Lodge from £250. Family room discount.
- **Public Transport** - Coach station 5 min walk. Buses from Taunton, Exeter and Tiverton. Train station: Taunton (26 miles). Steam railway from Taunton to Minehead.
- **Directions** - With the sea behind you, drive/walk up The Parade until you reach Park Street, continue straight on until you reach a fork. Take the right fork into The Parks (Baptist Church on your right). Only limited parking is available.

CONTACT: Wendy or Graham
Tel: 01643 703520 or 0773 1651536
togooutdoors@hotmail.com www.togooutdoors.co.uk/BaseLodge/Base Lodge
Web-page.html
16 The Parks, Minehead, Somerset, TA24 8BS

A small family run farm in West Somerset, on the edge of Exmoor. Providing inexpensive basic accommodation, with an emphasis on a warm and dry place to stay after a day out in the locality. So if you're looking to have a day hiking on Exmoor, or training for the UK 70.3 IRONMAN, or just spending time in the countryside this could be the place for you. The Hay Barn, is a dormitory style open plan barn with bunks, two bathrooms with showers, a kitchen and seating area for up to 12 people, more by prior arrangement. It is centrally heated, with hot and cold running water at no extra charge. The Cart Shed is more of an open plan chalet with a kitchen, bathroom with shower, seating area and bunks for four people, if you require extra beds for this barn there is a sofa bed (double). Also centrally heated with hot and cold running water. You will need to bring everything as if you were camping, mattresses are provided but no pillows

DETAILS

- **Open** - All year.
- **Number of beds** - 16: The Hay Barn 12, The Cart Shed 4.
- **Booking** - Book via website or phone
- **Price per night** - The Hay Barn £15pp, sole use £160, £1000/week. The Cart Shed: £15pp, sole use £50, £350/week
- **Public Transport** - Train to Taunton, local buses to Wiveliscombe. pick up available from here for a small fee
- **Directions** - Don't use sat nav. From B3190 Raleigh's Cross to Bampton road at crossroads take turning for Huish Champflower and Wiveliscombe, Chitcombe is the second left about three hundred yards from cross roads. Chitcombe is down a steep bumpy lane, about half a mile.

CONTACT: Sam Kennen
Tel: 01398 371274 or 07866 852 699.
stkennen@hotmail.co.uk chitcombebarns.co.uk/
Chitcombe Farm, Huish Champflower, Taunton, Somerset, TA4 2EL

CAMPBELL ROOM
ENGLAND GROUP ACCOMMODATION

The Campbell Room offers self-catering group accommodation for youth organisations, schools and universities, training courses, groups of walkers, cyclists and others. Sheltered at the mouth of a rural valley on the edge of the Quantock Hills AONB, the building offers a main activity hall which can also sleep 18 on comfortable mattresses, 2 bedrooms each sleeping 3, a multi-use cabin, fully equipped kitchen, washrooms, showers, drying room, campfire area and space for 1 or 2 tents. Many walking, hiking and mountain biking routes pass close to the centre, a swimming pool is nearby and the forest is within 10 minutes' walk. Other attractions and activities in the area include horse riding, high ropes, water sports, beaches with rock pools and fossils, the coastal resort of Minehead, the West Somerset Railway, Wells Cathedral, Glastonbury Tor, Wookey Hole, Cheddar Gorge, Dunster Castle, Tropiquaria Animal and Adventure Park, Exmoor and the county town of Taunton.

           GROUPS ONLY

DETAILS

- **Open** - All year, by arrangement. Check current availability on the website.
- **Number of beds** - 24 recommended (but see website). 2x3, 1x18 max, 1x8 max
- **Booking** - Essential one month in advance with deposit. Bridgwater YMCA, Friarn Avenue, Bridgwater, Somerset, TA6 3RF.
- **Price per night** - £4.50 pp (2 leaders free for groups over 12), min £54 per night.
- **Public Transport** - Buses Mon to Sat from Bridgwater. Details on website.
- **Directions** - 10 miles from the M5 (junction 23 or 24). Centre is at T junction west of Aley, 1.5 miles south of Nether Stowey (on the A39 Bridgwater to Minehead road). GR ST187381. TA5 1HB / TA5 1HN. Full directions on our website.

CONTACT: Thomasina Williams
Tel: 01278 726 000
info@campbellroom.org.uk www.campbellroom.org.uk
Campbell Room Group Accommodation, Aley, Over Stowey, Somerset.

Larkshall (Mendip Bunkhouse) is the Cerberus Spelaeological Society's headquarters and offers excellent modern facilities. As well as for members it is available for use by guest individuals or groups wanting accommodation on Mendip. It makes an ideal base for caving as well as many other outdoor activities including walking, cycling, climbing etc. It is also a good base for anyone wanting to explore the Somerset countryside and within very easy reach are the famous tourist attractions of Wells, Wookey Hole, Cheddar Gorge and caves, and the city of Bath. The accommodation provides all the home comforts with a kitchen/dining room, large lounge, showers and changing facilities. For anyone so inclined the central corridor can be traversed using the climbing holds fitted along the wall. There are two guest communal bunkrooms sleeping 12 and 19 respectively, with ample space to sleep large groups in comfort. For those that prefer, it is possible to camp. There is a large car park.

DETAILS

- **Open** - All year, 24 hours. Key available by prior arrangement.
- **Number of beds** - 31 (1 x 12 + 1 x 19). Unlimited camping available.
- **Booking** - Advisable. Email preferred, deposit required. Availability on website.
- **Price per night** - £5 per person. Sole use of bunkrooms £60 and £95 per night. Minimum charge £10 per person per stay.
- **Public Transport** - There is a bus stop near the crossroads in Oakhill on the A367. Taxis are available in Shepton Mallet, Wells and Frome
- **Directions** - Larkshall is 4 miles north of Shepton Mallet and 15 miles south of Bath off the A367. At the crossroads in Oakhill take road to Stoke St Michael. Larkshall is about one mile from Oakhill on the right (ST 6505 4720).

CONTACT:
Tel: 0845 475 0954
hostelbookings@cerberusspeleo.org.uk www.cerberusspeleo.org.uk
Cerberus Spelaeological, Larkshall, Fosse Road, Oakhill, Somerset, BA3 5HY

GOBLIN COMBE
LODGE

Just 10 miles outside Bristol, Goblin Combe Lodge is set in 8 acres of its own grounds with stunning views across the Severn Estuary and beyond. Set in 130 acres of woodlands, rich in history and geology with 80 acres designated as a site of special scientific interest, it offers something for everyone. The timber framed building is clad in larch and has a biomass central heating system, rainwater harvesting and a sewage treatment plant. Groups of up to 38 can be accommodated in 10 bedrooms sleeping 2, 4 & 6 people. The cottage alongside the Lodge provides a lounge, dining and catering facilities and is the ideal place to relax and warm yourself after a long day of activities or to prepare for an exciting night walk where you might meet the resident owls. The 18ft yurt is a great place for a drumming workshop, a day of meditation or just a get-together.

Fire pits and a BBQ area are included in the price. Smaller groups may be accommodated, camping available for the overspill of larger groups - please contact for information.

DETAILS

- **Open** - All year. Please contact for opening times.
- **Number of beds** - 38
- **Booking** - By phone/email. Booking address Plunder Street, Cleeve, BS49 4PQ.
- **Price per night** - Ask for prices.No min stay. Reductions for charities and schools.
- **Public Transport** - The bus X1 between Bristol & Weston Super Mare stops at the end of Cleeve Hill Road on the A370. Nearest train station - Yatton - 3 miles.
- **Directions** - Detailed directions to the site will be given upon booking

CONTACT:
Tel: 01934 833723
enquiries@goblincombe.org.uk www.goblincombe.org.uk
Goblin Combe Lodge, Cleeve Hill, North Somerset, BS40 5PP

BRISTOL
BACKPACKERS HOSTEL ENGLAND

Bristol's most central backpacker hostel.

- clean & comfy beds - mixed/single sex dorms - private rooms
- individual bathrooms & free hot showers - free linen
- large kitchen - free tea, coffee & hot chocolate
- indoor bicycle storage.

Late night basement bar - piano & guitar room - DVD lounge - cheap internet machines - free WiFi - luggage storage room - laundrette.
Run by backpackers for backpackers - no curfew after check in.

            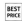

DETAILS

■ **Open** - All year, reception hours 9am -11.30pm (no curfew).
■ **Number of beds** - 90: Bunk bed accommodation in private twin, private triple or 6, 8 and 10 bed dorms.
■ **Booking** - Most cards, phone or walk in.
■ **Price per night** - £18pp. Private rooms from £41. See website for discounts.
■ **Public Transport** - See below.
■ **Directions** - Located in 'Old City', the historic centre of Bristol. From Bristol Central Bus Station (Marlborough St) 7 minutes' walk. Follow pedestrian signs to 'Old City' then see map above. From Bristol Temple Meads train station 12 minutes' walk. Follow pedestrian signs to 'Old City' then see map above. Or take bus number 8 or 9 to the 'Centre Promenade'. Disembark at The Bristol Hippodrome. From Airport take the 'Shuttle' to the Central Bus Station. By road follow signs for Baldwin Street in the city centre.

CONTACT:
Tel: 0117 9257900
info@bristolbackpackers.co.uk www.bristolbackpackers.co.uk
17 St Stephen's Street, Bristol, BS1 1EQ

ROCK AND BOWL

ENGLAND

In a huge 1930's building in the heart of Bristol you'll find Rock and Bowl hostel, the Lanes and the GimmeShelter Vintage shop all in one the perfect base for your stay in the city. A variety of rooms from private doubles to 20 bed dorms (including female only) means there will be a bed at a price to suit your budget. You can enjoy your free time bowling at The Lanes (20% discount for hostel guests -FREE on Mondays) or playing pool or ping pong. The Lanes has club nights so Friday and Saturday nights in particular are quite noisy until about 3am but free earplugs are available. Facilities include a well equipped large kitchen, lounge with TV etc., free Wifi, towels, ironing equipment, hair dryer as well as laundry facilities and great discounts from local food outlets. Groups of 5 or more people get room discounts plus continental breakfasts, packed lunches and party activities if required.

DETAILS

- **Open** - All year, 24 hour reception.
- **Number of beds** - 1x20, 3x12, 1x10, 3x10 weekly bed dorm, 2x8, 1x6, 3x4, 1x4 female, 1xdouble/twin/3bed, 1xdouble
- **Booking** - Book online via the website
- **Price per night** - Dorms from £10pp. Private rooms from £39. Weekly rooms from £90. Discounts for groups.
- **Public Transport** - Bristol Temple Meads: 20 mins, Coach station: 5 mins' walk.
- **Directions** - From train station walk toward the wharf, cross the river, walk along High Street to Vine Street, left onto Pithay, left onto All Saints, then left into Nelson Street. From bus station turn left onto Whitson St, turn left onto Lower Maudlin St, turn right onto The Haymarket turn left onto Silver St, turn right onto Nelson St.

CONTACT: Alfredo Esposito
Tel: 0117 325 1980
bookings@rocknbowlmotel.com www.thelanesbristol.co.uk/hostel
22 Nelson Street, Bristol, BS1 2LE

BATH
YMCA

Bath YMCA offers a warm welcome and the best value accommodation. From its central location all the sights of this World Heritage City are easily reached on foot. Bath is also an ideal base for the explorer. Staying longer brings Stonehenge, Wookey Hole caves, Cheddar Gorge, the southern reaches of the Cotswolds, and more exciting destinations all within reach. With a total of 210 beds, Bath YMCA has a great deal of experience in making guests feel comfortable. There is a fully air conditioned lounge area with TV. Laundry, lockers, pool and football table, fax and internet facilities are available. The Health and Wellbeing Centre provides up to date equipment and qualified staff who work hard to provide 'Fitness with Fun'. Couples, families, groups and backpackers are all welcome. All these facilities and the YMCA's traditional sense of community will make your stay a truly memorable one. Awarded 3 stars by VisitBritain.

DETAILS

- **Open** - All year, 24-hour reception.
- **Number of beds** - 210: Dorms: 1x10, 3x12, 1x15, 1x18. Rooms: 7 x quad, 6 x triple, 29 x twin, 5 x double, 9 x single
- **Booking** - Credit card guarantees.
- **Price per night** - From: Dorm £21pp. Single £32pp. Twin £28pp. Double £30pp. Triple £23pp. Quad £22pp. Includes light breakfast.
- **Public Transport** - Bath has a train station and is served by National Express.
- **Directions** - Located approximately ½ mile from rail and bus station. Broad Street is located near the Podium Shopping Centre off Walcott Street.

CONTACT: Reception
Tel: 01225 325900
stay@bathymca.co.uk www.bathymca.co.uk
International House, Broad Street Place, Bath, BA1 5LH

This Victorian-Gothic mansion is located in Dorset's Area of Outstanding Natural Beauty, with easy access to the Jurassic Coast at Lyme Regis, and the Wessex and Monarch Ways further inland. Our dorm room is mixed gender, camping is available, and guests can use our vegetarian self-catering kitchen. Catered vegetarian meals are available at an extra cost (advance booking essential).

Monkton Wyld Court is a charity promoting ways of living sustainably. Volunteers live communally to minimise resource use. As much as possible, we heat and cook using wood; fresh water comes from our wells; we use compost loos and waste water passes through a reed bed filtration system; fruit and vegetables are grown in our organic garden; and eggs come from our free-range chickens. Tenant farmers keep 3 Jersey cows which provide all our milk, yoghurt and cheese. Bed and Breakfast private rooms are also available.

DETAILS

- **Open** - Year-round. Office opening hours: 9am-5pm.
- **Number of beds** - 11 beds in 2 mixed-gender dorm rooms
- **Booking** - Book via website, by email or by phone.
- **Price per night** - £20 per person per night.
- **Public Transport** - Train to Axminster. First Bus from station (direction Lyme Regis / Bridport) to Hunter's Lodge (10 min) + 40 min walk along B-road and lanes.
- **Directions** - Off A35 between Bridport (East) and Axminster (West), about 4 miles north of Lyme Regis. Monkton Wyld is sign-posted from the A35; 1 mile up the lane you will see St Andrew's Church on your left, driveway is just beyond it on your right.

CONTACT: Office Coordinator
Tel: 01297 560342
info@monktonwyldcourt.org www.monktonwyldcourt.co.uk
Elsdon's Lane, Charmouth, Bridport, Dorset, DT6 6DQ

Located in the heart of Weymouth, the gateway to the beautiful and exciting Jurassic coastline and the host of the 2012 Olympic Games, Bunkhouse Plus has a mixture of bunk rooms with the 'Plus' of double en suites rooms making it a versatile accommodation for your stay. Children over 5 are welcome accompanied and supervised by adults. Situated close to the beach and town centre with safe waters to swim, whilst the old harbour hosts fantastic festivals of the sea. Why not get involved in wind and kite surfing, fishing, sailing, diving or rock climbing? Whatever your sport or hobby, the friendly hostel staff are more than happy to link you to venues and organisers to help make your stay as exciting or peaceful as you wish. The building is available for exclusive use. Sleeps either 15 (winter) or 25 all year round. Facilities include large self-catering kitchen with free tea/coffee, lounge with TV, dining area and equipment wash down and drying room. Bedding & linen included, towel hire. No curfew.

DETAILS

- **Open** - All year, reception times 4pm to 11pm daily.
- **Number of beds** - 22: 2x4, 2x3, 2x2, 2x double en suites
- **Booking** - via website, email or telephone.
- **Price per night** - Double en suite from £40 per room. Dorm from £18pp. Self-catering only. Sole use for 25 people from £200 or £1600 per week.
- **Public Transport** - Trains, bus and coach from all areas.
- **Directions** - 5 minute walk from train/bus station. Follow Ranelagh Road to Walpole Street on right. From sea front head north, at Queen Victoria statue turn left into William Street across crossroads then bear to the left into Walpole Street.

CONTACT: Bunkhouse Plus
Tel: 01305775228
bunkhouseplus@gmail.com www.bunkhouseplus.co.uk
Bunkhouse Plus, 47 Walpole Street, Weymouth, DT4 7HQ

MYTIME
OUTDOOR CENTRE

MyTime Outdoor Centre, previously know as the David Donalds Field Studies Centre or the Poole and the Dorset Adventure Centre, provides accommodation for groups. It is a converted 1940's radar station with central heating and double glazing. There are beds for 24 but up to 40 can be accommodated if some wish to camp and share the indoor facilities. There is a well equipped kitchen, a spacious community room, a drying room, picnic area, BBQ, campsite, lots of space to run around and plenty of parking. There are ramps to the main building and adapted toilets for wheelchair users. This is a brilliant area for environmental studies and is popular with groups and families enjoying the coast, walking, outdoor activities or just relaxing. It is within an SSSI, and is close to Lulworth Cove, Durdle Door, The Arne Nature Reserve, Purbeck Marine Reserve, Corfe Castle, Swanage Heritage Railway and Poole Harbour.

DETAILS

- **Open** - All year.
- **Number of beds** - 40: 24 inside: 1x2, 1x4 en suite, 1x8, 1x10. 16 camping.
- **Booking** - Booking required with £200 deposit. Phone for availability, then download form and return to 37 Commercial Road, Poole, Dorset BH14 0HU.
- **Price per night** - Whole centre from £315 per night (24 people). 16 more can camp (bring your own tents) at £5pp Bedding set hire £5 per person. Winter fuel supplement £5 per night (October - March)
- **Public Transport** - Train to Wareham. Wilts & Dorset Buses to Worth Matravers.
- **Directions** - Arriving in Worth Matravers from Kingston bear right by duck pond into Pikes Lane. After Renscombe Farm road turns sharp right then left onto Renscombe Rd. 200m further the driveway to the base is on the right. OS SY967777

CONTACT: MyTime Outdoor Centre (Poole & Dorset Adventure Centre)
Tel: 01202 710701
enquiries@mytimecharity.co.uk www.mytimecharity.co.uk/Outdoor_Centre.html
Off Renscombe Rd, Worth Matravers, Isle of Purbeck, Dorset. BH19 3LL

Based in Wareham Forest, Dorset, Carey Outdoor Education Centre has been running for over 65 years. The centre has two bunkhouses each providing basic group accommodation for up to 12 people with en suite toilets and separate showers. There is a self-catering cabin with domestic kitchen facilities as well as the wash down facilities and covered hanging space for drying equipment. All bunkhouse bookings come with exclusive use of the entire site. Carey Outdoor Centre is a perfect base for groups wanting to visit Swanage (20 mins drive) for climbing, Poole Harbour for watersports, the Jurassic Coast (20 mins), Portland (45 mins), Arne Nature Reserve (10 mins) for birdwatching and wildlife as well as Wareham Forest, Purbeck Ridges and Puddletown (30 mins), all great for mountain biking. On site instructors can help with arranging and leading activities from as little as £12 per person. Bell tent hire in the secluded Purbeck woodland is also available for up to 40 people .

DETAILS

- **Open** - All year.
- **Number of beds** - Bunkhouses 24: 2x12, Bell tents 40: 8x5
- **Booking** - By telephone or email
- **Price per night** - One bunkhouse - £150; two bunkhouses - £300. Bell tents £250 for up to 20 people then £10 per per extra person (under 3s free) All rates plus VAT (unless an instructor is also booked.)
- **Public Transport** - Trains at Wareham 1.5 mile walk
- **Directions** - From north on A531 on arriving in Wareham go right on first and second roundabouts then first left onto Carey Road. Follow until arriving at the centre on the left.

CONTACT: Paul
Tel: 01929 552265
careyoec@dorsetcc.gov.uk www.dorsetforyou.com/carey
Carey Rd, Wareham, Dorset, BH20 7PB

SWANAGE AUBERGE
BUNKHOUSE
ENGLAND

Swanage Auberge, the bunkhouse that cares, is a refuge for climbers, walkers and divers, situated at the eastern end of the Jurassic Coast with excellent walking, diving and rock climbing on the doorstep. The bunkhouse is in the centre of Swanage town, a stone's throw from the South West Coast Path and all local amenities - pubs, shops, restaurants etc. Swanage Auberge is family run and self-contained with central heating, fully equipped self-catering kitchen, drying and laundry facilities and a meals service if required. There are two bunk rooms, one with 4 standard bunks and the other with 6 alpine style places (3 and 3).There is also a 5 bed dorm in the adjoining house. Towel, plus pillows are provided and bedding is included. There are three showers, loos and washrooms and an area to hang and wash wet-suits. Once booked in, the Auberge is available 24 hours a day. Parking is available for 2 vehicles and is allocated on a first come, first served basis. Price includes cereal breakfast and beverages. Packed lunches available (see website for further details).

             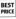

DETAILS

- **Open** - All year (phone mobile if no reply). Access all day.
- **Number of beds** - 15: 1x6, 1x4,1x5
- **Booking** - By phone (mobile in day time), email or online. Deposit required.
- **Price per night** - £20pp (one night), £18 if staying more than one night. Includes bedding, cereal breakfast, tea or coffee. Group rates available. No credit cards.
- **Public Transport** - Trains to Bournemouth, Poole or Wareham, bus to Swanage
- **Directions** - Turn left off High Street (opposite Earth Lights Café) into Mount Pleasant Lane. First left into Hardy Close. Swanage Auberge is at the end on the left.

CONTACT: Pete or Pam
Tel: 01929 424368, mobile 07711 117668
bookings@swanageauberge.co.uk www.swanageauberge.co.uk
45 High Street, Swanage, Dorset, BH19 2LX

AVON TYRRELL
ACTIVITY CENTRE

Set in 65 acres of private grounds, in the heart of the New Forest National Park, Avon Tyrrell Activity Centre offers an extensive range of outdoor adventure and learning activities for groups and individuals as well as various on site accommodation options. The Grade I listed house provides full or part board catering for large groups. Dormitory style bedrooms sleep between 2-10 people. B&B for smaller groups and individuals is also available. On site are 6, 12 and 14 berth self-catering lodges, plus the exclusive Escape Camping site with ready pitched tents, beds and electric hookups. Camping is available between March and October. In this stunning location there is so much to do on site including; fundays, courses, family events, bike hire and tracks, Go adventure days and drop in activities for day visitors and on site guests. Step over the stile and you are in the heart of the New Forest where you can enjoy long walks, explore local villages and enjoy some of the many cycling trails. Everyone is welcome at Avon Tyrrell and all of the activities and facilities are fully accessible so everyone can enjoy their time here.

DETAILS

- **Open** - All year (March–Oct Escape Camping and camp-site). Offices 08:30-17:00.
- **Number of beds** - 110: Main house. Plus 6,12 and 14 berth lodges, 3 tipis sleeping 4 people in each and campsite.
- **Booking** - Booking essential.
- **Price per night** - Please visit the website for prices, special offers and late deals.
- **Public Transport** - Trains at Christchurch, New Milton & Brockenhurst (6,7&10 m)
- **Directions** - GR SU185003. Half way between Burley and Bransgore.

CONTACT: Guest Services
Tel: 01425 672347
info@ukyouth.org www.avontyrrell.org.uk
Bransgore, Hampshire, BH23 8EE

An award winning example of eco-renovation and part of The Sustainability Centre which promotes environmental awareness and low impact living in the heart of the South Downs National Park. We're right on the South Downs Way National Trail and ideal for walkers, cyclists, business away-days and family get-togethers. The Lodge has a fully equipped self-catering kitchen, a communal area, comfortable bedrooms with linen & towels provided, and shared bathrooms/toilets. A 'help yourself' breakfast is included. The centre has large grounds with woodland trails and a café open every day. The camp-site has tipis and yurts, secluded woodland pitches and solar showers, offering a peaceful real camping experience. Within 2 miles there are country pubs, local shops and take-aways/deliveries.

DETAILS

■ **Open** - Hostel and camp-site open all year. Tipis & yurts closed from Nov to April.
■ **Number of beds** - 38: 10 x 3, 4 x 2
■ **Booking** - Book online via our website. Groups book by telephone or email.
■ **Price per night** - Single occupancy £33 adult, additional adults £20 each. Additional children £12.50 (2-17). Children under 2 £5. Inc linen and breakfast. Camping: £12/adult £7/child (reductions Nov-Mar). Lge Yurts: £33/adults; £12.50/child. Tipis: £22/adult, £10/child. Under 2 free.   Exclusive use of either the campsite or Lodge £700 per night.
■ **Public Transport** - Trains at Petersfield, 6 miles (£20-25 by taxi). 38 bus to Clanfield, 67 to East Meon, 41 bus to Clanfield from Portsmouth Harbour .
■ **Directions** - GR 676 189. From A3 take Clanfield turn (brown sign). Turn right after Rising Sun in Clanfield. At top of hill, turn left signed Droxford.

CONTACT: Tony or Dave
Tel: 01730 823549
accommodation@sustainability-centre.org www.sustainability-centre.org
The Sustainability Centre, Droxford Road, East Meon, Hampshire, GU32 1HR

THE PRIVETT
CENTRE

Situated mid-way between Alton and Petersfield in glorious Hampshire countryside, the Privett Centre offers lowest cost, comfortable short-stay accommodation in a unique rural setting. The centre is a picturesque converted Victorian school and schoolhouse located next to the church in a farming hamlet which lies within the East Hampshire 'Area of Outstanding Natural Beauty'. Sleeping a maximum of 26 dormitory style with 1 twin bedroom (with disabled access en suite) and one single room, the centre is designed to accommodate small to medium-sized groups who prefer the freedom of hiring a small centre all to themselves. The centre provides the basics – a self-catering kitchen, bunk beds mainly in bedrooms, a large common room, games room and shower rooms all under one roof. Outside a large paddock and asphalt playground provide secure and spacious recreational and parking space. Available for weekday, weekend and day use all year, the Privett Centre is an ideal residential setting

DETAILS

- **Open** - All year.
- **Number of beds** - 29: 1x1, 1x2, 2x4, 1x6, 1x12
- **Booking** - Phone or email
- **Price per night** - From £13 pppn with a minimum charge of £150 per night. (please contact the centre for exact prices applicable to your group)
- **Public Transport** - Nearest train station - Petersfield, approx 6 miles from centre.
- **Directions** - From the A272 follow signs to Petersfield. Go straight across crossroads, centre is signposted on left after approx 2 miles.

CONTACT: Angela Grigsby
Tel: 01730 828238
info@privettcentre.org.uk www.privettcentre.org.uk
Church Lane, Privett, Hampshire, GU34 3PE

Gumber Bothy is a converted Sussex flint barn on a working sheep farm within the National Trust's Slindon Estate. It provides simple overnight accommodation or camping for walkers, horse riders and cyclists, just off the South Downs Way, or a tranquil and remote location to get away from it all.

Five minutes' walk from Stane Street, the Roman Road that crosses the South Downs Way at Bignor Hill, facilities include sleeping platforms in 3 dorms sleeping up to 25, basic kitchen and bathroom facilities, BBQ, drying room, bike racks, payphone. Wheelchair accessible (please phone for details).

Sorry, but as the bothy is on a sheep farm, no dogs and most definitely NO CARS. Not suitable for under fives.

DETAILS

- **Open** - March to October (inclusive), flexible opening hours.
- **Number of beds** - 25: 1 x 16, 1 x 5, 1 x 4 plus overflow area
- **Booking** - Booking by phone or email. Booking required for groups with 50% deposit.
- **Price per night** - £12 (adults), £6 (under 16s).
- **Public Transport** - Train stations, Arundel (urban) 5 miles, Amberley (rural) 5 miles, Chichester (8 miles). National Express stop at Chichester. Buses 84 and 85 from Chichester, stop at Fontwell and then it is a 3 mile walk to the Bothy. Taxi fare from Arundel to Northwood Farm is approx £10, followed by a 2 mile country walk.
- **Directions** - OS Map LR197 or E121 GR 961 119. Nearest car park GR 973 129. No vehicular access. One mile off South Downs Way on Stane Street bridleway

CONTACT: Bothy Ranger
Tel: 01243 814484
gumberbothy@nationaltrust.org.uk www.nationaltrust.org.uk/slindon-estate
Slindon Estate Yard, Slindon, Arundel, West Sussex, BN18 0RG

PUTTENHAM
ECO CAMPING BARN

Puttenham Eco Camping Barn offers simple overnight accommodation and a warm welcome for walkers and cyclists - individuals, families or groups - in the Surrey Hills Area of Outstanding Natural Beauty. Located on the North Downs Way and Sustrans NCN22 cycle route, the Barn has a fully equipped self-catering kitchen, a shower, toilets and foam covered sleeping platforms, as well as a garden with picnic benches. Electricity and hot water included but bring your own towel and sleeping bag (or hire one - £3 a stay). Evening meals are available in the village. The Barn has many sustainable features including solar panels and rainwater collection for flushing toilets. NO CARS ON SITE. Excellent cycle shed. Young people are welcome but must be accompanied by a responsible adult. The Barn is wardened. Lights out 11.30 pm.

DETAILS

- **Open** - Easter to October, arrive after 5pm leave before 10am. No access 10am-5pm.
- **Number of beds** - sleeping platforms for 11.
- **Booking** - Essential. No stag or hen parties.
- **Price per night** - £15 adults; £12 under 18 (accompanied by adult). Sole use by arrangement. £3 `green` refund if arriving by foot, bicycle or public transport.
- **Public Transport** - Trains (08457 484950) at Wanborough (3.5 km), Guildford (7 km) and Farnham (9 km). Bus 65 (0845 1210190) from Guildford and Farnham stops within 1 km of Barn, or bus 46 to Watts Gallery, Compton & follow North Downs Way 2 miles west.
- **Directions** - GR SU 933 479. In Puttenham village (halfway between Farnham and Guildford) the Camping Barn is on North Downs Way - opposite the church.

CONTACT: Bookings
Tel: 01629 592 700 or 0800 0191 700
bookings@puttenhamcampingbarn.co.uk www.puttenhamcampingbarn.co.uk
The Street, Puttenham, Nr Guildford, Surrey, GU3 1AR

COURT HILL
CENTRE

Just 2 miles south of Wantage, and only a few steps from the historic Ridgeway National Trail, The Court Hill Centre enjoys breathtaking views over the Vale of the White Horse.

Reclaimed barns surround a pretty courtyard garden, on the site of a disused rubbish dump! Offering accommodation to families, groups and individuals, a popular year-round destination.

The centre offers evening meals, breakfasts, and picnic lunches. Meals are served in the beautiful high-roofed dining room which retains the impressive proportions and atmosphere of the old barn. There is also the option to self-cater. There is a small sunken lounge to relax in. Camping is an option. A meeting/classroom is also available.

DETAILS

- **Open** - All year, to check availability please call 01235 760253.
- **Number of beds** - 59: 1x15, 1x9, 1x6, 1x5, 6x4, 1x2
- **Booking** - Essential 24 hours in advance.
- **Price per night** - Adult £19.50. Under 18 £15.50
- **Public Transport** - Train, Didcot Parkway 10 miles. Stagecoach, 32/A, X35,36 from Didcot Parkway to Wantage 2 miles. There is no direct connection to the centre.
- **Directions** - From the M4 Jct 14, follow signs to Wantage. From Oxford A420 and A338 through Wantage. The Court Hill Ridgeway Centre is accessed from the A338 close to Letcombe Regis

CONTACT: Reception
Tel: 01235 760253
info@Courthill.org.uk www.Courthill.org.uk
Court Hill, Letcombe Regis, Wantage, OX12 9NE

KIPPS
BRIGHTON

Kipps Brighton is situated in the centre of Brighton, with views of the Royal Pavilion and close to all of Brighton's attractions including the beach, Brighton Pier, The Lanes and The Brighton Eye. We offer great value accommodation with excellent facilities, including a lounge, games room, & self catering kitchen. Staff offer nightly events, from pizza night to pasta night, a great way to meet the other guests and the staff. Dormitory rooms come with secure free lockers and en suite facilities, suitable for individuals and groups. Private rooms, all feature digital televisions/ bluetooth speakers/ tea & coffee making facilities, and combination safes. Friendly staff look forward to welcoming you to Brighton and to Kipps Brighton. Kipps also have a hostel in Canterbury, a short walk from the town centre and historic attractions. See page 88 for details.

DETAILS

- **Open** - All year. Reception 8am-2am – No Curfew.
- **Number of beds** - 47: 1x1, 6x dbl, 4x twin, 2x3, 2x10.
- **Booking** - Please book by phone, email or online (5% discount if booked online).
- **Price per night** - Dormitory rooms from £15 per person. Private rooms from £21 per person.
- **Public Transport** - Close to Brighton train station and bus station. From train station: exit and walk ahead down the main street for a few minutes, turn into Church Street (on your left) and walk along Church Street until the end, the hostel is opposite. From bus station: exit onto Old Steine Road and turn left towards the Royal Pavilion. At the far end of the Pavilion and opposite is the hostel.
- **Directions** - Take the M23, then A23 towards Brighton town centre. The hostel is opposite the Royal Pavilion on Grand Parade.

CONTACT: Reception
Tel: 01273 604182
kippshostelbrighton@gmail.com www.kipps-brighton.com
76 Grand Parade, Brighton, BN2 9JA

PALACE FARM
HOSTEL

Palace Farm Hostel is a relaxing and flexible four star hostel on a family run arable and fruit farm. It is situated in the village of Doddington, which has a pub, in the North Kent Downs Area of Outstanding Natural Beauty. The area is great for walking, cycling (cycle hire available £5 a day) and wildlife. The location is central for exploring Canterbury, Rochester, Chatham, Leeds Castle and the many other historic towns, villages and castles in Kent. The accommodation, in converted farm buildings, consists of ten fully heated en suite rooms sleeping up to 39 guests. The rooms surround an attractive courtyard garden with lawns, patio and barbecue area, ideal for families and groups. The en suite rooms cater for all age groups and those with disabilities. There are quality double beds, single beds & 3ft bunk beds. Duvets, linen and continental breakfast are included. There is also a small tent only camp-site. Green Tourism Business Scheme GOLD Award winner.

DETAILS

- **Open** - All year, 8am to 10pm flexible, please ask.
- **Number of beds** - 39: 1x8, 1x6, 2x5, 1x4, 1x3 and 4x2
- **Booking** - Advised.
- **Price per night** - From £16 to £30 (all private en suite rooms). Reduction for groups, see website.
- **Public Transport** - Trains: Sittingbourne (London Victoria to Dover). Buses from Sittingbourne station to Doddington two hourly (Mon-Sat), last buses 16.30 & 17.30.
- **Directions** - From A2 between Sittingbourne and Faversham turn south at Teynham, signed to Lynsted. Go through Lynsted and over M2 bridge, take 2nd turning right into Down Court Rd. Farm is 90 metres on left.

CONTACT: Graham and Liz Cuthbert
Tel: 01795 886200
info@palacefarm.com www.palacefarm.com
Down Court Road, Doddington, Sittingbourne / Faversham, Kent, ME9 0AU

KIPPS
CANTERBURY

Kipps is an ideal home-from-home for backpackers, visitors or small groups looking for self-catering budget accommodation in Canterbury. It is a short walk to the town centre and the historic attractions including the renowned Canterbury Cathedral. Canterbury also makes an ideal base for day trips to Dover, Leeds Castle and the many local beaches.

Facilities include dining room, TV lounge with digital TV, a garden, a fully equipped kitchen, a small shop offering breakfast and other food items, bicycle hire. Free WiFi & broadband access. Rooms include single/double/twin/family & dorms of up to 8 beds (most en suite). Camping available in summer. Free on-street parking. Kipps also have a hostel / hotel in Brighton, opposite the Royal Pavilion and close to town. See page 84.

DETAILS

- **Open** - All year, no curfew, reception 7.30am to 11pm.
- **Number of beds** - 51:- 2x1, 2x2, 1x3, 1x5, 1x6, 1x7, 2x8, 1x9
- **Booking** - Advance booking recommended. Book online.
- **Price per night** - From: dorms £14pp, singles £22pp, doubles £37, quads £50. Weekly and winter rates available. Credit cards accepted.
- **Public Transport** - Canterbury East train station on London Victoria to Dover line, is ½ mile by footpath (phone hostel for directions). The local C4 bus stops by the door of the hostel. Taxi from coach/rail stations is £3.
- **Directions** - By car :- Take B2068 to Hythe from City Ring Road (A28). Turn right at first traffic lights by church. Kipps is 300 yds on left.

CONTACT: Reception
Tel: 01227 786121
kippshostel@googlemail.com www.kipps-hostel.com
40 Nunnery Fields, Canterbury, Kent, CT1 3JT

ALPHA
HOSTEL

A hostel by the sea, next to the Viking way for walkers and cyclists and just 50m from a Blue Flag, safe swimming beach, Alpha Hostel has been providing great budget accommodation in a friendly flexible atmosphere for over 20 years. Children love the beach which is only 50m from the front door- so parents be ready to help build those sand castles! The beach is also used by a number of different water sports enthusiasts. Facilities include; two lounges, a dining room, and large self-catering kitchen, washbasins in rooms, en suite family rooms. Secure bike storage. On street car/coach parking. Risk assessed for council, European schools and group use. Catering available for large groups (20+),exclusive hostel use with classroom available. Group self-catering also an option. Families and individuals also welcome. Why not visit the area or just stay on your way to Europe (1/2 hour to Dover by car)?

DETAILS

■ **Open** - All year, 08.00 to 10.00hrs ,17.00 to 22.30 hrs.
■ **Number of beds** - 60: 2x6, 2x5, 4x5, 2x3, 6x2
■ **Booking** - Individuals/families: 25% deposit via website, balance on arrival, Groups: 25% deposit, balance 1 month before arrival.
■ **Price per night** - £16.00pp. accommodation only groups please call/email hostel direct with requirements for meals etc. to obtain the best price.
■ **Public Transport** - Train to Margate, bus to central Margate - Stagecoach, taxi, local buses and private hire. 10 minute walk to stations and town centre.
■ **Directions** - By car: From A28 follow brown hostel signs. By foot from Margate walk to sea front. Turn left (to the west) and follow the prom. Take second set of stairs to the higher walkway. Hostel is across the road 25m away.

CONTACT: Suzy Shears
Tel: 01843 221616
info@margatehostel.com www.margatehostel.com
3 Royal Esplanade, Westbrook Bay, Margate, Kent CT9 5DL

HARLOW
INTERNATIONAL HOSTEL ENGLAND

Harlow International Hostel is situated in the centre of a landscaped park and is one of the oldest buildings in Harlow. The town of Harlow is the ideal base from which to explore London, Cambridge and the best of South East England. The journey time to central London is only 35 minutes from the hostel door and it is the closest hostel to Stansted Airport. National Cycle Route 1 passes the front door. There are a range of room sizes from single to eight bedded including two rooms with double beds. Self-catering facilities, refreshments and a small shop are all available. During your visit you can relax with a book or game from the large collection. A children's zoo, orienteering course and outdoor pursuit centre are available in the park as well as pleasant river walks. Meals can be provided for groups. New for 2016 is a free outdoor gym in the neighbouring park.

DETAILS

- **Open** - All year. 8am - 10.30pm (check in 3-10.30pm).
- **Number of beds** - 30: 2x1, 5x2, 1x4, 1x6, 1x8
- **Booking** - Advance booking is recommended (can be taken 18 months in advance).
- **Price per night** - Please check the hostel website for all prices.
- **Public Transport** - Harlow Town rail station is only 800m from hostel with direct links to London, Cambridge & Stansted Airport. Buses connect to London and airports.
- **Directions** - J7 of M11 take A414 into Harlow. At the 4th roundabout take 1st exit (First Ave). Drive to 4th set of traffic lights. Immediately after lights turn right (School Lane). Hostel is on left of Greyhound Pub.

CONTACT: Richard Adams
Tel: 01279 421702
mail@h-i-h.co.uk www.h-i-h.co.uk
13 School Lane, Harlow, Essex, CM20 2QD

DOVER CASTLE
HOSTEL AND FLATSHARES

Dover Castle Hostel and Flatshares, located close to London Bridge in Central London (Zone 1), offers backpackers great value, short and long stay accommodation. Located in the centre of the city. It is walking distance to sights such as Tower Bridge, St Paul's Cathedral, London Dungeon, Shakespeare's Globe, Tate Modern and the London Eye. Prices include free breakfast and free WiFi. The hostel has a guest kitchen and common room, free luggage room, a laundry service as well as a late guest bar with pool table and super drink offers.

Guests wanting to stay in London for longer can rent rooms in Dover Castle house / flatshares. These furnished houses and flats are a short bus ride to London Bridge in Zone 2 (South East London). Single occupancy double rooms cost £145 per week and twin rooms cost £95 per week per person inclusive of bills and WiFi for a 6 week minimum stay. See www.london99.com for more info on the flatshares. Short or long term guests can find their home in London with Dover Castle!

DETAILS

- **Open** - All year 24 hours. No Curfew.
- **Number of beds** - 86: 1x4, 2x6, 2x8, 3x10, 2x12
- **Booking** - Booking advisable. Credit card secures bed.
- **Price per night** - £15-£25 pp incl. breakfast. Discounted weekly rates available.
- **Public Transport** - Nearest main line station: London Bridge. Take underground Northern Line to Borough Station. Hostel is opposite Borough Underground Station between London Bridge and Elephant and Castle. 10 mins from Waterloo Station.
- **Directions** - From Borough station cross to Great Dover Street, 1 min on right.

CONTACT: Reception
Tel: 020 74037773
stay@dovercastlehostel.com www.dovercastlehostel.com
6A Great Dover Street, Borough, London, SE1 4XW

CLINK78

Clink78 is a social backpackers' hostel in a vibrant area, just a stone's throw from the hip borough of Hackney, within easy reach of London's main tourist attractions, and close to the transport hub of King's Cross. Set in a 200-year-old magistrates' courthouse, where Charles Dickens was inspired to write Oliver Twist and The Clash stood trial. Original Victorian features combine with cool and colourful design, facilities are modern, beds are comfortable and the Clink team are always happy to help. The atmosphere is lively, especially down at ClashBAR where guests head for happy hour, DJs and live music. Cook a budget dinner in the well-equipped kitchen and meet up and share stories with other travellers in the TV/film lounge and internet rooms, both in original courtrooms. Innovative pod beds have a personal reading light and USB ports. Dorms, private rooms and en suites available and you can sleep in one of the original prison cells. Come and get locked-up at Clink78 and judge for yourself!

DETAILS

- **Open** - All year, 24 hours - no curfew or lockouts.
- **Number of beds** - 500: 4-16 bedded, triple, twin, single, en suite, cell rooms(for 2)
- **Booking** - Online, by email or phone. with full payment by credit or debit card.
- **Price per night** - From £13pp incl FREE breakfast, FREE bed linen, FREE WiFi and FREE London walking tour. Group discounts.
- **Public Transport** - Round the corner from King's Cross-St Pancras with direct links to Heathrow, Luton, Gatwick, Victoria, Eurostar and one change to Stansted.
- **Directions** - King's Cross station is 10 minutes away by foot. Exit the station, walk down King's Cross Road for 500m and you'll find Clink78 on your left.

CONTACT: Reservations
Tel: 020 7183 9400
reservations78@clinkhostels.com www.clinkhostels.com
78 Kings Cross Road, King's Cross, London, WC1X 9QG

VENI, VIDI, DORMIVI - I CAME, I SAW, I SLEPT

I AM A LIGHT SLEEPER BUT A HEAVY DREAMER

Clink261 is one of London's best established independent backpacker youth hostels, offering trendy and stylish accommodation in the very centre of London. This rather glamorous boutique hostel offers a very cosy and intimate atmosphere, combined with a personalised service. Clink261 attracts a diverse mix of individual and group travellers of all ages from around the world. You'll also find yourself a stone's throw from the British Museum, Covent Garden, Bloomsbury and Camden Market or just minutes away from the bright lights of Piccadilly Circus and Leicester Square on the tube. An improved security system gives you key card access to the building, your room and the self-catering kitchen and the tour desk will ensure you have everything you need for a great and unforgettable stay in London! All beds were upgraded in summer 2014 with LED lighting, power sockets and USB charge points.

DETAILS

■ **Open** - All year (except for Christmas), 24 hours - no curfew or lockouts.
■ **Number of beds** - 170: 4-6 8-10 & 18 bed dorms, 4 private rooms (up to 3 beds)
■ **Booking** - Advanced booking recommended.
■ **Price per night** - From £13pp including FREE breakfast & WiFi. Group discounts.
■ **Public Transport** - Just beside King's Cross / St.Pancras which houses the Eurostar station and has UK mainline trains, underground, local buses and direct links with all major airports - Heathrow, Gatwick, Luton and Stansted. .
■ **Directions** - Only 3 mins' walk from Kings Cross / St Pancras. From the station take the Gray's Inn Road exit, Keeping McDonald's on your right, walk straight ahead, past an exchange bureau, the police station and KFC. Gray's Inn Road curves to the right - the hostel is on the right 200m further on, opposite the hospital.

CONTACT:
Tel: 020 7833 9400
reservations261@clinkhostels.com   www.clinkhostels.com
261-265 Gray's Inn Road, King's Cross, London, WC1X 8QT

TRAVEL JOY
HOSTEL

Travel Joy Hostels are relaxed and chilled-out hostels which focus on personal service. Travel Joy is the only London hostel overlooking the river, centrally located between Chelsea and The Houses of Parliament. There is bicycle dock and a 24-hour bus outside the door that goes every ten minutes to Victoria Station, Houses of Parliament, Trafalgar Square, Soho, Oxford Street and Camden. On-site European restaurant and tour/theater-tickets desk. PCs in the lounge area (small fee) and € exchange with no commission/spread. Free tea/coffee/soft drinks at all times, free linen/towels, free WiFi in the entire building and free continental breakfast. There are no hidden costs. Other facilities include post, card phones, washing machine/dryer/iron, hair dryers, on-street parking and free luggage storage.

The hostel has a large bar, a great place to relax and socialize, with guest drink specials. You can BBQ on the terrace or hang out in the common room.

DETAILS

- **Open** - All year, reception open 7:30am - 5am. Contact in advance if arriving later.
- **Number of beds** - 74
- **Booking** - recommended, by email or online
- **Price per night** - Dorm beds from £18. Includes breakfast, bed linen & towel.
- **Public Transport** - Pimlico tube station (Victoria Line) is 5-7 minutes' walk away. Victoria Station 10-15 minutes' walk. Bus 24 runs into central London 24 hours a day.
- **Directions** - From Pimlico tube take Bessborough St South exit, follow Lupus St, turn left onto Claverton St and then right onto Grosvenor Rd. Look for King William IV.

CONTACT: Reception
Tel: 0207 834 9689
info@traveljoyhostels.com www.traveljoyhostels.com
111 Grosvenor Rd. London SW1V 3LG

STOUR VALLEY
BUNKHOUSE

Opened in 2007, and fitted with a wide range of modern facilities, Stour Valley Bunkhouse is set in peaceful surroundings on an historic 1000 acre working farm, an ideal base for exploring Constable Country. Close to the Stour Estuary, there are excellent opportunities for bird watching, walking and cycling on the doorstep. Alton Water is only 3 miles away for sailing and windsurfing. Ipswich is 6 miles away. For children of all ages there is a huge choice of local attractions, such as Jimmy's Farm or Colchester Castle. Colchester Zoo and Sutton Hoo are good options for a wet day, and there are excellent beaches at Dovercourt, Frinton and Walton. The bunkhouse sleeps up to 20 in 5 rooms. It is self-catering, with a shop and pub within a mile. The bunkhouse is unsuitable for stag parties or groups that are likely to be very noisy or drink heavily.

             GROUPS ONLY

DETAILS

■ **Open** - All year round (sole use groups only). Arrivals 4pm-9pm, depart by 10 am.
■ **Number of beds** - 20 beds: 2 x 6, 1 x 4, 2 x 2
■ **Booking** - Advance booking essential. Sole use group bookings only.
■ **Price per night** - 2 nights from £430 - £620, 3 nights from £530 - £825 for a maximum of 20 guests.
■ **Public Transport** - Manningtree Station 2.4 miles (less using bridle path) with regular service to London Liverpool St (1hr), Harwich Port and Ipswich. Taxis from Manningtree Station about £6.
■ **Directions** - Grid Reference: TM120340. Six miles south of Ipswich on A137. Look out for The Bull pub, then cross the railway bridge and turn left after 200 yards, between white railings. Follow the drive to the crossroads, turn left and the bunkhouse is on the right hand side.

CONTACT: Caroline
Tel: 01473 327090 / 07857 630692
stourvalley@yha.org.uk www.yha.org.uk/hostel/stour-valley-bunkhouse
Brantham Hall, The Chase, Brantham, Nr Manningtree, Suffolk, CO11 1PT

The 1912 Centre is the former town Fire Station situated within the heart of the Harwich Conservation area and just 50m from the sandy beach and promenade. Harwich owes much of its charm to its medieval origins, the grid pattern on which the original 13th century town was built still survives and there are over 200 listed buildings within half a square mile. The centrally heated hostel is laid out around the old engine garage, which now forms the central dining and recreational area. The upper floor has access to four cabin style sleeping areas, whilst additional beds are available on the ground floor allowing access for the disabled. All cabins have bunk beds. Facilities include a fully equipped kitchen, showers & drying room. Visitors can bring their own sleeping bags, or can hire duvets from the Centre. The Centre is compact and easily managed, groups are expected to undertake certain domestic duties during their stay, and are responsible for leaving the Centre in a clean and tidy condition.

DETAILS

- **Open** - All year apart from 24th-27th December. Centre users have all day access.
- **Number of beds** - 26: 3 x 6, 2 x 2, 1 x 4.
- **Booking** - Sole use groups only. No stag/hen groups. Pre booking essential.
- **Price per night** - Friday - Sunday (2 nights) £450, 1 Night - £240, 5 Nights - £900, 7 Nights - £1150. Other prices on application
- **Public Transport** - Harwich Town Station is a short walk from the Centre, direct trains to London Liverpool Street. The bus station is also within walking distance.
- **Directions** - Follow A120 to Harwich Quay, follow the road round past the Navy Yard Wharf. The Centre is on the right (adjacent to the Electric Palace Cinema).

CONTACT: Debbie Rotchell
Tel: 01255 552010
d.rotchell@harwichconnexions.co.uk www.harwichconnexions.co.uk
Cow Lane, Off Kings Quay Street, Harwich CO12 3ES

Croft Farm is located just outside Tewkesbury in the scenic River Avon Valley, with a caravan and camping park adjacent to the sites own lake. Accommodation is in cabins, a pod village, chalets and camping. The wide range of watersports activities and tuition on offer provide added interest for those wanting a more active holiday. A footpath meanders through the meadow to the River Avon, and free river fishing is available to all our guests.

Croft Farm is ideally placed as a centre for touring, with the Cotswolds, Malverns, Bredon Hill and the Forest of Dean within easy reach. Local towns include Pershore, Evesham, Cheltenham, Gloucester and Tewkesbury. We also offer a full range of activity holidays and events, from corporate team-building events to stag and hen groups.

DETAILS

- **Open** - All year, 0900-2100.
- **Number of beds** - 250: 58x4 9x2
- **Booking** - £15 deposit on individual bookings. £50 deposit on groups.
- **Price per night** - Bed £12, B&B £18, half board £24, full board £30
- **Public Transport** - Bus stop 100 yards from site entrance. Train station 2 miles Ashchurch for Tewkesbury
- **Directions** - M5 jnct 9. towards Tewkesbury. Turn right at the lights, (Shannon Way). At next lights turn right and go over the motorway bridge. Take the first turning left, through housing estate and over the motorway again. Turn right onto the B4080 and then first left into Croft Farm. From Tewkesbury take the B4080 north (Bredon). Croft Farm is on the left hand side after about 1.5 miles.

CONTACT: Martin Newell
Tel: 07736036967
alan@croftfarmleisure.co.uk www.croftfarmleisure.co.uk
Bredons Hardwick, Near Tewkesbury, Gloucestershire GL20 7EE

YE OLD FERRIE INN
BUNKHOUSE

This beautiful riverside pub has been standing on the banks of the River Wye since the 15th Century. With charming traditional features, warming open fires and stunning views across the valley, Ye Old Ferrie Inn is the ideal base for your exploration of the Wye Valley.

Ye Old Ferrie Inn Bunkhouse, adjoining the inn, is the perfect place for you to hang up your rucksack, kick off your walking boots and relax. There are two bunkrooms, sleeping 6 and 12, which are cosy, practical and affordable. You can watch the world float by on the two riverside terraces and meals are available in the inn which serves traditional pub food, locally sourced.

The inn also has double B&B rooms with riverside views. The area is ideal for canoeing, walking and rock climbing.

DETAILS

- **Open** - All year, all day.
- **Number of beds** - 20 (1x14, 1x6) plus double B&B rooms
- **Booking** - Book by phone or email.
- **Price per night** - From £15 per person. For sole use please ring to enquire.
- **Public Transport** - Train stations at Newport, Lydney, Hereford or Gloucester. Regular buses from Monmouth or Ross-on-Wye.
- **Directions** - From A40 Ross-on-Wye to Abergavenny road take junction signed Whitchurch/Symonds Yat West (B4164). Stay on B4164 and take slight left at Ferrie Lane and continue onto Washings Lane.

CONTACT: Jamie
Tel: 01600 890 232
hello@yeoldferrieinn.com www.yeoldferrieinn.com
Ferrie Lane, Symonds Yat West, Herefordshire HR9 6BL

Located on a working family farm, Haye Farm Sleeping Barn offers bunkhouse accommodation finished to a very high standard. It has a fully equipped self-catering kitchen, dining room and lounge. Bedrooms range from double/twin en suite to a 6 bedded dormitory. The barn is central heated throughout. Covered decking, patio, lawn and a BBQ provide ample opportunity to enjoy the quiet rural location. A great location to enjoy the surrounding countryside, the Wyre Forerst being one of the largest remaining ancient forests in England. The Worcestershire Way footpath follows the boundary of the farm and both the Severn Way and Mercian Way (NCN route 45) pass through Bewdley.

The georgian town of Bewdley located on the river Severn is just 1 mile away, the West Midland Safari Park and Severn Valley Railway are also very close

DETAILS

- **Open** - Open all year 24 hour access.
- **Number of beds** - 15: 1x2, 1x3, 1x4, 1x6
- **Booking** - advance booking required
- **Price per night** - From £15pp. Can book bed in dormitory, private room or exclusive use of whole barn. Visit website for full prices
- **Public Transport** - Train station Kidderminster 4 miles. Bus stop Bewdley 1 mile
- **Directions** - One mile from Bewdley town centre, within 30 minutes' drive of both the M5 and M42. From Bewdley town centre take the B4194 southbound for ½ mile. At top of bank turn right (signposted Heightington/outdoor centre). Farm entrance on the right after ½ mile

CONTACT: Stuart Norgrove
Tel: 01299 403371
enquiries@haye-farm.co.uk www.haye-farm.co.uk
Haye Farm, Ribbesford, Bewdley, Worcestershire, DY12 2TP

BERROW HOUSE

ENGLAND BUNKHOUSE & CAMP SITE

Berrow House is situated between Rugged Stone Hill and Midsummer Hill in the Malvern Hills. An Area of Outstanding Natural Beauty close to the Forest of Dean, the Welsh border and the start of the Worcestershire Way Walk. In the garden around Berrow House there is a selection of simple accommodation and camping with a wildlife picnic area, woodland, star gazing and grass sledging. The Bunkhouse has two rooms and shares the toilets and showers in the yard with the camp-site. It's kitchen has a table and benches, hot water, fridge freezer, microwave and a cooker. It's sitting room has easy chairs, four beds and steps leading up to a small loft area with 3 mattresses. The Fold has a toilet and shower and two small bunkrooms each sleeping two. Adjacent is a kitchenette with fridge, toaster, small cooker and utensils. The Bandsaw Barn is a meeting room for use by groups on request.(seats 16) and can also be used as overflow accommodation for 3. The Nook (caravan) has one double and a single bed (sharing main bunkhouse cooking and toilet facilities). Heating provided (fan heaters). Bring you own sleeping bag or can be hired.

DETAILS

- **Open** - All year, 24 hours.
- **Number of beds** - 7 (Bunkhouse), 4 (Fold), 3 (Nook), 3 (Bandsaw Barn) & 8 tents.
- **Booking** - Not required for individuals
- **Price per night** - £13 per person
- **Public Transport** - Trains and National Express in Ledbury (3 miles £5 in a taxi).
- **Directions** - Take A449 from Ledbury towards Malvern. Turn right on to A438 through Eastnor. Berrow House is behind phone box in Hollybush (yellow sign).

CONTACT: Bill or Mary Cole
Tel: 01531 635845
berrowhouse@tiscali.co.uk www.berrowhouse.co.uk
Hollybush, Ledbury, Herefordshire, HR8 1ET

WOODSIDE LODGES
BUNKHOUSE
ENGLAND

Woodside Lodges is a landscaped park with lakes, grass and woodland managed to encourage wildlife. In addition to the Scandinavian lodges, campsite and camping pods there is a modern barn converted into 5 self-catering units. 3 units sleep 2, 1 unit sleeps 3 and 1 unit sleeps 4 (additional camp beds are available). Each unit has a cooking area with kettle, toaster, microwave, 2 electric rings, fridge and basic utensils. Electricity is by coin meter and bedding can be provided for an extra charge (or bring your own sleeping bag). The bunkhouse has a small common room, the toilets and showers are shared with the campsite. Close to the Herefordshire Trail, the Malvern Hills and the Forest of Dean the area is ideal for walkers. Nature lovers will enjoy the site with its backcloth of mixed woodland, wild flowers, pools and waterfalls where fishing, wild swimming and picnics can be enjoyed. The nearby town of Ledbury is famous for its black and white buildings, cobbled streets and Poetry Festival.

DETAILS

- **Open** - All year, all day.,
- **Number of beds** - 13 : 3x2, 1x3, 1x4 (max 20 using camp beds)
- **Booking** - Booking in advance advised.
- **Price per night** - From £12.50 pp based on 4 sharing a room, weekend supplement, phone/website for full prices. Can be booked for exclusive use.
- **Public Transport** - Public transport is available within 1/2 mile.
- **Directions** - From Junction 2, M50 take the A417 to Ledbury. At the first roundabout turn left following Leadon Way (the by-pass). At the third roundabout turn left into Little Marcle Road. Go past the factory and take the right turn signposted Falcon Lane & Baregains Lane. Woodside Lodges is the sixth entrance on the right.

CONTACT: Woodside Lodges Country Park
Tel: 01531 670269
info@woodsidelodges.co.uk   www.woodsidelodges.co.uk
Woodside Lodges, Falcon Lane, Ledbury, Herefordshire, HR8 2JN

LUDLOW MASCALL
CENTRE

Located in the heart of this beautiful market town, with ample free parking, Ludlow Mascall Centre is within walking distance of the restaurants, markets, shops, pubs, museum, castle and church. The Shropshire Hills are close by, with miles of beautiful countryside and stunning landscapes to explore. Built in 1857 as a national school, this beautiful Victorian building has been extended to provide residential accommodation with twin rooms, a family room, and a room which has been designed for those with limited mobility in mind. All rooms have en suite toilets, basins and showers. Continental breakfasts are included and home cooked breakfasts using locally sourced produce are available for a small extra charge. Packed lunches, half board and full board are also available by arrangement. Tea and coffee making facilities are available in the residents lounge along with a television. The pretty courtyard garden with seating, won 'Best Community Garden' during 'Ludlow in Bloom 2012'. Guided cycling routes are available by prior arrangement.

DETAILS

- **Open** - All year except Christmas.
- **Number of beds** - 19: 7x2, 1x1, 1x4
- **Booking** - Bookings taken via telephone, email or website.
- **Price per night** - From £40.00 B&B single per night.
- **Public Transport** - Ludlow railway station is five minutes' walk away.
- **Directions** - From A49 take Sheet Road towards Ludlow (The first roundabout from the south and second from the north) Continue along Sheet Road towards the town centre. The Centre is on the left hand side after the police station.

CONTACT:
Tel: 01584 873882
info@ludlowmascallcentre.co.uk   www.ludlowmascallcentre.co.uk
Lower Galdeford, Ludlow, Shropshire SY8 1RZ

FOXHOLES CASTLE
BUNKHOUSE

Foxholes Castle Bunkhouse at Bishops Castle is situated within a relaxed, family-run camp-site, surrounded by glorious views of South West Shropshire's beautiful hill country. Within a few minutes' walk of the Shropshire Way, Offa's Dyke Path, the Sustrans cycle network and the lively town of Bishops Castle it is ideal for families, couples, walkers, cyclists and photographers. The bunkhouse is heated, divided in half by a partition with an open doorway. There is a single bed and 3 sets of bunks (no bedding is provided) and television. In a heated buildings next to the bunkhouse (shared with the camp-site) you will find 3 wet rooms,and a room with fridge, kettle and washing-up sink. A second set of showers and toilets are 30 seconds' walk away. There is good accessibility for wheelchair users. There is an outside table seating area and space for a BBQ. There are no cooking facilities but there are lots of pubs, restaurants, cafés and take-aways 10 minutes' walk away in Bishops Castle.

DETAILS

- **Open** - All year.
- **Number of beds** - 7
- **Booking** - Bookings by email.
- **Price per night** - £10 per person or £60 for whole bunkhouse (sleeps 7).
- **Public Transport** - Trains at Craven Arms (12 miles). Buses from Shrewsbury to Bishops Castle (5 minutes' walk from bunkhouse) every 2 hours.
- **Directions** - Bishops Castle is on the A488 about 20 miles south of Shrewsbury, and 35 miles from the M54. Foxholes is on the B4385 Montgomery Road just north of the town. Look for our sign, and follow our driveway for half a mile. GR SO 324 897

CONTACT: Chris or Wendy Jones
Tel: 01588 638924, mobile 07890 231351
foxholes.castle@googlemail.com www.foxholes-castle.co.uk
Foxholes Camping, Montgomery Rd, Bishops Castle, Shropshire, SY9 5HA

Broughton Bunkhouse offers comfortable accommodation in a 17th century barn with a wealth of exposed beams and full of character. The bunkhouse is clean and cosy, central heating, hot water and showers are all inclusive. There is a fully-equipped kitchen with cookers, fridge-freezer, dishwasher and all the utensils you will need. Clothes washing and drying facilities are also provided.

Broughton Bunkhouse is just outside Bishops Castle in South Shropshire, an excellent area for walking on the nearby Stiperstones and Long Mynd. Ideal for cycling around Clun or just enjoying the real ale brewed in two of Bishop Castle's own pubs.

DETAILS

- **Open** - All year, 24 hours.
- **Number of beds** - 12: 2 x 6
- **Booking** - Check availability and arrange check-in by phone or email. A deposit is required for advance bookings.
- **Price per night** - From £10pp. Sole use hire by groups for a night, weekend or week is welcomed. Please telephone for prices.
- **Public Transport** - National Coach stop in Shrewsbury. Train Station at Craven Arms (12 miles). Local Bus service from Craven Arms to Bishops Castle. Ask hostel about free collection from Bishops Castle. You may also be able to arrange collection from Craven Arms by the hostel for a fee of £10.
- **Directions** - GR 313 906. From Bishops Castle take B4385 (signed Montgomery). Lower Broughton Farm is 2 miles out of town on the right (on the B4385).

CONTACT: Kate
Tel: 01588 638393
lbrfarm@fastmail.co.uk www.broughtonfarm-shropshire.co.uk
Lower Broughton Farm, Nr Bishops Castle, Montgomery, Powys SY15 6SZ

BRIDGES LONG MYND YOUTH HOSTEL

This small hostel, once the old village school, is tucked away in the Shropshire hills with the Long Mynd to the east and Stiperstones to the west. It is an ideal spot for ramblers with the Shropshire Way passing close by and a great network of uncrowded paths to explore. Ideally situated for the End to End cycle route and plenty of mountain biking opportunities. The nearby small towns of Church Stretton, Ludlow, Much Wenlock, Bishops Castle and sleepy Montgomery are all worth a visit. There's also the Acton Scott working farm museum and Snailbeach former lead mines close by. The hostel has a good kitchen, lounge with wood fire, books and games, a drying room, a food shop and a large garden. One en suite room has some facilities for the disabled, phone to discuss your requirements. Meals are available, camping is allowed and there is a pub nearby.

DETAILS

- **Open** - All year. Reception open 8-10 am and 5-10 pm. Hostel closes at 11pm.
- **Number of beds** - 38: 2x4 en suite, 1x6 or 8, 1x10, 1x12
- **Booking** - Telephone to book. No credit or debit cards accepted. Cheques must be made payable to Bridges Youth Hostel not YHA.
- **Price per night** - Adults £19 single night, £16 two or more nights. Under 18's £13 single night, £11.50 two or more nights. Camping £8
- **Public Transport** - Trains at Church Stretton (5 miles) with a shuttle bus to Bridges at weekends from April to September.
- **Directions** - From Church Stretton, take 'The Burway' road uphill. Take right fork at top of Long Mynd. From Shrewsbury take road via Longden and Pulverbatch, then left by Bridges Pub. Access from Church Stretton over the Long Mynd Hill is not advisable in bad weather during winter.

CONTACT: Bridges Youth Hostel
Tel: 01588 650656
Ratlinghope, Shrewsbury, Shropshire, SY5 0SP

Situated on the Dudmaston Estate, a National Trust property 4 miles east of Bridgnorth, Big Mose Basecamp accommodates groups of up to 20 people in 4 bunkrooms of varying sizes. The converted Tudor farmhouse offers a large living area with a TV/DVD and lots of games for those rainy days, a dining area where everyone can sit together and enjoy reflecting on the day's adventures and a fully equipped kitchen area. Sleeping bags required.

Situated next to the Basecamp is a large camping area which, with the outside toilet block attached to the Basecamp, can accommodate additional members to your group. Having your annual meeting where you decide your events for the year? Then why not hire the meeting room, this beautiful airy room is perfect for all occasions.

DETAILS

- **Open** - All year.
- **Number of beds** - Basecamp 20: 1x2, 1x4, 1x6, 1x8, Mose cottage 10: 1x6, 2x2
- **Booking** - Essential
- **Price per night** - £550.00 per week (Mon - Fri 4 nights) £300.00 per weekend (Friday to Sunday 2 nights) £137.50 per night.
- **Public Transport** - Train stations at Telford, Wolverhampton or Kidderminster.
- **Directions** - From Bridgnorth take A458 towards Stourbridge. Travel 3 miles and after a small pine wood on right, take right hand turning to Mose. Approx 1/4 mile along take a left down a track with a small National Trust sign leading to the basecamp.

CONTACT: Sarah Bailey
Tel: 01746 780866
bigmosebasecamp@nationaltrust.org.uk www.nationaltrust.org.uk/dudmaston-estate
Big Mose Basecamp, Quatford, Bridgnorth, Shropshire, WV15 6QR

ALL STRETTON
BUNKHOUSE

All Stretton Bunkhouse offers comfortable self-catering accommodation with underfloor heating for individuals and small groups of up to 10 people. It has easy access to the Long Mynd which offers walks and bike rides for all levels of fitness. It is within easy reach of the busy town of Church Stretton and all its facilities, and just 10 minutes' walk from the local pub (but please always book meals as it is not very big). Take-away food is available in Church Stretton. There are three bedrooms in the bunkhouse: Synalds and Cardoc have two bunks (sleeping 4) and Novers has two singles. A cot is also available. The well-equipped kitchen has cooker, microwave, toaster, kettle and fridge. There is a shower, two toilets and a tumble dryer. The track up to the property is steep and rough so wheelchair access is difficult. Groups booking the complete bunkhouse may bring dogs.

DETAILS

- **Open** - All year. Winter 4:00pm-10:30am; Summer 5:00pm-10:30am. Extra access negotiable.
- **Number of beds** - 10 plus 1 cot.
- **Booking** - Book by phone, post or online.
- **Price per night** - £19 per person per night; children half price; Under 5s free. £1 per person per night discount for those arriving without a vehicle.
- **Public Transport** - Trains to Church Stretton from Shrewsbury, Hereford and Cardiff. Station 1.2 miles walk (or taxi) from bunkhouse. National Express buses to Shrewsbury, hourly local buses from Shrewsbury to Church Stretton via All Stretton.
- **Directions** - 300m on right going up Batch Valley bridleway (off the B5477, a mile north of Church Stretton).

CONTACT: Frankie Goode
Tel: 01694 722593   Mob: 0781 5517482
info@allstrettonbunkhouse.co.uk www.allstrettonbunkhouse.co.uk
Meadow Green, Batch Valley, All Stretton, Shrops, SY6 6JW

ENGLAND

STOKES BARN
BUNKHOUSES

Stokes Barn is located on top of Wenlock Edge, Area of Outstanding Natural Beauty, in the heart of Shropshire countryside. Two bunkhouses are available; the Threshing Barn (sleeping 28) and the Granary (sleeping 16).

These offer comfortable, centrally heated, dormitory accommodation for a wide range of groups and provide an ideal base for corporate groups, field study groups, universities, schools, stag and hen parties, walkers or just a relaxing reunion with friends or family. The Ironbridge World Heritage Site is only 6 miles away and is a great attraction. Walk to the historic town of Much Wenlock to visit shops, pubs and sports facilities. Situated only a few miles from Church Stretton and the Long Mynd the barn is in a walking / cycling haven. Many activities available. Have a relaxing and enjoyable stay.

DETAILS

- **Open** - All year, all day.
- **Number of beds** - Threshing Barn 28: 1x12,1x10,1x6 Granary 16: 1x10,1x4,1x2
- **Booking** - Deposit required. Minimum stay 2 nights.
- **Price per night** - Minimum of two nights. Barn £540 two nights mid week, £880 two nights weekend. Granary: £384 two nights mid week, £595 two nights weekend.
- **Public Transport** - Trains at Telford (10 miles) and Shrewsbury (10 miles). National Express coaches call at Shrewsbury from London, call 0839 142348 for information. Midland Red buses stop in Much Wenlock, enquires 01952 223766.
- **Directions** - GR 609 999. From the M6 take M54 Telford following Ironbridge Gorge signs. A4169 to Much Wenlock, joining A458 for Shrewsbury. The Barn is signed at Newton House Farm (TF13 6DB) on the Much Wenlock to Shrewsbury Rd.

CONTACT: Chris
Tel: 01952 727491
info@stokesbarn.co.uk www.stokesbarn.co.uk
Stokes Barn, Newtown Farm, Much Wenlock, Shropshire, TF13 6DB

WOMERTON FARM
BUNKHOUSE

Womerton Farm Bunkhouse is situated right next to the Long Mynd, Area of Outstanding National Beauty in the heart of the Shropshire Hills. It offers small select accommodation to sleep eight; six in bunks downstairs and two in a double sofa bed upstairs. There is a fully equipped kitchen and living area upstairs. The bunkhouse is 3 miles from Church Stretton, 12 miles from historic Shrewsbury and 15 miles from Ludlow, food capital of Shropshire. There are many local attractions such as Acton Scott Working Farm Museum, Stokesay Castle, Museum of Lost Content and Discovery Centre. The Long Mynd is fantastic for walking, mountain biking and horse riding. Horses can be field-accommodated if arranged in advance. Well behaved dogs that are not moulting allowed. For photo gallery, directions and details please visit website.

DETAILS

- **Open** - All year, all day. Closed from 11 am to 4pm on change over days.
- **Number of beds** - 8: 1x6, plus double sofa bed in living area .
- **Booking** - Booking recommended to guarantee a place.
- **Price per night** - £80 Christmas / New Year, £80 Easter to Sept, £60 off peak. Stay 3 nights get next 1 to 3 nights half price. Phone or email for midweek offers.
- **Public Transport** - Nearest train and bus station is Church Stretton (3 miles). Taxi fare is about £10.
- **Directions** - From Church Stretton follow A49 north. Past coffee shop and craft centre take a left turn signed Lower Wood. From Shrewsbury on A49 south, pass though Leebotwood then take the right turn signed Lower Wood. Follow this road for 1 mile, cross a cattle grid onto the Long Mynd and we are the first farm on the right.

CONTACT: Ruth or Tony
Tel: 01694 751260
ruth@womerton-farm.co.uk www.womerton-farm.co.uk
Womerton Farm, All Stretton, Church Stretton, Shropshire, SY6 6LJ

BUNKHOUSE

Springhill Farm Bunkhouse is on a Welsh hill farm at 1475ft above sea level, on the Welsh/Shropshire border with beautiful views over the Ceiriog Valley and Berwyn Mountains. Great for walking, riding, cycling, team building, meetings, or just to relax.

Self catering, the main bunkhouse sleeps around 21 in 5 bedrooms. The 2 smaller self catering cottages can sleep 12 more. There is also a heated games and lecture room. The bunkhouse has under-floor heating, entrance hall with w/c and drying room, large kitchen, dining room and sitting room. Outside is a large patio and lawn, BBQ and hot tub. Available on site, horse riding for all ages and abilities, archery and cycle hire. Horses and pets welcome on request.

DETAILS
- **Open** - By arrangement.
- **Number of beds** - 30+: 21 (bunkhouse) + two cottages
- **Booking** - Advisable, deposit required
- **Price per night** - £20pp (including bedding but not towels)
- **Public Transport** - Nearest train station Chirk (8 miles). Nearest bus service is in the village Glyn Ceiriog (2.5 miles). Transfer can be arranged.
- **Directions** - GR SJ 210 346. On the A483 from Wrexham, take the third exit on the first roundabout (McDonalds). At the next roundabout take the first exit, continue into Chirk, and then turn right for Glyn Ceiriog. After 6 miles you will arrive at Glyn Ceiriog. At the mini roundabout turn left, go over the bridge, and then straight away turn right into a small lane. Continue up the hill for about two miles, do not turn off.

CONTACT: Sue Benbow
Tel: 01691 718406
sue@springhillfarm.co.uk www.springhillfarm.co.uk
Springhill Farm, Selattyn, Oswestry, Shropshire, SY10 7NZ

HATTERS
BIRMINGHAM

Your ideal choice for city central accommodation, Hatters Birmingham has combined hotel quality en suite rooms with the social atmosphere of an international travellers' hostel. Catering for groups of all sizes and independent travellers, you can enjoy the comforts of FREE WiFi, breakfast, en suite rooms, large communal areas and enthusiastic, informative staff. Full board or half board options are available for groups of over 15 people. Conveniently located for all city centre attractions and transport links, ask our reception staff about discounts to Cadbury World, Warwick Castle, Sealife Centre, and many other FREE adventures, including our FREE city walking tours and quiz nights. If you are into the outdoors we have the largest bouldering complex just around the corner, or try out your mountain biking skills at Cannock Chase (30 mins' drive). So come and stay with us and we'll show you what's fun in Brum.

DETAILS

- **Open** - All year. Reception available, 24 hours. Check in 2pm, check out 11am.
- **Number of beds** - 100: single, double, twin, triple, 4, 6, 8 and 12 bed rooms.
- **Booking** - Booking not essential but recommended, especially at weekends. Photo ID (ie passport, ID card or driving license) required at check in.
- **Price per night** - From £12 dorms, from £32 private rooms, inc b/fast & linen. For group prices and bookings see www.hattershostels.com/groups or email: groups@hattersgroup.com
- **Public Transport** - Easy walking distance from all public transport hubs: New Street Station 15mins, Snow Hill Station 5mins, Digbeth Coach Station 20mins. Local taxi service @ £5.00 for all city centre travel. Taxi service: BB's Taxi 0121 693 3333
- **Directions** - Please contact the hostel reception for directions.

CONTACT: Reception
Tel: 0121 236 4031
birmingham@hattersgroup.com www.hattersgroup.com/#bham
92-95 Livery Street, Birmingham, B3 1RJ

IGLOO
HYBRID

Located on Market Square, right in the centre of Nottingham, Igloo Hybrid is Nottingham's most popular choice for budget-minded travellers. Opened in 2015, it offers a clean, safe and warm overnight stay for great value prices. Facilities include a fully-equipped self-catering kitchen, free Wi-Fi throughout, power showers, lockers, lounge with internet access, outdoor courtyard and laundry facilities. There are dorms beds with memory foam mattresses and reading lights, inspired SleepBox quarters for 1 or 2 people as well as twins, doubles, triples, quads and family rooms (some en suite). Igloo Annexe & Pods (100 Mansfield Road NG1 3HD), also centrally located, offers further accommodation with the same standards and facilities. All rooms are inspired by travelling, fellow explorers and a real passion for value. Created using locally sourced, up-cycled and second-hand furniture (with added touches of personality and top notch comfort) and featuring local street art murals.

DETAILS

- **Open** - All year, all day. Reception open 7am-1am weekday, 24hrs Fri / Sat.
- **Number of beds** - 49: singles, twins, doubles, triples, quads and family rooms.
- **Booking** - Essential - especially during summer months. Groups require deposit.
- **Price per night** - Dorms: £18pp. £95 per week after 10 nights stay. Singles from £32.00. Other private rooms from £18 pp. Seasonal discounts.
- **Public Transport** - 5 mins' walk from the train and Broadmarsh bus stations or take FREE Centrelink bus to Market Sq. Direct trains/coaches from London, etc.
- **Directions** - From the Tourist Info Centre in Market Square turn left, walk across the square to Starbucks and Costa Coffee. Take the road between coffee shops (Wheeler Gate). Hostel on right in a courtyard, between Cafe Nero and Specsavers.

CONTACT: Igloo Hybrid
Tel: 01159 483822
hybrid@igloohostel.co.uk www.igloohostel.co.uk
Igloo Hybrid, 4-6 Eldon Chambers, Wheeler Gate, Nottingham, NG1 2NS

Greatly improved over the last few years, inc adding en suites, Hunstanton Backpackers is 3* VisitEngland approved. An ideal affordable family break or activity getaway for walking, cycling, bird watching or fun on the beach. The Norfolk Coast Path, serviced by Coasthopper Bus, goes through stunning beaches, great for wildlife spotting, or take a boat to Seal Island. Rooms are bunkrooms of various sizes or family rooms, some doubles, some en suite. Hire the property for sole use, for groups, friends reunions and family get-togethers. Self-catering kitchen, large lounge, conservatory dining area and an optional classroom/training area. Meals and drinks (including alcohol) can be provided (5* food hygiene). The garden has patio, benches & sea views. A 3 minute walk will take you to the sea front or town centre with a Sealife sanctuary, fantastic beaches and cliff top walks. A friendly, family welcome awaits you at Hunstanton Backpackers a great home-from-home on the east coast

DETAILS

- **Open** - All year (call if online booking not available). Reception 8-10am 5-9:30pm.
- **Number of beds** - 47: 1x double (en suite), 1x 3-bed, 3 double/ WC, 2x4, 1x4 (en suite), 1x4D(family) inc WC, 1x5/6, 2x6/8 (en suite). 1 Ground Floor 2 bed (en suite)
- **Booking** - By phone or email
- **Price per night** - Adults from £24. 2 bed from £55, 4 bed from £80. Enquire for multi night discounts, family rooms & sole use, schools/groups full board packages.
- **Public Transport** - Coast Hopper. Trains at Kings Lynn with bus to Hunstanton.
- **Directions** - Follow the coast road to Hunstanton, then signs for South Beach (Southend Rd). Turn right into Park Road, then first left, hostel is 20 yds on the left. Brown youth hostel signs on route

CONTACT: Neal or Alison Sanderson
Tel: 01485 532061 Mob: 07771 804831/07737 642828
enquiries@hunstantonhostel.co.uk www.norfolkbeachholidays.co.uk
15-17 Avenue Road, Hunstanton, Norfolk, PE36 5BW

DEEPDALE GRANARY
GROUP HOSTEL

A perfect base for groups to stay, explore and absorb the stunning North Norfolk coast. Deepdale Granary is a self-contained 17th century building sleeping 18 in four bedrooms with a fully fitted kitchen and dining/sitting room. Part of the award winning Deepdale Farm, right on the coast in the heart of an Area of Outstanding Natural Beauty. There are excellent pubs nearby, both traditional and chic, great restaurants and miles of unspoilt beaches and dunes. The Norfolk coast is perfect for walking and cycling with miles of coast path and picturesque villages. Take time to discover our heritage sites including the Sandringham and Holkham estates or enjoy birdwatching in the tranquil beauty of the unique saltmarsh. The Granary is fully heated, has showers, a drying room and solar water heating. Next door Dalegate Market has shops, a supermarket, and a brilliant café serving locally sourced food. Camping and tipis also available.

DETAILS

- **Open** - All year, all day. Collect key from Deepdale Information.
- **Number of beds** - 19: 2x6, 1x4, 1x3.
- **Booking** - Essential, 20% deposit, balance in advance. See website for details
- **Price per night** - From £150 per night, for up to 19 people.
- **Public Transport** - Trains / coaches at King's Lynn (25 miles) then excellent Coastal Hopper bus to Burnham Deepdale. Coastal Hopper services the coast from King's Lynn to Cromer, including Sandringham. Travelline 0870 608 2 608.
- **Directions** - GR 803443. On A149 coast road, halfway between Hunstanton and Wells-next-the-Sea. Beside Deepdale Garage & opposite Deepdale Church.

CONTACT:
Tel: 01485 210256
info@deepdalebackpackers.co.uk www.deepdalebackpackers.co.uk
Deepdale Information Centre, Burnham Deepdale, Norfolk, PE31 8DD

Escape to this eco-friendly award-winning backpackers' hostel on the beautiful North Norfolk coast. Deepdale Backpackers offers private en suite rooms (double, twin, triple, quad and family), single sex and mixed dorms. Deepdale is a perfect base for walking and cycling with miles of coast path, the famous big skies and quaint fishing harbours. You will also be happy if you want adrenaline sport, great pubs and restaurants and miles of sandy beaches. A fully equipped farmhouse kitchen and cosy lounge with a TV and a wood burner for cooler nights, complement the lovely courtyard with barbeques for summer evenings.

Deepdale is an eco-friendly working farm with recycling, underfloor heating and solar water. Next door Dalegate Market has shops, a supermarket, and a café serving locally sourced food. Camping and tipis are also available. The hostel is now available as a whole unit perfect for a large family get together.

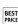

DETAILS

- **Open** - All year, all day, collect key from Deepdale Information.
- **Number of beds** - 50: 5xdbl, 1twin, 1triple, 1quad, 2 family rms up to 6, + dorms
- **Booking** - Pre-booking recommended. Max group size 12, unless you hire the whole hostel which is avalable certain dates on request. - See website
- **Price per night** - From £15(£105 per week) dorm room. £30 twin/double room.
- **Public Transport** - Train / coaches at King's Lynn (25 Miles). Coast Hopper bus from King's Lynn to Cromer stops at Burnham Deepdale. Traveline 0870 6082608.
- **Directions** - GR 803443 On A149 coast road halfway between Hunstanton and Wells-next-the-Sea. Beside Dalegate Market, opposite Deepdale Church.

CONTACT:
Tel: 01485 210256
info@deepdalebackpackers.co.uk www.deepdalebackpackers.co.uk
Deepdale Information Centre, Burnham Deepdale, Norfolk, PE31 8DD

BRANCASTER
ACTIVITY CENTRE (BAC)

This Grade 2 listed flint cottage is located within the picturesque harbour of Brancaster Staithe on the North Norfolk Coast. Guests are never disappointed by the stunning sea views across the beautiful marshes. Brancaster Activity Centre offers group accommodation for up to 22 guests, in 4 newly furbished bedrooms with en suite facilities. Larger groups of up to 48 are also welcome, across 9 bedrooms. Your group can be creative in the self-catering kitchen, or sample the local flavours in nearby pubs and café's. The upstairs 'snug' has a TV and wood burner and there is a garden with seating and gas BBQ. The perfect spot for activities such as sailing, walking, kite surfing and more; the Norfolk Coast Path runs by the door, as does the Coasthopper bus service and some of Norfolk's finest birdwatching reserves are only a stones' throw away.

DETAILS

- **Open** - All year, by arrangement.
- **Number of beds** - 48: 1x8, 1x7, 2x6, 3x5, 1x4, 1x2
- **Booking** - Booking is essential. Call booking office on 0344 335 1296.
- **Price per night** - Oct-Mar: Half centre from £647 (2 nights) to £1848 (7 nights). Full centre from £823 (2 nights) to £2351 (7 nights). Apr-Sep: Half centre from £862 (2 nights) to £2464 (7 nights). Full centre from £1293 (2 nights) to £3695 (7 nights).
- **Public Transport** - Train: King's Lynn 25 miles away. The Coasthopper bus stop is 200 metres away.
- **Directions** - Situated on the seaward side of the A149 200m on the left hand side of "Harbour Way" (the turning to Harbour Way is opposite the Northshore Sailing Shop). Visitors are encouraged, where possible to share cars.

CONTACT:
Tel: 0344 335 1296
bunkhouses@nationaltrust.org.uk www.nationaltrustholidays.org.uk/
bunkhouses/brancaster-bunkhouse/
Dial House, Harbour Way, Brancaster Staithe, Nr Kings Lynn, Norfolk PE31 8BW

OLD RED LION

ENGLAND

Visitors to Castle Acre are entranced by the special atmosphere of this medieval walled town which lies within the outer bailey of an 11th century castle. Castle Acre is on the Peddars Way, an ancient track now a long distance path. The Old Red Lion, a former pub, is centrally situated and carries on the tradition of serving travellers who seek refreshment and repose. Guests can stay in private rooms or dormitories, where bedding and linen are provided free of charge. There are quiet areas (with wood burning stoves) for reading, meeting other guests and playing. There are two large areas: the flint and timber walled converted pub cellar, suitable for yoga and The Garden Room with kitchen and toilet adjacent, ideal for group use: celebrations, classes, courses, workshops and retreats. There is a ground floor room with double bed. Drying facilities. Local shops and pub. No smoking.

DETAILS

- **Open** - All year, all day access. Arrival times by arrangement.
- **Number of beds** - 22: 1x8, 1x6, 1x double, 2 x double en suite, 2 x twin
- **Booking** - Useful but not essential
- **Price per night** - Price includes self service, wholefood breakfast, bedding, towel, all day access and parking. Twin £50, double en suite £65, double £60 per room. Single occupancy supplement. Dorm beds £22.50.
- **Public Transport** - Trains at King's Lynn & Downham Market . Peterborough to Lowestoft X1 bus by Excell stops at Swaffham. Daily National Express coach between London Victoria & Swaffham. Norfolk Bus 0500 626116.
- **Directions** - GR 818151. Castle Acre is 3.5 miles north of Swaffham (A47) on the A1065. The hostel is on left, 75yds down from Bailey Gate in village centre.

CONTACT: Alison Loughlin
Tel: 01760 755557
oldredlion@yahoo.co.uk www.oldredlion.org.uk
Old Red Lion, Bailey Street, Castle Acre, Norfolk, PE32 2AG

BROOK HOUSE
BARN

Comfortable, self-catering accommodation ideally suited for families, groups or individuals. This high standard barn conversion has a fully equipped kitchen/ dining area, drying room, utility, and a large lounge with panoramic views over the Wolds countryside. There are 2 bedrooms on the ground floor and 3 bedrooms and a small lounge on the first floor. The bedrooms have a mix of beds and bunks, bed linen is provided and all have en suite shower rooms. A two bedroom (4/5 person) cottage converted to a similar standard (graded VisitBritain 4*) is also available. The village of Scamblesby, at the heart of the Lincolnshire Wolds and on the Viking Way, has footpaths, bridleways and meandering country lanes. The historic market towns of Louth and Horncastle are 10 minutes' drive, 1/2 hour to Lincoln, Boston and the coastal beaches. Cadwell Park racing circuit, Market Rasen racecourse and the Battle of Britain and Aviation Heritage centres are nearby. See website for activities in the area

DETAILS

- **Open** - All year, flexible accesss.
- **Number of beds** - 22 (27 including adjoining cottage).
- **Booking** - Booking necessary, 20% deposit, balance 1 month prior to visit.
- **Price per night** - From £20pp, family and group rates available. Whole barn hire: Full week £1650, Mon,Tues,Wed,Thurs £275 per night (minimum of 2 nights) reducing to £250 per night for longer stays, Weekends (Fri, Sat) £850 for 2 nights. Sundays £270. Bond of £150 required.
- **Public Transport** - Trains: Lincoln, Grimsby. Coaches: Louth, Horncastle. Interconnect 6 (0845 234 3344) calls at Scamblesby and other villages in the Wolds.
- **Directions** - Scamblesby village is just off the A153 Horncastle to Louth road.

CONTACT: The Strawsons
Tel: 01507 343266
enquiries@brookhousefarm.com   www.barnbreaks.co.uk
Watery Lane, Scamblesby, Nr Louth, Lincolnshire, LN11 9XL

GLENORCHY
CENTRE

The Glenorchy Centre is situated in the heart of the Derbyshire countryside on the edge of the Peak District National Park. Suitable for self-catering groups wishing to explore this attractive area. A few minutes' walk in any direction will find you in the rolling Derbyshire countryside. Within walking distance of the High Peak Trail for walking, pony trekking and cycling, and Black Rocks - great for bouldering and climbing. Nearby Cromford has Arkwright's mills and Cromford Canal to explore. The fully heated accommodation comprises 8 and 12 bed dormitories, one 4 bed and one 2 bed room, all with showers and toilets. Sheets and duvets provided, but not towels. There is a fitted kitchen with dining area and a large multi-purpose room with a large stage, ideal for recreation, conferences etc. There is a TV, DVD player, table tennis and a snooker table. Disabled access is possible to the main hall and dining area. All groups must include at least 4 adults. Graded as 3 star by Tourism England

DETAILS

- **Open** - Mid Feb to Early Dec, 24 hours.
- **Number of beds** - 26: 1x12, 1x8, 1x4, 1x2
- **Booking** - Book with 25% deposit. Booking form on website or ring 01629 824323. WDURC, Coldwell Street, Wirksworth, Derbyshire, DE4 4FB
- **Price per night** - Mon 12am - Fri 12am £910; Fri 4pm - Sun 4pm £560; Sat 2pm - Sat 10am £1310. Smaller groups £16.50pp, minimum £360 over 2 nights. Incl. 9hrs heating per day, extra heating £5 per hour.
- **Public Transport** - Frequent local buses run to Belper and Matlock. Nearest trains at Cromford (2 miles).
- **Directions** - From the town centre go down past Red Lion pub then take next left.

CONTACT: The Secretary
Tel: 01629 824323
secretary@glenorchycentre.org.uk www.glenorchycentre.org.uk
Chapel Lane, Wirksworth, Derbyshire, DE4 4FF

THE RECKONING
HOUSE

The Reckoning House camping barn has been renovated to a high standard including double glazing and insulation. It is situated on the edge of Lathkill Dale, 3 miles from Bakewell. Lathkill Dale is a nature reserve managed by English Nature to protect a variety of flora and fauna as well as some outstanding geological features. Horse riding, fishing, golf and cycle hire are all available locally. There are also many local walks including the Limestone Way.

It has a cooking area, 4 calor gas rings (gas supplied), a washing up sink with hot water, a toilet, wash basin, storage heaters in all rooms and shower inside the barn. Upstairs there are two separate rooms with bunkbeds.

DETAILS

- **Open** - All year, by arrangement.
- **Number of beds** - 12
- **Booking** - Sole use bookings only, in advance (min 2 nights at weekends). £50 deposit, balance 4 weeks before arrival.
- **Price per night** - £15 per person. Sole use £95 per night.
- **Public Transport** - Train stations at Buxton (10 miles) and Matlock (13 miles). National Express drop at Bakewell. Local buses (enquiries 01332 292200) go to Bakewell from Monyash, Over Haddon, Matlock and Buxton.
- **Directions** - GR 184 666. Take the B5055 out of Bakewell towards Monyash. Continue for 3 miles. After passing Haddon Grove Farm holiday cottages (the second set of cottages on right), take the first turn left at the signpost to Haddon Grove. Bear left at the bottom of the lane. The camping barn is the first on the left in a half mile.

CONTACT: Rachel Rhodes
Tel: 01629 812416 / 07540839233
mandalecampsite@yahoo.co.uk www.mandalecampsite.co.uk
Mandale Farm, Haddon Grove, Bakewell, Derbyshire, DE45 1JF

BARN FARM
BARNS AND CAMPSITE

Barn Farm is in the village of Birchover with fine views over the Derwent valley. A few minutes' walk from the farm is Stanton Moor with Victorian stone carvings and the Nine Ladies stone circle. Robin Hood's Stride and other bouldering and climbing are an easy walk away. The Limestone Way passes by the village and there are two local pubs serving food. Barn Farm has four camping barns - Sabine Hay sleeps 15 in triple bunk beds, Hill Carr and Warren Carr sleep 12 in single beds, Stables sleeps 6 in bunk beds. All the barns have fully fitted kitchens, TV, heating and some have private bathrooms and showers. The Gatehouse, a double bed unit with kitchen, bathroom and lounge/living area, is also available. Camping is available (no single sex groups). Caravan, motorhome and campervan pitches available with electric hook ups. Laundry facilities, games room, childrens' play area, shop, showers & toilets are on site. AA 5 star rated and VisitEngland 4 star rating.

DETAILS

- **Open** - 1st April - 31st October, enquire for opening hours.
- **Number of beds** - 47: 1x15, 1x12, 1x12, 1x6, 1x2 plus camping.
- **Booking** - Deposits required: barns 50%, camping £10/tent/ngt all non refundable
- **Price per night** - Hill Carr £160, Sabine Hay £150, Warren Carr £240, Stables £100, Gatehouse £85, all per night (min. 2 nights). Camping £8.50pppn (£5.50pppn D of E groups).
- **Public Transport** - The 172 bus runs from Bakewell to Matlock.
- **Directions** - From the A6 Matlock to Bakewell take the B5056. Follow signs for Birchover, go through the village, Barn Farm is on the right at the top of the village.

CONTACT:
Tel: 01629 650245
gilberthh@msn.com www.barnfarmcamping.com
Birchover, Matlock, Derbyshire, DE4 2BL

THORNBRIDGE
OUTDOORS

Thornbridge Outdoors offers excellent flexible accommodation for family and friends reunions, parties and retreats. In a fantastic location in the heart of the Peak District, Thornbridge Outdoors is a perfect base to access the wonderfully diverse countryside and interesting towns/villages of the Peak District. The Monsal Trail is accessible from the grounds; popular with walkers and cyclists, this flat, traffic free route travels 8.5 miles between Bakewell & Blackwell Mill near Buxton. The gritstone edges of Froggatt and Stanage are within easy reach. The Lodge and the Farm House buildings sleep 38 and 31 people respectively and are self contained, each having its own kitchen and dining/ lounge area. The Lodge is all on one level and has a disabled toilet/shower room, making it suitable for wheelchair users, whilst the Farm House, a Grade 2 listed 19th century building is characterful with some quirky shaped rooms in the attached roundhouse. The camp-site & tipis can be booked along with the Base Camp building that contains toilets, showers, kitchen and dining room. Outdoor activities led by qualified instructors can be provided.

              GROUPS ONLY

DETAILS

- **Open** - All year, all day.
- **Number of beds** - 69 plus camping: Lodge 38: 4x5, 4x3, 1x6; Farm House 31: 3x6, 1x5, 1x4, 2x2; Tipis & camping; 45: 9 x 4/5.
- **Booking** - Via website contact form, phone or email.
- **Price per night** - Weekend breaks from £720 per building. Ask for activity costs.
- **Public Transport** - Buses from Bakewell. Trains at Grindleford (7 miles).
- **Directions** - Between Great Longstone and Ashford in the Water on Longstone Ln

CONTACT: Reception
Tel: 01629 640491
info@thornbridgeoutdoors.co.uk www.thornbridgeoutdoors.co.uk
Great Longstone Bakewell Derbyshire DE45 1NY

SHEEN
BUNKHOUSE

Sheen Bunkhouse is a newly converted barn in a quiet corner of the Peak District, close to the beautiful Dove and Manifold valleys. Comprehensively equipped, it offers a large TV lounge, well-equipped self-catering facilities and two bunkrooms with wash basins. Toilets and showers are conveniently located for both rooms.

Passing close by the barn, the Manifold Valley Track, Tissington Trail and High Peak Trail provide easy access to beautiful countryside, ideal for families and cyclists. Dovedale, the Upper Dove Valley and the remote and mysterious moorlands around Flash and Longnor offer stunning scenery for walkers. Visit the markets and parks at Buxton (8 miles), Leek (10 miles) and Bakewell (12 miles) for a great day out. Other attractions include Alton Towers (20 mins by car) and the famous Opera House and show caves at Buxton.

DETAILS

- **Open** - All year, 24 hours access, reception 8am - 9pm.
- **Number of beds** - 14: 1x8, 1x6
- **Booking** - Book by phone or email
- **Price per night** - From: adults £16, under 16s £11.
- **Public Transport** - Train station at Buxton. Daily bus operated by Bowers from Buxton to Hartington passes close to bunkhouse.
- **Directions** - On the B5054 between Hartington and Hulme End take the turning to Sheen (also signposted for 'Staffordshire Knott'). The bunkhouse is on the right 200yds after the pub.

CONTACT: Jean or Graham Belfield
Tel: 01298 84501
grahambelfield@fsmail.net
Peakstones, Sheen, Derbyshire, SK17 0ES

ILAM
BUNKHOUSE

Ilam bunkhouse is located in an 18th century stable block which originally formed part of the Ilam Hall Estate. The estate is now managed by the National Trust and the bunkhouse sits within the grounds of Ilam Park. Ilam bunkhouse was refurbished in April 2012 and now provides high quality group accommodation for up to 16 people. There are 3 bedrooms with bunk beds, with each bunk provided with a locker, night light and plug socket, there is also a hand basin in each room. There is a sociable main living area comprising of a large dining table with benches, an open plan kitchen area with dishwasher and 2 large comfortable fitted sofas in the sitting room area. There are 3 individual toilet and shower rooms and an additional toilet room. A good base to explore the Peak District National Park, in particular the limestone hills and gorges, meandering rivers and beautiful woodland of the White Peak. Explore nearby Dovedale with it's famous stepping stones and our own Ilam Park with it's beautiful views, popular tea room and shop. Dogs welcome.

DETAILS

- **Open** - All year, all day.
- **Number of beds** - 16: in three rooms
- **Booking** - Via National Trust central booking system 0344 335 1296
- **Price per night** - Weekdays £170pn. Weekends £250pn. A minimum of 2 nights at a weekend and 3 nights on bank holidays. Dogs £15 per dog per stay
- **Public Transport** - Trains at Uttoxeter (12 miles), Bus; Moorlands Connect service – bookable service stops in Ilam village 0300 111 8003.
- **Directions** - In Ilam follow signs for National Trust Ilam Park. Use main car park.

CONTACT: National Trust Holiday Bookings
Tel: 0344 335 1296
bunkhouses@nationaltrust.org.uk www.nationaltrustholidays.org.uk
Ilam Bunkhouse, Ilam Park, Ilam, nr Ashbourne, DE6 2AZ

ST MICHAELS
CENTRE

St Michaels Centre is at the heart of the bustling Peak District village of Hathersage on the Hope Valley train line. It is an ideal base to explore the Derwent Valley reservoirs, the gritstone edges, Chatsworth estate and the caverns of Castleton, with limitless walking from the doorstep. Regular trains to local villages in the Hope Valley makes it possible to explore the area without a car. The centre provides high quality, warm, welcoming accommodation for large families or groups of around 20 or more. It can accommodate up to 38 people in bunk-bedded rooms with 4 extra beds available in an adjacent cottage. There is a self-catering kitchen (catering provided on request), a dining room and lounge area with TV/DVD and music, WiFi, a classroom, showers, toilets, drying room and a car park for 12 cars. Shops, pubs, cafés, rail station, bus route, tennis court and a fabulous open air heated swimming pool are all a few steps away. The centre may be able to arrange instruction and equipment for caving, climbing, rock hopping, abseiling, gorge walking and orienteering.

DETAILS

- **Open** - All year, all day.
- **Number of beds** - 38: 2x2, 1x4, 2x6, 1x8, 1x10. Plus 4 in adjacent cottage.
- **Booking** - Advanced booking available.
- **Price per night** - £21 per person with a minimum of £420 a night. Minimum of 2 night's hire. Activities: £280 per day (for maximum of 12 people).
- **Public Transport** - On the Hope Valley line with regular trains from Manchester and Sheffield. Buses daily to Sheffield, Hope, Castleton, Eyam, Bradwell, Bakewell.
- **Directions** - On the Main Road opposite Brookfield Manor and Catholic Church.

CONTACT: Gary Richards
Tel: 01433 650309

stmichaels@nottscc.gov.uk www.nottinghamshire.gov.uk/learning/outdoor-and-environment-education
St Michaels Centre, Main Road, Hathersage, Derbyshire, S32 1BB

THORPE FARM
BUNKHOUSES

Thorpe Farm Bunkhouses are situated a mile northwest of Hathersage, on a family-run mixed dairy farm which makes its own ice cream.

The bunkhouses are 2 miles west of Stanage Edge. Other popular climbing and walking areas are nearby. Castleton is 6 miles up the Hope Valley and Eyam is 6 miles southwest. Each bunkhouse has dormitories with individual bunks each with mattress and pillow. There is some sleeping space in the sitting rooms and room for camping outside. The bunkhouses have heating, drying facilities, hot showers, toilets, electric / gas cooking, fridges, freezers, electric kettles, toasters etc. The Byre is all on one level with disabled facilities.

DETAILS

- **Open** - All year, no restrictions.
- **Number of beds** - Old Shippon 32: 2x12, 2x4. Byre 14: 1x6, 1x4. Living room 4. Old Stables 14: 1x8, 1x6. Pondside 14: 1x8, 1x6
- **Booking** - Essential for weekends.
- **Price per night** - See own website.
- **Public Transport** - Train station at Hathersage, 10 mins' walk from bunkhouse. Bus service 272 operates from Sheffield to Hathersage. Details phone Busline 01298 230980 or 01246 250450.
- **Directions** - GR 223 824. If walking from A6187/A625 in Hathersage turn right (just past the George Hotel) up Jaggers Lane, turn second right up Coggers Lane and fifth turning on left (signed Thorpe Farm). If driving follow the road from Hathersage towards Hope for ¾ mile, then turn right into private drive (signposted Thorpe Farm).

CONTACT: Jane Marsden
Tel: 01433 650659
jane@hope-valley.co.uk www.thorpe-bunk.co.uk
Thorpe Farm, Hathersage, Peak District, Via Sheffield, S32 1B

ROYAL OAK
BUNKBARN

Eat, drink, be merry and stay in a refurbished stone barn with a traditional award winning Peak District country pub on site. The Royal Oak serves fantastic pub grub and local cask ales (Multiple Winner of 'Derbyshire Pub of the Year Awards'). The Royal Oak has direct access to the High Peak and Tissington Trails which use disused railways to provide easy off road cycling. The area is also ideal for climbing and walking with stone circles and limestone gorges to explore. The bunk barn is perfect for any number from 1 to 34 (small and large groups welcome) wanting comfortable, clean, private bunk bed style rooms. The five separate bunk rooms are all heated and lockable. All the bunk beds have comfortable mattresses, a pillow and fresh linen, just bring a duvet or sleeping bag. There is a small communal kitchen ideal for basic meals with fridge, oven and kettle and seating for 5/6 people. Separate ladies and gents toilets and hot showers are included in the simple per person tariff. Camp-site and holiday cottages (some sleeping large groups) available.

DETAILS

- **Open** - All year, all day.
- **Number of beds** - 34: 3 x 8 (bunks), 1 x 6 (bunks), 1 x 4 (bunks)
- **Booking** - Booking in advance by phone or email
- **Price per night** - April to Sept £16pppn, Oct to March £14pppn.
- **Public Transport** - Nearest trains Buxton (8 miles). Local bus no.42 (Buxton to Ashbourne) drops off 15 minutes' walk away on A515
- **Directions** - From the A515 Buxton to Ashbourne road take road to Hurdlow oposite to B5055 road to Bakewell.

CONTACT: The Royal Oak
Tel: 01298 83288
hello@peakpub.co.uk www.peakpub.co.uk
The Royal Oak, Hurdlow, Nr Buxton, SK17 9QJ

High Peak and Tissington Trails

Managed by the Peak District National Park Authority and Derbyshire County Council, these are former railway lines, converted for use by walkers, cyclists and horse riders. Please respect other users. Cyclists give way to walkers and horse riders - keep to the left of the Trail and overtake others slowly in single file.

Take extra care on bridges and embankments.

You are advised NOT to cycle down inclines

MOORSIDE
FARM BUNKHOUSE

Moorside Farm is a 300-year-old farmhouse set 1200 feet up in the beautiful Peak District National Park on the Derbyshire / Staffordshire border and approximately five miles from the historic town of Buxton. Sleeping accommodation is provided in two areas, one for 14 - this is alpine style with pine clad ceiling and a pine floor with bunk beds. The second area has 6 beds, also in bunks and is an ideal room for a small group or family. Downstairs there are showers, toilets and a large dining / general room. The farmhouse has full central heating and drying facilities are available. Provided at the bunkhouse is a three course breakfast, packed lunch and a substantial dinner in the evening, vegetarians are catered for. A small kitchen is available for making tea and coffee. Ample parking space is provided. All bookings have sole use of the accommodation.

DETAILS

- **Open** - All year, 24 hours.
- **Number of beds** - 20: 1 x 14, 1 x 6
- **Booking** - Deposit required with minimum two weeks' notice.
- **Price per night** - £35.00 per person per night, includes bed, breakfast, packed lunch and evening meal. Bed and breakfast only £24.00 per person per night. Minimum booking 4 persons.
- **Public Transport** - Nearest train station Buxton. Take bus to Longnor or Travellers Rest. Bus enquiries 01332 292200.
- **Directions** - GR SK 055 670. Leave A53, Buxton to Leek road at Travellers Rest, take 4th lane on left, down to T junction, take first left, Moorside Farm is first right entrance.

CONTACT: Charlie
Tel: 01298 83406
charliefutcher@aol.com www.moorsidefarm.com
Hollinsclough, Longnor, Buxton, Derbyshire, SK17 0RF

'We found it - the most beautiful site we've ever encountered'.

Upper Booth Camping Barn is located adjacent to a small camp-site alongside Crowden Clough. It is possible to hire the barn and additional pitches on the camp-site. There is space for cooking and tables for eating. Toilets, handbasins, washing up sinks and showers are shared with the camp-site.

Upper Booth camping barn is located on a working hill-farm. Walking and biking are available from the farm, the Pennine Way passes through the farmyard. An ideal base for outdoor enthusiasts.

DETAILS

■ **Open** - March-November. Arrival between 3pm and 9pm. Departure before 10am. Not suitable for late night parties.
■ **Number of beds** - Sleeping space for 12
■ **Booking** - Pre-booking essential for weekends & bank holidays. Provisional booking held for 7 days. Confirmed if full payment is received within that time.
■ **Price per night** - Exclusive use (up to 12 persons) from £90 per night plus vehicles. Individual spaces from £10 per person per night.
■ **Public Transport** - Nearest station, Edale (Sheffield/Manchester line) approx 40 minutes' walk on footpaths to Upper Booth. Nearest bus stop Barber Booth (15 minutes' walk). Service 260 weekdays. 3 buses a day go to Upper Booth.
■ **Directions** - GR103 853. Follow signs for Edale village, then for Barber Booth, immediately after river bridge turn right for Upper Booth.

CONTACT: Robert, Sarah or Alice
Tel: (01433) 670250
mail@helliwell.info www.upperboothcamping.co.uk
Upper Booth Farm, Edale, Hope Valley, Derbyshire, S33 7ZJ

PINDALE FARM
OUTDOOR CENTRE

A mile from Castleton in the heart of the Peak District. Pindale Farm comprises a farmhouse pre-dating 1340 and lead mine buildings from the 1850s, which have been completely rebuilt from near dereliction. The centre offers 5 different kinds of accommodation. The farmhouse offers traditional bed and (an AGA cooked) breakfast. The Barn has 6 independent self-catering units, 3 of these can accommodate people with certain physical disabilities. The Old Lead Mine Engine House is a self-catering unit sleeping 8. The Powder House, originally the mine's explosive store, is a small camping barn with basic facilities for up to 4 people. A camp-site, adjacent to the centre, has showers, hot water, and toilet facilities. All rooms have Freesat TV, WiFi is available in the barn and most of the camping areas (£2 a day). The ideal base for walking, climbing, caving, horse riding etc. Instruction is available if required. Well behaved pets welcome. Scouts, Cadets and DofE expeditions welcome, camping or in the bunkhouse.

DETAILS

- **Open** - All year (camping March-October), 24 hours.
- **Number of beds** - 64 bunkbeds plus camping and B&B
- **Booking** - Early booking (deposit) is best.
- **Price per night** - Camping £8 pp (£4 for hook up). Barns £16 pp plus £1 electric tokens for cooker, shower and sockets. B&B with four poster bed and AGA breakfast enquire for prices.
- **Public Transport** - Train station in Hope. On local buses ask for Hope. Hope is 15 minutes' walk from the hostel. National Express Sheffield (taxi fare £15-£20).
- **Directions** - GR 163 825. From Hope follow cement works signs, turn off main road between church and Woodroffe Arms.

CONTACT: Alan Medhurst
Tel: 01433 620111
pindalefarm@btconnect.com www.pindalefarm.co.uk
Pindale Road, Hope, Hope Valley, Derbyshire, S33 6RN

HOMESTEAD
AND CHEESEHOUSE

These two bunkhouses are situated on a small mixed farm in the middle of Bamford, just 3 miles from Stanage Edge. The Derwent Dams are between 1.5 and 7 miles further up the valley. Castleton is 5 miles to the north, Chatsworth House and Park 10 miles to the southwest.

Both bunkhouses have individual bunks with mattress, fitted sheets and pillow (bring your own sleeping bags), gas central heating and drying facilities. Homestead has 22 beds in 3 rooms, and 2 bathrooms with 2 toilets and showers in each, a large dayroom with oak seating and a fully equipped kitchen with gas cooker. Cheesehouse is a self-contained bunkhouse with four bunks, ideal for a small family or group. It has a shower and toilet and is equipped with a kitchen having cooking rings, a microwave oven, toaster and kettle. The bunkhouses are 2 mins walk from a pub. Sorry, no dogs (working dogs on site)

DETAILS

- **Open** - All year, arrive after 2pm on day of arrival and leave by 11am on departure.
- **Number of beds** - Homestead 22: 1x10, 2x6. Cheesehouse 4: 1x4.
- **Booking** - Recommended for weekends.
- **Price per night** - From £15 per person. Sole use: Homestead £195, Cheesehouse £45. Minimum of 2 night booking for Homestead at weekends or phone for a quote for a single night fee.
- **Public Transport** - Nearest train station Bamford, 10 minutes' walk. Bus 274 & 275 operates Sundays Bamford to Sheffield or Castleton. Bus 272 Bamford to Sheffield and Castleton. Bus 241 Bamford to Bakewell.
- **Directions** - The farm is in the centre of Bamford on South View Lane (turn off A6013 at the 'Country Stores').

CONTACT: Helena Platts
Tel: 01433 651298
The Farm, Bamford, Hope Valley, S33 0BL

DALEHEAD
BUNKHOUSE

Dalehead Bunkhouse is a renovated gritstone farmhouse on a working hill-farm at the remote head of Edale Valley. Providing basic but comfortable accommodation heated by log burner supplemented by infrared radiant heat. There is a kitchen with fridge/freezer, a lounge, dining room and plenty of parking. Visitors must bring their own sleeping bags, pillows and towels. Edale is a very popular destination for walkers, climbers, mountain bikers, hang-gliders or for just enjoying the magnificent scenery. It lies between the gritstone of the peat-topped Kinder moors to the north and the cave-riddled limestone of the White Peak to the south. Despite its proximity to major cities and the straightforward rail service to Sheffield and Manchester, the Dark Peak remains unspoilt, with many places where it is possible to enjoy a sense of remoteness. Dogs are welcome on the ground floor of the bunkhouse.

DETAILS

- **Open** - All year, 24 hours.
- **Number of beds** - 20: 1x6, 1x8, 1x6
- **Booking** - Via National Trust central booking system 0344 335 1296
- **Price per night** - Weekdays (Mon-Thurs) £190 per night. Weekends (Fri-Sun) £275 per night. single night bookings available Mon –Thurs, a minimum of 2 nights at a weekend and 3 for a bank holiday.   Dogs £15 per dog per stay.
- **Public Transport** - Trains at Edale (2 miles) to Sheffield and Manchester. Taxi service only available from Hope Station. Nearest bus station at Castleton (3 miles).
- **Directions** - SK101841 (OS map no. 110). At the western end of the dale 2 miles from Edale church .

CONTACT: National Trust Holiday Bookings
Tel: 0344 3351296
bunkhouses@nationaltrust.org.uk www.nationaltrusholidays.org.uk
Dalehead Bunkhouse, Upper Booth, Edale, Hope Valley, S33 7ZJ

JOHN HUNT
BASE

The John Hunt Base, part of Hagg Farm Outdoor Education Centre, offers comfortable accommodation in a converted 19th century hill farm in the Upper Derwent Valley, with unparalleled views across the open moors of the Dark Peak. Walks from the door lead onto the high moors of Kinder and Bleaklow and around the Ladybower reservoirs and dams. The Hagg Farm descent cycle route passes close by and there is secure storage for mountain bikes. The Base has a lounge, TV/DVD, payphone, showers & toilets, drying room and kitchen, with good wheelchair access throughout. Dormitory accommodation consists of two rooms with bunks sleeping 6 and 8. In addition there are 2 rooms with 2 single beds in each. Groups have sole use during their stay, and all bedding is provided. In the grounds are a wildlife garden, field, artificial climbing boulder, jacobs ladder, climbing tower and access to woodland. Instructional support for various outdoor activities such as climbing, caving, gorge walking, canoeing etc may be booked in advance. The site is also ideal for quiet pursuits and retreats.

DETAILS

- **Open** - All year. Office open Mon - Fri, 9am - 4.30pm.
- **Number of beds** - 18: 1 x 8, 1 x 6, 2 x 2
- **Booking** - Advance booking essential.
- **Price per night** - £265 minimum 2 night stay. Outdoor activity instruction for 12 people from £280 per day. Hire of boots & equipment £5 per person per day.
- **Public Transport** - Trains at Bamford (7 miles away) on the Hope Valley Line.
- **Directions** - From Ladybower Reservoir junction take the A57 3 miles west towards Glossop, lookout for a sign to Hagg Farm on the right.

CONTACT:
Tel: 01433 651594
haggfarm@nottscc.gov.uk www.nottinghamshire.gov.uk/haggfarm
Hagg Farm OEC, Snake Rd, Bamford, Hope Valley, S33 0BJ

FOUNDRY ADVENTURE CENTRE

Foundry Activity Centre has 2 units, Kinder; 31 beds and Howden; 21 beds, they can be combined to provide total 52 beds. With easy access to all parts of the Peak District National Park, the centre is an ideal location for outdoor activities and touring, welcoming a wide range of groups including schools, universities, corporate, clubs and large families. The spacious centre includes; comfortable lounges with a library, TV and wood burning stove, equipped kitchens and dining areas, four bathrooms and warm drying facilities. Bunks in rooms of 2 - 8 have optional bedding provision. There is parking for 20 plus vehicles with flat hard surfaced and grass areas for activities on site. Surrounding farmland and woodland can be accessed via an extensive network of footpaths. The centre is an AALA licensed provider and can also offer a wide range of adventure activities including abseiling, caving, climbing, hill walking, mountain biking & watersports. These can be combined to create a range of team building and personal development courses.

DETAILS

- **Open** - All year, all day.
- **Number of beds** - 52
- **Booking** - Group bookings for minimum 20 people.
- **Price per night** - From £17 per person per night
- **Public Transport** - Buses and trains via Hope Valley
- **Directions** - A623 (Chesterfield to Chapel en le frith), follow to Tideswell junction. Turn for Bradwell, take first right for Great Hucklow. On approaching the village, turn right at Queen Anne pub, then first right after 100m.

CONTACT: Tim Gould
Tel: 01298 873029 Mob: 07786 332702
info@foundrymountain.co.uk www.greatadventures.co.uk/foundrymountain
The Old Playhouse, Great Hucklow, Derbyshire, SK17 8RF

THE STABLES
BUNKHOUSE

The Stables Bunkhouse is a centrally heated barn located in the heart of the stunning Peak District countryside. Situated on a working hill farm which dates back to the 16th century, the barn is close to the start of the Pennine Way and offers easy access to Kinder Scout. The village of Edale is half a mile away, with a village store, two pubs serving food, a railway station and the Moorlands Information Centre. This is ideal walking country, with a network of footpaths direct from the doorstep, including a pleasant hike with stunning views over the Mam Tor ridge to Castleton, a pretty tourist village famous for its Christmas lights, with show caves and gift shops. Buxton, Bakewell and Chatsworth House which are all within 40 minutes' drive. The bunkhouse sleeps 16 in 4 rooms sleeping 4. The bunks have a bottom sheet and pillow case, bring your own sleeping bag. There is a fully equipped kitchen, dining area, 3 showers, 2 toilets, drying facilities, cycle store and car parking. Book sole use or book by the bed and share the barn. Weekends reserved for groups until close to date.

DETAILS

■ **Open** - All year, all day. Arrive after 4pm depart before 10.30am.
■ **Number of beds** - 16: 4x4
■ **Booking** - Booking required with deposit, remainder to be paid 4 weeks in advance of stay. Weekends reserved for groups until 3 weeks prior to stay.
■ **Price per night** - Sole use Mon to Thurs £180 per night, weekends (Friday to Sunday) £200 per night. See website or enquire for prices per bed or per room.
■ **Public Transport** - Less than half a mile from Edale train station
■ **Directions** - Follow signs for Ollerbrook Booth from Edale or footpath from station.

CONTACT: Sheila
Tel: 01433 670235 Mob: 07971 865944
ollerbrookfarm@gmail.com www.edalecottagesandbunkhouse.co.uk
Ollerbrook Farm, Ollerbrook Booth, Edale, Hope Valley, Derbyshire, S33 7ZG

BUSHEY HEATH
FARM

Bushey Heath Farm is a family-run smallholding in the heart of the Peak District, central to all the popular visitor centres, Offering a pre-booking group summer camp-site and bunkbarns for up to 28 people in three self contained units. The farm has been developed in an environmentally sensitive way with ground source heating, a wind turbine for electricity and rainwater harvesting for wc flushing, so visitors can experience practical sustainable ideas. The Hen House bunk barn has two bedrooms with bunks for 4 in each. The Little Barn has a large single bedroom with bunks for 6 people. Hadfield Barn sleeps 14 in two rooms of 6 and 8. All have luxury shower rooms and a combined fully equipped kitchen/diner open area. Sleeping bags/duvets/sheet required. Well behaved dogs accepted by prior arrangement.

DETAILS

■ **Open** - All year. Group only camp-site May - October. Opening hours by arrangement.
■ **Number of beds** - 8: Hen House, 6: Little Barn, 14: Hadfield Barn.
■ **Booking** - Camping: always. Bunkhouse: early with deposit advisable.
■ **Price per night** - Bunkbarns: for sole use, Hen House: £160. Little Barn: £120. Hadfield Barn: £280. All per night (min. 2 night)
■ **Public Transport** - Nearest trains at Hope (4 miles). Nearest buses in Tideswell (2 miles). Bus numbers 65, 66, x67, 173, 177, 197, 202.
■ **Directions** - GR SK 146 785. From Tideswell take Manchester Road past Star Pub and cross over A623, road stops at farm. Going west along A623, 1.5 miles past the Anchor Pub turn right at crossroads in 's' bends.

CONTACT: Rod or Lisa Baraona
Tel: 01298 873007 9am-8pm only.
busheyheathfarm@gmail.com www.busheyheathfarm.com
Tideswell Moor, Tideswell, Buxton, Derbyshire, SK17 8JE

With its own crags, streams, lakes and over 100-acres of mature woodland, the hidden Shining Cliff Hostel has nature on its doorstep. Completely refurbished in 2009, the hostel is ideal for groups wishing to enjoy time away in a peaceful woodland setting. The entrance porch, with space for hanging coats and boots, leads into the open plan kitchen, dining and lounge area. In the well equipped kitchen, there is a 6 ring gas hob, electric oven, microwave, fridge, freezer, dishwasher and water boiler. The dining area comfortably seats 20 people whilst the lounge provides seating and space to relax. Shining Cliff hostel offers a full range of activities, some are on-site such as bushcraft, abseiling, ecology and environmental art, while climbing, caving or canoeing can be enjoyed a little further afield. Activities must be booked in advance.

Nestled within 100 acres of woodland and a ten minute walk, down a very rough track, from the nearest parking area. Paths lead through the woods to the A6 at Ambergate (20 mins' walk) which has a food shop, pubs, buses to Derby and a train station with connections to Derby, Nottingham and London.

DETAILS

- **Open** - All Year.
- **Number of beds** - 20: 1 x 4, 2 x 6, 2 x 2
- **Booking** - Phone or email
- **Price per night** - Enquire for prices.
- **Public Transport** - Ambergate rail station (1 mile). Transpeak bus on A6 (1 mile)
- **Directions** - See website for directions. Sat Navs NOT recommended.

CONTACT:
Tel: 01433 620377
enquiries@shiningcliff.org www.lindleyeducationaltrust.org/shining
Jackass Lane, Alderwasley Belper, DE56 2RE

UNDERBANK
CAMPING BARN

Located on Blaze Farm, a dairy farm, café, ice cream parlour and pottery painting studio on the western edge of the Peak District National Park. This lovely little barn overlooks the Wildboarclough Valley and is close to the stunning viewpoint on Shuttlingsloe Fell.

The barn provides the perfect, simple base for walking, climbing, fell-running and mountain biking in and around in this beautiful landscape. The sleeping area is on the first floor, with the living area and a kitchen area with fridge. There is a toilet and shower below. Bring your own sleeping bag, camping mattresses and a stove plus all cooking equipment if you wish to self cater. Blaze Farm ice-cream parlour and café serves snacks and light meals from 10am, and there are several good pubs nearby. Come and explore the farms own nature trails.

DETAILS

■ **Open** - All Year, arrive at 4pm leave at 10am (earlier arrivals by arrangement).
■ **Number of beds** - 10
■ **Booking** - Book via the YHA on 0800 0191 700 contact barn direct before arrival
■ **Price per night** - From £9.50. Sole use of 10 bed barn: £95.00 per night. Electricity is metered, so please bring change.
■ **Public Transport** - Train at Macclesfield (7 miles)
■ **Directions** - 10 miles from Congleton and 7 miles from Buxton and Macclesfield. Travelling on the A54 from Congleton, Blaze Farm is the second farm access on the left hand side after the Rose and Crown pub. When travelling from Buxton, Blaze Farm is the second farm access on the right hand side after the turning for Wildboarclough.

CONTACT: Caroline & Marshall Waller
Tel: 01260 227 266
thesheeponthehill@gmail.com   www.underbankbarn.co.uk
Blaze Farm, Wildboarclough, Macclesfied, Cheshire, SK11 0BL

Wandering Duck is a unique hosted canal boat experience of 2 or 3 nights on board a 69ft narrowboat. It's like a floating backpacker's hostel.

Trips take place around Manchester, Cheshire and Derbyshire. Come on your own and join a tour, or charter Wandering Duck for your own small group (max 10 people). These experiences are very hands on and you'll be shown how to work the locks and encouraged to have a go at steering the 69ft boat. Choose between the 3 Night Canal Boat Adventure (Manchester to the Peak District) or the 2 Night Canal Boat Escape (Marple, Manchester to Congleton, Cheshire). Most meals are included in the price of the trip, as are hot drinks and home-made cake. On board you will find an honesty bar, games, and an ipod dock. As well as many walking options, fishing gear is available free of charge or you can go for a paddle in the 3-man canoe (£6pp unlimited use).

       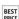

DETAILS

■ **Open** - March to October, 24 hrs.
■ **Number of beds** - 8: 2x4
■ **Booking** - Website or phone
■ **Price per night** - 2 night tour £145: 3 night tour £195: Charter the boat from £920. Tours include: accommodation on the boat, fully hosted experience, meals & cake.
■ **Public Transport** - All trips are one-way and start and finish within walking distance of train stations.
■ **Directions** - See website for details. Detailed directions sent with your booking confirmation.

CONTACT: Roberta
Tel: 07584 122614
duckmail@wanderingduck.co.uk www.wanderingduck.co.uk
Blackbrook House, Bugsworth Basin, Brookside, High Peak, SK23 7NE

HATTERS
ON HILTON STREET

Hatters on Hilton Street brings new meaning to 'flash packing'! Your ideal choice for city centre accommodation in the heart of the bohemian Northern Quarter, with a combination of hotel quality en suite rooms with the social atmosphere of an international travellers' hostel. Catering for groups of all sizes and independent travellers, you can enjoy the benefits of WiFi, breakfast, en suite and standard rooms, large communal and outdoor areas, and enthusiastic, informative staff. Full board or half board options for groups of over 15. Convenient for all city centre attractions and transport links. Ask about discounts to Alton Towers, and about Man Utd and City football stadium tours and lest we forget, all that is FREE to do in Manchester...We are more than happy to help. Also a great base for day trips to the Peak District. Come and enjoy our hospitality and explore all that Manchester has to offer!

DETAILS

- **Open** - All year, 24 hour reception. Check in 2pm, check out 11am.
- **Number of beds** - 155; single, twin, double, triple, 4, 6, 8, and 12 bed rooms
- **Booking** - Booking not essential but recommended especially at weekends, with credit/debit card. Photo ID (eg. passport, driving license) required on check in. For group bookings please contact groups@hattersgroup.com
- **Price per night** - From £12 dorms, from £32 private rooms. All rooms include en suite, linen and breakfast. For group prices and bookings see http://www.hattershostels.com/groups or email: groups@hattersgroup.com
- **Public Transport** - Only 5 minutes' walk from Picadilly train and bus stations and Shudehill bus station, and 10 minutes' walk from Victoria train station.
- **Directions** - Please contact the hostel reception for details.

CONTACT: Reception
Tel: 0161 236 4414
hilton@hattersgroup.com www.hattersgroup.com
15 Hilton Street, Manchester, M1 1JJ

HATTERS
ON NEWTON STREET

Recently refurbished to its 100 year old splendour and winner of the Manchester Tourism Customer Care award, Hatters has firmly established itself as the city's favourite funky hostel. The city centre location makes it the ideal spot to start exploring the north west of England. Hatters caters for independent travellers and groups. It has a fully serviced kitchen with seating for groups of up to 50 and free all-day continental breakfast. Enjoy the FREE all-day coffee while using the FREE WiFi, or choose to socialise with other like-minded travellers and staff. We also offer full board or half board options for groups over 15 people. Let the knowledgeable and friendly staff guide you to the best that this great city has to offer, from live music and football to restaurants, shopping, museums, pubs and clubs.

DETAILS
- **Open** - All year. 24 hour reception. Check in 2pm, check out 11am.
- **Number of beds** - 170. Private double/ single rooms. Dorm sizes include 18 bed, 10 bed, 6 bed and 4 bed.
- **Booking** - Booking recommended, with credit/debit card, especially at weekends. Photo ID is required at check in. Group bookings contact groups@hattersgroup.com.
- **Price per night** - From £12 for dorms and from £32 for private rooms. Overnight price includes linen and breakfast.   For group prices and bookings see http://www.hattershostels.com/groups or email: groups@hattersgroup.com
- **Public Transport** - Easy walking distance from all public transport hubs: Picadilly Train Station 5mins, Picadilly Bus Station 5mins, Shudehill Bus Station 5mins, Victoria Train Station 10mins
- **Directions** - Please contact the hostel reception for directions.

CONTACT: Reception
Tel: 0161 236 9500
Manchester@hattersgroup.com www.hattersgroup.com
50 Newton Street, Manchester, M1 2EA

EMBASSIE

The Embassie is a terraced house in an unspoilt Georgian square used in the filming of 'In the Name of the Father'. The house was built in 1820 and until 1986 it was the Consulate of Venezuela. Only 15 minutes' walk from the centre of Liverpool, known for its nightlife. A large student population ensures a lively scene, with late night bands and bars. The hostel has been refurbished and there are new kitchen facilities, a brand new shower suite and an all new games room and relax area with Sky Sports and HD television. Hostellers have a key to come and go. The hostel is clean, safe and staffed 24 hours. Bedding is provided (including sheets) and free coffee, tea, toast and jam are available 24 hours, eat as much as you want. International, or UK regional travellers only. Free Beatles guided tour every Thursday night at 8pm including free admission to the world famous Cavern Club (and free piece of Beatle memorabilia). The only tour given by a tour guide who saw the Beatles perform.

DETAILS

- **Open** - All year, 24 hr access.
- **Number of beds** - 50
- **Booking** - not essential for individuals. Groups over 6 should book (25% deposit).
- **Price per night** - £16 (Sunday to Thursday), £21 (Friday and Saturday).
- **Public Transport** - Liverpool has a train station and is served by National Express Coaches. A £3.50 taxi fare will bring you from the train or bus station to the hostel door, (good idea if you have a heavy rucksack).
- **Directions** - From the Anglican Cathedral (the third largest in the world) continue uphill along Canning Street away from the city centre. This will bring you into Falkner Square (15-20 mins). The hostel has a red door and is by a phone box.

CONTACT: Kevin
Tel: 0151 7071089
embassie@gmail.com www.embassie.com
1 Falkner Square, Liverpool, L8 7NU

HATTERS
LIVERPOOL

Your ideal choice for city central accommodation, Hatters Liverpool has combined hotel quality en suite rooms with the social atmosphere of an international travellers' hostel. Catering for groups of all sizes and independent travellers, you can enjoy the comforts of WiFi, continental breakfast, en suite rooms, large communal areas and enthusiastic, informative staff. We also offer full board or half board options for groups of over 15. Conveniently located for all city centre attractions and transport links, ask the reception staff about discounts to Alton Towers, Beatles tours, football stadium tours, Albert Docks, or many other FREE adventures....The perfect base for day trips to the historic city of Chester, Chester Zoo, or the majestic Lake District. Come and stay and enjoy what is making Liverpool one of the UK's top tourist destinations!. Three star graded by Quality in Tourism.

DETAILS

■ **Open** - All year, 24 hour reception. Check in after 2pm, check out 11am.
■ **Number of beds** - 300 beds; single, double, twin, triple, 4, 6, 8 and 12 bed rooms.
■ **Booking** - Booking not essential but recommended, especially at weekends. We require photo I.D (passport/drivers' licence) and credit/ debit card. For all group bookings please contact groups@hattersgroup.com
■ **Price per night** - From £12 for dorms and from £32 for privates. Prices include en suite, linen and breakfast. For group prices and bookings see http://www.hattershostels.com/groups or email: groups@hattersgroup.com
■ **Public Transport** - Within walking distance of all public transport hubs. Liverpool Lime Street Station – 5mins, Northern Street Coach Station – 15mins
■ **Directions** - Please contact the hostel reception for directions

CONTACT: Reception
Tel: 0151 709 5570
liverpool@hattersgroup.com www.hattersgroup.com/#lpool
56-60 Mount Pleasant, Liverpool, L3 5SH

THE OLD SMITHY
CAMPING BARN

The Old Smithy camping barn was at one time the village fire station. This "stone-tent" is situated in the village of Burwardsley, Cheshire, mid-way along the Sandstone Trail, one of the finest long distance walks in North West England. The barn is also on NCN route 45 Mercian Way. The Old Smithy offers affordable country accommodation for up to 8 people. Ideal for families or groups of walkers, cyclists and others visiting this part of Cheshire or wanting to get closer to nature. There is an area for cooking & washing up, a toilet and an insulated sleeping platform. There is no electricity or hot water, nor beds; Bring your own sleeping bag and roll mat. Lighting is via lanterns (candles and matches provided). You can pre-order bacon and sausage sandwiches at an extra cost when booking. You can also pre-book or buy food and hot drinks at Burwardsley Post Office & Village Shop (5 min walk). The nearest pub is The Pheasant Inn. Also close by is the Candle workshop, Cheshire Fishery and the Ice Cream Farm. Bikes can be locked away overnight. Dogs welcome.

DETAILS

■ **Open** - All year, 24 hours. Pre-arrange arrival times.
■ **Number of beds** - 8: 1 x 8
■ **Booking** - By phone or email. All bookings must be paid in full to be guaranteed.
■ **Price per night** - £8 per person per night. Exclusive use £50 per night.
■ **Public Transport** - The nearest train station is Chester (10 miles) with an hourly bus service to Tattenhall (2 miles).
■ **Directions** - The Barn is on Burwardsley Road, close to the Post Office. Grid reference: 513 569 OS Landranger No.117

CONTACT: Rachel and Phillip
Tel: 01829 770359
rachel_hoarau@yahoo.co.uk
Burwardsley Post Office & Village Store, Harthill Road, Burwardsley, Cheshire CH3 9NU

Once a 17th century water mill, set on a quiet riverside, 1½ miles north of the town centre and 15 minutes' walk from Scalby Mills and the North Bay beach. Scarborough Hostel provides quality low-cost accommodation popular with families, school, college, university and sports groups as well as individuals who wish to enjoy, explore, or simply unwind on the beautiful North Yorkshire coast. Two long sandy beaches, miles of rugged coastline, and some of the UK's largest areas of forest and moorland, make Scarborough the perfect base for activity breaks with excellent walking, cycling, surfing and sailing. There is plenty for those interested in birds, wildlife, history, geology and the seashore. Scarborough regularly hosts quality live concerts and festivals, TT racing, surf competitions and theatre productions. A well equipped kitchen is available or enjoy a cooked breakfast in the dining room. Sole use available for large groups as are school/group packages inc breakfast, pack lunch & evening meals.

DETAILS

- **Open** - All year, 7.30 - 10.00 am and 5.00 - 10.00 pm.
- **Number of beds** - 46: 5x6, 4x4.
- **Booking** - Phone 01723 361176 or search for Scarborough on YHA website.
- **Price per night** - Beds from £15, rooms from £45, discounts for YHA members
- **Public Transport** - Bus or train to Scarborough, No 3 or 3A bus from York place to Sea Life Centre, alight at The Ivanhoe. Hostel is a 5 minute walk from The Ivanhoe
- **Directions** - On A165 two miles north of town centre sharp left after the brick bridge (or make U-turn after the hostel and turn from the left). By foot: leave the Cleveland Way at the Helmsley sign, walk to Burniston road turn left down the hill to the hostel drive.

CONTACT: Robert Fletcher
Tel: 01723 361176
scarboroughhostel@gmail.com www.scarboroughhostel.com
The White House, Burniston Road, Scarborough, YO13 0DA

BANK HOUSE
FARM HOSTEL

A luxury Bunk Barn and a simple Camping Barn on a working organic farm with farmhouse B&B. Set in beautiful Glaisdale Dale, with stunning views of the North York Moors. The Bunk Barn is a modern barn conversion with under-floor heating, large comfy kitchen/dining/living room with sofas, drying room, showers and private toilets. Picnic/ BBQ area and garden with panoramic views. There is one large dorm with 9 single beds and one bunkbed, each equipped with sheet and pillow. Bring your own sleeping bag/duvet and towel. All bookings get sole use of the Bunk Barn. The Camping Barn provides simple, single-night shelter for those walking or cycling with their own sleeping bags, mats and cooking equipment. The farm's beef & lamb is available for sale, bring all other food with you, or arrange a delivery. Wainwright's Coast to Coast route 1m, Whitby & Jurassic coast 12 m, steam trains 3m, Esk Valley walk 3m.

              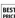 **BEST PRICE**

DETAILS

- **Open** - All year. 9am-9pm for phone calls.
- **Number of beds** - 1 x 11
- **Booking** - Booking essential. Deposit required, balance 4 weeks before arrival.
- **Price per night** - Bunkbarn: Weekends £400 (2 nights), Bank Hols £600 (3 nights). Midweek adult £20, child (6-16) £12. Single night supp. £5/adult, £3/child. Midweek term-time 3-to-5 nights for 2-11 people £15pppn. Camping Barn: £12pp.
- **Public Transport** - Glaisdale train station 3miles. 'M&D Transport' minibus from Castleton to Whitby in Glaisdale village (2.5 miles). Nat. Express coaches at Whitby.
- **Directions** - From Glaisdale station go uphill through village and turn left at T junction 'Glaisdale Dale Only'. After 1 mile turn left by Witchpost Cottage. Pass New House Farm then turn left and follow farm track 1/3 mile to farmyard.

CONTACT: Chris or Emma Padmore
Tel: 01947 897297
info@bankhousefarmhostel.co.uk www.bankhousefarmhostel.co.uk
Bank House Farm, Glaisdale, Whitby YO21 2QA

COTE GHYLL
MILL

Situated in a beautiful and secluded valley in the North Yorkshire Moors National Park, this converted linen mill is a perfect location for those wishing to explore the whole of the Yorkshire Moors/Dales & Coast. Close to walking and cycling routes as well as orienteering at Cod Beck Reservoir, mountain bike routes, pony trekking, fishing & golf clubs. Osmotherley, offers pubs, a tea room and shops. The stream and woodlands in the mill grounds, provide an exciting exploring ground for children and adults. The Mill is bookable as a whole, by room (some en suite) or by bed. Great for educational groups, families, outdoor clubs and friends who wish to get together in a comfortable, great value venue. Fully catered or self-catering available in a well equipped kitchen. Bedrooms and shower rooms newly refurbished in 2015. Other facilities include licensed bar and lounge, TV/games room, pool table, free WiFi, large garden, bike store, meeting rooms,laundry & drying room.

DETAILS

- **Open** - All year, 7am -10am, 5pm-9pm.
- **Number of beds** - Sleeps 68: 1x2,3x4,2x4(en suite),7x6(en suite), +4 rollout beds
- **Booking** - Advanced booking recommended – especially for groups
- **Price per night** - Adults from £20.00. Under18's from £13. Family rooms from £33. For group and sole occupancy please contact the Mill.
- **Public Transport** - Train to Northallerton, from the station the 80 or 89 bus (for Stokesley) stops in the centre of Osmotherley the hostel is a 10 min walk (1/4mile).
- **Directions** - From A19 or Northallerton A684 towards Osmotherley or Teeside into Osmotherley. At the T junction/village cross turn left. Cote Ghyll Mill is ¼ mile out of the village on the right, just after the Caravan and Camping Park

CONTACT: Reception
Tel: 01609 883425
mill@coteghyll.com www.coteghyll.com
Osmotherley, Northallerton, North Yorkshire, DL6 3AH

WEST END
OUTDOOR CENTRE

Situated in the Yorkshire Dales amidst stunning landscape overlooking Thruscross Reservoir in an AONB on the edge of the Dales National Park, this self-catering centre offers excellent facilities for up to 30 people in 9 bedrooms with bunk beds. The centre is fully centrally heated. Accommodation is in small dorms of 2 to 6 beds and the leaders' en suite accommodation has dining and lounge facilities. The main kitchen is well-equipped with a 4-oven Aga cooker, two fridges and a freezer, together with all the cooking utensils and equipment. There are 4 showers, 4 hand basins and 4 toilets. There are no extra charges for heating, lighting and hot water. Ideal for team building courses, schools, Scouts, Guides and family parties etc. Located only 12 miles from Harrogate and Skipton, 30 miles from the City of York. Managed by the owners for 20 years. All groups must be accompanied by an adult (25+). No stag or hens.

DETAILS

- **Open** - All year, flexible.
- **Number of beds** - 30: 4x2, 3x4, 1x6, 1 x 4 en suite
- **Booking** - Advisable at weekends
- **Price per night** - £15pp (minimum charge £30). Sole use (Fri, Sat & bank holidays) £350 per night (min stay 2 nights), Midweek £230 (minimum stay 2 nights) or £350 for one night. £780 for 4 nights midweek, £1100 for 7 nights not starting on a Saturday.
- **Public Transport** - Nearest train stations are at Harrogate and Skipton, both 12 miles from the hostel. Taxi fare from either station would be approximately £22.
- **Directions** - GR 146 575. Leave A59 at Blubberhouses, signed West End 2.5 miles. Do not turn off, centre is on left side.

CONTACT: Hedley or Margaret Verity
Tel: 01943 880207
info@westendoutdoorcentre.co.uk www.westendoutdoorcentre.co.uk
West End, Summerbridge, Harrogate, HG3 4BA

HEBDEN
BRIDGE HOSTEL

Hebden Bridge Hostel (aka Mama Weirdigan's) is located in a former concert hall adjacent to a Grade II listed Baptist Chapel. The hostel provides accommodation in small dorms, private rooms and a 6-bed bunkroom, all en suite. Nestled into woodland only a short walk from the town centre, the hostel makes a good base for hiking, sight-seeing, shopping or experiencing Hebden Bridge's vibrant music and arts scene. Close to the Pennine Way, Calderdale Way, Hardcastle Crags, canal, river and popular cycle routes. 10am-5pm access is to the lobby only. No evening curfew but please respect other guests. Bed linen provided in dorms and private rooms. Bring sleeping bag and pillow for the bunkroom. Free internet, WiFi. Self-catering, vegetarian-only kitchen. Light breakfast & tea/coffee included.

DETAILS

■ **Open** - Easter to November. Whole-hostel bookings possible in closed season. Check-in 5-8pm, check-out by 10am.

■ **Number of beds** - 33 : 6x4 (or 2), 1x3 (or 2), 1x6

■ **Booking** - recommended but not essential (full payment on booking).

■ **Price per night** - Bunk-room £14pp. Small dorm £20pp. Twin £55. Double £60. Private 4-bed room £75. Sole use available..

■ **Public Transport** - 15 minutes' walk from Hebden Bridge train station (frequent, quick service to Leeds and Manchester). Buses from the station stop outside the Birchcliffe Centre (Dodd Naze Circular). Coach stations in Bradford and Leeds.

■ **Directions** - From train station turn left onto main Burnley Rd, then right (towards Keighley), right again (Birchcliffe Rd). Hostel is 400m up hill, behind Birchcliffe Centre.

CONTACT: Em or Dave
Tel: 01422 843183
mama@hebdenbridgehostel.co.uk www.hebdenbridgehostel.co.uk
The Birchcliffe Centre, Hebden Bridge, W Yorks, HX7 8DG

AIRTON BARN
FRIENDS MEETING HOUSE

The recently renovated Airton Camping Barn offers overnight accommodation for up to 16 people. The barn is situated in the quiet village of Airton in central Malhamdale, on the Pennine Way and the Way of the Roses cycle route. It is an easy walk from Malham Cove, Gordale Scar and Janet's Foss. The Three Peaks and Bronte Country are a short drive away and the barn is in 1652 country where the first Quakers gathered. The Meeting House has been used by Quakers since the 1650s, and now offers a warm welcome to cyclists, walkers, mountaineers and family groups. There is a bunk room with 6 beds and two multi-purpose rooms for which airbeds can be provided. The enclosed flat garden is ideal for tents. There are two fully-fitted kitchens, two bathrooms and a separate toilet. Bedding can be provided on request, and there is a small store of basic non-perishable food supplies on site. Food can be ordered and collected from the village farm shop. Secure cycle storage available.

DETAILS

- **Open** - All year, friend resident on site.
- **Number of beds** - 6 bunk beds + 10 air mattresses. Camping in the garden
- **Booking** - Please contact the Friend in Residence. Prior booking recommended.
- **Price per night** - £17 per person, reductions for groups over 6.
- **Public Transport** - Trains at Skipton (11 miles) and Gargrave (7 miles by road, 4 miles by Pennine Way). Limited buses from Skipton (via Gargrave) and Malham.
- **Directions** - Coming into Airton from Gargrave take the first right. Barn is the fourth building on the right. Leave the Pennine Way at Airton Bridge, walk towards the village. Barn is first building on the left. Knock on the white door. GR SD 904592

CONTACT: Friend in Residence
Tel: 01729 830263
airtonbarn@gmail.com www.airtonbarn.org.uk
The Nook, Airton, Skipton, North Yorkshire, BD23 4AE

At almost 1000 feet, with spectacular views of Wharfedale, Grassington Bunkbarn offers comfortable accommodation for groups of up to 32 people in a magnificent location. The ground floor has 3 bunk rooms and a leader/disabled bedroom with private toilet/shower. On the upper floor there is a large dining area with open plan kitchen equipped for groups and a lounge/games area with Freeview TV, although you may be content with the dramatic views from the window! The barn has free WiFi and good mobile coverage. The ground floor has 3 bathrooms with 5 showers and 5 WCs along with a large drying room. The barn is heated by an environmentally sustainable wood pellet biomass boiler which fuels radiators in all the rooms and constant hot water. Outside there is a barbecue area, a large locked bike store and a large car park area. With walking, cycling, climbing, fishing, horse riding, archaeology, bird watching, geology, botany and even golf, the area has something for everyone.

             GROUPS ONLY

DETAILS

■ **Open** - From June 2014. Reception 9am - 5pm Mon - Fri, Sat Sun 10am - 2pm.
■ **Number of beds** - 34: 2 x 12, 1 x 6, 1 x 4
■ **Booking** - 25% deposit, with balance 2 weeks before stay.
■ **Price per night** - Weekends £950(2 nights). Bank holidays (Friday 3 pm to Monday 11am) £1150. Mon–Thurs £320 per night. 4 night stay £265 per night. 7 night stay from £1900. Individual beds: please ring for availability @ £20 per night.
■ **Public Transport** - Train to Skipton and then an hourly bus to Grassington. The bunk barn is about 1.25miles from the nearest bus stop.
■ **Directions** - Take B6265 to Grassington, turn up Main St. through village to the Town Hall, then carry on up the hill (Moor Lane) for 1/2 mile bunk barn is on the left .

CONTACT: Paul or Janet Kent
Tel: 01756 753882
enquiries@grassingtonbunkbarn.co.uk www.grassingtonbunkbarn.co.uk
Spring Croft, Moor Lane, Grassington, BD23 5BD

KETTLEWELL
HOSTEL

The Kettlewell Hostel has 40 beds spread over eight bedrooms, a large dining room, serving the best cooked breakfasts, a bookshop, a well-equipped self-catering kitchen, a lovely lounge with wood-burning stove and a nice garden to sit out in during the summer. There are dormitory rooms and private rooms, most with bunk beds and shared bathroom facilities. The hostel offers really good value, delicious home cooked evening meals and a great range of local ales and carefully selected wines. It is in the heart of Kettlewell which is well served by three great pubs and a village shop. There are lovely walks to be had right out of the front door including Great Whernside and Buckden Pike or you can join the Dales Way for a more gentle walk along the river Wharfe or over to Grassington. Kettlewell also makes a great base for touring the Yorkshire Dales, from here you can easily drive to Hawes, Malham or Skipton. There is a large cycle shed and some of the country's most fabulous riding including Park Rash, Fleet Moss and Buttertubs all right around the corner.

DETAILS

- **Open** - All Year. Reception times: 08.00 - 10.30 16.00 - 22.00.
- **Number of beds** - 40: 1x2, 1x4, 2x5, 4x6
- **Booking** - Email to hire whole hostel or via YHA website for individual bookings.
- **Price per night** - Beds from £18, private rooms for 2 from £49
- **Public Transport** - Bus number 72 from Skipton train station.
- **Directions** - From Skipton travel north towards Grassington then follow signs to Kettlewell. In the village, cross two bridges then turn right in front of the Bluebell pub. At the T junction turn left. The Hostel/Post Office is the second building on right.

CONTACT: Saul & Floss Ward
Tel: 01756 760232
saulward@hotmail.com www.yha.org.uk/hostel/kettlewell
Whernside House, Kettlewell, Skipton, North Yorkshire, BD23 5QU

SKIRFARE
BARN

Skirfare Barn is a traditional stone barn and is a distinctive feature of the beautiful Dales landscape, standing at the confluence of Upper Wharfedale and Littondale with the Climbers Challenge, Kilnsey Crag, providing a spectacular backdrop. The area is famous for walking, cycling and touring with several footpaths easily accessible from the barn including the Dales Way. Kilnsey is nearby where you can find The Kilnsey Park providing day fishing and food as well as The Tennant Arms Hotel for those who prefer a bar snack. Pony trekking is available at Conistone. Although altered little on the outside, the Barn has been converted to provide centrally heated accommodation with fully equipped kitchen, common room with TV and DVD player and showers on the upper floor, and 5 bedrooms & drying room on the ground floor. Ample car parking and a grass recreation area. Free WiFi available. Perfect accommodation for cycling or walking holidays or friends and family-get-togethers

DETAILS

- **Open** - All year.
- **Number of beds** - 20: 2x2 (twin), 2x4, 1x8
- **Booking** - Essential, up to 6 months in advance for weekend block bookings.
- **Price per night** - From £13 per person
- **Public Transport** - Skipton trains (12 miles). Buses from Bradford, Keighley and Harrogate. Dales buses pass Barn (01756) 753123 or (01535) 603284.
- **Directions** - From Skipton take B6265 to Grassington then the B6160 towards Kettlewell. In Kilnsey, 400m after the Crag turn into Skirfare Barn just before the T junction.

CONTACT: Matt & Bev
Tel: 07597 645254
skirfarebarn@gmail.com www.skirfarebarn.com
Kettlewell Rd, Kilnsey, North Yorkshire, BD23 5PT

WHITEFIELDS
COTTAGE

Situated in a medieval deer park, Whitefields Cottage offers self-catering accommodation within Fountains Abbey and Studley Royal Estate. Cared for by the National Trust and awarded World Heritage Site status in 1986, the estate contains a beautiful water garden, Elizabethan mansion and a Cistercian abbey. Whitefields is a 19th century cottage on the edge of Studley Royal Deer Park, home to around 350 red, fallow and sika deer.

Whether you want to explore the water gardens and impressive abbey, or walk around the North York moors (1hr drive) or Yorkshire Dales, Whitefields is ideal. It offers groups of up to 16 people inexpensive but comfortable accommodation.

DETAILS

■ **Open** - All year, except Christmas and New Year, no restrictions.

■ **Number of beds** - 16: 1x6, 1x8, 1x2.

■ **Booking** - Bookings required 1 week in advance, non refundable deposit £60.

■ **Price per night** - Mid week £140. Weekend (Fri/Sat) £180. Bookings of 7 nights or more charged at £140.00 night. £50 extra charge for 1 night stays at weekends

■ **Public Transport** - Train station and National Express coaches at Harrogate (15 miles). Regular bus service between Harrogate and Ripon. Taxis Ripon to Whitefields £8 - Harrogate to Whitefields £20.

■ **Directions** - From B6265 turn to Studley Roger. Drive through village, bear sharp right, before the National Trust sign, into deer park. Half a mile up main avenue turn right sign-posted 'estate vehicles only'. Turn right up the track at the end of this road, Whitefields is at top of track.

CONTACT: Andrew Moss
Tel: 01765 643172
andrew.moss@nationaltrust.org.uk www.nationaltrust.org.uk/fountainsabbey
Fountains Abbey and Studley Royal Park, Fountains, Ripon, HG4 3DY

Dalesbridge is located on the A65 at Austwick, on the edge of the Yorkshire Dales National Park, just five miles from both Ingleton and Settle. It is a comfortable venue for those visiting the Yorkshire Dales, whether you are a family, a group or an individual. The six bed units have a kitchen area with a cooker, fridge, washing up sink, shower and toilet. Crockery, cutlery and cooking pots are provided and there is a seating area in the middle of the room. The four bed units have a shower and toilet, small seating area with kettle, toaster, microwave, crockery and cutlery. These rooms are ideal for the smaller group not requiring full self-catering facilities. Utilising all the units provides group accommodation for up to 40. You will need to bring your own sleeping bag and pillow, alternatively bedding is available to hire. Dalesbridge has a great deal to offer: function bar, drying room, function catering, B&B and camp-site.

DETAILS

- **Open** - All year, reception open 9am - 5pm,
- **Number of beds** - 40
- **Booking** - Advance booking with first night payment as deposit.
- **Price per night** - £13-£19 per person per night dependent on season, usually let by the unit. Check our website for your dates, or ring us on 015242 51021
- **Public Transport** - Settle railway station is 5 miles away and Clapham station 1.5 miles. There are infrequent buses but if you would like collection from either railway station please give us a call.
- **Directions** - GR 762 676. Dalesbridge is on the main A65. When travelling from Settle towards Ingleton it is situated on the left hand side between the two turnings into Austwick.

CONTACT: Jon
Tel: 01524 251021
info@dalesbridge.co.uk www.dalesbridge.co.uk
Austwick, Nr Settle, LA2 8AZ

HORNBY LAITHE
BUNKHOUSE BARN

Simple, comfortable accommodation in the Yorkshire Dales National Park Hornby Laith Bunkhouse Barn has been converted from original farm buildings, and occupies a secluded position within easy walking distance of both the pretty village of Stainforth and traditional market town of Settle. The perfect base for groups wishing to explore this beautiful area. Within easy access to a wide variety of routes for both the seasoned walker or climber and those wishing to explore the countryside at their leisure. Sleeping up to 50 there is also space for a marquee for events and weddings & ample parking. Full catering available by arrangement although a fully equipped kitchen is available for self catering. A separate barn contains a recreational area & camping is available. Stainforth Foss, a picturesque waterfall on the river Ribble, is just a short walk across the fields from the barn and in the right season you can see the salmon leap on their journey upstream to spawn. The owners also have a holiday cottage available in Cumbria. See selfcatering-windermere.co.uk for more details.

DETAILS

- **Open** - All year.
- **Number of beds** - 50
- **Booking** - Book by telephone
- **Price per night** - 36 people - £750 for the weekend 50 people - £1,000 for the weekend. Please call for prices for other party numbers
- **Public Transport** - Train at Settle, Bus No 11 from Settle to Stainforth from which it is approximately a 12 minute walk to bunkhouse..
- **Directions** - From the A65 follow the B6480 through Settle and Langcliffe. After crossing the railway contine for approx 1 mile. Hornby Laith is on the left up a track.

CONTACT: Neil and Enid Caton,
Tel: 01729 822240
Hornby Laithe, Stainforth, Nr Settle, North Yorkshire BD24 9PB

A Victorian house in private grounds, Greta Tower is situated on the edge of the Yorkshire Dales, in the pretty village of Ingleton. Surrounded by magnificent countryside with caves, waterfalls and mountains. Dominated by Ingleborough the best known of Yorkshire's Three Peaks, the area is known for its walking routes and waterfall trail. There is plenty to offer for walkers, climbers, mountain bikers and cavers and it makes a great base for the Yorkshire Three Peaks Challenge. The Yorkshire Dales, Lake District, Forest of Bowland and Morecambe Bay coastline are all only a short drive away. Whatever your agenda, you're sure of a relaxing stay. This licensed hostel serves tasty meals. There's an open-air swimming pool (summer only) and park next door. Great for family breaks and school trips. Dormitory-style bed rooms with bunks and shared bathrooms plus two private en suite rooms with 5 Beds (including one double bed). Exclusive hire is available. Free parking on site.

DETAILS

- **Open** - March to October. Reception 7-10am, 5-10pm.
- **Number of beds** - 64: 4x6, 7x4, 1x2, 2x5
- **Booking** - Recommended, essential for groups. By phone, e-mail or website.
- **Price per night** - Beds from £15, rooms from £30. Sole use bookings welcome.
- **Public Transport** - The Leeds to Morecambe train line stops at both Clapham & Bentham. Ribblehead train station is the closest stop on the Settle-Carlilse railway. All are within approx. 10 minutes drive of Ingleton. For convenient bus connections to Ingleton, the best stations are Settle or Lancaster.
- **Directions** - In centre of village, close to the outdoor pool and play area. Off the A65 Skipton to Kendal Road, 30 mins from Morcambe and 25 mins from Lancaster.

CONTACT: Manager
Tel: 015242 41444
ingleton@yha.org.uk www.ingletonhostel.co.uk
Greta Tower, Sammy Lane, Ingleton, North Yorkshire, LA6 3EG

THE OLD SCHOOL
BUNKHOUSE

Situated 4.5 miles from Ingleton in Yorkshire Dales limestone country, between Ingleborough and Whernside with superb views of both, the bunkhouse makes an ideal base for sporting or nature holidays.

The area is well known for its scenery including the Three Peaks walk, (Ingleborough, Pen-y-ghent and Whernside), the Waterfalls walk and some of the best caves and potholes in the country including the famous Gaping Ghyll system and the White Scar show cave. This is a stone property, which has been converted from an old school, with much of the character remaining. It provides self-catering accommodation for up to 30 people and has a lounge, drying room, 4 shower rooms with hand basins and toilets, well equipped kitchen / dining room with industrial cooker, toasters, fridge, freezer, dishwasher, microwaves and payphone. No pets allowed. Nearest pub 100 yds.

DETAILS

- **Open** - All year, 24 hours.
- **Number of beds** - 30 (5 x 6)
- **Booking** - Early booking advised for popular times. £150 deposit for 2 nights. 25% for 3 nights or over.
- **Price per night** - £320 per night (sole use) for up to 20 people with an extra £16 per person for groups over 20 people. Minimum of 2 nights at weekends.
- **Public Transport** - Ribblehead station 1 mile. No buses.
- **Directions** - 4.5 miles on the B6255 Ingleton to Hawes Road, just after Chapel-Le-Dale village on left hand side. 11 miles from Hawes on B6255.

CONTACT: Clare and Peter Fox
Tel: 01729 823835
pfox119@btinternet.com www.oldschoolbunkhouse.co.uk
Chapel-le-Dale, Ingleton, Carnforth, Lancs, LA6 3AR

OLD SCHOOL BUNKHOUSE ENGLAND

Adjacent to the Pennine Way, on the edge of the picturesque village of Hardraw, The Old School Bunkhouse offers well-appointed, practical accommodation for individuals and groups of up to 26. The two new smaller bunkrooms are ideal for families or staff. The large school hall and enclosed field are perfect for communal activities. Off road parking, drying room, secure bike storage and bike wash area are all available. Hardraw village has a camp-site, café, the famous Green Dragon Inn and Hardraw Force waterfall, whilst the small town of Hawes is a 1.5 mile walk across fields. Andy and Helen, qualified instructors, offer days out underground, and other adventurous activities for families and groups with discounts available to bunkhouse guests. Hardraw Bunkhouse is a perfect overnight for individuals walking the Pennine Way. It is also ideal for groups booking sole use for outdoor pursuits, family get-togethers, educational visits and D of E. Call for mid-week deals for groups.

DETAILS

- **Open** - All year, 24 hours.
- **Number of beds** - 26:1x8,1x9,1x6,1x3 (2 tent spaces / 4 mattresses for groups)
- **Booking** - Advance booking preferred. 25% deposit for sole use. Total fee payable for 1 night bookings but short notice bookings may be available.
- **Price per night** - £15 pppn (£12 under 12s), exclusive use £175-£275pn.
- **Public Transport** - Trains: Garsdale (6 miles). Little White Bus outside bunkhouse connects with Leeds - Carlisle services. Buses to Bedale & Leyburn from Hawes.
- **Directions** - Turn north off A684 approx. 1 mile west of Hawes and proceed for ½ mile. Hardraw Old School Bunkhouse is on the left as you enter the village.

CONTACT: Andy or Helen
Tel: 01969 666034 Mob: 07546894317
enquiries@hardrawoldschoolbunkhouse.co.uk www.hardrawoldschoolbunkhouse.co.uk
Schoolhouse, Hardraw, near Hawes, Wensleydale, North Yorkshire, DL8 3LZ

THE JONAS
CENTRE

At the heart of Wensleydale in the tranquil beauty of the Yorkshire Dales, The Jonas Centre is uniquely positioned to provide all that is needed for those seeking relaxation and to enjoy all that the area has to offer. An ideal centre for cycling, walking and sightseeing, with routes direct from the door. Activities can be arranged independently with local providers on or off site. Close to Redmire station on the Wensleydale Railway and near to Castle Bolton & Aysgarth Falls. Good pub for meals in Redmire village. 12 self-catering log cabins with bathroom, well equipped kitchen & TV sleep 5-7. Heated by night storage (additional heaters available). Freezer, coin operated washing machine & dryer are available. Meeting facilities and large kitchen available to groups. Linen and towels can be hired. Pets allowed (nightly charge). Children's playground, table tennis hut, ball games area, camp fire area as well as space just to relax in the peaceful surroundings. An ideal venue for conferences, training, teaching and fellowship as well as wedding receptions and family celebrations.

DETAILS

- **Open** - Open all year. Office open from 9am - 5pm Monday to Saturday.
- **Number of beds** - 60
- **Booking** - Minimum 2 nights. The person making the booking must be over 18.
- **Price per night** - See website for special offers. Discounts for full site use.
- **Public Transport** - Train at Darlington & Northallerton (25 miles) local buses
- **Directions** - A684 westbound to Wensley, right toward Redmire. Entrance is on left after railway arch. A684 eastbound follow signs to & through Redmire entrance is directly ahead, drive carefully down to reception, or park by top steps and walk.

CONTACT: Simon Eastwood
Tel: 01969 624900
stay@jonascentre.org www.jonascentre.org
The Jonas Centre, Redmire, Leyburn. North Yorkshire, DL8 4EW

In the tiny village of Fremington in Swaledale, Yorkshire Dales, surrounded by the best biking in Yorkshire in a stunning landscape, criss-crossed by ancient lanes, moorland tracks and roads, this is the perfect venue for cycling, mountain biking, trail running and walking. The 2014 Tour de France Yorkshire Grande Depart route runs right past the door. 14 bed bunk accommodation, café, bike shop, hire, workshop and secure storage, bike wash, drying room and a wealth of knowledge about the Dales. 14 beds, in smart 2 and 4 bedded rooms, warmly decorated and with amazing views across the Swaledale. Bedding is provided, as well as a kitchenette with free tea and coffee. The café lounge can be used by guests, with magazines, free WiFi internet, internet radio and 24 hour cake access! A hearty breakfast is included. Evening meals are available in pubs and restaurants in Reeth, a five minute stroll away. On route for a Reeth stopover on Wainwright's famous Coast-to-Coast walk, the infamous Woodcocks off-road Coast-to-Coast mountain bike trip and the Yorkshire Dales Cycle Way.

DETAILS

- **Open** - All year, 24 hours.
- **Number of beds** - 14: Old barn 1x4, 1x2; New barn 1x4, 2x2,
- **Booking** - online via website, by phone or by email.
- **Price per night** - Bunkroom + B&B: 2 bed £68, 4 bed £116. Single £39.
- **Public Transport** - Trains Darlington (25 miles). Buses X26 & X27 every 15 mins from Darlington to Richmond. Bus 30 from Richmond to Reeth (7 per day till 6.15pm).
- **Directions** - 20 mins from A1M: from Richmond take A6108 then B6270 signed to Reeth. Once through Grinton, DBC is on left at end of a row of tall trees.

CONTACT: Stu Price
Tel: 01748 884908
enquiries@dalesbikecentre.co.uk www.dalesbikecentre.co.uk
Parks Barn, Fremington, Richmond DL11 6AW

RICHMOND
CAMPING BARN

East Applegarth Camping Barn, Richmond is converted from 3 former byres which are part of a listed, traditional dales, longhouse. It is situated at East Applegarth Farm, 3 miles west of the town of Richmond on the Coast to Coast walk. Grid ref NZ135017 OS Map 92. The farm borders the Yorkshire Dales National Park, with panoramic views over the lower valley of Swaledale and the River Swale. The barn is a great base for exploring the historic town of Richmond and The Yorkshire Dales National Park with all it has to offer. Sleeping accommodation is in two rooms on raised platforms with mattresses, pillows and lightweight sleeping bags. Heating and cooking facilities are available on a meter. Lighting is not metered and is included in the price. The shower is available on a separate meter. Cutlery, crockery and pans are provided.

DETAILS

- **Open** - 1st March to 30th November, access after 4pm and departure by 10.30am unless otherwise arranged.
- **Number of beds** - 12: 1 x 8, 1 x 4
- **Booking** - Book by phone or email
- **Price per night** - £10 per person. £120 sole use of barn.
- **Public Transport** - Nearest railway 15 miles away at Darlington. Bus service 3 miles away at Richmond. Local taxi service is available.
- **Directions** - On the A6108 in Richmond at the petrol station (Victoria Road) turn right into Hurgill Road. Continue for 3 miles. Farm entrance is on the left in a dip in the road 200 yds past the 2 radio masts on the right. The barn is at the end of the tarmac road ignoring the T-junction.

CONTACT: Mrs J Atkinson
Tel: 01748 822940
rebekah.atkinson@virgin.net
East Applegarth Farm, Westfields, Richmond, North Yorkshire DL10 4SD

FELL END
BUNKHOUSE

Overlooking the unspoilt Howgill Fells, these two 18th century buildings provide comfortable bunkhouse accommodation for people wishing to explore this beautiful area. Perfect for mixed groups, DofE, families and people with special needs. Great for walking & cycling, canoeing & caving nearby, the Lake District is only 1 hour away. The Schoolhouse sleeps 8 in bunks in the central area with an extra bed in an adjoining room. There are two toilets, one shower and four wash basins and a fully equipped kitchen with a fridge, freezer, microwave and cooker. The living room has a multi-fuel stove, which also heats the radiators. Greenslack has a further 2 bunks and 1 single bed plus a bathroom for people with mobility problems. Get in touch if your group has fewer than 8 people but you require Greenslack for these facilities. Entry into both buildings is by a touch lock system. Dogs allowed under strict supervision. Fell End is owned by the Bendrigg Trust, a charity offering outdoor activities for disabled people.

            GROUPS ONLY

DETAILS

- **Open** - All year.
- **Number of beds** - 14: 1x8, 1x5, 1x1.
- **Booking** - Completed booking form with 20% deposit to Bendrigg Trust, Old Hutton, Kendal, Cumbria, LA8 0NR. Payment by cheque or BACS
- **Price per night** - £11.50 + VAT. Minimum booking: 6 for Schoolhouse, 8 for both buildings, 12 people if booking 1 night, (no charge under 5yrs).
- **Public Transport** - Nearest train station: Kirkby Stephen (6 miles) on the Carlisle/Settle/Leeds line. Taxis only to Fell End.
- **Directions** - Bunkhouse 6 miles NE of Sedbergh, just off A683. GR:723983

CONTACT: Lynne Irish
Tel: 01539 723766
lynne@bendrigg.org.uk www.fellend-bunkhouse.org.uk
Ravenstonedale, Kirkby Stephen, Cumbria, CA17 4LN

BENTS
CAMPING BARN

Bents Camping Barn was formerly a shepherds' cottage in the 1600s. There are 2 sleeping rooms on the first floor with bunk beds. On the ground floor there is a kitchen with cooking area, a dining area with tables and benches and a WC with washbasins. Other facilities include electric lighting and power points throughout (£1 coin meter), crockery, cutlery, toaster, fridge, microwave, 3 electric cooking rings, 2 electric kettles, 2 electric convector heaters and parking. You will need sleeping bags, walking boots and warm clothes. The barn is accessible from the Coast to Coast path and there is good fell walking in the Howgill Fells, Wild Boar Fell and Crosby Garrett Common. Smardale Gill Nature Reserve and Sunbiggin Tarn are nearby. The area is ideal for mountain biking and the Settle to Carlisle Railway is five miles away at Kirkby Stephen. There is a shop 2 miles away.

DETAILS

- **Open** - All year, all day.
- **Number of beds** - 12 to 14: 1x10, 1x6
- **Booking** - Booking is essential for groups in advance with full payment. Individuals are advised to phone first.
- **Price per night** - £10 per person. Full barn £144 per night.
- **Public Transport** - Train station at Kirkby Stephen (5 miles). Local buses to village of Newbiggin-on-Lune.
- **Directions** - GR MY 708 065 OS map 91. From Junction 38 of the M6 take the A685 to Newbiggin-on-Lune. Take Great Asby Road on left then first right through tall gate. Follow tarmac road past Tower House and follow signs to Bents Farm up track.

CONTACT: Dorothy Ousby
Tel: Booking 017687 74301   Dorothy 01768 371760
www.lakelandcampingbarns.co.uk/barns/bents-camping-barn
Newbiggin-on-Lune, Kirkby Stephen, Cumbria, CA17 4NX

Wythmoor Camping Barn is on the Walney to Wear coast to coast cycle route and a few hundred metres from the Dales Way long distance footpath. It enjoys great views of the Howgill Fells and the distant mountains of the Central Lakes. Being only 4.5 miles from Kendal and less than 10 mins from the M6 this is an ideal location for exploring the Lake District and the Yorkshire Dales. The 19th century barn has hot water provided by solar panels (immersion heater backup), underfloor heating powered by ground source heat pump and mains electricity supplemented by wind turbine. The barn is generously sized for twelve people and includes facilities for wheelchair users, two separate heated shower rooms and a food preparation area with sinks and cooking slabs (bring your own camp-stove).Kettle and microwave are provided. Local taxis available for transport to Kendal and Sedburgh. Holmescales Farm Outdoor Centre is close by.

DETAILS

- **Open** - All year, all day.
- **Number of beds** - 12: 1x12 (10 single beds, 1 double)
- **Booking** - Book online, by phone or email. Booking not always required
- **Price per night** - £10 per person.
- **Public Transport** - Oxenholme (6.5 miles) and Kendal (4.5 miles) have stations.
- **Directions** - Take Appleby Road (A685) from Kendal. After 2.5 miles turn right signed 'Docker' (single track). Opposite Docker Hall Farm, take left fork signed Lambrigg. Continue for 2 miles, barn is on left next to white farmhouse. From M6 Junction 37 take A684 towards Sedbergh; then direct left signed Lambrigg/Beck Foot. After 1.5 miles take left signed Lambrigg and Docker (single track). Barn is on right in half a mile next to white farmhouse. Sat Navs will direct you to a private drive.

CONTACT: Bruce Withington
Tel: Booking office 017687 74301
info@lakelandcampingbarns.co.uk www.lakelandcampingbarns.co.uk
Wythmoor Farm, Lambrigg, Kendal, LA8 0DH

LONGRIGG
RESIDENTIAL CENTRE

Longrigg Residential Centre, within walking distance of Sedbergh, only 10 miles from Kendal and less than 10 minutes from the M6, is an ideal location for exploring the Lakes and the Yorkshire Dales. Standing in its own grounds and overlooking the unspoilt splendour of the Howgill Fells the centre is perfect for mixed groups or families. Walking, cycling, canoeing and caving are nearby. Recently refurbished the centre has two six bed dorms in the main building and a larger separate building sleeps 20 in dorms of 2,4,6 and 8. There are ample shower and toilet facilities, a drying room and tumble drier. Sleeping bags and pillowcases are required. The large kitchen is equipped for group catering. The lounge has easy chairs and gives access to the patio area. A separate games room has pool table, TV and table football. The centre holds an Adventure Activity Licence and can offer instruction and equipment. Entry is by a touch lock system. The centre is owned by Action 4 Youth a registered Charity (No 1033626) and complies with relevant health and safety requirements.

DETAILS

- **Open** - All year, all day.
- **Number of beds** - 32: 1x8, 3x6, 1x4, 1x2
- **Booking** - Book by phone or email
- **Price per night** - £17 per head for a minimum of 12 people. £16 per head for 20 or more. £15 per head for groups of 25 or more.
- **Public Transport** - Trains at Oxenholme on the West Coast Line.
- **Directions** - Near the village of Sedbergh which lies on the edge of the Yorkshire Dales and is just 30 minutes from the Lake District. Easy access via M6 junction 37.

CONTACT: Dave Hollingham
Tel: 01539 621161
longrigg@action4youth.org www.longrigg.org.uk
Frostrow Lane, Sedbergh, Cumbria, LA105JT

Kirkby Stephen Hostel, is a former YHA hostel converted from a Methodist Church and has been independent since 2010. The old chapel has a range of accommodation for individuals, families and groups amongst beautiful authentic features; stained glass windows, arches, oak panels and stone covings. The chapel houses a large dining room and kitchen, with a lounge/reading room in the gallery. The bedrooms and dormitories are in a building at the rear, with ample lavatories and showers, WiFi and a drying room. Kirkby Stephen is a pleasant market town in the upper Eden valley, situated 15 miles from Kendal, 15 miles from Hawes and on Wainwright's coast to coast path and the W2W cycle path. It enjoys easy access to the Lady Ann Clifford Walk, the Walney to Wear Bike Ride, the Howgill Hills, the Dales National Park and the Lake District. Paragliding is also available. The hostel stands prominently on the main street of Kirkby Stephen, with a range of restaurants, cafés, pubs, take aways (including fish and chips) and food shops on the doorstep.

DETAILS

■ **Open** - All year, please arrive after 5pm (or ring to arrange arrival).
■ **Number of beds** - 38: 1x8, 3x6, 2x4, 1x2, 1x2 en suite
■ **Booking** - Book by phone or email. Booking advised but not essential.
■ **Price per night** - £20pp. Reductions for groups.
■ **Public Transport** - One mile from Kirkby Stephen train station on the Leeds-Carlisle line. Regular buses from Penrith, Kendal and Appleby stop outside hostel.
■ **Directions** - In the centre of town on main road. From M6 leave at junction 38 and follow signs towards Appleby.

CONTACT: Denise
Tel: 01768 371793 or 07812 558525
kirkbystephenhostel@btconnect.com www.kirkbystephenhostel.co.uk
Market Street, Kirkby Stephen, Cumbria, CA17 4QQ

NEW ING
LODGE

New Ing Lodge is a 18th century grade 2 listed farm. Now operating as a 10 bedroom, 9 bathroom B&B and hostel offering friendly flexible accommodation with food. It has been awarded Gold Green Tourism and is the only winner of the Above & Beyond Outstanding Commitment to Responsible Tourism. Based in Shap in the Eden Valley, on the edge of the Lake District National Park, the Howgills and the Pennine Fells, New Ing Lodge offers comfort at an affordable price just minutes from the M6. Available for exclusive use it is perfect for large groups looking for a peaceful retreat. Situated on Wainwright's Coast to Coast path, the Westmorland Way and the Miller's Way it is ideal for walking and cycling. Run by outdoor enthusiasts who can give advice on what to do. There is an acre of well kept field with volleyball court and a walled orchard. Sole hire gives use of 10 bedrooms, the bar, commercial kitchen, dinning room, games/ cinema room, volleyball court and the grounds. Quality Cumbria accredited

DETAILS

- **Open** - All year, all day.
- **Number of beds** - 34. 2x twin, 3xdouble, 2x double and single, 1x double and 2 singles, 1x 6 bedded dorm, 1 x 8 bedded dorm.
- **Booking** - Well in advance - deposit 50% via website or card payment by phone.
- **Price per night** - £18pp dorm with bedding, B&B (private rooms) from £30pp. Discounts available for larger groups and longer stays. Sole use from only £550.
- **Public Transport** - Bus from Penrith or Kendal station. Pick-up from station is possible. No buses on Sunday.
- **Directions** - North end of Shap village, opposite the Bampton and Haweswater junction. 5th building on the left hand side if travelling from the North.

CONTACT: Scott or Jamie
Tel: 01931 716719
info@newinglodge.co.uk www.newinglodge.co.uk
New Ing Lodge, Main Street, Shap, Penrith, Cumbria, CA10 3LX

GREENGILL
BARN

A converted traditional barn on the edge of Morland in Cumbria's rolling Eden Valley, close to the Lake District and handy for the M6. Great for weekend gatherings of family or friends wanting to visit the Lake District, the Pennines, the Yorkshire Dales and the Borders. Accommodating 16 in 2 bunk rooms, a large fully equipped kitchen/dining room and a huge beamed recreation room with sofas, armchairs, pool table, library, dartboard and card table and music system. A great space for a party. Night storage heating. 3 Mira sports showers, 3 loos. Small camp-site and two self-catering cottages next door. The Eden Valley is an idyllic cycling area with quiet rolling roads and wonderful views. Greengill Barn is on NCN route 71 and new Wiggo's Loop on C2C. Secure bike storage, ideal for road cyclists and mountain bikers. Good local walking, and easy access to lakes and fells. BYO food and drink or just 4 mins' walk to The Mill Yard Café for Friday night pizzas, full English breakfasts, coffees, lunches and take-aways. The Crown Inn opposite serves real ale, and weekend meals.

DETAILS

■ **Open** - All year.
■ **Number of beds** - 16: 2x8
■ **Booking** - Exclusive group use only. Minimum 2 nights. 30% non-returnable deposit to confirm. Balance due a month before arrival. Payable online or by cheque.
■ **Price per night** - £280 per night so £560 for 2 nights.(£17.50pppn for 16 people). Bunk sheet included. Own sleeping bags free or duvet, pillow, towel £5pp. Dogs £15.
■ **Public Transport** - Nearest rail station and bus station in Penrith, 7 miles
■ **Directions** - Last building in Morland on road to Great Strickland.

CONTACT: Freddy Markham
Tel: 01931 714244 Mob: 07831 428541
freddy@greengillholidays.co.uk www.greengillholidays.co.uk
Greengill Barn, Strickland Road, Morland, Penrith, Cumbria CA10 3AX

YEALAND
OLD SCHOOL

Yealand Old School hostel is located in the middle of the village of Yealand Conyers, and is part of the Quaker Heritage of the village. The hostel is run on a not-for-profit basis by the adjacent Quaker meeting house. The hostel offers simple self-catering accommodation for all sorts of groups.

Facilites include a well equipped kitchen, which provides good dining space. The upstairs provides 3 good sized spaces used in various ways by different groups. One is a sizable hall, and another a comfortable sitting room.

Groups normally have sole occupancy of the building. The hostel is well located for walking, cycling, the RSPB reserve at Leighton Moss and is on NCN6. Camping in the adjacent field may be possible. Resident warden.

DETAILS

- **Open** - All year, all day.
- **Number of beds** - 26: 1x4, 1x2, mattresses for 20+
- **Booking** - Contact warden for booking form.
- **Price per night** - £15/adult/night, £7.50 children 5 and over, min charge £100 for group Friday/Sat, £50 during week
- **Public Transport** - Carnforth station 3 miles, with a connection by local bus which stops outside the hostel.
- **Directions** - Exactly at the top of the hill on the main road through Yealand Conyers village, 5 mins from J35 M6

CONTACT: Sue Tyldesley
Tel: 01524 732336
yealandwarden@lancsquakers.org.uk www.lancsquakers.org.uk/simple-hostel.php
Yealand Rd, Yealand Conyers, Carnforth, LA5 9SH

LAKE DISTRICT
BACKPACKERS

Situated in the heart of Windermere and central Lakeland, you will find this cosy, friendly hostel ideally situated for exploring the surrounding area. The owners can advise you on routes for walks and cycle rides and provide you with maps. Staff can also help to organise abseiling, canoeing, sailing, windsurfing, even caving! There is easy access to the lake and fells from our door and the hostel is adjacent to the main 555 bus route through Lakeland.

The hostel with its cosy dormitories provides you with every comfort but at a budget price. The hostel is right next to a number of pubs, restaurants and take-aways and only minutes away from the rail and bus stations. Lockers are available. Internet access with WiFi and Sky TV keep you in touch! A well equipped kitchen and comfortable common room make your stay one to remember.

DETAILS

- **Open** - All year, 24 hours with key code for front door.
- **Number of beds** - 20:- 1x6, 2 x4, 2 x double with single above.
- **Booking** - Essential, 24 hours in advance.
- **Price per night** - £16.00 dorms/ £19.00 private rooms. £2 discount per night for stays of 3+ nights. Includes self service continental breakfast and free tea/coffee.
- **Public Transport** - Windermere train station is 2 minutes' walk. National Express coach stop 2 minutes' walk.
- **Directions** - Turn left out of the station, walk to the information centre, the hostel is opposite, between Open Door Properties and the Lamp Lighter Bar, 2 minutes' walk from station.

CONTACT: Paul
Tel: 015394 46374
info@lakedistrictbackpackers.co.uk www.lakedistrictbackpackers.co.uk
High Street, Windermere, Cumbria, LA23 1AF

ROOKHOW
CENTRE

Situated in the Rusland Valley, close to the heart of the Lake District, this small beautiful hostel has its own glorious woods where you can have a bonfire/BBQ or explore the woodland walks. Close to Coniston and Windermere and on the edge of the Grizedale Forest Park with its trails and sculptures, Rookhow is the perfect base for walking, orienteering, mountain biking, canoeing and all outdoor activities as well as quiet retreat, relaxation, study and artistic pursuits.

Converted from the stables of the nearby historic Quaker meeting house (available for conferences, seminars and group activities) the three sleeping areas can be rented as private or family rooms. Facilities: kitchen/dining area, cosy wood stove, picnic tables and BBQ. Private parking. WiFi by arrangement. Inn food 2/3 miles. Supermarkets 15mins or will deliver. Electric heating inc.

DETAILS

- **Open** - All year, all day.
- **Number of beds** - 20: 1x9, 1x8, plus extra on bed settees. Also camping.
- **Booking** - Booking is essential (deposit).
- **Price per night** - From :- Adult £16.00, £8.00 for under 16s. Sole use from £190 (minimum) per night. Camping rate half the above. Duvet hire £5 pp.
- **Public Transport** - Trains at Grange-over-Sands and Ulverston. (11 miles, approx £25 by taxi). A seasonal bus service sometimes operates - check with the warden.
- **Directions** - GR 332896. From M6, Junction 36, follow A590, signs for Barrow. Leave A590 at Greenodd (A5092) junction and follow sign for Workington for ¼ mile. Take minor road to right signed Colton / Oxen Park. Continue through Oxen Park for 2 miles. Centre on left. From Ambleside: to Hawkshead, then to Grizedale. Continue beyond Grizedale for 3.5 miles (Satterthwaite - Ulverston Road). Centre on the right.

CONTACT: Warden
Tel: 01229 860231 Mob: 0794 350 8100
straughton@btinternet.com www.rookhowcentre.co.uk
Rusland Valley, nr Grizedale, Ulverston, Cumbria, South Lakeland, LA12 8BLA

LOWICK SCHOOL
BUNKHOUSE

Lowick School Bunkhouse is based within the old primary school at Lowick Green which is nestled between Coniston and Ulverston. The bunkhouse has 20 beds in 3 rooms plus a lounge/meeting room with wood-burning stove, kitchen/dining room, great views of the mountains, an outdoor area with campfire and more!

River Deep Mountain High Activity Centre provides a wide variety of outdoor activities from gorge walking to mountain biking, kayaking to sailing and more. Group and family packages include activities in the price. Just 25 mins' drive from the M6 and only 4 miles from Coniston Water. It is less than a mile to 2 pubs – either a pleasant walk down a back lane to the Red Lion or down the main road to the Farmer's Arms.

DETAILS

- **Open** - All year.
- **Number of beds** - 20: 2x8, 1x4
- **Booking** - Package prices include an outdoor activity with River Deep Mountain High. Schools and youth/college groups can discuss how to fit a stay in their budget.
- **Price per night** - Whole bunkhouse available from £550 at weekends (Club scheme), from £800 Mon-Thurs. £250 deposit required for groups. Shorter stays available by negotiation. Family packages in school holidays
- **Public Transport** - Buses from Windermere and Ulverston
- **Directions** - From the M6, jn36, follow the A590 to Greenodd. Turn right onto A5092 after 2.5 miles Lowick school is on the right after Esps Farm. If you get to Woodgate, you have missed it!

CONTACT: Emma Hoving
Tel: 01539528666
info@riverdeepmountainhigh.co.uk www.riverdeepmountainhigh.co.uk
Lowick Old School, Lowick Green, Ulverston LA12 8EB

HIGH WRAY
BASECAMP

Situated in the heart of South Lakeland in secluded woodland, 4 miles from the village of Ambleside, High Wray Basecamp provides an ideal base for groups wishing to explore and take part in activities in the Lake District area. Local attractions include rambling, fell walking, climbing and water sports, with the Basecamp ranger being happy to assist with information on local walks and activities. The Longland Block has two separate fully centrally heated dormitories each sleeping 8, with a separate washing and living area/kitchen block. The comfortable living area is heated by a central wood burning stove and the kitchen has a commercial gas cooker, fridge freezer, microwave and utensils. The Acland block has two separate centrally heated dormitories sleeping 10 each, with toilet and shower room attached. The kitchen / lounge area is fitted with commercial gas cooker, fridges, microwave and utensils.

DETAILS

- **Open** - All year, 24 hours.
- **Number of beds** - 16 + 22
- **Booking** - by email or phone
- **Price per night** - Longland £11.00pp (Mon-Thur), £14.00pp (Fri-Sun). Acland £11.50pp (Mon-Thur), £15.00pp (Fri-Sun).
- **Public Transport** - Nearest train station Windermere 8 miles. Local bus (505 'Coniston Rambler' Windermere - Hawkshead) stops 2 miles away at turning to Wray Castle (Cumbria travel-line 0870 6082608)
- **Directions** - GR: 373 995 Take A593 from Ambleside towards Coniston, bear left onto the B5286 signed Hawkshead, fork left for High Wray village, signed Wray Castle. Basecamp is ¼ mile up dirt road on the left at the end of High Wray village.

CONTACT: Philippa Barber
Tel: 015394 34633
Philippa.barber@nationaltrust.org.uk
High Wray, Ambleside, Cumbria, LA22 0JE

LUMLEY FEE
BUNKHOUSE

Breathtaking views across the beautiful Lyth Valley provide a unique window over the lakeland hills and fells from Lumley Fee Bunkhouse. The perfect base for a group of friends or family looking for a happy hangout or for couples (or groups) wanting to experience the peace and tranquillity of this stunning landscape. Whether walking, climbing, cycling or just relaxing, Lumley Fee will be an individually different experience. The creative and charming interior of this former school house will welcome you with open arms. Each of its five rooms sleeps up to four people with en suite facilities. The old school room has been converted to a perfect communal area for relaxing and getting together with a wood burning stove, comfy sofas and plenty of games. The well equipped kitchen is also available to guests and the Wheatsheaf Inn just down the road in Brigsteer also serves breakfast and can provide packed lunches as well as evening meals.

DETAILS

- **Open** - All year. Guests can check-in from 3pm, departure is by 11am.
- **Number of beds** - 20: 5x4
- **Booking** - Via website, email or telephone
- **Price per night** - from £70 per room, sole use rate inc. meals also available.
- **Public Transport** - Bus and Train at Kendal (3 miles away) good taxi service. A mini bus service for dinners between Lumley Fee, The Wheatsheaf & The Masons Arms is available (Booking required).
- **Directions** - from A6 Kendal, follow signs for Brigsteer. nearing Brigsteer where road veers sharp right, turn left, (to Helsington Church) Lumley Fee is on the left by the Church.

CONTACT: Reception
Tel: 015395 68938
info@lumleyfeebunkhouse.co.uk www.lumleyfeebunkhouse.co.uk
Lumley Fee Bunkhouse, Helsington, Kendal, LA8 8AQ

FINE HAND PULLED CUMBRIAN

Dogs welcome! Great Ales

HOMEMADE PIZZAS

OPEN ALL Paper GREAT
Out DAY FOOD
door Proper
dining packed Log Fires
Lunches
Butters Cumbrian
Delicacies
FREE TAKEAWAY DISHES
WIFI Wine by the Glass
& BY THE BOTTLE TOO!
BEAUTIFUL BRIGSTEER
HOT BREWS, MUGS, CUPS & POTS
Muddy boots & cagoutes Welcome!
Super filled
SANDWICHES
GOOD BEAUTIFUL VIEWS
CAMP HALLOUS BEER
ERS, CARAVANER
WELCOME

KENDAL
HOSTEL

A Georgian town house next to the Brewery Arts Centre just 300 yards from the centre of the historic market town of Kendal, this family run, friendly hostel is a home from home. With a comfortable lounge, well equipped kitchen, dining room (seats 26), central heating, hot showers, secure cycle shed and drying room and a range of bedrooms all with wash basins and 5 en suite. There is free WiFi and a good selection of books about the surrounding area, walking and cycling routes. A Blue Badge guide is on site and the hostel staff are always happy to pass on their local knowledge. Kendal has many attractions including the castle ruins, Kendal Museum, Abbot Hall Art Gallery and more. A short drive, bus or train ride will take you to Lake Windermere and Bowness-on-Windermere for lake cruises and the famous Beatrix Potter exhibition. A great place to break a journey to and from Scotland as well as discovering this beautiful part of the country. Breakfast available on request. Whole hostel bookings taken.

DETAILS

- **Open** - All year, 7.30am to 10.30am, 4.30pm to 8.30pm and by arrangement.
- **Number of beds** - 70: 1 x 14, 1 x 8, 2 x 7 (family), 2 x 6, 1 x 5(family), 1 x 4, 1 x 3, 4 x 2, 1 x double. All family rooms have private shower room and double bed
- **Booking** - by phone, email, text or website. Booking is preferable but not essential
- **Price per night** - £20 Sunday to Thursday, £22 Friday and Saturday.
- **Public Transport** - National Express to Kendal bus station. (10 min walk), Kendal train station (15 min walk), Oxenholme (The Lakes Station) 5 mins by taxi.
- **Directions** - Junction 36 of M6, A6 into Kendal 300m from Parish Church on LHS, in front of Brewery Arts Centre. Directions on hostel website under the location tab

CONTACT: Jan or Kristina
Tel: 01539 724066; Mob: 07795 198 197
kristina@kendalhostel.co.uk www.kendalhostel.com
118-120 Highgate, Kendal, Cumbria, LA9 4HE

INSTITUTE OF TOURIST GUIDING

Jan Moffat

DACRES STABLE
CAMPING BARN

Although only 20 minutes' drive from Kendal, Dacre's Stable Camping Barn is located on the wonderfully isolated Grisedale farm on a gated road away from the main A6. It is the perfect base to explore the Yorkshire Dales National Park, the Lake District National Park and the Eden valley. Here there is abundant wildlife, fell walking, and cycling on quiet tracks and lanes, also space to gaze, read, sketch, dream and do nothing. Or with the Central Lakes less than an hour's drive away make the most of the nearby tourist attractions. The Stable is a flexible, friendly space for families or groups. Available only on a sole-occupancy, self-catering basis, the ground floor sleeps two in a double bed and is heated by wood burning stove and has a well equipped kitchen. Upstairs is a bunk room for 6 with additional mattresses. The big barn on the farm can provide overflow play space for children in bad weather as well as bike storage. Pillows are provided. Please bring towels, sleeping bags, warm bedding and pillow cases, torches and some dry kindling wood

DETAILS

■ **Open** - All year, all day.
■ **Number of beds** - 8 1X2 1X6
■ **Booking** - Please phone to book and discuss requirements
■ **Price per night** - Sole use only - from £55pn reductions for mid-week and longer stays (min 2 night stay, unless by special arrangement) Please phone to discuss.
■ **Public Transport** - Trains: Penrith & Oxenholme (30 mins' drive), Kendal (20 mins' drive). Car hire and National Express buses also at Kendal. No local buses.
■ **Directions** - 10 mins from A6, 7miles north of Kendal, please phone for directions.

CONTACT: Hilary Fell
Tel: 01539 823208   mobile: 07788 633936
dacresstable@gmail.com dacresstablecampingbarn.blogspot.co.uk/
Grisedale Farm, Whinfell, Kendal, Cumbria, LA8 9EN

Refurbished recently, Rydal Hall Youth Centre is situated in the centre of Rydal Hall estate, sheltered on three sides by the Fairfield Horseshoe and offering access to the best of Lakeland's activities. Facilities inside provide accommodation for groups of up to 29. There are 2 dormitories sleeping 9 and 10 in each and 2 leader rooms each sleeping 4 and 6. A large common room can be used for dining or recreation. A drying room on the ground floor. A welcoming log burner provides additional warmth to the ample heating powered by our nearby water turbine. The kitchen is fully equipped for cooking. Guests need to bring sleeping bags, pillow cases and extra blankets during winter.

Rydal Hall also offers camping to groups and families and there is residential accommodation for up to 56 at the Hall in single, twin, double and family rooms with private facilities.

DETAILS

- **Open** - All year, 24 hours.
- **Number of beds** - Dormitories 29: 1x10 , 1x9, 1x6, 1x4.
- **Booking** - Required with deposit. No bookings by email please.
- **Price per night** - Peak season 1st April to 31st October £295.00. Off Peak 1st November to 31st March £250. Late deals available please enquire.
- **Public Transport** - Trains at Windermere. National Express at Ambleside. Local Stagecoach service (555) from Lancaster to Keswick stops 200 yards from Hall.
- **Directions** - GR 366 064. Take the A561 from Ambleside to Grasmere, Rydal is reached after 2 miles. By the church turn right and go up lane for 200m.

CONTACT:
Tel: 01539 432050
mail@rydalhall.org www.rydalhall.org
Rydal Hall, Ambleside, Cumbria, LA22 9LX

GREAT LANGDALE
BUNKHOUSE

Great Langdale Bunkhouse offers great value accommodation for groups, families and individuals. Situated amidst some of the finest mountain scenery in England with immediate access to world class mountain biking, road cycling, walking, fell running and climbing. The whole place is set up to explore the amazing mountains and ideal for those who love the outdoors.

The bunkhouse has 21 beds divided into 3 twin rooms, 1 room of 7 and 1 room of 8 (all bunk beds). It has gas central heating throughout with separate male and female shower and toilet facilities. There is a drying room and secure bike storage. There are no cooking or dining facilities. The Sticklebarn Tavern is located right next door and serves good value lunch and dinners. Sheet, pillow and pillowcase are provided, bring your own sleeping bag and towels. Well behaved dogs are allowed in the bunkhouse in a private room with owner.

DETAILS

- **Open** - All year, all day.
- **Number of beds** - 21
- **Booking** - Booking is advised for all of summer, all weekends and for larger groups. 50% deposit required.
- **Price per night** - From £15pppn
- **Public Transport** - Bus service 516 to Great Langdale from Ambleside, ask for New Dungeon Ghyll Hotel, walk 2 mins (timetable 01946 632222).
- **Directions** - From the A591 Windermere to Keswick road at Ambleside take the A593 turn to Coniston / Torver. After two miles take the B5343 to Great Langdale via Chapel Stile. The bunkhouse is behind the Sticklebarn Tavern.

CONTACT:
Tel: 01539 437725
langdale.bunkhouse@gmail.com www.greatlangdalebunkhouse.co.uk
Great Langdale, LA22 9JU

ELTERWATER
HOSTEL
ENGLAND

Elterwater Hostel (formerly YHA Elterwater) is located in the peaceful village of Elterwater, in the Langdale valley, 15 minutes' drive from Ambleside. The area has many walks for people of all abilities, from gentle riverside meanders to the challenge presented by the Langdale Pikes, Bowfell and Scafell. Banks, shops and other amenities are available nearby.

The area is also a favourite for both on and off-road cycling, rock climbing and many other outdoor activities. An ideal overnight stop on the Cumbria way.

The hostel is an ideal venue for individuals, families, outdoor groups, schools and college trips.

DETAILS

- **Open** - All year (Nov-Feb Groups only). Access between 7:30am and 11:30pm. Reception open 7:30 to 10:00 and 17:00 to 22:30.
- **Number of beds** - 40: 6 x 2 beds, 1 x 4 beds, 4 x 6 beds
- **Booking** - Booking advisable all year round, via website or phone.
- **Price per night** - Beds from £18pppn. For exclusive hire please call. Low season discounts may be available
- **Public Transport** - From Ambleside: Stagecoach-in-Cumbria route 516 towards Dungeon Ghyll
- **Directions** - from Ambleside take the A593. After 2 miles, turn right onto the B5343. After 2 miles go over cattle grid, then next left. Go through the village, the hostel is right.

CONTACT: Nick Owen
Tel: 015394 37245
enquiries@elterwaterhostel.co.uk www.elterwaterhostel.co.uk
Elterwater Hostel, Elterwater, Ambleside LA22 9HX

AMBLESIDE
BACKPACKERS

The English Lakes National Park is one of the most scenic areas of the UK made famous by the likes of Wordsworth and Beatrix Potter. Ambleside Backpackers has a great central location, ideal for fell and mountain walking, climbing, boating, scenic drives, cycle touring, mountain biking and outdoor activities. Fell walks from the front door with lakes nearby yet just 4 minutes' walk from the centre of Ambleside with its many outdoor equipment shops,cafés, restaurants and pubs. The hostel is a large, old lakeland house featuring a great lounge with comfy chairs, fire and piano, dining room & large well equipped, self-catering kitchen, drying room, laundry facilities and secure bike store. Free light breakfast, tea/coffee and internet access. With 52 beds Ambleside Backpackers can accommodate individuals, couples, groups and families in rooms or dorms. Group and whole hostel bookings welcome. Sorry no stag, hen or drinking parties. Opening 19th March for 2016 season.

DETAILS

- **Open** - From 19th March 2016. Arrive after 4.30pm and depart by 10.30am.
- **Number of beds** - 56: 1x10, 1x8, 4x6, 2x4, 1x2
- **Booking** - Recommended, essential for groups. See website for availability
- **Price per night** - See website, reductions for three or more nights. All prices include light breakfast, tea, coffee, daytime and evening internet access.
- **Public Transport** - Windermere train station 4 miles then 555 bus to Ambleside.
- **Directions** - From Ambleside, Kelsick Rd bus stop: up hill to T junction turn right them immediately left into Old Lake Rd, hostel is 200m up on left. By road: A591 Windermere to Ambleside. At 2nd Hayes Garden Centre sign turn right into Old Lake Rd. Hostel is 300m on right.

CONTACT: David
Tel: 015394 32340
bookings@amblesidebackpackers.com   www.amblesidehostel.co.uk
Ambleside BPs, Iveing Cottage, Old Lake Rd, Ambleside Cumbria, LA22 0DJ

THORNEY HOW
INDEPENDENT HOSTEL

Thorney How offers clean and comfortable holiday accommodation in Grasmere, the heart of the Lake District. Family-run and welcoming it provides bed and breakfast and self-catering accommodation for individuals, families and groups. With the backdrop of magnificent fells, adjacent to the Coast to Coast path, local village amenities and lake, the tranquil location provides the perfect place from which to explore all the Lake District has to offer.

The main house, a 350 year old gentlemen's farmhouse, is charming with well proportioned rooms and fabulous views. There is some en suite accommodation. The newly refurbished bunkhouse overlooking the Easedale valley is ideal for smaller groups up to 16. Larger groups are automatically offered breakfasts and at least one evening meal as part of their booking price. Parking, electric car charging, bike hire, cycle store, drying room, licensed bar, café and spacious grounds complete the experience. No pets allowed.

DETAILS

- **Open** - Open all year. Closed 10.30am to 3.30pm – check in 3.30pm to 10.30pm.
- **Number of beds** - 42: Split between Main House 26 and Bunkhouse 16
- **Booking** - Booking online recommended, by phone or email. First night's accommodation non-refundable payment required to secure booking,
- **Price per night** - Bunkhouse from £20. Main House B&B from £25.50. Double en suite from £77.00. 4 person rooms from £76.00. Larger groups please contact hostel.
- **Public Transport** - National Express coaches stop in Grasmere. Local bus 555 to / from Windermere & Keswick. Train station at Windermere.
- **Directions** - Grid ref: 332084. Half a mile NW of Grasmere Village.

CONTACT: Taylor Nuttall
Tel: 01539 435597
enquiries@thorneyhow.co.uk   www.thorneyhow.co.uk
Thorney How Off Helm Close & Easedale Road Grasmere Cumbria LA22 9QW

GRASMERE
HOSTEL

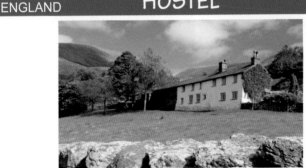

This small deluxe hostel, situated on a farm, is nestled in the heart of the Lake District National Park and a short stroll from the idyllic village of Grasmere. The only 4 star independent hostel in the Lake District, this family run hostel is ideal for individuals, couples, families and groups, especially if you want exclusive use of the whole place for a club, school or special event. For groups requiring more space, 3 luxury cottages are also available on the farm. The hostel's extensive facilities include en suite bedrooms, 2 fully equipped self-catering kitchens, dining room, lounge, laundry area, secure bike storage, drying room, LCD TV & DVD, free WiFi throughout and an Internet PC, private parking, BBQ area with seating for 24 and even a sauna. An adjacent conference/studio room is available for an additional charge. A stunning location midway between Windermere and Keswick makes Grasmere the perfect base for your holiday, whether you are on a quest for adventure, relaxation or celebration. Grasmere Hostel has been praised by the Guardian, The Rough Guide and others.

DETAILS

- **Open** - All year. Reception open until 9pm. 24hr Keypad entry system.
- **Number of beds** - 24: 1x3, 1x4, 1x5, 2x6.
- **Booking** - Advisable,
- **Price per night** - From £20 pppn. Sole use from £475 per night.
- **Public Transport** - Trains at Windermere. 555 bus from Windermere or Keswick, ask for Traveller's Rest pub. National Express coach from London to Grasmere daily.
- **Directions** - GR 336 094 1.25 miles north of the village. Stay on the A591 right to our drive, 400m north of Traveller's Rest pub on the right hand side.

CONTACT: Dave Keighley
Tel: 015394 35055
dave@grasmerehostel.co.uk www.grasmerehostel.co.uk
Broadrayne Farm, Keswick Road, Grasmere, Cumbria, LA22 9RU

GRASMERE
Independent
HOSTEL

BROADRAYNE
FARM

Tel: 015394 35055
www.grasmerehostel.co.uk

SHEPHERDS CROOK
BUNKHOUSE
ENGLAND

Noran Bank Farm is situated near Lake Ullswater just through Patterdale in Cumbria. Only 5 minutes' walk away from the Coast to Coast route as well as The Westmorland Way which is a 95 mile walk along generally good paths beginning in the famous horse fair town of Appleby and ending at Arnside, all within the old County of Westmorland.

Shepherd's Crook Bunkhouse is a barn conversion, converted to a very high standard and sleeps 8. Upstairs it has a two bedded room with en suite shower and a 6 bedded room. On the ground floor there is a fully equipped kitchen, seating area in which to relax, toilet and wet room with 2 showers. Duvets, linen and towels are provided. DIY breakfast and packed lunches are available if pre-booked. A well behaved dog considered at owners discretion. "Shepherd's Crook" is very popular with overnight stays on the Coast to Coast route and with week-end breaks for walking and cycling enthusiasts. It is also a fantastic meeting place for family and friends get-togethers

DETAILS

- **Open** - All year.
- **Number of beds** - 8: 1x6, 1x2
- **Booking** - Please book by phone or email.
- **Price per night** - £15pp (6 bed room), £20pp (double room). Sole use £120. Dog £4 per night. D.I.Y breakfast £6, Packed Lunch £5. Farmhouse B&B £30pp.
- **Public Transport** - Trains at Penrith (14 miles). Buses at Patterdale (half a mile).
- **Directions** - Take A592 from Patterdale south, farm is on right in half a mile.

CONTACT: Mrs Heather Jackson
Tel: 017684 82327 Mob: 07833 981504
heathernoranbank@fsmail.net www.noranbankfarm.com
Noran Bank Farm, Patterdale, Penrith, Cumbria, CA11 0NR

FISHER-GILL
CAMPING BARN

Situated in Thirlmere at the foot of the Helvellyn range of mountains, close to Sticks Pass and spectacular Fisher-gill waterfall, with numerous walks, hill and rock climbing from the barn, it's an ideal place for touring the Lake District being just off the A591 road, with local and national bus stops at the end of the lane. Accommodation consists of two rooms: a kitchen/diner with fridge, 4 ring calor gas stove, kettle, toaster, tables and chairs, and all pots, pans etc and a sleeping area consisting of 10 bunk beds with mattresses, pillows, blankets and duvets (sleeping bags/liners are required). Both rooms have a wood-burning stove with a daily allowance of wood included (extra is available from the farm). There's also a shower cubicle (metered), toilet, wash basin and a small seating area. Outside there is ample parking with a small patio area, tables and chairs. A pub serving meals is nearby (approx a quarter of a mile).

Keswick is 5 miles, Grasmere 7 miles. Open all year. Pets by arrangement. The barn is ideal for quite country retreats, not suitable for late night drinking parties.

DETAILS

- **Open** - All year, all day.
- **Number of beds** - 10
- **Booking** - Advanced booking recommended.
- **Price per night** - £15pp. £130 sole occupancy.
- **Public Transport** - Local and national buses stop at the end of the lane on A591.
- **Directions** - Travelling on the A591 SE from Keswick, after about 5 miles take 1st lane on left after junction with B5322. Barn is after about 100m.

CONTACT: Mrs Jean Hodgson
Tel: 017687 74391
stybeckfarm@btconnect.com www.stybeckfarm.co.uk
Stybeck Farm, Thirlmere, Keswick, Cumbria CA12 4TN

DERWENTWATER
INDEPENDENT HOSTEL

Family run and friendly, Derwentwater Independent Hostel is a Georgian mansion in 17 acres of grounds complete with its own waterfall. The glorious setting near the lake gives wonderful views of the surrounding mountains and is just 2 miles from Keswick. A great base for individuals, families, groups, family parties, reunions and conferences, the hostel has lounges, games rooms and free WiFi. It is licensed and offers a full meal service with a good reputation for home made food. Many of the spacious bedrooms have lovely original architecture. The grounds are teeming with wildlife including red squirrels, with plenty of space for children to play, football goals, picnic tables and open water access to launch canoes and boats onto the lake. Borrowdale has something for everyone; walks along the lake shore, challenging mountains, water sports, mountain biking, climbing, gorge scrambling and tourist attractions. Friendly staff are happy to help you organise your days. The C2C route passes close by.

DETAILS

- **Open** - Most of the year, 7am - 11pm.
- **Number of beds** - 88: 1x4, 2x5, 3x6, 3x8,1x10,1x22
- **Booking** - Advance booking recommended - especially for groups
- **Price per night** - From £22.50 (adult), £16 (child). Family rooms from £68 (for 4). The smallest rooms are for 4 & 5 but please ask if you want a room for 2 or 3.
- **Public Transport** - Train to Penrith then X4 bus to Keswick. From Keswick take the launch to the jetty 100 metres from hostel or bus no 78 to hostel drive.
- **Directions** - Two miles south of Keswick on the B5289 Borrowdale road. Hostel entrance is directly off the main road, 150m after the turning to Watendlath.

CONTACT:
Tel: 017687 77246
contact@derwentwater.org www.derwentwater.org
Barrow House, Borrowdale, Keswick, Cumbria, CA12 5UR

CARLISLE DIOCESAN YOUTH CENTRE

Carlisle Diocesan Youth Centre is located near St John's-in-the-Vale just four miles from Keswick. The centre offers flexible accommodation for a variety of groups in modern en-suite 4-6 bed bunkrooms. With fell walking, climbing, orienteering, geo-caching and cycling on the doorstep and freedom, space and amazing views from the buildings, this is the perfect place for a group retreat, large family get-together or activity field trips, Projection equipment, flip-chart easel and TV & video/DVD player are available by arrangement with the Chaplain. School House and Chapel House sleep 25 and 14 respectively with well equipped self catering kitchens, communal spaces and comfortable rooms. The buildings can be hired separately or together. Visitors must bring their own sleeping bag, pillowcase and towel etc. Groups are responsible for providing all consumable items including toilet rolls and cleaning materials.

DETAILS

- **Open** - All year, 24 hours.
- **Number of beds** - 39. School House 25 1x6, 1x5, 3x4, 1x2. Chapel House 14: 3x4 1x2
- **Booking** - Book via phone or email. Availability shown on website.
- **Price per night** - £13.50 pp for mixed groups (adults, children, young people, students) from outside Cumbria. £12.00 pp for mixed groups (adults, children, young people, students) from Cumbria. £17pp for all adult-only group
- **Public Transport** - The centre is well signposted from the A66 ('Youth Centre') and from the B5322 St John's in the Vale road ('Diocesan Youth Centre').
- **Directions** - Trains at Windemere and Penrith, Bus 555 Windemere to Keswick stops about 40 minutes' walk away.

CONTACT: The Revd. Peter Barnes
Tel: 017687 79714
carlisledyc@gmail.com www.cdyc.org.uk
Carlisle Diocese Youth Centre, St John's-in-the-Vale, Keswick, Cumbria, CA12 4UB

St John's-in-the-Vale Camping Barn is adapted from an 18th century stable and hayloft, in an idyllic setting. Overlooking St John's Beck, the peaceful hill farm has stunning views to Blencathra, Helvellyn and Castle Rock.

The Barn has a sleeping area upstairs (mattress provided) with a sitting and dining area below. Separate toilet, shower and cooking area (bring your own stove, cooking and eating equipment) are within the building. A wood-burning stove provides a focal point and warmth!

There is a BBQ and seating area outside and, as there is no light pollution, the star-filled night skies are magical. Northern Lights have been seen too! Low Bridge End Farm has a tea garden - all home baking. To see more and book online go to: www.lakelandcampingbarns.co.uk

DETAILS

- **Open** - All year, 24 hours.
- **Number of beds** - 8 : 1x8
- **Booking** - Advised in advance. Credit card booking available on 017687 74301
- **Price per night** - £10.00 per person.
- **Public Transport** - Trains terminate at Windermere. From there take a 555 bus towards Keswick. Get off at Thirlmere Dam Road End (Smaithwaite). Climb over ladder stile and we are ½ mile north along a footpath.
- **Directions** - Leave M6 at junction 40. Take A66 towards Keswick for 14 miles. Turn left onto B5322 St Johns-in-the-Vale Road. 3 miles along the road on the right.

CONTACT: Graham or Sarah
Tel: 017687 79242 (Bookings 017687 74301)
info@campingbarn.com   www.campingbarn.com
Low Bridge End Farm, St John's-in-the-Vale, Keswick, CA12 4TS

MAGGS HOWE
CAMPING BARN

Kentmere is a quiet, unspoilt valley within the Lake District National Park. It's a ramblers' paradise with woods, fields, lanes, a scattering of traditional lakeland farms and dwellings and of course the fells with their walks so favoured by Wainwright. The Lakeland to Lindisfarne long distance path passes this way as well as the mountain bikers' and horse riders' Coast to Coast. Kentmere offers plenty of activities which include biking, riding and fishing, but most of all quiet enjoyment. A pleasant day's visit can be found at the market town of Kendal and Lake Windermere which are only 20 minutes away. The converted barn has two sleeping areas, kitchen, two showers and toilets. All you need is your sleeping bag, mattresses are provided. Breakfasts and suppers are available next door at the B&B with notice.

DETAILS

- **Open** - All year, 24 hours.
- **Number of beds** - 14: 1 x 6   1 x 8
- **Booking** - Recommended with 50% deposit for groups. Individuals can book but not essential
- **Price per night** - £12 per person or £120 sole use.   Friday and Saturday night must be on a sole use booking at £120 per night or a surcharge of £60 added if only 1 night taken.
- **Public Transport** - Staveley 4 miles with train and bus service. Oxenholme train station is 10 miles. Kendal / Windermere National Express 8 miles.
- **Directions** - GR 462 041, MAP OS English Lakes South East. Green Quarter. Leave the A591 and come into Staveley, proceed to Kentmere for 4 miles, then take right fork to Green Quarter keeping right until you reach Maggs Howe.

CONTACT: Christine Hevey
Tel: 01539 821689
enquiry@maggshowe.co.uk
Maggs Howe, Kentmere, Kendal, Cumbria, LA8 9JP

DENTON
HOUSE

Denton House is a purpose built hostel and outdoor centre in the heart of the Lake District offering bunkhouse style accommodation designed for groups. There is plenty of hot water for showers, central heating throughout, a self-catering kitchen, a large dining room and solid bunk-beds. All linen provided. Breakfasts, packed lunches and evening meals are all available upon request.

The centre is also available for large groups looking for sole use. There is a car park for 40 cars and the outdoor centre provides traditional activities for groups seeking an adrenaline rush. Activities include Ghyll scrambling, climbing, abseiling, via ferrata and mountain challenge events. Storage for kayaks and bikes is available and there's access to the River Greta just across the road.

DETAILS

■ **Open** - Open all year round (including Christmas). Office hours 9.00am - 20.00pm everyday.

■ **Number of beds** - 56: 1x4, 2x6, 1x8, 2x10, 1x12.

■ **Booking** - Due to large number of school, youth and military groups, corporate team-builds and celebration weekends, early booking is advised. 25% deposit for groups with the balance due 28 days before arrival.

■ **Price per night** - £17 midweek, £19 weekend. Sole use £900 (midweek) £999 (weekend). Breakfast £6. Pack Lunch £6. Dinner £10. Activities £30/half day.

■ **Public Transport** - Nearest train station Penrith, buses hourly to Keswick.

■ **Directions** - Go out of Keswick towards Windermere, keep the river on your left (approx 10 mins). Denton House is on the right after post sorting office.

CONTACT: Libby Scott
Tel: 01768 775351
keswickhostel@hotmail.co.uk www.dentonhouse-keswick.co.uk
Penrith Road, Keswick, Cumbria, CA12 4JW

THE WHITE HORSE
INN BUNKHOUSE

The White Horse Inn Bunkhouse has been converted from the stables of this traditional Lake District inn at the foot of Blencathra. The White Horse is a country pub with great pub food, open fires, local ales and a warm welcome. Four of the stables have been converted into bedrooms, two sleeping 6 people in bunks, one sleeping eight and one sleeping four. There is a basic kitchen with electric hob, microwave and a coin operated clothes dryer and a communal dining area seating 16-20 people. The toilet block has male and female toilets, basins and showers. Guests are welcome to socialise in the pub which is open from 11am to 11pm and has free WiFi, hot drinks and good beer. Food is served 12-2pm and 6-9pm on weekdays and all day on weekends. The White Horse is just outside the picturesque village of Threlkeld at the foot of the Blencathra and Sharp Edge, ideal for trekking, with paths to the mountains immediately from the beer garden. The Coast to Coast (C2C) route snakes past the front door of the inn which remains a popular stop for thirsty cyclists and walkers alike.

DETAILS

- **Open** - All year, all day access.
- **Number of beds** - 24. 1 x 8, 2 x 6, 1 x 4
- **Booking** - Book by phone or email.
- **Price per night** - £10 pppn, 4 bunk room £40, 6 bunk room £60, 8 bunk £80, sole use £200. Pillow, sheet and duvet £5 for the stay. Enquire for Xmas/New Year prices
- **Public Transport** - From Penrith train station, 15 mins by taxi or catch the X5 or X4 bus from Penrith to Keswick and ask for Scales, stops outside pub on the A66.
- **Directions** - Just off A66 Penrith to Keswick road, 4m from Keswick (see signs).

CONTACT: Sophie, Cozmin or Ben
Tel: 017687 79883
info@thewhitehorse-blencathra.co.uk   www.thewhitehorse-blencathra.co.uk
The White Horse Inn, Scales, Nr Threlkeld, Keswick, CA12 4SY

Skiddaw House is a remote, mountain hostel, accessible only on foot or by mountain bike. At 1550 feet (470m), it is the highest YHA hostel in Britain and is an ideal base for exploring the quiet Northern Fells.

A former shooting lodge and shepherd's bothy on the Cumbria Way, the hostel offers simple, yet comfortable accommodation. Solar panels provide hot water and lighting, whilst wood-burning stoves provide the only heating. There is no mains electricity, phone signal, internet or TV to distract from the tranquil surroundings. The hostel is self-catering, but our small shop stocks everything you need to make a simple meal. The nearest road is 3.5 miles away.

Walkers and cyclists are advised to bring a map and torch. Camping available.

DETAILS

■ **Open** - March to Oct. Check in from 5pm, check out by 10am.
■ **Number of beds** - 22 : 1 x 8, 2 x 5, 1 x 4
■ **Booking** - Book by phone or email.
■ **Price per night** - £18 (adult), £9.50 (under 18). YHA members £1.50 - £3 discount. Camping £7. Credit / debit cards not accepted.
■ **Public Transport** - Nearest trains and National Express coaches at Penrith. From Penrith take X4 or X5 bus to Keswick. From Keswick it is a 5 mile walk to the hostel.
■ **Directions** - Grid reference: NY 288 291. No access for cars, nearest road 3½ miles. Vehicles can be left at Fell car park by Blencathra Centre above Threlkeld, at Lattrigg car park (end of Gale Rd near Applethwaite) or at Whitewater Dash Falls south of Bassenthwaite.

CONTACT: Martin or Suzy
Tel: 07747 174293
skiddawhouse@yahoo.co.uk www.skiddawhouse.co.uk
Bassenthwaite, Keswick, Cumbria, CA12 4QX

CATBELLS
CAMPING BARN

Catbells Camping Barn is part of a traditional set of farm buildings dating back to the 14th century. The barn is on the slopes of Catbells in the tranquil Newlands Valley, with magnificent views over the Lake District. The Cumberland Way passes through the farmyard. Keswick is only 4 miles away and both Borrowdale and Buttermere are within walking distance. The camping barn is on the ground floor and has sleeping accommodation for 10, with mattresses provided. Bring your own sleeping bags. The barn is heated with a multi-fuel stove (not suitable for cooking) and wood can be bought at the farm. In the adjacent building is a toilet and a cooking area suitable for a camping stove. Bring your own stove, cutlery, crockery and cooking utensils. It is possible to walk to a pub which serves food.

DETAILS

- **Open** - All year, 24 hours.
- **Number of beds** - 10: 1x10
- **Booking** - Advisable, groups require deposit.
- **Price per night** - £10.00 per person
- **Public Transport** - Trains at Penrith (20 miles). Regular buses (meet the trains) from Penrith to Keswick. Summer bus from Keswick to Buttermere stops ½ mile from barn. Summer ferry from Keswick to Hawes End (¾ mile from barn).
- **Directions** - GR 245211. Leave the M6 at Junction 40 and follow the A66 past Keswick. At Portinscale turn left, follow the Buttermere road for 3 miles. Turn sharp left at Stair, follow the sign for Skelgill, up the road for ½ mile and right into farmyard. Please follow these directions and not those from 'sat-nav'.

CONTACT: Mrs Grave
Tel: 017687 74301 or 0709 2031363
info@lakelandcampingbarns.co.uk www.lakelandcampingbarns.co.uk
Low Skelgill, Newlands, Keswick, Cumbria, CA12 5UE

Hawse End Centre, at the head of the magnificent Borrowdale Valley and directly across Derwentwater from Keswick, has stunning views and access to lakeside, mountains and Keswick (via launch or lakeside walk). The house is a large, comfortable, country mansion, ideal for groups. It has a well equipped and spacious self-catering kitchen with a professional catering oven & hob, a large dining room, lounge, games room, classroom and extensive grounds leading down to the lake shore. The Cottage for individuals, families and groups has a basic self-catering kitchen, living room and a patio with picnic tables and views of the lake. Two yurts with stunning views and transparent domes for star gazing, are on a wooden platform close to the house. These felt and wood structures have electricity, tables and chairs (optional) and mats for sleeping. Picnic tables, a gas barbeque and water are also on the platform with toilets close by. A catering service can be made available by prior arrangement. Outdoor activities can all be booked in advance and are led by experienced and well qualified outdoor leaders.

DETAILS

- **Open** - All year.
- **Number of beds** - House 49: (9 rooms) Cottage 24: (6 rooms). Yurts: 24 (2x12)
- **Booking** - Please book by phone or email. Deposit required.
- **Price per night** - Price on application, subject to availability and season.
- **Public Transport** - Trains at Penrith (18 miles). Keswick Launch passenger ferry from Keswick to Hawse End. Service buses within walking distance in high season.
- **Directions** - 4 miles outside of Keswick.

CONTACT:
Tel: 01768 812280
cumbriaoutdoors.enquiries@cumbria.gov.uk www.cumbria.gov.uk
Hawse End Centre, Portinscale, Keswick, Cumbria, CA12 5UE

LOW GILLERTHWAITE
FIELD CENTRE

Towards the head of Ennerdale valley, one of the most beautiful, least spoilt and quietest valleys in the Lake District, at the foot of Pillar and Red Pike sits Low Gillerthwaite Field Centre. An ideal base for fell walking, classic rock climbs, bird and wildlife watching, mountain biking, orienteering, canoeing and environmental studies.

Originally a 15th century farmhouse, the centre has group self-catering facilities, drying room, a library of environmental books, a large barn for indoor activities (ideal for barn dances), a group lecture room and two lounges with log burning fires. Due to its remoteness the centre generates its own electricity via a hydroelectric scheme. Vehicle access is by forest track and a BT payphone is on site (most mobiles do not work here). Low Gillerthwaite is an ideal base for clubs, extended family groups, school and youth groups.

DETAILS

■ **Open** - All year (except Christmas and Boxing Day), 24 hours.
■ **Number of beds** - 40: 2x4, 1x8, 1x10, 1x14
■ **Booking** - See booking link. Always phone to check availability
■ **Price per night** - From £11.50 per person (children and students), £15.50 (adults), camping is £5 per person.
■ **Public Transport** - Whitehaven Station 12 miles. Buses to Ennerdale Bridge from Cleator Moor or Cockermouth (5 miles).
■ **Directions** - GR NY 139 141. From Ennerdale Bridge take road east, via Croasdale, 3.5 miles to Ennerdale Forest. Continue on forest track 3 miles. Hostel is the first building below the RH road, 200m before the YHA.

CONTACT: Ellen or Walter
Tel: 01946 861229
Warden@lgfc.org.uk www.lgfc.org.uk
Ennerdale, Cleator, CA23 3AX

High House in Seathwaite, at the head of the popular valley of Borrowdale, offers comfortable bunkhouse/hostel self-catering accommodation in a converted 16/17 century farmhouse set within its own grounds. It is popular with walking and climbing clubs and is regularly used by outdoor education and corporate groups. Early booking is advised, especially for weekends. The building is let to one group at a time. Two dorms are available each with toilet, washbasin and shower. There is a third dorm reserved for K Fellfarers members and on some occasions club members may use this room during your stay. There is a common room with stove, easy chairs, library and dining area, a fully fitted kitchen and car parking. You will need to bring sleeping bags or duvets plus sheets, pillows, tea towels, firelighters and food. Basic food (eg. milk) is available from the café in Rosthwaite and the nearest supermarket is in Keswick. Eco friendly washing up liquid is provided to aid the septic tank.

DETAILS

- **Open** - All year, 24 hours.
- **Number of beds** - 26: 1x18, 1x8
- **Booking** - Early booking essential. Groups only. Min. 2 nights at weekends. £40pn deposit. Send to Briarcliffe, Carr Bank Rd, Carr Bank, Milnthorpe, Cumbria, LA7 7LE.
- **Price per night** - £145, irrespective of numbers, including electricity and heating. £50 key deposit is required.
- **Public Transport** - The nearest train station is in Penrith 26 miles away. Buses run from Penrith to Keswick, and from Keswick to Seatoller (1 mile from High House).
- **Directions** - OS Grid Ref NY235119

CONTACT: Hugh Taylor
Tel: 01524 762 067
jhugh.taylor@btinternet.com www.highhouse.talktalk.net/ff.htm
High House, Seathwaite, Borrowdale, Keswick.

SWALLOW BARN
CAMPING BARN

Lying in the picturesque Loweswater Valley, Swallow Barn is part of a traditional set of buildings dating back to 1670 on a working beef and sheep farm. The barn accommodates 18 people on mattresses in 4 sleeping areas.

There is a cooking and eating area with tables and chairs, 2 metered showers and a metered plug socket and 2 toilets. The barn is an excellent base for exploring the western fells with both high and low level walks and spectacular views, or you can enjoy the peace and tranquillity of the valley.

Fishing permits are available from the farm. The Coast to Coast cycle route is right on the doorstep. The Kirkstyle pub provides excellent food, just over a mile away and the market town of Cockermouth is only 8 miles. Check the website www.lakelandcampingbarns.co.uk and book online.

DETAILS

- **Open** - All year, all day.
- **Number of beds** - 18: 1x9, 3x3
- **Booking** - Book online in advance, especially for school and bank holidays.
- **Price per night** - £10 per person.
- **Public Transport** - The nearest train station is Penrith with a bus to Cockermouth, then a taxi costing approximately £25.
- **Directions** - Leave the M6 at junct. 40 and follow the A66 to the Egremont turn off at Cockermouth. Follow the A5086, Egremont road for 6 miles. Turn left at Mockerkin and follow road to Loweswater. The farm is just past the Grange Hotel on the left .

CONTACT: Kath Leck
Tel: Booking office 017687 74301, Farm 01946 861465
info@lakelandcampingbarns.co.uk www.lakelandcampingbarns.co.uk
Waterend Farm, Loweswater, Cockermouth, Cumbria, CA13 0SU

HILLSIDE FARM
BUNKBARN

A Georgian farmstead in a conservation area just steps away from Hadrian's Wall. Hillside Farm in the small village of Boustead Hill, near the Solway Coast AONB and RSPB nature reserve has stunning views over the Solway Firth marshes towards Scotland. Hadrian's Wall National Trail and Hadrian's Cycleway pass right by. Hillside farm is a working farm and the 4th generation of farmers welcome you to to the bunkbarn or the B&B rooms in the farmhouse. The bunkbarn, in a converted stable block, has cooking slabs, cutlery, crockery, a 2 ring gas stove, microwave and small electric oven. There are hot showers, towels and sleeping bags can be hired if required. The communal downstairs areas are heated but not the upstairs bunkroom. Shopping deliveries can be arranged via the farmhouse and with notice you can have breakfast or bacon sandwiches. Walking, cycling and family groups are most welcome.

DETAILS

- **Open** - All year, 10.00am to 21.00pm.
- **Number of beds** - 12
- **Booking** - Book by phone or email.
- **Price per night** - £12 per person including shower. £4 full English breakfast, £2 bacon/sausage sandwiches.
- **Public Transport** - Trains at Carlisle. Bus: Stagecoach 93 (NOT RUNNING ON SUNDAYS or BH's). Ask to get off at Boustead Hill not Burgh-by-sands.
- **Directions** - From Jnct 44 of M6 take the western bypass sign posted Workington. Follow until you reach a roundabout signed to Burgh-by-Sands and Bowness on Solway. Follow to Burgh and continue for 2 miles. After crossing cattle grid on to Marsh Road take next left to Boustead Hill then 2nd left under arches into farmyard.

CONTACT: Mrs Sandra Rudd
Tel: 01228 576398
ruddshillside1@btinternet.com www.hadrianswalkbnb.co.uk
Hillside Farm, Boustead Hill, Burgh-by-Sands, Carlisle, Cumbria, CA5 6AA

THE OLD SCHOOL
WYTHOP MILL

Once a Victorian village school, The Old School offers simple, heated, self-catering accommodation in a delightful rural setting in the northern Lake District. Ideal for family groups, school/youth groups, cycling/walking groups. Set on the flank of Ling Fell on the C2C cycle route, only a mile from the A66 between Keswick and Cockermouth and a few minutes' drive from Bassenthwaite Lake and Skiddaw. Whinlatter Forest Park is nearby for walking and mountain biking, with western fells, Keswick, Derwentwater, Borrowdale within easy reach. The main building has a fully equipped kitchen, common room, and three bedrooms with bunks. Outside is a Bothy and separate buildings for toilets, washrooms and showers. The Old School is managed by volunteers from the local 'Dewode' charity to fund a health centre in an impoverished Ugandan village, and to support a charitable Trust for the educational needs of local children.

DETAILS

- **Open** - All year.
- **Number of beds** - 20: Main building 18: 1x10, 1x6, 1x2   Bothy 2: 1x2
- **Booking** - Book by email. Availability shown on website.
- **Price per night** - £12 per person
- **Public Transport** - Trains at Penrith, buses hourly to Keswick. Bus X4 or X5 towards Workington, alight at Wheatsheaf Inn, Embleton. 1 miles walk to Wythop Mill.
- **Directions** - Leave M6 (Jct 40) and follow A66 westwards towards Cockermouth. Pass Keswick and Bassenthwaite Lake, Wythop Mill is signposted to the left. At crossroads in centre of hamlet, cross bridge and follow road through houses uphill. Turn left after last house, and look on the right. Marked 'school' on OS Maps.

CONTACT: John Atkinson
Tel: 07941 208 356
info@theoldschool-dewode.org.uk www.theoldschool-dewode.org.uk
The Old School, Wythop Mill, Embleton, Cockermouth, Cumbria, CA13 9YP

WAYFARERS
INDEPENDENT HOSTEL

Wayfarers Independent Hostel is situated close to Penrith town centre, providing excellent value accommodation to those visiting Penrith, the Eden Valley and the North Lakes. Penrith is on the edge of the Lake District National Park, close to the M6 and on the West Coast Mainline with shops, pubs, restaurants and a cinema all within 5 minutes' walk of the hostel. The Coast to Coast cycle route passes 100m from the doorstep, secure indoor bike storage, a drying room, and cleaning and maintenance facilities make this an ideal place to stay after a hard day's ride. Newly refurbished in a comfortable, modern style, facilities include a lounge, full kitchen and dining facilities and an outside seating area for guests to enjoy. All bedrooms are en suite with made up beds (sheets & duvets), lockers, bedside lights, towels for hire and have free WiFi available. Individuals, small parties and groups of up to 18 are welcome.

DETAILS

- **Open** - All year, reception open 8am-11am, 4pm-9pm.
- **Number of beds** - 16: 1x2, 1x6, 2x4.
- **Booking** - Recommended online, by phone or email.
- **Price per night** - From £22pp (dorm room bed). Sole use available from £320 pn. Family rates available Sun-Thurs from £55. Breakfast and packed lunches available.
- **Public Transport** - Trains and National Express to Penrith train station, 104 bus from Carlisle and X4-5 from Workington to Penrith bus station.
- **Directions** - M6 jcn 40 into Penrith along Ullswater Road. Past the station, bear left at first roundabout, straight over second heading down the hill past Booths and Morrisons. At bottom of the hill follow round to the left and take first turning on left.

CONTACT: Mark Rhodes
Tel: 01768 866011
guests@wayfarershostel.com www.wayfarershostel.com
19 Brunswick Square, Penrith, Cumbria, CA11 7LR

CARLISLE CITY
HOSTEL

Carlisle City Hostel is Carlisle's only independent hostel. Located on picturesque Abbey Street, the building is an old Georgian terrace that can accommodate up to 20 guests. There is a communal kitchen for you to prepare your own meals and communal lounge with TV, DVDs and book swap.

Free tea, coffee and WiFi is available in communal areas. Secure bicycle and luggage storage is located in the large cellar. Come and explore this wonderful city and its surrounds. The staff look forward to welcoming you as their guest in their hostel and their city. On street parking is free from 6.30pm-8.30am during the week and all day Sunday. Nearest carpark: Devonshire Walk.

DETAILS

■ **Open** - All year. Check in is between 3pm – 8pm ONLY (Sunday 4pm-8pm).
■ **Number of beds** - 22: 1x8 1x6 1x4 1x4 (family/triple/double)
■ **Booking** - by website with first night deposit. Cash only on arrival. Check before booking if you wish to arrive outside of check in times. Deposits are non-refundable
■ **Price per night** - From £18 to £25 pp. Groups of over 8 by pre-arrangement only.
■ **Public Transport** - Carlisle City Hostel is located in the city centre of Carlisle. Bus station and train station are 5 minutes' walk from the front door of the hostel.
■ **Directions** - From city centre: English Street bears left onto Castle Street, past cathedral. Left onto Paternoster Row which becomes Abbey Street. From M6 Jnc 43: follow signs for city centre. At Nando's traffic lights follow the road left. Get in the right hand lane and take a right through the old city walls. Turn left onto Victoria Viaduct then 2nd right -W Walls this becomes Annetwell Street. Turn right onto Castle Street. Take the first right onto Paternoster Row which becomes Abbey Street.

CONTACT: Jonathan Quinlan
Tel: 01228 545637 Mob: 07914 720821
info@carlislecityhostel.com www.carlislecityhostel.com
36 Abbey Street, Carlisle, CA3 8TX

HAGGS BANK
BUNKHOUSE & CAMPING

Set in the stunning North Pennines Area of Outstanding Natural Beauty, often described as England's last wilderness, this location is ideal for anyone who loves the great outdoors - walkers, cyclists and mountain bikers . The 36 mile Isaac's Tea Trail walk passes through the site; directly on the C2C and with bicycle hire (including electric bikes) available nearby.The bunkhouse sleeps up to 24 in 3 bunkrooms of 4/5, 9 and 10 and includes a relaxing lounge, self-catering kitchen, modern shower room and large conservatory for chilling out in! Breakfast and evening meals can be provided for larger groups if pre-booked. Nestled between a special nature conservation area and the wildflower meadow, the camp-site has been created with tiered pitches to enhance the infinite views across the Nent valley. Electric hook-ups for caravans and motorhomes are also available within the car park. The site has its own private supply of spring water, unique outdoor equipment washing area and secure bike and gear store. It has recently been awarded a Silver Green Tourism Award for commitment to sustainability.

DETAILS

- **Open** - All year, all day access.
- **Number of beds** - 24 in 3 bunkrooms
- **Booking** - Contact by email or phone
- **Price per night** - £18pppn. Discount for sole use. Camping £8pppn. Motorhomes/caravans £20pn for up to 2 people
- **Public Transport** - On 889 / 888 bus routes operated by Wright Bros, Nenthead
- **Directions** - Directly on the A689 between Alston and Nenthead.

CONTACT: Danny Taylor
Tel: 07919 092403/ 01434 382486
info@haggsbank.com haggsbank.com
Haggs Bank Bunkhouse, Nentsbury, Alston, Cumbria, CA9 3LH

Situated in the small town of Alston, Alston Youth Hostel is an ideal place to base your adventures in the North Pennines AONB. Right on the Pennine Way, the South Tyne Trail and the central point of the Coast to Coast Cycle Route Alston is the perfect destination for cyclists, walkers, families and school groups. The hostel was built by the YHA in 1975 as an overnight point for Pennine Way travellers and sold in 2006 to become an independent hostel. It is run by keen outdoor enthusiasts who know just what you need after a long day in the hills, a hot shower, comfortable bed, hearty home cooked food, large warm drying room and secure bike storage. There is a well equipped kitchen available for self-catering and the dining room and lounge overlook the River South Tyne. Don't forget to look out for the red squirrels feeding in the trees by the side of the Pennine Way.

DETAILS

- **Open** - All year
- **Number of beds** - 30: 2x2, 2x4, 3x6
- **Booking** - via hostel or YHA website or by phone
- **Price per night** - from £20.50pp discount for YHA members. • Private rooms from £36.00. Sole use from £380 for two nights.
- **Public Transport** - Train – There is no rail link to Alston – nearest stations are Haltwhistle, Penrith, Carlisle, Hexham or Langwathby on the Settle to Carlisle line. Bus – Service 680 from Carlisle via Brampton or the Service 889 to Hexham (Tuesday morning only)
- **Directions** - Car – From the West – A686 from Penrith or A689 from Carlisle. From the East A686 from Hexham (A69 from Newcastle).

CONTACT: Linda, Jenny or Neil
Tel: 01434 381509
Alston@yha.org.uk alstonyouthhostel.co.uk/
Firs Edge, The Firs, Alston, Cumbria, CA9 3RW

Book a bed, a room, or the whole hostel! This family run hostel is open to guests all year round. Catering available for groups and exclusive hire.

4-star rated Ninebanks Youth Hostel is a recently renovated and extended 18th century cottage in a stunning rural location. It's a great place to stay, with high quality en suite bedrooms and a spacious multi-use dining room - and it has high environmental credentials!

In the beautiful county of Northumberland, within the North Pennines and close to the iconic Hadrian's Wall, it provides the perfect base from which to explore this spectacular part of the country.

DETAILS

- **Open** - All year, open all day, reception from 5pm.
- **Number of beds** - 28: 2x2/3, 2x4, 1x6, 1x8
- **Booking** - booking is recommended
- **Price per night** - beds from £10.00, rooms from £34, whole hostel from £200
- **Public Transport** - Buses are few and far between and get no closer than 1.5miles from the hostel. See the Wright's bus website for the current information. Trains: the nearest train stations are Haydon Bridge 11 miles and Hexham 15 miles (more trains stop at Hexham)
- **Directions** - From A686 take turning signposted Ouston, Ninebanks, Carrshield (left from Northumberland, right from Cumbria) -look out for the blue and white YHA sign. Go down over the cattle grids turn right at the T junction, follow the road up the hill and the hostel and manager's cottage are the only buildings on the right.

CONTACT: Pauline Elliott
Tel: 01434 345288
pauline@ninebanks.com www.ninebanks.org.uk
Orchard House, Mohope, Hexham, Northumberland, NE47 8DQ

Edmundbyers Youth Hostel at Low House Heaven is now owned by a local farming family. It continues to offer friendly accommodation as part of the YHA and Independent Hostels networks. The hostel is a former 17th century inn in the centre of the village, with wooden beams and a cosy open fire. A self-catering kitchen is available and the local pub, The Punch Bowl Inn, serves home cooked meals and locally brewed beer. The village of Edmundbyers lies in moorland close to the boundary between Nothumberland and County Durham, with fine views over Edmundbyers and Muggleswick Commons. It is two miles from Derwent Reservoir, where sailing and fishing are available, and within an Area of Outstanding Natural Beauty. The location is ideal for walking holidays, and there are prehistoric remains to explore. The village is on the Coast to Coast cycle route and for a day out you could visit Hadrian's Walls or the Beamish outdoor museum. The hostel has a camp-site within a walled garden, with mature trees and stunning views. Roadside parking available.

DETAILS

- **Open** - All year (camping Apr-Oct). Check in 5-10pm, check out 8-10am.
- **Number of beds** - 28: 2x6, 2x5,1x4,1x3. Eight pitches for camping.
- **Booking** - Book by email, phone or online.
- **Price per night** - From £23 (adult), £19 (under 18). Discounts for YHA members: £3 adult, £1.75 under 18. Room for 3 £60, for 4 £70, for 5 £80 and for 6 £90.
- **Public Transport** - Service 773 from Consett to Townfield calls at Edmunbuyers. Operated twice a day by Weardale Travel.
- **Directions** - Opposite the shop at the centre of the village of Edmunbyers.

CONTACT:
Tel: 01207 255651
lowhousehaven@outlook.com www.lowhousehaven.co.uk
Low House, Edmundbyers, Consett,Durham,DH8 9NL

ALLENDALE
BUNKHOUSE

The Allendale Bunkhouse opened in October 2014, being completely refurbished and thoroughly modernised. Its sits on the market square in Allendale, overlooking the hustle and bustle of a small countryside town and the fells and river beyond. An oasis for walkers, cyclists, horse riders, families, groups of friends and youth & school groups alike. Allendale tea rooms, the Forge art gallery & café, a quirky gift shop, pharmacy, Allendale medical pratice and the library are all a stone's throw away. There is also bike hire (electric, mountain and hybrid bikes) and the C2C cycle trail runs close by. Art, heritage and music events run throuout the year across the valley. Book a bunk, a room, a floor (up to 18) or the whole bunkhouse for your group.

Downstairs is a large open plan area with a brand new fully equipped kitchen, dining area with seating for up to 34 and a lounge area with comfortable sofas to relax. Double french doors lead onto a BBQ, seating and patio area with steps into the large landscaped garden.

 BEST PRICE **GROUPS ONLY**

DETAILS

■ **Open** - All year, 8am-8pm.
■ **Number of beds** - 37: 2x6, 2x4, 1x7, 1x2, 1x3, 1x5
■ **Booking** - via telephone or email. A deposit will be required.
■ **Price per night** - From £14 - £30 per person per night.
■ **Public Transport** -   Nearest train stations: Hexham or Haydon Bridge. Buses available to Allendale Market Place. Pick up service can be arranged.
■ **Directions** - on the market place in Allendale, 12 miles from Hexham.

CONTACT: Linda Beck
Tel: 01434618579
info@allendalebunkhouse.co.uk www.allendalebunkhouse.co.uk
Market Place, Allendale, Hexham, NE47 9BD

BARRINGTON
BUNKHOUSE

Situated in the pleasant sleepy village of Rookhope in the stunning surroundings of Weardale. Next door is The Rookhope Inn for a welcome pint and substantial meals. The bunkhouse provides clean, comfortable accommodation with a self service continental breakfast ready for your day's activities. There are kettles, toasters and a microwave. Eggs are supplied as well as a microwave poacher. All welcome, especially cyclists on the Coast 2 Coast (C2C), walkers on the Pennine Journey, Weardale Way, and groups visiting the area. There are 12 bunk beds each with a personal reading light and an additional fold-up bed plus a fully fitted disabled wet-room with toilet, basin and shower and one able bodied shower and separate toilet. The large cast iron multi-fuel stove is used from October to March and oil-filled radiators provide extra warmth. There is a tumble dryer and a hair dryer is available on request. Visitors can also camp on the lawns - some camping equipment is available.

DETAILS

- **Open** - All year, all day.
- **Number of beds** - 12 (+1): 1 x 12 plus 1 fold up bed
- **Booking** - Booking recommended, by phone or email. 50% non-refundable deposit for weekdays, and full payment in advance for weekends and bank holidays.
- **Price per night** - £24pp incl. continental breakfast. Camping £14 with breakfast, £10 without. Sole use rates negotiable depending on group size and time of year.
- **Public Transport** - Nearest train stations: Hexham 17 miles, Durham 25 miles, Bishop Auckland 23 miles. Buses to Crook, Durham and Bishop Auckland.
- **Directions** - Next door to Rookhope Inn in Rookhope.

CONTACT: Valerie Livingston
Tel: 01388 517656
barrington_bunkhouse@hotmail.co.uk www.barrington-bunkhouse-rookhope.com
Barrington Cottage, Rookhope, Weardale, Co. Durham, DL13 2BG

SLACK HOUSE
FARM

Slack House Farm is a working, organic dairy farm overlooking Birdoswald Roman Fort on Hadrian's Wall. It is on the NCN 72 cycle route and is only 0.5km from the Hadrian's Wall National Trail. The bunk-barn is adjacent to The Scypen licensed café and farm shop and Birdoswald cheese is made on the farm. Accommodation consists of 3 dorms; a 10 bed space with 6 put-up beds and blow-up floor mattresses provided, a 5 bedded room, and a 3 bed family room (+ child's bed and travel cot). Sheets and shower towels available to hire. Each room has its own shower, toilet, hot water, heated towel rail and electric lighting. There is a worktop with kettle, microwave, fridge and crockery in the shared kitchen/ sitting area.The wood pellet fired stove warms the shared area and provides under-floor heating. Cooked breakfasts, farmhouse suppers and packed lunches can be provided. There is a laundry with powerful drying room. This is a lovely cosy place to base your Hadrian's Wall stay.

DETAILS

- **Open** - All year. Check in from 17.00hrs, check out by 10.00hrs.
- **Number of beds** - 18: 1x10, 1x5, 1x3 (family)
- **Booking** - Individuals: advisable, credit card confirms. Sole use: essential.
- **Price per night** - Beds £15.00 pp, space on camping loft £10.00pp, Sole use of 5 bedded room £50.00, sole use of family room £45.00.
- **Public Transport** - Carlisle-Newcastle train line 9km, bus 5km. AD122 bus (April-October) request stop 200m. (Kiln Hill junction).
- **Directions** - On B6318, GR NY670613, From A69, west take turning for Gilsland & Spadeadam. From east take right turn signed Greenhead. Follow Hadrian's Wall signs to Birdoswald. Do not turn left to the Fort but continue a further 200 metres.

CONTACT: Dianne Horn
Tel: 01697 747351 Mob: 07900472342
postmaster@slackhousefarm.plus.com www.slackhousefarm.co.uk
Slack House Farm, Gilsland Brampton, Cumbria, CA8 7DB

GREENHEAD
HOSTEL

Greenhead Hostel is a converted Methodist Chapel in the village of Greenhead on Hadrian's Wall. It is ideal for those walking the Pennine Way or The Wall and is in a great location for those exploring the nearby Roman heritage sites. The church was built in 1886 to serve the village miners and gave its last service in 1972. It has been a YHA hostel since 1978.

Greenhead Hostel has a self-catering kitchen and guest lounge. There are 40 beds in four rooms of six beds and two rooms of eight beds. These can be booked as family rooms, by groups or by the bed for individuals. Above the hostel is a self contained flat with kitchen, lounge, two double rooms and a single room. Evening meals, breakfast and packed lunches are available. The hostel is operated by Greenhead Hotel (over the road) with a welcoming bar and restaurant. VisitEngland approved.

DETAILS

- **Open** - All year (groups only in winter, please enquire), hostel is open all day.
- **Number of beds** - 45: Hostel 40: 2x8, 2x6. Flat 5: 2dbl, 1 single.
- **Booking** - Book by phone or email.
- **Price per night** - Bunkhouse adult: £15, under 18 £10. Flat £35pp. Reductions for large groups or full rooms. Sole use of hostel £400, £450 including flat.
- **Public Transport** - Trains: Haltwhistle 3 miles, Carlisle 19 miles, Newcastle 45 miles. Bus: May to Sept Stagecoach AD 122 from Newcastle to Bowness-on-Solway. Arriva 685 Carlisle-Newcastle passes Haltwhistle station and runs hourly all year.
- **Directions** - On the A69 between Carlisle and Newcastle. Turn off at sign for Greenhead. Turn right at the T junction, the hostel is opposite the Greenhead Hotel.

CONTACT: Diane and family
Tel: 01697 747411
diane@greenheadhotelandhostel.co.uk www.greenheadhotelandhostel.co.uk
Greenhead Hotel, Greenhead, Brampton, Cumbria, CA8 7HG

GIBBS HILL
FARM HOSTEL

Gibbs Hill Farm Hostel is a new conversion of a barn on a traditional working hill farm near Once Brewed on Hadrian's Wall. The hostel is designed to reduce energy consumption and is centrally heated throughout. There are 3 bunkrooms, 2 shower rooms, 2 toilets, a well equipped kitchen, comfortable sitting and dining area and a large deck where you can enjoy the evening sun.

The hostel has a drying room, lockers, laundry facilities and safe cycle storage. Ideal for families who may take a whole room with private facilities. Study groups welcome. Situated near Hadrian's Wall it is an excellent base for exploring the Roman sites, Hadrian's Wall Trail and Northumberland National Park. Basic items of food may be purchased and evening meals can be ordered the day before. Continental breakfast £5, packed lunches £6.

DETAILS

- **Open** - All year, hours flexible but no check in after 9pm.
- **Number of beds** - 18: 3x6
- **Booking** - Advisable, groups require full payment 4 weeks before arrival.
- **Price per night** - £18 adult, £12 child (under 12), including bedding.
- **Public Transport** - Trains at Haltwhistle 6 miles. Regular bus service along A69 between Newcastle and Carlisle, and in summer the Hadrian's Wall Bus runs between Newcastle and Carlisle. Alight at Once Brewed Information Centre and walk north to farm. Last bus 5.30pm from Haltwhistle.
- **Directions** - From the A69, turn north at Bardon Mill, signed 'Once Brewed'. Follow the signs towards 'Housesteads'. At the B6318, turn right and then immediately left towards 'Steel Rigg'. Follow for 1 mile, turn right to 'Gibbs Hill'.

CONTACT: Valerie Gibson
Tel: 01434 344030
val@gibbshillfarm.co.uk   www.gibbshillfarm.co.uk
Gibbs Hill Farm, Bardon Mill, Nr Hexham, Northumberland, NE47 7AP

DEMESNE FARM
BUNKHOUSE

This self-catering unit was converted in 2004 from a barn on a working hill farm in the centre of Bellingham in the Northumberland National Park. The farm is situated on the Pennine Way, Route 68, and the Reivers & Sandstone Way cycle routes. The bunkhouse is an ideal base for exploring Northumberland, Hadrian's Wall, Kielder Water and many climbing crags. It accommodates 15 and is perfect for groups, individuals and families. The bedrooms are fitted with hand crafted oak man-sized bunk beds, high quality mattresses, pillows, curtains and cushion flooring and full bed linen. Towels can be hired. Downstairs there is a large living room with wood burning stove and central heating with leather sofas and WiFi. The large kitchen with under floor heating has electric range cooker, microwave, fridge, freezer, kettle, toaster, crockery, cutlery, cooking utensils and farmhouse table & chairs to seat 15. It has 2 bathrooms with under floor heating, hot showers, basins, toilets. In the courtyard there is ample parking, bike lock up, drying room and a gravelled area with picnic tables.

DETAILS

- **Open** - All year, flexible but no check in after 9pm.
- **Number of beds** - 15: 1 x 8, 1 x 4, 1 x 3
- **Booking** - Please book in advance.
- **Price per night** - £20 per person, £15 under 18's (including linen).
- **Public Transport** - Trains at Hexham (17 miles), regular bus service from Hexham to Bellingham. Bellingham bus stop 100 metres from bunkhouse. By car: Newcastle 45 mins, Scottish Border 20 mins, Kielder Water 10 mins.
- **Directions** - 100 metres from centre of village, located next to the petrol station

CONTACT: Robert Telfer
Tel: 01434 220258 Mobile 07967 396345
stay@demesnefarmcampsite.co.uk www.demesnefarmcampsite.co.uk
Demesne Farm, Bellingham, Hexham, Northumberland, NE48 2BS

Houghton North Farm, partly built with stones from Hadrian's Wall, has been in the Laws Family for five generations. It is situated in the beautiful Northumberland countryside right on the Heritage Trail and 15 miles from the start of the Hadrian's Wall Trail. Within the region walkers can enjoy marked woodland trails, rugged moorland & hills and some of the most beautiful deserted beaches in the UK. This newly built, spacious accommodation can take a group of up to 23 and is also ideal for individuals and families. A 4 Star Hostel with Visit Britain, the bunk style rooms (some en suite) are located around the central courtyard and include the use of a self-catering kitchen where a continental breakfast is served. A well appointed TV lounge has a log fire and WiFi access, secure cycle storage and parking. Long-term parking, baggage transfer and packed lunches are available on request. Within 10 minutes' walk are pubs, a restaurant and shops in Heddon-on-the-Wall.

DETAILS

- **Open** - All year. Arrive after 3.30pm depart by 10am ,
- **Number of beds** - 22: 1x5, 3x4, 1x3, 1x2
- **Booking** - Book with a non-refundable deposit of £10 per person per night
- **Price per night** - From £25 (adult) incl breakfast. Group discounts.
- **Public Transport** - Trains at Wylam (2 miles) and Newcastle (7 miles). The 685/ X85/X84/ Newcastle-Carlisle bus stops right outside the farm. Baggage transfer is available.
- **Directions** - From Newcastle take the Heddon turn off the A69 to the B6528. Farm is 1/4 mile outside of the village of Heddon. From Carlisle take Horsley junction and continue approx 3 miles beyond Horsley. Farm is on the left at the top of a hill.

CONTACT: Mrs Paula Laws
Tel: 01661 854364
wjlaws@btconnect.com www.houghtonnorthfarm.co.uk
Houghton North Farm, Heddon-on-the-Wall, Northumberland, NE15 0EZ

TARSET TOR
BUNKHOUSE AND BOTHIES

Tarset Tor's striking timber eco-buildings integrate effortlessly into their natural surroundings deep in the Northumberland National Park, making the most of this remarkable location and providing the perfect base for outdoor adventures. The skies around Tarset Tor are now protected and are an International Dark Sky Reserve, making it the ideal spot from which to gaze at the stars. The stylish bunkhouse is a superb social space, offering comfortable, contemporary sleeping quarters together with shared cooking, eating, showering and lounge facilities. There is also a sauna and pool table. The incredibly versatile floorplan can be quickly adapted to create a welcoming venue for events, conferences and parties. The self-contained Bothy holiday homes enable guests to enjoy the peace and tranquility of Tarset Tor in a more private setting. A small number of campervan/camping pitches are also available.

DETAILS

- **Open** - Mid January - December.
- **Number of beds** - Bunkhouse: 16-20, Bothies: 2 x 8, 3 Campervan bays.
- **Booking** - Booking essential. Bothy 3 OPENS JUNE 2016
- **Price per night** - Bunkhouse £320 to £384 p/n. Lowest rate: Sun-Thur: Bothies: £160-£192pn. Lowest rate Sun-Thur. Campervans £20pn (Summer only)
- **Public Transport** - Nearest train station is Hexham 20 miles and a bus runs to Bellingham 3 miles. Pick ups and drop offs can be arranged.
- **Directions** - From A68 to Bellingham follow signs to Kielder Water. After 3 miles at Lanehead junction, look right to see Tarset Tor farmhouse. The bunkhouse and car park is just down the hill on the right.

CONTACT: Rob Cocker and Claire Briggs
Tel: 01434 240980
info@tarset-tor.co.uk www.tarset-tor.co.uk
Greystones Lanehead Tarset Hexham NE48 1NT

ALBATROSS

Fly high with the award winning "Albatross"! This clean and modern hostel is located in Newcastle's city centre. All in walking distance from sporting, musical and conference venues, art galleries, historical attractions, food markets and public transport facilities. We are open all year round. The Albatross is primarily designed to provide affordable accommodation in the city centre for the international travellers, walkers, cyclists and bikers, exchange student groups, sports teams, choirs etc. We provide rooms from 12 bed to 2 beds and anything in between for as little as £16.50. The overnight price includes; linen, 24hr reception, fully fitted self-catering kitchen with free tea, coffee and toast, free WiFi access and computer terminals, pool table, satellite TV, outside sitting/ barbeque area, free baggage storage and laundry facilities. A young dedicated international team is looking forward to welcoming you.

DETAILS

- **Open** - All year, 24 hours.
- **Number of beds** - 176:
- **Booking** - Recommended. Photo ID at check-in (passport or driving licence).
- **Price per night** - From £16.50pp (dorm) to £24.90pp (excludes 10th Sept).
- **Public Transport** - Five minutes' walk from central train, bus and metro stations.
- **Directions** - Central Station/Megabus drop off point: from main entrance, head right, take the first street on your left (Grainger St), you'll find us on your left 200m uphill. From National Express coach station: head down Scotswood Rd to Central Station. From Airport: take Metro to Central Station (20 mins' travel). From port (ferry): buses travel between the port and Central Station and take 20 mins.

CONTACT: Reception
Tel: 0191 2331330
info@albatrossnewcastle.co.uk www.albatrossnewcastle.com
51 Grainger Street, Newcastle upon Tyne, NE1 5JE

TOMLINSONS
CAFÉ AND BUNKHOUSE

A former schoolhouse in the historic town of Rothbury overlooking the River Coquet, Tomlinson's is a one-stop shop for low-cost accommodation, wholesome homemade meals and cycle hire. Ideal for families, groups and independent travellers, there are four flexible rooms most with en suite showers. Guests can mix in the communal TV lounge, enjoy the views or a homemade meal in the café. Big windows give beautiful views over the River Coquet. The bunkhouse has laundry facilities, a wash down area for bikes and boots, secure bike storage and drying room. A 50 capacity function room for hire for celebrations and meetings. Rothbury is becoming the Northumberland National Park's cycling hub and the bunkhouse is just metres from a string of off-road cycle tracks and public footpaths. The bunkhouse has a fleet of mountain bikes available to hire and instructors to lead cycle groups of all ages. The Cheviot Hills and the Northumberland Coast are within a 30 minute drive and the area is awash with castles including Alnwick featured in the Harry Potter films.

             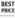

DETAILS

- **Open** - All year, all day.
- **Number of beds** - 22: 1x8, 1x7, 1x6 plus a double room
- **Booking** - Book by phone, online or email
- **Price per night** - From £20 per person, £450 for the whole bunkhouse.
- **Public Transport** - Trains at Morpeth (15 miles) and Alnmouth. Buses to Newcastle and Morpeth bus station run most days.
- **Directions** - Overlooking River Coquet, on the corner of Bridge Street and Haw Hill off the B6342 in Rothbury.

CONTACT: Jackie Sewell
Tel: 01669 621979
info@tomlinsons-rothbury.co.uk   www.tomlinsonsrothbury.co.uk
Bridge Street, Rothbury, Northumberland, NE65 7SE

Tomlinsons Cafe
and Bunkhouse

COQUET
VALLEY CYCLING
CLUB

Every Sunday
9.30am All Welcome

Road or Mountain Bike
ALL WELCOME!

find us on Facebook

ALNWICK
YOUTH HOSTEL

Once the town's Court House, today the accommodation offered by the Alnwick Youth Hostel is now somewhat less austere. Opened in 2011, this family friendly 4 star hostel is sure to meet the needs of every traveller, with a variety of en suite rooms, cosy lounge, games room and a bright and airy dining room.

The hostel's town centre location makes it ideal for a visit to historic Alnwick Castle, the medieval home of the Dukes of Northumberland, which had a starring role in the early Harry Potter films, as well as the neighbouring Alnwick Garden. A 15 minute car journey takes you to the beach with glorious views of Dunstanburgh and Bamburgh Castles and wildlife havens such as Holy Island and the Farne Isles. Only a short trip inland brings you to the stunning heather clad Cheviot Hills, Hadrian's Wall and Border Reiver country. Great for families, groups, cyclists and backpackers

DETAILS

- **Open** - All year. Reception open 08:00 to 10:00 and 16:00 to 21:00.
- **Number of beds** - 57: 1x1, 3x2, 1x3, 6x4,1x5, 3x6
- **Booking** - Booking advisable by phone or e-mail or book online via our website.
- **Price per night** - Adult dorm beds from £19.50, under 18 from £15. 2 bedded rooms from £49.00. Family 4 bedded rooms from £69.00.
- **Public Transport** - Bus - X15 / X18 / X20 Newcastle - Alnwick Train station - Alnmouth (4 miles) National Express 591/594 to Alnwick bus station.
- **Directions** - You will find the hostel opposite Alnwick library. A public car park is available at Roxboro Place, to the rear of the Job Centre.

CONTACT: Andrew Clarkson
Tel: 01665 660800
info@alnwickyouthhostel.co.uk www.alnwickyouthhostel.co.uk
34 - 38 Green Batt, Alnwick, Northumberland, NE66 1TU

The Hides, located in Seahouses and run by Springhill Farm, are a fantastic affordable accommodation option. The Hides are perfect for groups, families or independent travellers. The accommodation is great value for money, comfortable, and very conveniently located. The Hides have a quiet and secluded location within Seahouses but also the convenience of being no more than a five minutes' walk from the village centre, harbour, shops, restaurants and bars. All five Hides can sleep up to 4 guests each with en suite facilities and the use of an on-site fully equipped kitchen and dining area, cycle store, drying room and laundry. Guests at The Hides are also welcome to use the children's play area and seasonal farm shop at Springhill Bunkhouse, just five minutes' walk away (see page 286). The Hides are available to book as a block or per hide per night (minimum occupancy charge of 2 adults/night) .

DETAILS

- **Open** - All year, 9am - 6pm.
- **Number of beds** - 20: 5x4
- **Booking** - Online/phone; Min booking 2 nights. Deposit required when booking.
- **Price per night** - £19.50 adult, £14 under 14 (Under 1 free). Min charge 2 adults/night (£39). Christmas & New Year - £24/adult/night & £16/child/night min stay 3 nights. £5 pets/night. All 5 Hides £325/night. Sleeping bag & pillow hire £2.50/night
- **Public Transport** - Train station at Berwick upon Tweed. Buses run daily to Seahouses with the nearest bus stop being in North Sunderland which is the top end of Seahouses half a mile from Springhill.
- **Directions** - The Hides are on Main Street, Seahouses. From north or south follow B1340 to roundabout with large pub follow sign for riding centre to Main Street.

CONTACT: Miss Sarah Gregory
Tel: 01665721820
enquiries@springhill-farm.co.uk www.springhill-farm.co.uk
146 Main Street Seahouses Northumberland NE68 7UA

SPRINGHILL
BUNKHOUSE

Springhill's Bunkhouse & Wigwams are ideal for groups, families or independent travellers looking for great value comfortable accommodation which can be booked as a whole or on a per bed/night basis. Superbly located on the Northumberland heritage coastline and AONB coastal path with stunning views towards the Farne Islands and Cheviot Hills, only 1 mile from Seahouses and 3 miles from Bamburgh. The Lookout Bunkhouse has 8 rooms of 4 beds with en suite shower rooms, fully equipped kitchen, dining and sitting area with TV/DVD, free WiFi, BBQ and outdoor seating. The five Wigwams sleep 5 on platform beds with mattresses, electric heating, lights, sockets, fridge, kettle and a separate loo block. The Wigwams have the use of a fully equipped kitchen and dining area with WiFi, TV/DVD and an outdoor seating area with BBQ's and fire pits. Cycle store, drying room and laundry onsite. Pets welcome. Springhill Farm also run "The Hides" (page 384) just five minutes walk away.

DETAILS

- **Open** - All year round, arrive 3pm-6pm, departure by 10am. Cleaning 12pm-4pm.
- **Number of beds** - Bunkhouse 32: 8x4; Wigwams 25: 5x5
- **Booking** - Online, phone or email.
- **Price per night** - Bunkhouse £15 adult, £12 child (under 16). Wigwams £19.50 adult, £14 child. Prices constant all year round.
- **Public Transport** - Closest railway stop with easy bus transfers is Berwick upon Tweed. Buses run daily to Seahouses with the nearest bus stop being in North Sunderland which is the top end of Seahouses half a mile from Springhill.
- **Directions** - Springhill Farm is 0.75miles from the coast road, which runs between Seahouses 1mile and Bamburgh 3.5miles. Alnwick is 15 miles and Berwick 25 miles

CONTACT: Sarah or Julie
Tel: 01665 721820
enquiries@springhill-farm.co.uk www.springhill-farm.co.uk/bunkhouse
Springhill Farm, Seahouses, Northumberland NE68 7UR

BLUEBELL FARM
BUNKBARN

Bluebell Farm Caravan Park is in the centre of Belford, within walking distance of shops and pubs. It is ideally located for exploring Nothumberland's Heritage Coast, the Cheviot Hills and the historic Scottish Borders. The Bunkbarn sleeps 14, the Studio 4, the Ark 4 and there are 5 self-catering cottages. The Bunkbarn has a family room for 6, an 8 bed dorm and a fully equipped self-catering kitchen. The Studio has a bunkroom for 4 and kitchen, sitting and dining area with outside decking. The Ark has a sleeping platform for 4, fridge, microwave, toaster & kettle, with a patio area where you can use your own camping stove. There is a shared toilet block, renovated in 2015. Pillows and blankets provided and you can hire linen, duvets and towels or a sleeping bag. Activities include golf, climbing, canoeing, diving, horse riding, fishing, cycling and walking. Dogs welcome by arrangement. Duke of Edinburgh welcome. Two 1 man wooden tents are also available for hire with stove & utensils at £7.50 per night.

DETAILS

- **Open** - All year, check in by 9 pm, departure by 10 am.
- **Number of beds** - Bunkhouse 14: 1 x 8, 1 x 6, Studio 4: 1x4, Ark: 4: 1x4
- **Booking** - Recommended throughout school holidays and for weekends.
- **Price per night** - Bunkbarn: £12, under 16s £6. Studio and Ark : £15, under 16s £7.50. Linen and towel hire £6 person. Exclusive use rates available.
- **Public Transport** - Trains at Berwick upon Tweed. Buses from Berwick to Belford. Local bus from Newcastle.
- **Directions** - From the A1 take B1342 into the village. Turn onto B6349 signposted for Wooler. Bluebell Farm is first main driveway on right, almost opposite the Co-op.

CONTACT: Phyl
Tel: 01668 213362
corillas@icloud.com www.bluebellfarmbelford.com
Bluebell Farm Caravan Park, Belford, Northumberland, NE70 7QE

WOOLER
YOUTH HOSTEL

Wooler Youth Hostel & Shepherd's Huts is set in its own spacious grounds on the edge of the town. It has newly refurbished en suite bedrooms & Shepherd's Hut sleeping cabins, a huge dining and common room, excellent drying facilities and a large self-catering kitchen, making it great for groups & families. There is also an excellent value restaurant, on site car parking and secure cycle storage. Wooler has inns, grocery stores and specialist shops, and is an ideal base for exploring the Northumberland National Park, the Cheviot Hills (rich in archaeological sites), local castles and fine sandy beaches. For walkers there is the long distance St Cuthbert's Way and many shorter walks. For cyclists there are the Wooler cycle hub routes, Pennine Cycleway, the Sandstone Way and many quiet lanes to explore. Nearby there are bridleways perfect for mountain-biking, some of the best bouldering in the UK, riding centres and even a gliding school. Bird watchers can take a boat trip to the Farne Islands and visit the Cheviot Hills.

DETAILS

- **Open** - April until end Oct (open for group bookings Nov to March), 7am-11pm.
- **Number of beds** - 52: 3x2, 6x4,1x6,1x8. Shepherd's huts 3x2 & 1x3.
- **Booking** - Booking advised. Always call the hostel in advance of arriving.
- **Price per night** - From £15.50 adults, £12.00 children. Group booking discounts.
- **Public Transport** - Market Place, 400 yards from the hostel. Arriva Northumbria/ Travelsure 464, Border Village 267 from Berwick. Travelsure 470/3 from Alnwick.
- **Directions** - From the Market Place at the bottom of the high street go up Cheviot Street past The Anchor pub. The hostel is 300 yards up the hill on the right.

CONTACT: Mick
Tel: 01668 281365
wooler@yha.org.uk www.woolerhostel.co.uk
30 Cheviot Street, Wooler, Northumberland, NE71 6LW

Chatton Park Bunkhouse started life as a Smithy and has been converted into self-catering accommodation. It is situated on a mixed working farm which nestles around the River Till, half a mile from Chatton village.

Eight miles from the coast and five miles from the Cheviot Hills, Chatton Park is an ideal base for exploring Northumberland's vast empty beaches, heather clad hills & historic castles. Walking, water sports, climbing, fishing, golf and cycling are all available nearby. Accommodating 12, the bunkhouse is perfect for smaller groups, families & individuals. The 2 bedrooms are fitted with large custom made bunks and can be rented separately as secure units. Bedding can be provided at a small extra fee. The living area has a fully equipped kitchen & seating around the original blacksmith's fire. Wash & drying room with hot showers. Secure storage, ample parking. Room for 2 small tents. £10/dog/stay.

DETAILS

- **Open** - All year, flexible times but no check in after 9pm.
- **Number of beds** - 12: 2x6
- **Booking** - Booking recommended but not essential
- **Price per night** - £12 - £18 pp. Group bookings negotiable. Teenagers need to be accompanied by a responsible adult
- **Public Transport** - Nearest train station Berwick upon Tweed. Buses to Chatton from Alnwick / Berwick.
- **Directions** - From A1 take B6348 to Chatton. 4 miles at bottom of hill on right is Chatton Park Farm

CONTACT: Jane or Duncan
Tel: 01668 215247
jaord@btinternet.com www.chattonparkfarm.co.uk
Chatton Park Farm, Chatton, Alnwick, Northumberland, NE66 5RA

SPRUCE COTTAGE
AT FOREST VIEW INN

Spruce Cottage Bunkhouse is a former forestry workers cottage in the centre of Byrness on the edge of Northumberland National Park. Byrness is situated on the Pennine Way, and popular cycle routes. The bunkhouse is ideal for exploring Northumberland, Kielder Forest and the Scottish Borders. It is perfect for groups, individuals and families. The 9 full sized single beds (not bunks) in 3 bedrooms have high quality mattresses, pillows, full bed linen, curtains and carpets. There is also Z bed available as an extra that can go in a choice of locations downstairs. There is a large living room with original open fire and central heating. The kitchen has electric cooker, microwave, fridge, freezer, kettle, toaster, crockery etc. The dining room has another original open fireplace and large pine table to seat up to 10 people. Spruce cottage is in the heart of Byrness village directly opposite the multi award winning Forest View Inn with its famous real ale bar, food available if booked in advance.

DETAILS

- **Open** - April to October open to groups and individuals. November to March open to groups only. Opens at 4pm checkout is 9.30am.
- **Number of beds** - 10: 1x2, 1x3, 1x4 plus a z bed.
- **Booking** - Booking is recommended
- **Price per night** - Adults from £18. Under 16s £17.
- **Public Transport** - Nearest rail station Newcastle upon Tyne (40 miles) then National Express to lay-by 200yds from hostel.
- **Directions** - Spruce Cottage is just off the A68, 4 miles from the Scottish Border, 16 miles south of Jedburgh and 10 miles north of Otterburn.

CONTACT: Colin or Joyce
Tel: 07880711807
joycetaylor1703@hotmail.co.uk
2 Otterburn Green, Byrness Village, Northumberland, NE19 1TS

MAUGHOLD VENTURE
CENTRE BUNKHOUSE

Maughold Venture Centre Bunkhouse is built of Manx stone, overlooking farmland with views in the distance to the sea. It offers self-catering facilities with the option of purchasing meals from the neighbouring adventure centre if required (subject to availability). All bedrooms are en suite with full central heating.

Facilities include a basic but functional games room and kitchen. The local beach of Port e Vullen, 10 minutes' walk away, is popular with visitors and the bunkhouse is adjacent to the Venture Centre where you may arrange sessions of kayaking, abseiling, air rifle shooting, archery, gorge walking, dinghy sailing, and team events. It has its own stop, Lewaigue Halt, on the Manx Electric Railway giving access to Douglas, Ramsey and to mountain walks and tranquil glens. Ideal for groups, families and individuals.

DETAILS

- **Open** - January - December, 24 hours.
- **Number of beds** - 52: 2x2, 1x5, 4x8, 2x10
- **Booking** - Telephone reservation essential
- **Price per night** - £10-£15 per person
- **Public Transport** - No 3 bus or Manx Electric Railway from Douglas or Ramsey. Get off bus at Dreemskerry (5 minutes' walk); get off railway at Lewaigue Halt (nearby). Taxi from Ramsey £5. Taxi from Douglas £25.
- **Directions** - GR 469922. From Douglas take the A2 coast road. When the road begins to descend into Ramsey the Venture Centre is signposted on the right hand side. Follow the signs - it is the first building on the left.

CONTACT: Simon Read
Tel: 01624 814240
Contact@adventure-centre.co.uk www.adventure-centre.co.uk
The Venture Centre, Maughold, Isle of Man, IM7 1AW

South Wales

0 miles 25
0 kilometres 40

Aberystwyth 358
356

New Quay

340 A487

Cardigan

Lampeter

342
341

336 338
Fishguard

348

332
334
St Davids

Carmarthen

Haverfordwest A40 St Clears

325

Skomer Is.

326 327

Pembroke Tenby

Llanelli

330

328

324

322 320

KEY

45 - Hostel page number

45 - Page Number of group
only accommodation

360
Machynlleth
A487
A470
Newtown

351
A44

354
352
Rhayader
A470

Tregaron
Llandrindod Wells
350

344 346

Llanwrtyd Wells
Builth Wells
349

312 313,**310**
A438

307,308

Llandovery
306,309 **305**
A40
Brecon

304

316 318 302
A4067 Abergavenny

314 300 A40 298

A465 Tredegar

Merthyr
Tydfil
A470

Neath

Swansea 319
Port Talbot Pontypridd

M4 Newport

301 Cardiff

E N G L A N D

South Wales

North Wales

KEY

45 - Hostel page number

45 - Page number of group
only accommodation

Rhyl

Flint

A55

Queensferry

A494

Ruthin

Wrexham

376

Corwen   A5   374
                    373 Llangollen

370 A494
372 Bala

369

A458

Welshpool

A470

Newtown

E N G L A N D

North Wales

RICKYARD
BUNKHOUSE

Rickyard Bunkhouse is set amidst idyllic countryside and well away from the hustle and bustle. Offa's Dyke footpath passes the entrance and it is within 25 mins of Wye Valley, Symonds Yat and the Forest of Dean. Many outdoor pursuits can be enjoyed - canoeing, rafting, potholing, quad biking, rock climbing and paint balling to name but a few. The River Trothy borders the land; kingfishers and otters enjoy the peace and tranquillity of the Trothy valley. Buzzards circle high above, easily recognised by their distinctive call. The Bunkhouse holds 20 easily, has an excellent, very well equipped kitchen, a separate dining/relaxing area with TV, and background heating. Sleeping accommodation is split into several areas. It is totally self-contained, and is ideal for reunions, groups and families. There is a large secure area for camping where children can safely play and ample parking with hard standing. Luggage transfer, breakfasts and packed lunches can be arranged. Bedding supplied, towels £1. Come and enjoy the tranquil surroundings (loud music or wild parties are not welcome). Exclusive use available, please enquire.

DETAILS

- **Open** - All year, all day.
- **Number of beds** - 20: + camping.
- **Booking** - Deposit required, no credit cards.   Notice not always required.
- **Price per night** - £16.00pp. Prices include bedding, towels £1. Tents £5pp. Can be booked for sole use.
- **Public Transport** - Trains at Abergavenny (11m). Buses at Monmouth (3m).
- **Directions** - Next to the Hendre Farm House on the same side of the road.

CONTACT: Graham Edwards
Tel: 01600 740128
rickyardbunkhouse@googlemail.com www.rickyardbunkhouse.co.uk
Wonastow, Monmouth, NP25 4DJ

MIDDLE NINFA
BUNKHOUSE

Middle Ninfa Farm, situated on the edge of the Blaenavon Industrial Landscape World Heritage Site in the Brecon Beacons, offers bunkhouse/cottage accommodation, camping and hands-on training in coracle making and willow sculpture. The farm has fine views over the Usk Valley, of the Skirrid and rural Monmouthshire. The Bunkhouse provides comfortable self-catering accommodation for up to 6 people. The rustic charm of the stone building has been retained whilst ensuring modern comforts. The ground floor has a lounge / dining area with double futon and coal-effect gas fire; a well-equipped kitchen; and toilet / shower room. Upstairs (mezzanine floor) has 4 single beds, accessed by a spiral staircase. Outside there is a stone barbecue, table and duck pond. Guests should bring food, sleeping bags, towels & pillowcases. Home grown fruit, veg and local produce available.
Walkers and Cyclists Welcome.

DETAILS

■ **Open** - All year.
■ **Number of beds** - 6: 1x4, 1x2 [double] plus camping.
■ **Booking** - Book by phone or email
■ **Price per night** - £15pp or £60 sole use (Sun–Thurs nights) £70 (Fri & Sat nights). Sole use per week £300-£360. Camping £5 pp + pitch fee of £5/£10.
■ **Public Transport** - The nearest bus is at Llanfoist (1.5 miles). The train station is at Abergavenny (3.5 miles). Taxis from the station cost approximately £8
■ **Directions** - Approx. 2 miles from A465 (Hereford/Neath), A40 (Brecon/Monmouth and M50) and A4042 (Newport, M4). See website for map. The farm is reached by a steep winding road from Llanfoist, crossing the Monmouthshire and Brecon Canal.

CONTACT: Richard and Rohan Lewis
Tel: 01873 854662
bookings@middleninfa.co.uk www.middleninfa.co.uk
Middle Ninfa Farm, Llanellen, Abergavenny, NP7 9LE

RIVER HOUSE
HOSTEL

This is an award-winning family run 4 star hostel in the heart of Cardiff, voted number 1 in the Hostelworld list of best hostels. Opened in 2007 to rave reviews, the brother and sister team have made sure this will be the best hostel experience you will come across on your travels. With fabulous views of the world famous Millennium Stadium and River Taff and with the central train and bus stations just 5 mins' walk away, what's stopping you?

Facilities include well equipped kitchen, cosy TV lounge, decked garden with barbecue, free lockers and free wireless broadband. Bikes, irons and hairdryers available for hire. Linen, duvets and breakfast are included in the price and the beds are made up for you. Hostelworld awarded best Hostel in UK since 2008.

Treat yourself to a quality stay at budget prices.

DETAILS

- **Open** - All year, 24 hours.
- **Number of beds** - 50: 2 bed private rooms, 4 bed dorms and 6 bed dorms.
- **Booking** - Book by phone or online.
- **Price per night** - From £16pp. Private (twin) rooms from £36 for two people. All prices include breakfast.
- **Public Transport** - Cardiff Central coach and train stations, with regular services to UK cities and airports 5 minutes' walk away.
- **Directions** - From Central train station turn left and cross river on Tudor Street. Once over the river Fitzhamon Embankment is first turn on right.

CONTACT: Reception
Tel: 02920 399 810
info@riverhousebackpackers.com www.riverhousebackpackers.com
59 Fitzhamon Embankment, Riverside, Cardiff, CF11 6AN

WERN WATKIN
BUNKHOUSE

Wern Watkin Bunkhouse is located in the Brecon Beacons National Park, high up on Mynnedd Llangattock. It is also known as YHA Llangattock Mountain. There is direct access on foot to the mountainside and a flat mountain road to a National Cycle Route. The bunkhouse is a converted stone barn with bunks for 30 people in 7, mainly en suite, bedrooms. The massive dining room and seating area opens out onto ancient woodlands. It has under-floor heating throughout, excellent drying facilities and ample hot water. The location is ideal for caving, rock climbing, canoeing, abseiling, orienteering, pony trekking and mountain biking. Outdoor pursuit training can be arranged from local qualified instructors. The bunkhouse is within easy walking distance of Llangattock cave complex (one of Europe's most elaborate cave systems) as well as climbing crags and open moorland. A short drive away are the rest of Brecon Beacons, the scenic Wye and Usk river valleys and a wealth of industrial heritage at the World Heritage site of Blaenavon. Catering can be provided for groups.

DETAILS

- **Open** - All year, all day.
- **Number of beds** - 30: 4x6, 1x4, 2x2. All rooms except one are en suite
- **Booking** - Availability online. 20% deposit, balance three weeks in advance.
- **Price per night** - Sole use £450 week nights, £630 weekend nights. Smaller groups by negotiation £16pp week nights, £18.50 pp weekend.
- **Public Transport** - Trains Abergavenny (8miles). Nearest buses Crickhowell.
- **Directions** - Access can be either from Crickhowell or Brynmawr on small mountain roads. Detailed instructions will be sent with your booking.

CONTACT: Andrew Fryer
Tel: 01873 812307
enquiries@wernwatkin.co.uk www.wernwatkin.co.uk
Wern Watkin, Hillside, Llangattock, Crickhowell, NP8 1LG

THE STAR
BUNKHOUSE

Croeso i Fyncws y Seren. Welcome to The Star Bunkhouse. The Star Bunkhouse, in the village of Bwlch, is an ideal base from which to explore the beautiful Brecon Beacons National Park, and you can expect a warm and comfortable stay. The bunkhouse features spacious bedrooms, cosy lounge and dining areas, a fully-equipped kitchen, an outside BBQ area, hot showers, drying room, free WiFi and off-road parking. Sleeping up to 20 people in bunk beds spread over 6 bedrooms, bookings are welcome from individuals and couples as well as small & large groups. A popular choice for family get-togethers, reunions, birthday parties, hens & stags, school & youth groups, clubs & societies, and with all lovers of the great outdoors. Dog friendly by arrangement. The bunkhouse is situated alongside The Beacons Way long-distance footpath in the gap ('bwlch') between the Black Mountains and the Central Beacons mountain range (which includes Pen Y Fan). Meet and swap stories with fellow travellers if use of the bunkhouse is shared, or please ask if you would prefer exclusive use for your group.

DETAILS

- **Open** - All year, all day.
- **Number of beds** - 20: 1x4 (en-suite), 2x4, 2x2
- **Booking** - By email or telephone
- **Price per night** - Standard rate £19 per person
- **Public Transport** - Nearest train station, Abergavenny 13 miles. Bus route: X43 Abergavenny-Brecon. Nearest airport: Cardiff Airport 50 miles.
- **Directions** - On the A40 between Crickhowell and Brecon

CONTACT: Emma or Pete Harrison
Tel: 01874 730 080 Mobile: 07434 851 731
info@starbunkhouse.com www.starbunkhouse.com/
Brecon Road (A40), Bwlch, Brecon, Powys, LD3 7RQ

This old stone barn continues the tradition of 900 years when Llanthony Priory next door provided shelter and accommodation. Surrounded by the Black Mountains in the Brecon Beacons National Park, this spectacular setting is a superb base for walking, riding, pony trekking and other mountain activities.

Sixteen bunks are split into three separate areas for sleeping. There is a fully equipped kitchen, hot water for showers, heating throughout and a wood burning stove in the eating area. Small or large groups are welcome, but there is a minimum charge. Two pubs offer real ale and bar food.

Just 50 minutes from the M4 Severn Bridge and one hour from the M5/M50 junction, this must be one of the easiest bunkbarns to reach from the motorways - and yet you feel you are miles from anywhere.

DETAILS

- **Open** - All year, 24 hours, no restrictions.
- **Number of beds** - 16: 1 x 8 ; 1 x 4 ; 1 x 6.
- **Booking** - Booking and deposit required.
- **Price per night** - £30 per person for a two-night weekend, with a minimum charge of £300. Reduction for mid-week bookings.
- **Public Transport** - Abergavenny railway station 12 miles.
- **Directions** - GR SO 288 278 Map on website: Turn west off A465 Abergavenny/Hereford road at Llanvihangel Crucorney (5 miles' north of Abergavenny). Llanthony is 6 miles along country lane - follow signs to Priory. On cycle route 42.

CONTACT: Cordelia Passmore
Tel: 01873 890359
courtfarm@llanthony.co.uk www.llanthonybunkbarn.co.uk
Court Farm, Llanthony, Abergavenny, Monmouthshire, NP7 7NN

The Dragons Back (formerly The Castle Inn) is a pub with B&B rooms, camping & 3 self contained bunkrooms, located at over 1000ft above sea level in the stunning Brecon Beacons National Park. The bunkrooms are fully carpeted and centrally heated with en suite wet rooms. Book out the entire bunkhouse from just £350 per night (£12.50pp). A new fully fitted dining/kitchen complete with WiFi and large screen TV, is now located next to the bunkhouse so self-catering is an option, although meals are also available in the pub next door. The pub serves a range of local real ales and home cooked meals using locally sourced ingredients. There's a large log fire, fantastic beer garden, free WiFi in the bar, pool table & 50 inch TV. The bunkhouse's drying room and secure bike storage make it a great base outdoor activities. Groups welcome including stag/hen parties. Dogs £5 per night in the bunkhouse.

DETAILS

- **Open** - All year. Arrive after 2pm, depart before 11 am.
- **Number of beds** - 28 : 1x6, 1x10, 1x12
- **Booking** - Group bookings only. £100 non refundable booking deposit required. 28 days notice required for cancellation, otherwise full value of the booking (less deposit) will be charged.
- **Price per night** - £15pp, £20pp with breakfast. Minimum of 5 people required for 6 bunk room, 7 for 10 bunk room, or 9 for 12 bunk room.   Book entire bunkhouse for £350, or £500 with breakfast.
- **Public Transport** - Nearest trains: Abergavenny. Nearest bus: Talgarth (3 miles).
- **Directions** - Located on the A479 approx 3 miles South of Talgarth and 6 miles North of Crickhowell

CONTACT: Jill Deakin
Tel: 01874 711353
info@thedragonsback.co.uk www.thedragonsback.co.uk
The Dragons Back , Pengenffordd, LD3 0EP

Located close to the centre of Talgarth in the Brecon Beacons National Park, Joe's Lodge is the perfect holiday base for groups of up to 27 people. This former drill hall has been converted into a comfortable bunkhouse with a dining area, comfy seating, 4 bunkrooms, separate male and female wash rooms, drying room, lockable storage area and plenty of parking. The kitchen is well equipped with all you need to cater well for large groups. Those who fancy the excitement of outdoor pursuits can find all they need in the Black Mountains, Brecon Beacons, Llangorse Lake, and the River Wye, whilst the literary towns on Hay and Blaenavon (World Heritate site) are close by. There are several licensed adventure activity providers locally providing a full range of activities from pony-trekking and sailing or canoeing to caving, gorge walking, orienteering, mountain biking, kite flying, buggies, escape and evasion events and climbing. The ideal base for student field trips and workshops. Group only but group leaders can stay a couple of nights in advance by arrangement.

DETAILS

- **Open** - All year.
- **Number of beds** - 27: 2x10, 2x2-4
- **Booking** - via form on website, phone or email
- **Price per night** - £225. £450/weekend, reduced rates for longer stays
- **Public Transport** - direct buses to Hay, Brecon and Hereford
- **Directions** - By car from Talgarth Centre take Bronllys Road, take 2nd Right "New Street". Car park for lodge is on the left just before the end of the road. By foot take Hay Road from the centre of Talgarth, Joes Lodge is on the left.

CONTACT: Alison Wainwright
Tel: 07969447438
joeslodge@live.com www.joeslodge.org.uk
Hay Road, Talgarth, Brecon Powys LD3 0AL

THE TOWER
AT TALGARTH

Located in the centre of the Brecon Beacon's town of Talgarth, The Tower offers bunkhouse accommodation as well as private and family rooms in the hotel. The bunks are purpose made for adults and the rooms are serviced daily including fresh bedding, toiletries and clean towels.

Small groups of 2 - 16 people are welcome. Prices include breakfast whilst pub meals and packed lunches are available to order. Retaining many of its Victorian features, the Tower Hotel has been sympathetically updated with modern conveniences and boasts a multi Camra award winning public bar, licensed restaurant, home cooked food and a roaring log fire. They even have their own brewery. Being so close to the Brecon Beacons National Park Talgarth is the perfect base for walking (the town holds a walking festival in early May), cycling (the hotel is on NCN 8) and much more.

DETAILS

- **Open** - Check in from 2pm (leave by 11am). Private access to bunkhouse once checked in.
- **Number of beds** - 16
- **Booking** - via phone or email
- **Price per night** - Bunkhouse: From £20 (min charge £60), Hotel: from £45
- **Public Transport** - On the Stagecoach Red and White bus route. Tel 01633 266336 for more info. 63 miles from Cardiff International Airport. Nearest stations: Hereford (30 miles), Builth Wells (16 miles) and Abergavenny (17 miles).
- **Directions** - From the A479 follow Bronllys road into the centre of Talgarth. The Tower Hotel is on the Square in the centre of the town.

CONTACT: Jan or Pip
Tel: 01874 711253
mail@towerhoteltalgarth.co.uk www.bikesbunksbeer.co.uk
The Tower Hotel, The Square, Talgarth, BreconPowys, LD3 0BW

Brecon Bunkhouse is a spacious, comfortable and clean bunkhouse in the Brecon Beacons. Offering fantastic value for money with a large self-catering kitchen, big dining room with plenty of tables and separate sitting room with a cosy wood-burner (logs provided). Situated in a small valley in the Black Mountains, the eastern part of the National Park, with mountain walks from the door. The area is ideal for horse riding and mountain bikes, with a white water canoe centre nearby. There is a riding centre on the farm and the bunkhouse has a drying room and storage/cleaning facilities for bikes and canoes. The adult-sized bunk-beds come with a freshly laundered sheet, pillow and pillow-case. Bring a sleeping bag/duvet, or hire a duvet with cover for £5 per stay. The friendly, helpful staff will give advice or leave you to get on with it . The market town of Talgarth, 4 miles away, has Walkers Welcome status and planned walks. Camping available on the farm. Nice pub 15 minutes' walk.

DETAILS

- **Open** - All year. All day.
- **Number of beds** - 28+3: 1x10,1x2,1x2,1x6,1x8. Plus extra 3 bed room available.
- **Booking** - 40% deposit required to book, balance due before arrival.
- **Price per night** - £15 pp, minimum of 4 people. £250 for exclusive use plus £45 for extra en suite family room with 3 single beds.
- **Public Transport** - Train station at Abergavenny. Taxi to bunkhouse costs £25-30 or phone bunkhouse to enquire about minibus transfer (advance notice needed).
- **Directions** - Travelling south from Talgarth on A479 take first left after Castle Inn. The Bunkhouse is on this lane after Trans Wales Trails banner at entrance to farm.

CONTACT: Paul and Emily Turner
Tel: 01874 711500
breconbunkhouse@gmail.com www.brecon-bunkhouse.co.uk
Brecon Bunkhouse, Cwmfforest Farm, Pengenfford, Talgarth, Brecon, LD3 0EU

WYE VALLEY CANOES
BUNKHOUSE

WALES

In a converted Welsh Chapel, Wye Valley Canoes Bunkhouse is a warm, modern space with huge sofas and a slide to reach the ground floor. There is a small kitchen area, so it is possible to self cater, and the River Café next door can feed your group or serve food to you at the big bunkhouse dining table. The luxury bunks are in individual pods and there is a kingsize bedroom area. The beds, the sofas and the kitchen are all within one large first floor open plan area and there are three swanky bathrooms and a table tennis table downstairs. The bunkhouse has been graded 5 star by VisitWales and won the Gold Tourism of Wales Award in 2015.

Canoes, kayaks, mountain bikes and Vespa scooters can be hired from downstairs. Try paddling down to Hay on Wye and walking back along the Wye Valley Walk. It is a beautiful area to explore with the market town of Hay on Wye just 4 miles away. An inclusive package with accommodation, food and activities can be arranged or if you prefer just come and do your own thing!

              GROUPS ONLY

DETAILS

- **Open** - All year, all day.
- **Number of beds** - 14: 12x1 (pods), 1 x double
- **Booking** - Book via website, phone or email
- **Price per night** - From £1176 for a 2 night weekend.
- **Public Transport** - Trains at Hereford and Abergavenney direct bus from Hereford, bus via Brecon from Abergavenney.
- **Directions** - On A438 from Hereford to Brecon.

CONTACT: Jane Hughes
Tel: 01497 847213
info@wyevalleycanoes.co.uk   www.wyevalleycanoes.co.uk/bunkhouse.html
The Boat House, Glasbury-On-Wye, Herefordshire, HR3 5NP

TRERICKET MILL
RIVER CABIN

River Cabin, a traditional stone building with eco credentials, is set in an old cider orchard overlooking the mill stream. It sleeps up to 4 in a cosy bunkroom with bunk beds & a double futon. There is a kitchen/lounge area, sunny dining porch, patio & private garden with picnic table, fire pit and BBQ.

The price includes heating, hot water, showers & use of bike store.

From Easter - October a small camp-site is operated with a covered outdoor kitchen for simple cooking. Rent a Tent is also available.

Located on Wye Valley Walk & National Cycle Route 8 - fantastic exploration base for walkers and cyclists and anyone wishing to relax and explore this beautiful part of Mid Wales. Canoeing, pony trekking and riding, gliding, bike hire, rope and climbing centre all available locally.

DETAILS

- **Open** - All year, 24 hour access.
- **Number of beds** - 4: 1 x 4 plus camping
- **Booking** - River Cabin (sleeps 4) - minimum booking 2 people for 2 nights. .
- **Price per night** - From £19 per person per night.
- **Public Transport** - Trains: Builth (10 miles),Hereford (30 miles),Merthyr (30 miles). Daily bus service, ask for Trericket Mill. For info see:www.traveline-cymru.info.
- **Directions** - GR SO 112 414. Set back from the A470 Brecon to Builth Wells road between the villages of Llyswen and Erwood.

CONTACT: Alistair / Nicky Legge
Tel: 01982 560312
mail@trericket.co.uk www.trericket.co.uk
Erwood, Builth Wells, Powys, LD2 3TQ

Woodlands Bunkhouse is a converted stable in the grounds of Woodlands Centre, a late Regency building, set in 10 acres of grounds. Overlooking the River Wye and with wonderful views of the Black Mountains.

Woodlands is within easy reach of the spectacular limestone area to the south. Nearby is the historic town of Hay on Wye, famous for its vast array of bookshops. With its modern facilities, the Bunkhouse provides comfortable accommodation for families and a variety of groups. With recent renovations increasing the capacity to 22, the ground floor has a well-equipped kitchen and dining room. There are 3 bedrooms on the ground floor, one with en suite facilities and six first floor bedrooms and shared bathroom facilities on both floors. Camping is also available in the grounds. The bunkhouse can arrange courses in outdoor activities which are individually designed to suit groups of all ages and abilities run by their fully qualified instructors.

DETAILS

- **Open** - All year, 24 hours.
- **Number of beds** - 22 in rooms of 1 to 6 plus camping in the grounds.
- **Booking** - Booking essential. Phone or email.
- **Price per night** - £16 pp + VAT. Reduction for children and large group bookings.
- **Public Transport** - Trains to Hereford. A local bus then runs from Hereford to Glasbury on Wye, service 39.
- **Directions** - On the B4350 just through the village of Glasbury accessed via the A438 Brecon road.

CONTACT: Annie Clipson
Tel: 01497 847272
annie.clipson@oxfordshireoutdoors.co.uk www.woodlandsoec.org
Glasbury on Wye, Powys, HR3 5LP

CLYNGWYN
BUNKHOUSE, B&B AND HUT

Clyngwyn Bunkhouse is situated in the Brecon Beacons, in the heart of waterfall country, very near to the caves and waterfalls of Ystradfellte and close to the famous Sgwd Yr Eira waterfalls. The terrain is ideal for mountain biking, gorge walking, canyoning, caving, abseiling, climbing, quad biking, photography and painting. Clyngwyn Bunkhouse is perfect for groups of friends or family. It sleeps up to 19 with camping available to larger groups, three double B&B rooms in the farm house and a romantic shepherd's hut in its own private meadow. There is a fully equipped kitchen, central heating, lounge with TV-DVD, dining room for 20, four acres of land for ball games and a large decked out polytunnel acting as a marquee, lockable storage and drying area. Relax in the evenings and enjoy the mountain views by a fire or BBQ. The villages of Ystradfellte and Pontneddfechan (2½ miles by mini bus taxi) have pubs with restaurants. Four star graded by Visit Wales. Dog friendly.

DETAILS

■ **Open** - All year, all day.
■ **Number of beds** - Bunkhouse 19, B&B 6, Shepherds Hut 2
■ **Booking** - Booking essential. Only groups can book the bunkhouse at weekends. Credit/debit cards not accepted
■ **Price per night** - Weekdays: up to 19 people £265, up to 15 people £210 or £18pp. Fri or Sat: up to 19 people £305 up to 15 people £240. Extra charge for bedding or bring your own. B&B in Farmhouse £30pp. Shepherds hut £75 (sleeps 2).
■ **Public Transport** - Trains Neath or Merthyr (11 miles). Minibus can be arranged.
■ **Directions** - From A465 leave at Glenneath, drive through and take signs for Pontneddfechan. Then 2.5 miles up Ystradfellte road, turn right down small track.

CONTACT: Julie Hurst
Tel: 01639 722930
enquiries@bunkhouse-south-wales.co.uk www.bunkhouse-south-wales.co.uk
Clyngwyn Farm, Ystradfellte Rd, Pontneddfechan, Powys, SA11 5US

CRAIG Y NOS
CASTLE

Craig Y Nos Castle is situated on a sweeping mountain road that crosses the Brecon Beacons. Once a lavish home and then a sanatorium providing the fresh air cure, the castle has always been chosen for its location. In the grounds of the castle the 1920's Nurses Block has a lounge, a small self-catering kitchen, 10 twin rooms, 1 single room, showers, loos and a disabled bathroom. All the beds are made up with fresh linen and duvets. The kitchen has a 2 ring hob and 2 microwaves, bring your own plates, cutlery and pans. You are welcome in the Castle for hearty meals, cosy evenings by the wood burning stoves and a free history tour (some areas might be restricted if a wedding is taking place).

The Castle has a conservatory for parties, a unique period theatre, gardens with views across the river and a hot tub & sports room. The Gwyn Arms is five minutes' walk and there is a pub and other amenities in Pen Y Cae (1.5 miles). Local adventure companies offer outdoor activities, you can enjoy the mountain walks and waterfalls close by or take a 50 min drive to the Gower's sandy bays.

DETAILS

- **Open** - 1st April to 31st October 24 hours.
- **Number of beds** - Nurses Block: 21: 10x2,1x1. Plus 64 ensuite rooms in castle.
- **Booking** - Bookings only accepted within 6 months of the date of your visit.
- **Price per night** - Nurses Block sole use:- 1 night £350, 2 nights £500, 3 nights £600, 5 nights £700. B&B in Nurses Block per twin room: £67.50pn midweek, £87.50pn weekend. Breakfast for groups £6.50pp. Ask for Castle room rates.
- **Public Transport** - Half an hour by car from trains at Swansea or Neath.
- **Directions** - Between Swansea and Brecon at the foot of the Brecon Beacons.

CONTACT: Reception
Tel: 01639 730725
info@craigynoscastle.com www.groupaccommodationinwales.com
Craig Y Nos Castle, Brecon Road, Penycae, Powys, SA9 1GL

COED OWEN
BUNKHOUSE

Holiday on an idyllic Welsh hill farm in the heart of the Brecon Beacons National Park. Coed Owen Bunkhouse provides fully equipped self-contained accommodation suitable for large or small groups and families who wish to spend some time exploring this beautiful area of South Wales. Walkers, cyclists, fishermen and all who enjoy being in the countryside will be welcome at Coed Owen Farm. With a newly renovated interior to sleep up to 25 and fitted with all modern conveniences, the bunkhouse is perfect for family celebrations, getaways, group visits and school trips. Spend some time exploring the beautiful outdoors found right on the doorstep. Coed Owen provides an easy gateway between the city and the Brecon Beacons.

Enjoy walks, hiking, fishing, cycling and adventure activities, or simply relax in the warm bunkhouse with plenty of space to play outdoor games and BBQ.

DETAILS

- **Open** - All year, 8am - 10pm.
- **Number of beds** - 25: 2x6 bed dorm, 1x10 bed dorm, 1 double room and 1 single.
- **Booking** - Book by email or phone
- **Price per night** - From £20 pp which includes bed linen, tea and coffee. Minimum of two night stay at weekends.
- **Public Transport** - On route T4 in the area of Brecon, between the stops Storey Arms and Llwyn-on. Nearest railway station Merthyr Tydfil 10 minutes away. 1 hour from Cardiff International Airport
- **Directions** - On A470 between Brecon and Merthyr Tydfil at Nant Ddu.

CONTACT: Molly or Netty Rees
Tel: 07508544044   01685 722628
info@breconbeaconsbunkhouse.co.uk www.breconbeaconsbunkhouse.co.uk
Coed Owen Farm, Cwmtaff, Merthyr Tydfill, CF48 2HY

L&A
OUTDOOR CENTRE

L&A Outdoor Centre is a friendly family-run destination offering quality affordable accommodation and activities in the Swansea Bay area. Tailor-made for family holidays, the 6 and 8 bed two-storey self-catering cabins have upstairs bedrooms sleeping 2-3 in each room and downstairs, the toilet and shower, lounge with TV, fully equipped kitchen and dining area, all overlooking a tree-lined mountain stream.   The bunkhouses, which sleep between 10 and 40, are clean and warm with access to self-catering. L&A facilities include a 10,000 sq.ft. activity hall, a large dining hall with professional catering, the Watering Hole bar/café, meeting rooms and over 50 acres of woodland and pasture with play area, open air swimming pool, campfire, pets corner, kennels, BBQs, bike wash and are dog friendly.   For any number up to 250, L&A is the perfect base for conferences, training courses, summer camps and retreats. Activity Packages can be arranged. The area is ideal for mountain biking with Afan Aergoed and Glyncorrwg Trails just 10 mins. away and the Millennium and Liberty Stadia are within 30 mins.

DETAILS

- **Open** - All day.
- **Number of beds** - Cabin: 117: 6/8 bed units. Bunkhouse: 175:10,16,24,30,40 bed.
- **Booking** - Book or enquire by phone or email.
- **Price per night** - Bunkhouses: £12pp, £15 with bedding. Cabins: 6 bed £90 to £150, 8 bed £100 to £180, depending on length of stay. Groups please enquire.
- **Public Transport** - Nearest rail station is Port Talbot Parkway (two miles).
- **Directions** - One mile from Junction 40 of the M4

CONTACT: Nigel
Tel: 01639 885 509
info@landaoutdoorcentre.co.uk www.landaoutdoorcentre.co.uk
Goytre, West Glamorgan SA13 2YP

EASTERN SLADE
BARN

Eastern Slade Farm Barn is a luxury conversion of a 15 century farmhouse on a working dairy farm in the Gower peninsula. Under floor heating, powered by air source heat pump, provides year round warmth and the barn is ideal for groups of families or friends who like to holiday together. There are 3 wet rooms and 4 bedrooms sleeping 13 people. Two extra fold up beds are available in the lounge when the whole barn is booked. The beds are made up with fresh sheets and pillow cases and you are invited to bring your own sleeping bags or duvet covers (duvets available). The well equipped kitchen has a range style stove (electric oven and gas hobs) and granite work tops. The comfy lounge has leather sofas and a wood burning stove for cosy evenings. The Gower has glorious beaches and castles to explore and a network of traffic free lanes, ideal for mountain bikes. The Coastal Path passes through the farm. Port Eynon seaside village is 30 mins walk west. Oxwich Bay, 20 mins walk east, has a castle, beach and a hotel with bar and meals. Camping is also available.

DETAILS

- **Open** - All year, 24 hours.
- **Number of beds** - 15: 1x5, 2x 2/3 (double with bunk above), 1x2, 2 in lounge
- **Booking** - Please phone or email to book
- **Price per night** - £15pp, £180 sole use. High season £20pp, £240 sole use.
- **Public Transport** - Buses 118 and 114 from Swansea travel to Oxwich Cross once a day. Slade is a 20 minute walk from Oxwich Cross.
- **Directions** - From Oxwich follow the sign for Slade marked no through road. Pass Oxwich Castle and as the road descends look for Eastern Slade Farm on right.

CONTACT: Kate
Tel: (01792) 391374, Mob: 07970 969814
tynrheol@hotmail.com   www.easternsladebarngower.co.uk
Eastern Slade Farm, Oxwich, Gower, Swansea, SA3 1NA

RHOSSILI
BUNKHOUSE

Situated at the end of the Gower Peninsula, in the UK's first Area of Outstanding Natural Beauty, Rhossili Bunkhouse is within easy walking distance of three glorious beaches, including Rhossili Bay (TripAdvisor: UK's #1 Beach 2013) and ideally located for a range of outdoor activities including walking, surfing, cycling, climbing and flying. The Gower Way starts nearby. This 4 star Visit Wales bunkhouse is great for groups of friends or families. It is run for the benefit of the community by Rhossili Bunkhouse Ltd on behalf of Rhossili Village Hall Trustees. Duvets and pillows provided. Bring single bed linen or sleeping bags. Central heating throughout. Self-catering in fully equipped kitchen. Lounge/dining room opens onto patio and garden. Games and books in lounge. Free WiFi. Secure store for bikes and boards, with drying room for coats and boots. Outside area for rinsing/drying wet suits. Card locks on all doors. Hall and meeting room for hire. Car park. No pets. No smoking.

DETAILS

■ **Open** - All year except January. Check in 4-9pm; check out by 10:30am.
■ **Number of beds** - 18: 1x4, 2x3, 4x2. 4 sofa-beds in lounge (Sole use).
■ **Booking** - Advance booking recommended. Check our website for availability. Online form and virtual tour. Deposit 30%. Minimum booking: 2 people for 2 nights
■ **Price per night** - Shared (small groups) £16-£20. Full (group of 18) £340. Sole (group of 22) £390.
■ **Public Transport** - Regular buses (118) from Swansea stop outside. www.visitswanseabay.com/explorebybus www.traveline-cymru.info
■ **Directions** - On the B4247 in Middleton, Rhossili. GR SS 421 878

CONTACT: Josephine Higgins
Tel: 01792 391509
bookings@rhossili.org www.rhossilibunkhouse.com
Rhossili Bunkhouse, Rhossili, Swansea, SA3 1PL

HARDINGSDOWN
BUNKHOUSE

Hardingsdown Bunkhouse provides comfortable accommodation for families or groups in a tastefully restored stone barn on an organic farm. The Gower has National Nature Reserves, outstanding coastal scenery, family beaches, castles and ancient monuments. Llangennith beach is one of the best surfing beaches in the south west, Mewslade Bay and Fall Bay are popular with climbers, while walkers and bikers can use the local network of footpaths and bridleways. The ground floor consists of a fully equipped kitchen, 2 shower/toilet rooms, a living room with 2 single sofa-beds and comfy chairs. Off the living room is a bedroom with a bunkbed sleeping 2 people. A spiral staircase leads upstairs where there are 3 bedrooms sleeping 5, 3 and 2 in bunks and single beds. Separate drying room and a lock-up for storing bikes, surfboards, canoes etc. Ample parking and a patio area that catches the evening sun. Shops and pubs nearby. A new bunkhouse sleeping approximately 10 people will be available from July 2016.

              GROUPS ONLY

DETAILS

- **Open** - All year, 24 hours.,
- **Number of beds** - 14: 1x5, 1x3, 3x2. Plus 10: In new bunkhouse from July 2016.
- **Booking** - Booking essential by phone or email and confirmed by 30% deposit.
- **Price per night** - SOLE USE £220pn (weekends, bank holidays and school holidays), £190pn (midweek). Weekly rates available. INDIVIDUALS Mid week, shared use, £18 per person. Enquire for rates in the new bunkhouse.
- **Public Transport** - Regular bus 116 from Swansea. Traveline 0871 200 22 33.
- **Directions** - Turn left off the B4295 ½ mile AFTER Burry Green (by bus shelter and post box). Follow lane 400m. End of tarmac road (and before rough track beyond) turn right into Lower Hardingsdown Farm. Bunkhouse is on left of farmyard.

CONTACT: Allison Tyrrell
Tel: 01792 386222
bunkhousegower@btconnect.com www.bunkhousegower.co.uk
Lower Hardingsdown Farm, Llangennith, Gower, Swansea, SA3 1HT

Llansteffan is a beautiful, quaint village set at the tip of the Towi River and Carmarthen Bay. The sandy beaches nestled below the castle offer swimming and relaxation. The virtually traffic free country lanes make this area ideal for cycling. For the walker we are on the Wales Coastal Path. Carmarthen, Wales' oldest city and ancestral home to Merlin of King Arthur's legends, offers most social and cultural activities. The Pantyrathro International Hostel provides dorm accommodation, private rooms, and also has 3 new en suite units of 6, 9 and 12 beds. Facilities include self-catering kitchen, dining area, TV lounge, showers and free WiFi. Our two Mexican bars offer pool, darts, TV, weekly drink specials and food (eat-in or take-out). Horse riding and excursions for trekking, canoeing and surfing offered. Take a day trip, relax on the beaches or have a drink in our bars - something for everyone.

DETAILS

- **Open** - Febuary to January. 24 hours.
- **Number of beds** - 50: 1 x 12, 1 x 9, 2 x 6, 4 x 4, 1 x 3.
- **Booking** - Booking recommended. 50% deposit required in advance for groups.
- **Price per night** - £16pp dorm. Group discounts.
- **Public Transport** - Carmarthen has both coach and train stations serving South Wales, SW England and London. Local bus runs six times a day to Llansteffan. Ask driver to let you off at Pantyrathro.
- **Directions** - Pantyrathro is six miles from Carmarthen on the B4312, midway between Llangain and Llansteffan. Two miles from Llangain you will see the hostel signposted, turn right and follow hostel signs to top of lane.

CONTACT: Ken Knuckles
Tel: 01267 241014
kenknuckles@hotmail.com www.backpackershostelwales.com
Pantyrathro International Hostel, Llansteffan, Carmarthen, SA33 5AJ

UPPER NEESTON
LODGES

WALES

Environmentally sensitive barn conversions on a small family run sheep farm, close to the Milford Haven Waterway in the Pembrokeshire Coast National Park. Ideal for divers, climbers, walkers or for family and friends having a get-together. The four independent units, all have access to garden/patio, laundry/drying room, wash-down area, secure storage and ample parking. THE COWSHED BUNKHOUSE- single storey with disabled access. Large sitting room and kitchen/dining area, and two bedrooms each with en suite shower rooms. THE BARN BUNKHOUSE has an upstairs sitting room and kitchen/dining area whilst the two downstairs bedrooms have en suite shower rooms. THE GRANARY LODGE also has an upstairs sitting room/kitchen. The ground floor bedroom sleeps up to 3 people and has an en suite shower room. The DAIRY LODGE is single story with bathroom, 2 single beds and diner kitchen. All units have fully fitted kitchens, fridge freezers, microwave, toaster, crockery, TV, CD player and wood burning stove. Graded 5 Star bunkhouse by Visit Wales.

DETAILS
- **Open** - All year check in from 4pm. Check out before 10.30am.
- **Number of beds** - Cowshed 10 1x6,1x4. Barn 8 1x6,1x2, Granary 1x3. Dairy 1x3
- **Booking** - Provisional booking taken by phone/email and confirmed by deposit.
- **Price per night** - £16pp (inc linen). Min 2 nights at weekends (3 nights bank hols). Exclusive use: min 6 Barn, 8 Cowshed.Smaller groups / individuals by agreement.
- **Public Transport** - Puffin coastal shuttle passes farm www.traveline-cymru.org.uk
- **Directions** - Follow A4076 through Milford Haven to roundabout by Docks. Take first exit (signed Hakin). Follow for 2 miles, look for first farm on left (next to layby).

CONTACT: Sean or Mandy Tilling
Tel: 01646 690750
mail@upperneeston.co.uk www.upperneeston.co.uk
Upper Neeston Farm, Dale Road, Herbrandston, Milford Haven, SA73 3RY

LAWRENNY
MILLENNIUM HOSTEL
WALES

Set in a picturesque village, surrounded by organic farmland and ancient oak woodland, this relaxed and friendly hostel is a great base for launching into everything Pembrokeshire has to offer. The hostel is warm, clean and comfortable, with modern facilities. There are 22 beds in 5 rooms, all of which can be reserved as family rooms. There's a large open plan kitchen and living room as well as a drying room, large car park and cycle shelter. Once a Victorian village school, the hostel is superbly placed for walking, boating, bird watching and kayaking, and is close to many top family attractions and the beautiful beaches of south Pembrokeshire. Groups are welcome and the whole hostel can be hired for holidays, training courses and events. WiFi is available. The adjoining village hall is available to rent. The hostel is run as a charitable trust and is a Friends of Nature hostel. The village has a community shop, pub and an award-winning tearoom.

DETAILS

- **Open** - All year. Arrange check in with warden/all day access.
- **Number of beds** - 22: 2x4, 2 x double + bunks (4), 1 x double/singles + bunks (6)
- **Booking** - Online, email or telephone
- **Price per night** - Adults £16, children (4-17) £10. Double rooms £37 (couple), £50 (with children). Sole use of hostel £250 per night.
- **Public Transport** - Not easy! Coach/train to Kilgetty (8m). Get the 381 bus (Tenby to Pembroke Dock) and from Cresswell Quay it's a 2.5 mile walk to the hostel.
- **Directions** - From A40 St Clears to Haverfordwest road take A4075 signed Tenby and Oakwood. Just past the turning to Oakwood, turn right and follow signs to Lawrenny. Bear right in front of church and follow the car park signs.

CONTACT: Laura Lort-Phillips
Tel: 01646 651270
hostel@lawrennyvillage.co.uk www.lawrennyhostel.com
Lawrenny Millennium Hostel, Lawrenny, Pembrokeshire, SA68 0PW

STACKPOLE
WALES OUTDOOR LEARNING CENTRE

The 137-bed, platinum eco-award-winning, Stackpole Outdoor Learning Centre is in the heart of the Stackpole estate. Just a stone's throw from the banks of the Bosherston lakes. It's the perfect venue for large families, groups, special interest breaks and outdoor activities. The estate of countryside and coast includes a National Nature Reserve, ancient settlements, towering cliffs, wild woodlands and two stunning sandy beaches. The accommodation has been developed from a range of stone farm buildings. It comprises four large houses, three cottages and a manor house. Facilities include a theatre and bar. Adventurous activities such as coasteering, kayaking and surfing are available by arrangment. There are more than 30km of footpaths that criss-cross the estate

DETAILS

- **Open** - All year, all day. Reception 9am - 6pm.
- **Number of beds** - Swan House 13 bedrooms (sleeping 24 persons), Shearwater House 7 bedrooms (13 persons), Kestrel House 12 bedrooms (29 persons), Kingfisher 10 bedrooms (44 persons), Manor House 3 bedrooms (9 persons), 3 cottages 9 bedrooms (18 persons)
- **Booking** - Bookings are made through reception.
- **Price per night** - Minimum of two night's stay. Please contact bookings team for a quote. Prices range from £30 per person per night.
- **Public Transport** - Trains Pembroke (5 miles). Bus from Pembroke: Silcox 387 Coastal Cruiser.
- **Directions** - On the B4319 from Pembroke to Stackpole and Bosherton (various entry points onto estate).

CONTACT: Stackpole Reception
Tel: 01646 661425
stackpole@nationaltrust.org.uk www.nationaltrust.org.uk/stackpole-centre
The Old Home Farm Yard, Stackpole, nr Pembroke, Pembrokeshire, SA71 5DQ

WARREN FARM
GLAMPING

Beautiful big bell tents, cosy bunkhouse & unique pods right on the Pembrokeshire Coast Path with great views out to sea, close to fantastic climbing at Castlemartin Range, excellent surfing at Freshwater West & Broadhaven South and within striking distance of many of Pembrokeshire's beaches, countryside, wildlife, castles, river walks, charming pubs, film locations and other places of interest. The well-appointed 6m bell tents, which each sleep up to 8, and pods for individuals & couples are on secluded pitches with their own outside dining area, camp fire, fully equipped camp kitchen, and off grid shower & compost loo. The bunkhouse has purpose-built robust and good-sized bunkbeds for up to 12 adults, complete with wet room, toilets and courtyard campfire cooking. Pedestrianised, step-free & dog-friendly site with plenty of parking, grassy lawns and garden games. All mattresses are orthopedic & hypo-allergenic, so you'll get a good night's sleep even after the most energetic day. Please note: this is a remote rural location near an active military training range with no mobile signal, there is usually WiFi in the farmhouse.

DETAILS

■ **Open** - All year. Flexible check in by arrangement.
■ **Number of beds** - Bunkhouse: 12, Bell Tents: 6x8, camping, plus an expanding range of pods for couples & individuals
■ **Booking** - via website. Bunkhouse sole use only. Camping also available.
■ **Price per night** - Check website for latest accommodation & prices. From £12ppn
■ **Public Transport** - Train & Ferry Pembroke. Bus route: 387/388 Coastal Cruiser
■ **Directions** - Take the B4319 from Pembroke and follow red-edged signs to Castlemartin Range. Then turn right through Merrion, Warren Farm is on the right.

CONTACT: Jane, Hannah or Amy
stay@warrenfarm.wales www.warrenfarm.wales
Warren Farm, Warren, near Castlemartin, SA71 5HS

OLD SCHOOL HOSTEL
FORMERLY YHA TREFIN

WALES

Escape to this wonderful, wild and rugged corner of the Pembrokeshire Coast National Park. The Hostel is in Trefin, a pretty village which has a pub and a café, just a quarter of a mile from the world famous coast path. Circular walks from the door take you to stunning wild beaches and interesting small harbour villages. The cathedral city of St. David's and the popular family and surfers' beach at Whitesands Bay are only 20 minutes by car.

This characterful 4 star hostel has unique double and twin rooms with en-suite showers from £18 pppn. Travelling solo? This hostel has a rare find, great value single rooms from only £23 and budget family/friends rooms too. A light breakfast is included in the price. For groups exclusive use rates offer excellent value as well. Check out the (mostly!) excellent guests reviews on Tripadvisor (120 out of 124) and it's easy to book on-line via the hostels new website.

DETAILS

- **Open** - March to October and Xmas / New Year. Check in from 5pm.
- **Number of beds** - 25: 1 x 6/7 (3 bunks, one with 4' double lower bed); 1x2 (bunk); 1x2 (double); 2 x 2/3 (bunk with double lower bed); 1 x 3/4 (bunk with double lower bed & guest bed); 1 x 4 (1 double + 1 bunk). Rooms available for single occupancy.
- **Booking** - Book on-line via our website or phone.
- **Price per night** - From £18. Kids £10. Exclusive use of hostel from only £150.
- **Public Transport** - Train to Fishguard & Goodwick then bus 413 or train to Haverfordwest then bus 411 then bus 413. See www.travelinecymru.info
- **Directions** - M4/A48/A40 to Letterston. Turn left onto the B4331 for 5 miles then left onto the A487. After 3 miles turn right after the petrol station/shop for Trefin.

CONTACT: Sue or Chris
Tel: 01348 831800
oldschoolhostel@btconnect.com   www.oldschoolhostel.com
Ffordd-yr-Afon, Trefin, Haverfordwest, Pembrokeshire, SA62 5AU

CAERHAFOD
LODGE

Ideally situated between the famous cathedral city of St Davids and the Irish ferry port of Fishguard, the Lodge overlooks the spectacular Pembrokeshire coastline. Within walking distance of the well known Sloop Inn at Porthgain and the internationally renowned Coastal Path. An ideal stopover for cyclists with The Celtic Trail cycle route passing the bottom of the drive. The Lodge is a great base for all outdoor activities: boat trips around Ramsey Island, coasteering, kayaking, surfing or just lazing on the beach. The lodge sleeps 23 in 5 separate rooms, all en suite with great showers. There is a modern fully equipped kitchen/diner with sea view patio & picnic tables with a panoramic view from the Preseli mountains to Strumble Head and the North Bishop with glorious sunsets over the Irish sea. There is also a sitting room for cosy evenings, on-site washing/drying room and secure storage area. Dogs welcome by prior arrangement. Smoking outdoors. Visit Wales graded 4 star.

DETAILS

- **Open** - All year, check in from 4pm, check out 10.30 am. All day access.
- **Number of beds** - 23: 3x4 : 1x5 : 1x6.
- **Booking** - Advised in high season. 50% deposit.
- **Price per night** - Adult £18. Under 16 £14.50. Group rates available.
- **Public Transport** - Trains at Fishguard (9m) and Haverfordwest (17m). Fishguard/Rosslare ferry. National Express: Haverfordwest. 413 Bus: St Davids-Fishguard 50yds from Lodge. Seasonal coastal shuttle service for walkers.
- **Directions** - GR Landranger 157, SM 827 317. A40 from Haverfordwest, left at Letterston (B4331) to Mathry. Left onto A487 to St Davids, right in Croesgoch for Llanrhian, at crossroads right for Trefin. Lodge is on right after ½ mile.

CONTACT: Carolyn Rees
Tel: 01348 837859
Caerhafod@aol.com www.caerhafod.co.uk
Llanrhian, St Davids, Haverfordwest, Pembrokeshire, SA62 5BD

HAMILTON
BACKPACKERS

Hamilton Backpackers Lodge, Fishguard, a cosy base with free WiFi, close to the Pembrokeshire Coastal Path. Perfect for walkers, cyclists, golfers and family groups. The Lodge is comfortable and friendly. It sleeps nine in an en suite double room and two dormitories (1 x 3 beds, 1 x 4 beds). Groups of up to 18 are welcome in collaboration with James John Hamilton House hostel next door (See Page 338). All rooms are centrally heated and recently redecorated. Fully equipped kitchen, dining area and lounge with PC. Secluded private garden and covered patio with seating. Free tea, coffee and light breakfast provided. Parking close by. Two minutes walk from the centre of town and close to a number of good pubs. No curfew. Smoking is permitted in the garden/patio. Dog friendly - owner "Q" has a very friendly and laid back labrador.

             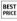

DETAILS

- **Open** - All year.
- **Number of beds** - 9 (+10): 1 x 4, 1 x 3 and 1 x 2. (Plus 10 next door)
- **Booking** - Booking advised to confirm beds. 50% deposit required from groups.
- **Price per night** - £19 to £20 pp in dorms, £24pp in double en suite.
- **Public Transport** - Fishgaurd has train station and ferries to Rosslare in Ireland. Port is 1 mile away (approx taxi fare £7). National Express coaches at Haverfordwest (15 miles). For local buses in Pembrokeshire phone Richard Bros 01239 613756.
- **Directions** - From Haverfordwest (A40) to Fishguard Square (A487), straight across roundabout then take first right (Hamilton Street), Hostel is 150m on left. From Cardigan A487, through Lower Town, up steep hill, turn left 100m after Globe Pub. From Ferry port 1 mile to Fishguard Town Centre (Square), turn left, then first right.

CONTACT: Quentin Maclaurin
Tel: 01348 874797 / 07505562939
hamiltonbackpackers@hotmail.com www.hamiltonbackpackers.co.uk
23 Hamilton Street, Fishguard, Pembrokeshire, SA65 9HL

JAMES JOHN
HAMILTON HOUSE

James John Hamilton House is a brand new conversion of the first free school in Fishguard, built in 1850 by James John Hamilton. The house sleeps 10 people in four private rooms. Upstairs is a large open plan lounge with exposed beams, comfy sofas and dinning table. Next to this is a self catering kitchen and a double bedroom. The three other three bedrooms, a twin, a double and a four person family room are downstairs and are all en suite. There is a patio with picnic table and across the garden is Hamilton House Backpackers (See page 336) where rooms are available for a further 9 people. There is free parking for one car, with a town car park only 40m away. Dogs welcome. Close to the town centre with a choice of pubs. Fishguard is a natural harbour surrounded by the sweeping sands of Cardigan Bay. The Pembrokeshire Coastal Path passes through the town and communities of grey seals and dolphins are regularly seen in its harbours.

DETAILS

■ **Open** - All year. OPEN NOW.
■ **Number of beds** - 10 (+9): 1 x twin, 2 x double, 1 x 4 (double & bunk bed) plus 9 beds next door.
■ **Booking** - Please book by phone or email.
■ **Price per night** - From £20 to £28 per person.
■ **Public Transport** - Fishguard has excellent new train links and operates a regular ferry service to Rosslare in Ireland. For local buses in Pembrokeshire phone Richard Bros 01239 613756.
■ **Directions** - Look for entrance to old school building behind Hamilton Backpackers on Hamilton Street.

CONTACT: Steve Roberts
Tel: 01348 874288 Mob: 07813 687570
stephenism@hotmail.com www.jamesjohnhamilton.co.uk
19A Hamilton St, Fishguard SA65 9HL

PIGGERY POKE
4 STAR HOSTEL

Piggery Poke is a 16 bed, 4 star hostel on the public footpath that loops from the Ceredigion Coast Path between Mwnt and Aberporth. Local cycle routes link the road at the top of the entrance drive to long distance cycle routes Lôn Teifi (within 4 miles) and the Celtic Trail (see Sustrans Route 82). Piggery Poke is a new conversion of an old building and has 3 dormitories sleeping up to 8, 5 and 3, each with en suite facilities. The dining room seats 16 at one sitting. There is a drying room on the ground floor and wireless broadband is available by arrangement. There is a large garden area with sea views and barbeque and there is a secure cycle store. Courtesy collection and delivery service is usually available from points within 15 miles along the coast for walkers or cyclists and/or their cycles/luggage. Ample parking is provided.

DETAILS

■ **Open** - All year round, 7.30am to 10am and 4pm to 10pm.
■ **Number of beds** - 16: 1 x 8, 1 x 5, 1 x 3.
■ **Booking** - Book by phone or via our website.
■ **Price per night** - £24 per person.
■ **Public Transport** - Trains at Aberystwyth and Carmarthen. From Aberystwyth station take the X50 bus to Blaenannerch or 550 bus to Felinwynt, via Aberporth. From Carmarthen station take the 460 or 461 bus to Cardigan (Finch Square) then change to the 550 bus to Aberystwyth via Aberporth, alighting at Felinwynt.
■ **Directions** - Piggery Poke hostel is part of Cardigan Coastal Cottages, at Ffrwdwenith Isaf, Felinwynt, half-way between Mwnt and Aberporth, 4 miles along the coast north of Cardigan. Lat: 52.13108, Long: -4.58939. Map X222837, Y251268.

CONTACT: Paul or Angela
Tel: 01239 811777
hostel@piggerypoke.co.uk www.piggerypoke.co.uk
Ffrwdwenith Isaf, Felinwynt, Cardigan, SA43 1RW

This budget bunkhouse is nestled in the Teifi valley, perfect for exploring the local area.

Bedding is included and facilities include a self-catering kitchen and a lounge, with terraced garden and BBQ area.

Twenty five minutes' drive will get you to the stunning Ceredigion coastline.

There are many village pubs and restaurants within walking distance.

Shaggy Sheep are expert in organising adventure activity holidays ideal for hen & stag weekends, corporate team building, youth groups, couples and families.

Get in touch to find out more.

DETAILS

- **Open** - Jan-Dec, 24hrs.
- **Number of beds** - 22 (5x4, 1x2)
- **Booking** - book by email or through the website
- **Price per night** - email with numbers and stay length for a quote
- **Public Transport** - No
- **Directions** - Take A484 from Carmarthen to Saron. Turn right at Rhos. Through Pentrecwrt to Llandysul, turn right at Half Moon pub, see us on the left or follow Sat Nav to SA44 4AJ.

CONTACT: Chris
Tel: 01559 363911
bookings@shaggysheepwales.co.uk www.shaggysheepwales.com/
Old Commerce House, Pontwelly, Llandysul, Carmarthen SA44 4AJ

THE LONG BARN

WALES

Penrhiw is a working organic farm in beautiful countryside with views over the Teifi Valley. The stunning Ceredigion Coast and the Cambrian Mountains are an easy drive away and the busy small town of Llandysul (1.5 miles) has all essential supplies. The Long Barn is a traditional stone barn providing comfortable, warm self catering bunkhouse accommodation for 31 people. The Cowshed provides self catering accommodation for 6 and the bedsit (or flat) has a double bed and single bed with kitchenette. Each unit can be hired separately or combined for larger groups. The farm's location is ideal for exploring, studying or simply admiring the Welsh countryside. Activities enjoyed by guests in the surrounding area include fishing, swimming, climbing, abseiling, canoeing, farm walks and cycling. The accommodation is available all year, having adequate heating with lovely warm log fires, roof insulation and double glazing throughout.

DETAILS

■ **Open** - All year, all day.
■ **Number of beds** - 40: Long Barn 31: 1x15,1x14,1x2. Cowshed 6:1x6. Bedsit: 3: 1x3 (dbl+single).
■ **Booking** - Essential, deposit required
■ **Price per night** - £15pp . Discount for groups and mid week bookings.
■ **Public Transport** - Trains and National Express at Carmarthen (16 miles). Local bus service at Landysul (1.5 miles) details/booking 0871 2002233 www.bwcabus.info
■ **Directions** - OS map 146, GR 437 417. In Llandysul, at the top of the main street, take right hand lane. Turn sharp right down hill. After 100 yds turn sharp left. Another ½ mile turn first right. Continue for 1 mile and Long Barn is on your right.

CONTACT: Tom or Eva
Tel: 01559 363200 Mob 07733 026874
cowcher@thelongbarn.co.uk www.thelongbarn.co.uk
Penrhiw, Capel Dewi, Llandysul, Ceredigion, SA44 4PG

TY'N CORNEL
TYNCORNEL HOSTEL

Ty'n Cornel Hostel is an isolated former farmhouse in the hills, with a cosy open fire. Favoured by walkers, cyclists, bird watchers and lovers of solitude it is in the beautiful Doethie valley on the Cambrian Way long distance footpath.

There are comfortable wooden bunk beds and good self-catering facilities. You can enjoy the wild open moorlands of the Elenydd uplands. Other attractions include the Cors Caron National Nature Reserve, the Red Kite Centre and museum in Tregaron, Teifi Pools, Llyn Brianne reservoir, Dolaucothi Roman gold mines, Strata Florida Abbey and the National Trust's Llanerchaeron country house.

DETAILS

- **Open** - All year, 24 hours. Reception 5pm -11pm, 7am -10am.
- **Number of beds** - 16: 2x8.
- **Booking** - Booking advisable; essential mid November to mid March. Book online at www.yha.org.uk, ring YHA booking office on 0800 0191700 or ring hostel managers on 01980 629259.
- **Price per night** - £12 per adult, £9 (under 18s). Block bookings negotiable.
- **Public Transport** - Trains: Aberystwyth 28m, Llanwrtyd Wells 16m, Cynghordy 12m. Coach: X40 (Cardiff – Aberystwyth) Lampeter 15m. Bus: 585 (Lampeter – Tregaron) Llanddewi-Brefi 7m.
- **Directions** - Road from Llanddewi-Brefi, near Tregaron: follow hostel signs SE 7m (last mile track). Bridle-path S up Doethie valley on the Cambrian Way (Llandovery 15 m) or byway 2m NW from Soar y Mynydd chapel.

CONTACT: YHA booking office
Tel: 0800 0191700 or 01980 629259
tyncornel@yha.org.uk www.elenydd-hostels.co.uk
Llanddewi Brefi, Tregaron, Ceredigion, SY25 6PH

DOLGOCH
HOSTEL

Come and experience the peace of this unique location in the remote Tywi valley. A stay in this 17th century farmhouse will take you into an era before electricity, with a log burner for heat. Dolgoch is a traditional simple hostel owned by the Elenydd Wilderness Trust. It has hot showers, a self catering kitchen/dining room and 20 beds in 3 dormitories and has been refurbished to include new toilets and showers and less able accommodation. Private rooms are also available and the access track has been upgraded. The Lôn Las Cymru (Welsh National Cycle Route) and the Cambrian Way pass nearby and there are many other mountain tracks to explore on foot, by mountain bike or pony. The hostel is ideal for bird-watchers and lovers of solitude and is close to an old drovers' track which leads over the scenic Cambrian mountains for 5 miles to the equally remote and simple Ty'n Cornel Hostel. Why not stay a night in each hostel and follow in the treads of the old drovers?

DETAILS

- **Open** - All year 24 hours. Reception 5pm -11pm, 8am -10am.
- **Number of beds** - 20: (in 3 rooms). Private rooms available.
- **Booking** - Booking information on yha.org.uk or from Gillian Keen
- **Price per night** - £12 per adult, £9 (under 18). Campers £8.
- **Public Transport** - Train to Aberystwyth, Carmarthen or Llanwrtyd Wells. Bus X40: Cardiff/Carmarthen to Lampeter/Aberystwyth, Bus 585: Lampeter/Aberystwyth to Tregaron. Postbus 287: Llandovery to Rhandirmwyn.
- **Directions** - SN 806 562. You can walk to Dolgoch over the hills from Tregaron or take the winding Abergwesyn mountain road. The hostel is ¾ mile south of the bridge, along an unsurfaced track.

CONTACT: YHA Booking Office or Gillian Keen
Tel: 01440730226
dolgoch@yha.org.uk www.elenydd-hostels.co.uk
Dolgoch, Tregaron, Ceredigion, SY25 6NR

GILFACH WEN
BARN

Gilfach Wen Barn has been converted to provide competitively priced homely self-catering accommodation for individuals, extended families or groups on a working farm adjacent to Brechfa Forest. Graded as a 4 star bunkhouse it sleeps up to 32 in 7 bedrooms and has a large kitchen/dining room, lounge and drying room. There is a downstairs bedroom and shower room for disabled. The facilities are walker, cyclist and equestrian friendly.

Adjacent to Brechfa Forest, the Cothi Valley and Llanllwni Mountain, Gilfach Wen Barn is a perfect venue for a holiday or weekend away – you need never leave the valley. The barn is WiFi enabled, fully equipped and Brechfa village with its shop and pub is within walking distance (1 mile). This is a stunningly beautiful area close to Brecon Beacons National Park, in the foothills of the Cambrian Mountains but only a short drive to Cefn Sidan Sands - an award winning 7 mile long beach. Virtual tour available on the barn's website.

DETAILS

- **Open** - All year, all day.
- **Number of beds** - 32: 3x6, 1x5, 1x4,1x3,1x2 in 10 double beds and 12 singles.
- **Booking** - Advance booking required.
- **Price per night** - From £17.50 pp, During school holidays and at weekends minimum numbers apply for advance bookings. Last minute bookings at weekend may be available at £20 pp for individuals and small groups.
- **Public Transport** - Trains and coaches at Carmarthen. Daily bus from Carmarthen to Brechfa passes gate. Bus is a request stop service. You can ask to be dropped off and can catch the bus at the bottom of the drive.
- **Directions** - GR SN 513 292 On the B4310 between Horeb and Brechfa.

CONTACT: Jillie
Tel: 07780 476737
info@brechfa-bunkhouse.com www.brechfa-bunkhouse.com
Gilfach Wen, Brechfa, Carmarthenshire, SA32 7QL

Stonecroft Lodge self-catering guest house is situated in Llanwrtyd Wells, 'the smallest town in Britain'. Surrounded by the green fields, mountains and glorious countryside of mid Wales, Llanwrtyd is in renowned Red Kite country and is a great centre for mountain biking, walking, pony trekking, etc. The town hosts many annual events such as the Man v Horse Marathon, World Bog Snorkelling Championships and the mid-Wales Beer Festival.

The hostel offers a warm welcome and a comfortable stay. It is Wales Tourist Board Star Graded and has private and shared rooms with fully made-up beds. There is a fully equipped kitchen, a lounge with TV and video, free laundry and drying facilities, central heating, a large riverside garden and ample parking. The hostel adjoins our Good Beer Guide pub, Stonecroft Inn (where great food is available), and is truly your 'home away from home', offering the best of everything for your stay.

          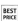

DETAILS

- **Open** - All year, all day - phone on arrival.
- **Number of beds** - 27: 1 x 1 : 3 x 4 : 1 x 6 : 4 x (dbl + 1 sgl)
- **Booking** - Welcome, 50% deposit.
- **Price per night** - £16. Discounts for 3+ nights. Phone for exclusive-use rates.
- **Public Transport** - Llanwrtyd Wells station on the Heart of Wales line is a few minutes' walk from the hostel.
- **Directions** - GR 878 468. From Llanwrtyd town centre (A483) take Dolecoed Road towards Abergwesyn. Hostel is 100 yds on left. Check in at Stonecroft Inn.

CONTACT: Jane Brown
Tel: 01591 610327
party@stonecroft.co.uk www.stonecroft.co.uk
Dolecoed Road, Llanwrtyd Wells, Powys, LD5 4RA

NEW INN
BUNKHOUSE

Stay at the 16th century New Inn on the River Wye and discover the forgotten countryside of mid Wales. The New Inn has a bunkhouse ideal for parties of walkers and cyclists as well as double, twin and family B&B rooms. The bunkhouse has its own entrance and a large lobby which can be used for boots and waterproofs. Secure storage is available for cycles and motor-cycles. The bunkhouse is self-contained with toilets and showers.

There are no self-catering facilities but the inn specialises in serving imaginative home-cooked locally grown food. A Welsh breakfast of home-made sausages and dry cured bacon is available for £5.50. Explore the surrounding countryside, inhabited by red kites, or relax in the secluded beer garden. There is plenty of parking and a large function room for parties

DETAILS

■ **Open** - All year, all day. Pub closed 3pm - 5pm some days.
■ **Number of beds** - Bunkhouse 10: 1x6, 1x4; B&B 11: family rooms, double & twin
■ **Booking** - Book by phone or email.
■ **Price per night** - £12 pp (Bunkhouse), £60 sole use of 6 bed room, £40 sole use of 4 bed room. Breakfast £5.50pp. En suite B&B in inn £60 double/twin. Family rooms also available from £80.
■ **Public Transport** - Trains at Llandrindod Wells (5 miles). Infrequent bus service.
■ **Directions** - Newbridge-on-Wye is on the A470 between Builth Wells and Rhayader. Travelling north on the A470 take a right turn in Newbridge and the New Inn is on the right.

CONTACT: Debbie and Dave
Tel: 01597 860211
dave@pigsfolly.orangehome.co.uk www.pigsfolly.co.uk/bunkhouse.htm
New Inn, Newbridge-on-Wye, Llandrindod Wells, Powys, LD1 6HY

PLASNEWYDD
BUNKHOUSE

Set in the beautiful mid-Wales countryside on the Glyndwrs Way the bunkhouse is an ideal location for exploring or unwinding. Built to the highest standards, with 4 star tourist board rating, it provides high quality accommodation for groups or individuals. It can also be booked for conferences and seminars. There is a well equipped kitchen and a large communal area with fabulous elevated views over the mid-Wales countryside. The bunk beds are large with comfortable mattresses. Pillows and pillowcases are included, sheets and duvets can be hired for £3 per set. Attractions close by include sailing, golf course, outdoor pursuit centre, shooting range, motorbike school and the picturesque market town of Llanidloes (0.5 mile) with many places to eat and drink. You will need to bring your own soap and towels. Boots and dirty footwear must be kept in the drying room so please bring footwear for indoors. Taxis for walkers and cyclists to / from routes available.

DETAILS

- **Open** - All year 24 hours. Arrival and departure times by arrangement.
- **Number of beds** - 27 in 2 dormitories and 1 family room.
- **Booking** - Booking is required (with non-refundable deposit) by phone, email or booking form on plasnewyddbunkhouse.co.uk.
- **Price per night** - Sole use £403 per night. Individuals £20 pp.
- **Public Transport** - Caersws train station (7 miles), Llanidloes bus station (0.5 mile). Pick ups can be arranged from these points if required.
- **Directions** - From Llanidloes take the Gorn Road and Plasnewydd is signposted on the left hand side after about half a mile.

CONTACT: Susan
Tel: 01686 412431 or 07977 508 648 / 07975 913049
susanvaughan67@aol.co.uk www.plasnewyddbunkhouse.co.uk
Gorn Rd, Llanidloes, Powys, SY18 6LA

BEILI NEUADD
BUNKHOUSE

Beili Neuadd Bunkhouse is a converted 18th century stone barn beautifully positioned in quiet, secluded countryside with delightful views, its own paddocks, stream, pools and woodland. The centrally heated barn sleeps 16 in 3 en suite bunkrooms and includes a fully equipped kitchen/dining room and drying room. The bunks have full sized mattresses, bed linen is included and towels can be hired. Accommodation is also available in an adjacent chalet, there is B&B in the main house and space to camp in the paddock. The paddock has picnic tables and a BBQ and there is ample parking in the yard. The barn is 2.5 miles from the small market town of Rhayader - the gateway to the Elan Valley reservoirs, 'the Lakeland of Wales'. A wide range of activities are possible including cycling, mountain biking, fishing, pony trekking, canoeing, bird watching and walking. Perfect for celebrations and get togethers.

DETAILS

- **Open** - All year, all day access.
- **Number of beds** - 16: 2x6,1x4. Chalet: 1 double, 2 singles. B&B 3 double rooms
- **Booking** - Booking preferred (with deposit).
- **Price per night** - Bunkhouse: £18 per person, sole occupancy £260. Chalet £20pp or £80 full occupancy (4 people). B&B £50pp.
- **Public Transport** - Nearest trains at Llandrindod Wells -12 miles. Some buses from Rhayader. Taxi from Rhayader about £4. Assistance with transport available.
- **Directions** - OS Explorer 200/OS147 GR 994698. Take the A44 east bound from Rhayader town centre (clock). After 0.4 miles turn left on unclassified road signposted Abbey Cwm-hir with Beili Neuadd sign. Take 1st left after 1.5 miles. Beili Neuadd is 2nd farm on right after 0.4 miles.

CONTACT: David and Alison Parker
Tel: 01597 810211
info@beilineuadd.co.uk www.beilineuadd.co.uk
Beili Neuadd, Rhayader, Powys, LD6 5NS

MID WALES
BUNKHOUSE

Mid Wales Bunkhouse, offers affordable, warm and comfortable accommodation for individuals or groups. Set in outstanding hill country, convenient for the Elan Valley, Wye Valley, Trans Cambrian Trail, Glyndwrs Way and Cycle Routes 8 and 81. There are lots of circular walks and rides from the door and with the Cambrian mountains just to the west the whole area is ideal for walking, mountain biking, cycling, horse riding, bird watching, fishing and trekking. Grazing for horses available by arrangement. Fully equipped kitchen for self-catering or meals available if arranged in advance. Outside there is a covered veranda and garden with barbeque and pizza oven. Access to the River Marteg where otters and many bird species have been spotted. Covered cycle storage. An ideal base for DofE, scout groups etc. Camping and tipi hire also available.

              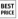

DETAILS

■ **Open** - All year, 24 hours. Arrivals after 3pm (advise if after 7pm) , depart by 11am.
■ **Number of beds** - 20
■ **Booking** - At short notice please phone to check availability. Otherwise book online, email or phone with deposit.
■ **Price per night** - £15pp, £75 for private 6-bed room. Sole use of dormitory area (sleeps 14) £170 per night, sole use of entire bunkhouse (20 people) £240 per night.
■ **Public Transport** - Trains at Llandrindod Wells/Newtown. NE coach to Llanidloes. Buses from Llandrindod to Rhayader and limited service to St. Harmon and Pant Y Dwr. We can collect from Llandrindod, Llanidloes or Newtown by arrangement.
■ **Directions** - From Rhayader take A44/A470 towards Llangurig then B4518 towards St Harmon. At the Mid Wales Inn turn right, After a mile turn right, Bunkhouse on right in half a mile. SatNav use is not advised. GR SN998750.

CONTACT: John or Steph
Tel: 01597 870081
enquiries@bunkhousemidwales.co.uk www.bunkhousemidwales.co.uk
Woodhouse Farm, St Harmon, Rhayader, LD6 5LY

MAES-Y-MOR

Maes-y-Mor offers superior accommodation at a budget price. A 4 star double room apartment and new 4 star boutique self-catering house which sleeps 7 is also available. Ideally situated near the town centre, around the corner from the beach and 5mins' walk to train and bus stations. Accommodation at the hostel is room-only. There is a large kitchen/diner with fridge-freezer, hob oven, microwave and toaster enabling guests to prepare their own food. Bedrooms have TV, tea/coffee making facilities and beds of a superior quality to ensure a good night's sleep. Free WiFi internet and towels are provided. There is a car parking area at rear and secure shed for bikes. Aberystwyth is an ideal base for exploring Wales. Visit Devil's Bridge with its dramatic waterfalls, the Vale of Rheidol narrow gauge railway, the National Library of Wales, the castle and the harbour. Aberystwyth is a university town with plenty of night life. Personal and helpful service. Croeso Cymraeg Cynnes i bawb / A warm Welsh welcome to all!

DETAILS

- **Open** - All year, 8am to 10pm.
- **Number of beds** - 19 : 7 x 2 (twin), 1 x 2 (double), 1 x 3 (family en-suite)
- **Booking** - Booking advisable.
- **Price per night** - Twin and double rooms from £50. Single room from £30. Discount for larger groups.
- **Public Transport** - Bus and train stations are within approximately 400 mts.
- **Directions** - From bus and train stations follow Terrace Road in a straight line towards beach. Turn right at Tourist Board shop, then Maes-y-Mor is about 30 mts along, next to the cinema.

CONTACT: Mererid or Alaw
Tel: 01970 639270 or 07966 502715
maesymor@hotmail.co.uk www.maesymor.co.uk
25 Bath Street, Aberystwyth, Ceredigion, SY23 2NN

PLAS DOLAU
COUNTRY HOUSE HOSTEL

Plas Dolau is set in 25 acres of quiet countryside just 3 miles from the popular coastal town of Aberystwyth. Ideal for exploring West Wales, walking, cycling, riding, fishing and golf etc. The holiday centre includes a warm country mansion (WTB 4 star hostel) with mainly dormitory style accommodation and an adjoining Scandinavian style farmhouse (WTB 3 star guest house). Plas Dolau includes meeting rooms, dining rooms, games room, outdoor areas and walks. The centre can accommodate groups of up to 45 people. Various options for accommodation, provision of food, cooking facilities, etc are available. Ideally suited for youth groups, field courses, retreats, house parties and many other groups or individuals. WiFi available to all from the guest house. Please feel free to phone to discuss your requirements.

DETAILS

- **Open** - All year, 24 hours.
- **Number of beds** - 45: + cots etc. Plus 16 in farmhouse.
- **Booking** - Recommended.
- **Price per night** - From £20 (including basic breakfast) to £35 (private room, en suite with full breakfast). From £650 per night for the whole mansion
- **Public Transport** - Nearest train station is in Aberystwyth. Taxi from the station will cost £5-6. National Express coaches and local buses (525 and 526) will set down at the end of the hostel drive.
- **Directions** - GR 623 813, OS map 135. On the A44, 3 miles from Aberystwyth, 1 mile from Llanbadarn railway bridge, 0.6 miles from turning to Bow Street. Sign on roadside says 'Y Gelli', B+B. Reception in 'Y Gelli'.

CONTACT: Pat Twigg
Tel: 01970 617834
enquiry@plasdolau.co.uk www.plasdolau.co.uk
Lovesgrove, Aberystwyth, Ceredigion, SY23 3HP

TOAD HALL
HOSTEL

Toad Hall is a family owned hostel in the Dovey Estuary close to Snowdonia. It is close to the centre of the lively town of Machynlleth, which has an alternative feel and an annual comedy festival. NCN Cycle route 8 and Glyndwrs Way route pass through Machynlleth. Cader Idris mountain is 6 miles away. Toad Hall Hostel has a four bed-roomed self contained accommodation unit above the family home. There is a mixture of double, twin and bunk beds and bedding is supplied for a small cost. The small self catering kitchen has a table seating 4 and there is a basic shower room with an antique toilet. There is a large games room with seating around an open fire which is available until 9pm at night. The hostel is a centrally heated older building providing simple accommodation. There is a flat garden for camping or bike/canoe storage and a workshop for bike repairs. Under 18s and well behaved dogs welcome by agreement. Guests must book in advance.

DETAILS

■ **Open** - Not always open, please phone to find out and always pre-book. Please vacate rooms from 12 -3 pm for cleaning. No arrivals after 11pm.
■ **Number of beds** - 10: 1x4 (family), 1x2 (twin), 1x2 (dbl), 1x2
■ **Booking** - Advance booking necessary - phone on the day if necessary. Payment in advance. Email is a good way to book as the phone is not always manned.
■ **Price per night** - £16 pp + £2 per stay for bedding. Reductions for groups.
■ **Public Transport** - 200m to train station (services to the Midlands, North Wales and Aberystwyth). 100m to Lloyds coaches depot and local bus stop
■ **Directions** - Situated behind the Texaco filling station directly opposite the railway station turning. Go into the petrol station car park, the hostel is directly behind.

CONTACT: Will
Tel: 01654 700597 Mob: 07807 849216 or 07866 362507
willcoyn@hotmail.com
Toad Hall, Doll St, Machynlleth, Powys, SY20 8BH

BRAICH GOCH
BUNKHOUSE & INN

The Braich Goch is a 16th century coaching inn situated 3 miles from Cadair Idris. There are stunning views of the Dulas Valley and Dyfi Forest. The Braich has been specifically set up with outdoor enthusiasts in mind. Facilities include drying room, secure bike storage and large well equipped self-catering kitchen. There are 6 bedrooms, 4 en suite and a further two bathrooms. WiFi. See a 360 degree virtual tour on our website. The location is ideal for walking, mountain biking, cycling, climbing and canoeing at all levels as well as bird watching or simply chilling out. The Cli-machx Trail & Dyfi Forest mountain bike trails are on the doorstep. The Braich is also a pub with pool table, darts and other games to keep you entertained in the evening! In the area are King Arthur's Labyrinth and Corris Craft Centre, Centre for Alternative Technology, Coed-y-Brenin Forest Park, Nant yr Arian and the coast. Wales Tourist Board 4 stars. Walkers & Cyclists Welcome Awards.

DETAILS

- **Open** - All year, all hours by arrangement.
- **Number of beds** - 26: 5 x 4, 1 x 6
- **Booking** - Essential for groups. 20% deposit, balance 4 weeks before arrival.
- **Price per night** - Sole occupancy (26 beds) 2 or more nights, £468pn. Sole occupancy 1 night, £494. Small group/individuals 2 or more nights, £18.50 pppn. Small group/individuals 1 night, £19 pp.
- **Public Transport** - Nearest train station to Corris is Machynlleth. Bus stop outside the 'Braich Goch' Inn. Taxis can be hired from Machynlleth.
- **Directions** - GR 754 075 On A487 between Machynlleth and Dolgellau at Corris turning. 2.5 miles north of Centre for Alternative Technology.

CONTACT: Ann or Andy
Tel: 01654 761229 Mobile: 07881 626734
annbottrill123@btconnect.com www.braichgoch.co.uk
Corris, Machynlleth, Powys, SY20 9RD

CORRIS
HOSTEL

Perfect for group activity and family gatherings, Corris Hostel offers a very special atmosphere that disengages the stresses of the outside world. The award winning hostel is renowned as a spiritual haven with its caring, easy going atmosphere, friendly staff, meditation areas, cosy wood fires and collection of inspiring books, games and artefacts.

Outdoors the terraced landscaped gardens provide a serene, inspirational environment for even the largest groups. An added bonus are the barbecue and camp fire areas. Nestled in the foothills of Cadair Idris, the hostel enjoys splendid views over the Dyfi Valley in the Snowdonia National Park. Down river are the Dyfi Biosphere nature reserves and miles of golden beaches at Aberdyfi, while the lofty Cadair Idris nestles in the next valley. Close by is the Centre for Alternative Technology and a range of environmental activities.

DETAILS

- **Open** - All year, all day access.
- **Number of beds** - 42/44
- **Booking** - Phone to check.
- **Price per night** - Adult £16 child £13. Breakfast £4.25. Private rooms extra.
- **Public Transport** - Transport: Buses 30, T2, 34 and X28 pass Machynlleth train station on the Cambrian Coast line with connection to Aberystwyth and Birmingham.
- **Directions** - GR 753 080. We are in the mountain village of Corris 6 miles north of Machynlleth. At Braich Goch turn off A487 into Corris. At Slaters Arms pub turn left, hostel is 150m uphill just beyond a small private car park. Guests' cars can be parked in private car park.

CONTACT: Michael or Debbie or Jackie
Tel: 01654 761686
mail@corrishostel.co.uk www.corrishostel.co.uk
Old School, Corris, Machynlleth, Powys, SY20 9TQ

TY'N Y BERTH
MOUNTAIN CENTRE

Ty'n y Berth is a former school at the foot of Cadair Idris on the southern edge of the Snowdonia National Park. Surrounded by mountains, valleys and crystal clear rivers, yet only 12 miles from the coast, it's a great location for outdoor activities and family holidays. The spacious accommodation sleeps up to 46 and there is a sperate unit sleeping 8 also for hire. The main room is divided into dining and lounge areas. There is a commercial kitchen, recently renovated, with large oven, hob and microwave, plenty of toilets & showers, drying room, pay phone, lockable storage for boats & bikes and parking for 10 cars. Corris is within walking distance and has two pubs: the Slaters Arms, which does bar meals, and the Braich Goch Inn, which regularly has live music. Courses are also available in climbing, mountain walking, abseiling, gorge scrambling, mine exploration, ropes courses, orienteering, and team building. Accommodation for a further 36 is available at the Bryn Coedwig Centre (also run by Wide Horizons), four miles from Ty'n Y Berth in Aberllefenni.

DETAILS

- **Open** - All year, all day.
- **Number of beds** - 46: 2x8, 4x6, 2x2, 2x1 plus Rugog: 8.
- **Booking** - Book by phone/fax or email.
- **Price per night** - £360+vat, sole use self catering. Rugog unit £110+vat.
- **Public Transport** - Trains run from London to Machynlleth with a change at Birmingham New Street.
- **Directions** - On entering Corris Uchaf from north on A487 you will enter a 30 mph speed limit. Ty'n y Berth is the old school on the right, just inside the 30mph signs.

CONTACT: Jane
Tel: 01654 761678
info@corris-bunkhouse.co.uk www.corris-bunkhouse.co.uk
Corris Uchaf, Machynlleth, Powys, SY20 9RH

HyB Bunkhouse is on Heol y Bont (Bridge St) in the old market town of Dolgellau, mid Wales, nestling at the foot of Cader Idris. It is centrally located above Medi gift shop, and has free parking at rear, for up to four cars. Near pubs, shops and restaurants, HyB backs onto the Mawddach trail near the river Wnion. It is 10 minutes' drive to Coed y Brenin mountain biking centre. This quirky listed building has original features such as oak floors, beams and panelling and consists of four bunk rooms, sleeping 16 in total. Each room has a mini-kitchen for basic self-catering with fridge, hob, toaster and kettle. One room is en suite and there are also two other bathrooms. Bring your own bedding or rent on request The entrance is at the rear of the building. Take a sharp first left at the corner of the public toilet block on the Marian car park, and sharp second right through double wooden gate into private car park. The key pad entry code is on single yellow door where there is 24 hour access. Strictly no stag parties...

DETAILS

- **Open** - Closed Xmas and New Year. Book before 4.30 pm, key pad entry code.
- **Number of beds** - 16: 4 x4.
- **Booking** - Please phone or email before 4.30pm.
- **Price per night** - £20 per person. Limited bedding sets available @£5.
- **Public Transport** - Buses stop at Eldon square (1 minute walk) and link with train stations at Machynlleth and Barmouth for connections to Midlands and London.
- **Directions** - HyB is above Medi - the last shop before the main bridge on the one way system out of Eldon square. By car turn into Y Marian car park and take a sharp left behind the public loos into HyB car park through the double wooden gates.

CONTACT: Nia
Tel: 01341 421755
post@medi-gifts.com www.medi-gifts.com
2-3 Heol y Bont (Bridge St), Dolgellau, Gwynedd, LL40 1AU

BUNKORAMA

Some places you will stay at for a short while, but they will stay with you for ever. The Bunkorama at Gwastad Agnes is such a place. This converted stone stable provides comfortable and well equipped accommodation for cyclists, backpackers, climbers and explorers. At the end of a day's expedition you can sit at the Bunkorama, cuppa in your hands and trace your route across from Cader Idris. You can gaze out across Cardigan Bay and wonder why you had never discovered Gwastad Agnes before. You certainly won't forget it.

The Bunkorama provides accommodation for individuals or groups in Snowdonia close to the Cambrian Way, Cycle route 8 and the Ardudwy Way.

For mountain goats the rock climbing of the Barmouth Slabs is a 5 minute walk and for mountain bikers you are only 20 minutes by car to Coed y Brenin, the UK's first dedicated mountain bike centre.

DETAILS

- **Open** - all year round.
- **Number of beds** - 2 rooms each sleeping 4. Plus sofa bed in lounge
- **Booking** - phone, email, post or on site
- **Price per night** - £15 pp + £5 per stay if bedding needed
- **Public Transport** - Bus and train to Barmouth approx 40 mins' walk to hostel.
- **Directions** - From the A496 out of Barmouth turn left up Panorama Road and after approximately 1 mile turn sharp left after small car park on right. The hostel is second entrance on left after about 200 metres

CONTACT: Graham
Tel: 01341 281134 or 07738467196
thebunkorama@gmail.com www.bunkorama.co.uk
Gwastad Agnes Off Panorama Road, Barmouth, Gwynedd, LL42 1DX

The newly refurbished and well equipped bunkhouse at Y Dolydd Llanfyllin Workhouse offers a unique holiday experience. Stay in one of the last remaining Victorian Workhouses still open to the public, which is now a developing community centre and venue for the arts, music, creativity and education, with a strong commitment to green hub principles. Y Dolydd is owned, managed and supported by the Llanfyllin Dolydd Building Preservation Trust (registered charity no.1091097) and is available all year round for individuals, families or groups, Y Dolydd is the perfect base for your holiday and is also available for exclusive hire for your private party or function. Close to the Berwyn Mountains National Nature Reserve, it has access to a range of outdoor and adventure activities. Nearby attractions include Pistyll Rhaeadr waterfall, the tallest single drop waterfall in the UK and Lake Vyrnwy, a hidden gem with array of walks to suit all abilities, cycle hire, water sports, sculpture park, tea rooms.

DETAILS

- **Open** - All year.
- **Number of beds** - 24: 1x4, 1x8, 1x12
- **Booking** - via phone, email or website
- **Price per night** - £15 including linen/duvets/pillows. Groups discounts may apply.
- **Public Transport** - Nearest trains at Shrewsbury & Welshpool. Bus connections to Welshpool. The Tanat Valley Bus service runs a request stop service from Welshpool which will drop at the hostel gate.
- **Directions** - Do not use Satnav. Llanfyllin is clearly sign posted from the A490 Oswestry to Welshpool. The Workhouse is the large Victorian building on the right just before you enter town.

CONTACT: Tree Marshall
Tel: 07534 354 082
bunkhouse@the-workhouse.com www.the-workhouse.org.uk/
Y Dolydd, Workhouse, Llanfyllin, SY22 5LD

BALA
BACKPACKERS

For outdoor adventures within the Snowdonia National Park, Bala Backpackers offers good value 'hostel-style' accommodation, including; 30+comfy SINGLE BEDS in bedrooms of 3,4 or 5, with two washrooms of cubicle-showers, wet-room, 3 private TWIN ROOMS and 3 new EN SUITES. The 19th century character buildings are located in a quiet, sunny, chapel square, in the bustling market town of Bala, mid North Wales. It is clean, safe and nice for the price, with a fully-fitted self-catering guest kitchen. Catering is available on demand, and in a BRAND NEW ECO-Caffé opposite. Bala boasts a five-mile-long lake, a white-water river for raft rides, and nestles beneath three 900 metre peaks. The lakeside, river and leisure pursuits are 5 mins' walk away. Plan your activities or just soak up the atmosphere in town, where new Tourism Attractions include Mary Jones World, Gorwellion Gardens, Lottery Play Park and the Sailing Club.

DETAILS

- **Open** - All year by arrangement, 8.30-20.30. Front door lock 00.30 – 6.00am.
- **Number of beds** - 45: 2x3, 3x4, 3x5 + 3 twin rooms + 3 en suites
- **Booking** - On-line or by answerphone or email.
- **Price per night** - 1 night £21, 2 nights £39, 3 nights £49, weekly £89. Twin room: £49 or en suites from £59 . Double holiday-let: £220/4 nights. Hostel sheet-bag hire £3/week or bring sheets/sack & pillowcase .
- **Public Transport** - Trains: Wrexham (30 miles) or Barmouth (30miles). Bus no 94 every 2 hours daily from Wrexham and Barmouth.
- **Directions** - GR 926 358. Bala is on A494. Turn in the middle of Bala High Street, opposite the White Lion Royal Hotel, down Tegid Street to see HOSTEL Sign. Unload outside Hostel, but park round corner, in FREE overnight pay & display.

CONTACT: Stella Welch
Tel: 01678 521700
info@Bala-Backpackers.co.uk www.Bala-Backpackers.co.uk
32 Tegid Street, Bala, LL23 7EL

BALA
BUNK HOUSE

The bunkhouse is a converted 200-year-old Welsh stone building, set back from the road in over an acre of picturesque grounds with private parking.

Modernised to provide accommodation for outdoor activity groups, it is light, airy and comfortable with storage heating. There is a large lounge/dining area and bunk rooms for 2, 4 and 8 plus annexe for 6. Separate ladies' and gentlemen's toilets have washing areas and hot showers. Fully equipped self-catering kitchen. Also there is a self-contained bunkroom sleeping 6, with small kitchenette, shower and toilet/washing area which is ideal for smaller groups and families. Sheets, pillows & pillowcases are provided - bring a sleeping bag.

There is a splendid view of the Berwyn Hills; together with the Aran and Arenig hills they provide superb walking. Bala Lake and the National White Water Centre are brilliant for water sports. Good pubs, restaurants and shops in Bala.

DETAILS

- **Open** - All year no restrictions.
- **Number of beds** - 26 : 1x2, 1x4, 1x6, 1x8, 1x6 self-contained
- **Booking** - Book if possible, ring or write with 20% deposit. Weekends are busy.
- **Price per night** - Single night £16 pp, two or more nights £15 pp per night.
- **Public Transport** - Trains at Wrexham (30 miles). National Express at Corwen (10 miles). Local buses call at Bala (1.6 miles from hostel). Call hostel for a taxi.
- **Directions** - GR 950 372. From England take M6, M54, A5 through Llangollen then A494 for Bala. We are on the A494 1.5 miles before Bala.

CONTACT: Guy and Jane Williams
Tel: 01678 520738
thehappyunion@btinternet.com www.balabunkhouse.co.uk
Tomen Y Castell, Llanfor, Bala, Gwynedd, LL23 7HD

NANTYR
OUTDOOR EDUCATION CENTRE WALES

Nantyr OEC has excellent bunk house facilities with 22 beds, toilets and showers, fully equipped self-catering kitchen and dining area, activity room/ lounge including TV/DVD, drying room & a small camping area with fire pit and separate toilets and showers. The centre is situated above the beautiful Ceiriog valley, 3 miles from Glyn Ceiriog and 6 miles from Llangollen and the River Dee. Located at the foot of the Berwyn Mountains, it is ideally positioned to utilise the local area's many wonderful outdoor locations and resources. Nantyr is committed to providing high quality, challenging outdoor educational opportunities for all, in a safe and enjoyable learning environment. The centre is licensed to provide a wide variety of outdoor activities including: hill walking and rock climbing, kayaking, canoeing, gorge scrambling, improvised rafting, bushcraft and mountain biking (all activities are at an extra cost).

           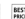

DETAILS

- **Open** - All year, all day.
- **Number of beds** - 20 - 2x8, plus 2x2
- **Booking** - Booking essential by email or phone
- **Price per night** - £200 sole use of centre. Small groups please contact for rates.
- **Public Transport** - Public transport to Glyn Ceiriog (3.5 miles) but not to Nantyr
- **Directions** - Sat-Nav directions are inaccurate please use the following: B4500 from Chirk to Glyn Ceiriog; at Glyn Ceriog roundabout, go straight on, signposted Llanarmon DC. After approx 0.2 miles take the right hand fork in the road signposted Nantyr. After 3 miles, the road begins to slope down hill. Nantyr OEC is at the bottom of the hill, on the right hand side, opposite a phone box and a Chapel.

CONTACT:
Tel: 01691 712833
nantyr@wrexham.gov.uk   www.nantyr.co.uk
Nantyr Outdoor Education Centre, Nantyr,nr Glyn Ceiriog,Wrexham LL207DL

LLANGOLLEN
HOSTEL

Llangollen Hostel offers clean and comfortable twin and double rooms, en suite family rooms, private four-bed and six-bed en suite rooms, and a great value six-bed dorm. There is a fully-fitted kitchen and all prices include a complimentary breakfast. You can enjoy your meals in the dining room, then relax in the spacious lounge by the log fire. We have a book exchange, free WiFi, plenty of games, laundry facilities, a drying room, and bicycle/canoe storage. Perfect location for walking, climbing, canoeing and mountain biking in the Vale of Llangollen. Families will love visiting the steam railway, horse drawn canal boats and Pontcysyllte Aqueduct - a World Heritage Site. The town offers a great choice of restaurants/pubs and is home to a fringe music and arts festival and the International Eisteddfod. Llandegla, Chester, Wrexham and Offa's Dyke Path are all nearby. You are assured of a happy and comfortable stay, freedom to come and go as you please, and above all, a warm welcome.

DETAILS

- **Open** - All year, all day.
- **Number of beds** - 32.
- **Booking** - Internet, email or phone.
- **Price per night** - From £18pp dorm. £20pp for a private 3,4,5 or 6 bed room. £45 Twin/Double or £50 en suite. Family of 4 £60, £10 per extra child. Inc light breakfast.
- **Public Transport** - Daily National Express from London. Trains Ruabon (5 miles). Buses all day.
- **Directions** - From the A5 heading west the hostel is located 50 yards past the main set of traffic lights on the right. Parking is at the rear of the hostel on Market Street – at the main traffic lights, turn right then first left.

CONTACT: Arlo Dennis
Tel: 01978 861773
info@llangollenhostel.co.uk   www.llangollenhostel.co.uk
Berwyn Street, Llangollen, LL20 8NB

TYDDYN
BYCHAN

Tyddyn Bychan is an 18th century traditional Welsh farmhouse and barns set in private grounds and surrounded on all sides by farmland. Situated in an excellent central location, for mountain biking, road cycling, canoeing, walking, climbing, fishing and numerous watersports including whitewater rafting.

The main bunkhouse sleeps 18 in two en suite rooms. All the bunks are handmade and of a very high standard. The smaller bunkhouse sleeps 9 in two en suite rooms and has its own kitchen, conservatory and lounge. All bedding is included.

Delicious homemade food is available if booked in advance. The bunkhouses are ideal for self-catering with very well equipped kitchen/dining rooms. There is a good parking area well away from the road.

DETAILS

■ **Open** - All year, all day.
■ **Number of beds** - 28: 1x10; 1x8; 1x6; 1x3
■ **Booking** - Booking is essential
■ **Price per night** - £15 pp including bedding.
■ **Public Transport** - Nearest train station is at Betws-y-Coed. Nearest National Express service at Llandudno. Phone 01492 575412 for details.
■ **Directions** - GR 931 504. Turn off A5 at Cerrigydrudion. Take B4501 out of village for Llyn Brenig, take the turning on left for Cefn Brith. After about 2 miles you will see a phone box on left, chapel on right and the road widens for a layby. The gate for Tyddyn is on the left directly opposite junction on the right.

CONTACT: Lynda
Tel: 01490 420680 Mob: 07523 995741
lynda@tyddynbychan.co.uk www.tyddynbychan.co.uk
Cefn Brith, Cerrigydrudion, Conwy, LL21 9TS

HENDRE ISAF
BASECAMP

377

WALES

This converted Grade II listed stone farm building offers the perfect base for enjoying the Snowdonia National Park. In a rural setting on the 8,000 hectares Ysbyty Estate it has easy access to the A5 and is only six miles from Betws-y-Coed. The 400 year old building offers group accommodation with lots of character, substantial dining and social space and a large private car park. The large enclosed garden at the rear of the bunkhouse has picnic benches and a barbecue area. There is excellent access to outdoor activities in the surrounding area including walks from the door of the bunkhouse so you can forget your car for a few days. Local attractions include the Tree Top Adventure Course at Betws-y-Coed, Zip World at Penrhyn Quarry, Bethesda, Zip World and Bounce Below at Llechwedd Slate Caverns, Blaenau Ffestiniog, the Plas y Brenin National Mountain Centre at Capel Curig, shops, leisure centre, swimming pool at Llanrwst and the seaside resort of Llandudno. No pets.

DETAILS

- **Open** - All year, 24 hours.
- **Number of beds** - 18: 2 x dormitories + 1x1 single bedroom.
- **Booking** - Early booking recommended (March to October is very busy).
- **Price per night** - Short breaks: 2 nights from £495. 7 nights from £1,295.
- **Public Transport** - Trains at Betws-y-Coed (6 miles), Llandudno Junction (20 miles) and Llanrwst (10 miles); National Express bus station at Llandudno. Some local buses to Betws-y-Coed, but we advise bringing your own transport.
- **Directions** - Situated 6 miles SE of Betws-y-Coed near the junction of the A5 and the B4407 (signposted Ysbyty Ifan and Ffestiniog). GR855511 (OS sheet 116).

CONTACT: National Trust Cottages Group Accommodation Team
Tel: 0344 3351296
group.accom@nationaltrust.org.uk www.nationaltrustholidays.org.uk
National Trust Ysbyty Estate Office, Dinas, Betws-y-Coed, Conwy, LL24 0HF

TREKS
BUNKHOUSE

Treks Bunkhouse, 900 feet above sea level, is high in the mountains near the Welsh-speaking village of Blaenau Ffestiniog. It is ideal for people who enjoy the rugged beauty of Snowdonia and a short airy walk to the pub of an evening. The bunkhouse is a modern conversion of a golf club house and is set in a wild area on the outskirts of the village. Opened in November 2015 the bunkhouse provides year round accommodation for individuals and groups. There is a self catering kitchen and five bedrooms sleeping between 1 and 6 people, ideal for groups, families or groups of families. The beds are fully made up with sheet and duvets and towels are available to hire for a small charge. The is a large lock up ideal for canoes and bikes. There are many tourist attractions available within a short drive: Llechwedd Slate Caverns, Bounce Bellow, Zipp World Titan, Antur Stiniog, Coed y Brenin Mountain Bike Centre, Portmeirion Italian Village, Bala White Water Rafting and Harlech Castle.

DETAILS

- **Open** - All Year, check in 3.30pm-6.30pm,
- **Number of beds** - 16: 1x6, 1x4, 1x3, 1x2, 1x1
- **Booking** - Online, by phone or email.
- **Price per night** - £18 per person.
- **Public Transport** - Express Motors Bus 35 from Dolgellau (4 times a day), bus 1B from Porthmadog (hourly). Trains from Llandudno Juction and Ffestiniog Railway narrow gauge trains from Porthmadog. Station/buses 20 mins walk from bunkhouse.
- **Directions** - Two thirds of a mile from the centre of Ffestiniog on the B4391 towards Bala. Look for a cattle grid and small lane on the right with catle gird.

CONTACT: Dyfed
Tel: 07796 172 318
treksbunkhouse@gmail.com www.treksbunkhouse.co.uk
Y Cefn, Ffestiniog, Gwynedd, LL41 4PS

Maentwrog bunkhouse is a newly renovated 200 year old cowshed situated on a working beef and sheep farm.

It has a fully equipped kitchen, underfloor heating, TV/DVD player, BBQ area, laundry facilities, power washer and lockup available for bikes.

Local activities range from hill walking (Moelwyn and Cnicht are 10 minutes away), white water rafting, Coed y Brenin cycling centre, Blaenau Ffestiniog down hill cycle track, RopeWorks, canyoning, Ffestiniog narrow gauge railway and several beautiful beaches are all within 15 to 20 minutes' drive as well as the Welsh costal path passing at the end of the lane.

Please contact direct for any other information

DETAILS

- **Open** - All Year.
- **Number of beds** - 4
- **Booking** - booking essential
- **Price per night** - £18 pppn bring sleeping bags or hire bed linen @£3 pp
- **Public Transport** - Public bus to bottom of lane 400m walk. Arriva Wales train to Penrhyndeudraeth
- **Directions** - Turn into Maentwrog village then follow the A496 towards Harlech for 1 mile with lay-by on right, take immediate left up small lane for 400m, first farmhouse on right

CONTACT: Mrs Eurliw M Jones
Tel: 01766590231
emj2@hotmail.co.uk www.bunkhousesnowdonia.com
Felen Rhyd Fach, Maentwrog, Blaenau Ffestiniog, Gwynedd, LL41 4HY

LLEDR HOUSE

Lledr House is nestled in the heart of Snowdonia National Park. A former YHA, this newly refurbished hostel is delightfully situated in its own woodlands in the beautiful Lledr Valley just outside the picturesque village of Dolwyddelan. Guests come back year after year, having delighted in the huge improvements, including luxury memory foam mattresses, modern bathrooms, well equipped kitchen, free WiFi and an extended car park also suitable for motorbikes. Whether you are a lone traveller, large family, DofE, college or a group of friends, Lledr House offers clean, cheap, comfortable accommodation. All bedding is provided in private single, twin and family rooms plus one nine-bed dorm. There is also a luxury self-contained cedar log cabin, sleeping 5, in the grounds. Enjoy the riverside garden, patio and BBQ area. Woodland walks and cycle trails surround the hostel. Views of Moel Siabod and surrounded by forest. Pub and Spar shop within walking distance. Betws-y-Coed, stunning Llyn Elsi and Tree Tops High Rope course just 4 miles away.

DETAILS

- **Open** - All year (except Christmas week), check in from 5pm till 10.30pm.
- **Number of beds** - 31: 1x9, 2x4,1x6, 3x2, 2x1.
- **Booking** - Book by phone/email with credit card. First night's deposit for groups.
- **Price per night** - From £18pp Sole use £550 +£50 at bank hol. Cabin from £100.
- **Public Transport** - Pont-y-Pant station on the Conwy Valley Line is ¾ mile away.
- **Directions** - On the A5 from Llangollen to Bangor turn left just before Betws-y-Coed onto the A470 (signed Dolgellau). The hostel is 4 miles on right side of road. Walking from Pont-y-Pant station, turn left and left again after stone road bridge.

CONTACT: Brian or Melanie Quilter
Tel: 01690 750202 Mobile: 07915 397705 or 07915 397660
Lledrhouse@aol.com www.ukyh.com
Pont-y-Pant, Dolwyddelan, North Wales, LL25 0DQ

PLAS CURIG
HOSTEL

This five star hostel has been stylishly refurbished since its previous existence as Capel Curig YHA and provides luxurious comfort in stunning surroundings. With views of Snowdon, the hostel is in the village of Capel Curig, the heart of Snowdonia National Park, and only 10 mins' drive from the Snowdon Horseshoe path. Plas Curig is the only five star hostel in Wales and welcomes individuals, couples, families and groups. The dorm rooms sleep from 4 to 8 people in bunks and family rooms, doubles and twins are also available. Each bunk has a comfy mattress, curtains for privacy, light, socket and is ready made with hypo-allergenic bedding. There is well equipped self-catering kitchen and dining facilities to sit 40 people. The TV room, lobby, lounge and library have free WiFi and there are private shower rooms with WC and basins. There is a drying room, outside storage for bikes/canoes and car parking. Well behaved dogs welcome in private rooms. Pubs and cafés close by. Snowdonia has it all!.

DETAILS

- **Open** - All year. Check in between 5-10pm.
- **Number of beds** - 59: 1x8, 2x6, 4x4, 1x 4/5, 2x 3/4, 2x 2/3,1xdouble, 1xtwin
- **Booking** - Book online with card.
- **Price per night** - Dorms from £22.50. Family rooms from £90 per room. Doubles & twins from £50 per room. Dogs £5. Exclusive hire of hostel from £1000 per night.
- **Public Transport** - Trains at Betws-y-Coed (5 miles). Buses: Snowdon Sherpa 97A Portmadog to Betws-y-coed, S2 Pen-y-Pass to Betws-y-Coed and S6 from Bethesda (with connections to Bangor) all run past the hostel.
- **Directions** - On the A5 in the centre of Capel Curig village.

CONTACT:
Tel: 01690 720 225
info@snowdoniahostel.co.uk www.snowdoniahostel.co.uk
Plas Curig, Capel Curig,Betws-y-Coed,North Wales, LL24 0EL

CABAN CYSGU
GERLAN BUNKHOUSE

Caban Cysgu offers comfortable, purpose-built accommodation at the foot of the Carneddau in the Welsh-speaking village of Gerlan. A warm welcome is guaranteed at this community run bunkhouse. An ideal location for walking in Snowdonia, providing an great base for the 'Fourteen 3000ft Peaks' long-distance challenge. For the adrenalin junky, it's just a 5 minute drive to Zip World; the longest and fastest zip line in Europe, "The Nearest Thing to Flying!!" Brilliantly located for mountain biking with plenty of off road trails nearby. And for road cyclists the bunkhouse is ideal for exploring Snowdonia, whilst for leisurely rides the hostel is within a mile of Sustrans route 'Lôn Las Ogwen'. Rock-climbing at Idwal is close at hand, as well as Ysgolion Duon for the dedicated winter climbers. The nearby Afon Ogwen provides a popular venue for canoeists. For more leisurely pursuits, try visiting Coed Meurig, Penrhyn Castle or the Greenwood Centre. Shops, pubs and cafés in Bethesda are within walking distance.

DETAILS

- **Open** - All year all day.
- **Number of beds** - 16 : 1x5, 1x2, 1x1, 1x8
- **Booking** - Not essential, but recommended (with 20% non-returnable deposit).
- **Price per night** - From £14 - £16
- **Public Transport** - Bangor train station is 6 miles. Catch a bus from Bangor bus station to Gerlan (66), or Bethesda (fare £1.40). Taxi from Bangor approx. £15.
- **Directions** - GR 632665. A5 southbound, turn left in Bethesda centre just before Spar. Bear right, up hill over 2 cross-roads. Hostel is 300m at the old school on left.

CONTACT: Dewi Emyln, Manager
Tel: 01248 605573   Mob: 07464676753
dewi@cabancysgu-gerlan.co.uk www.cabancysgu-gerlan.co.uk
Ffordd Gerlan, Gerlan, Bethesda, Bangor, LL57 3ST

CONWY VALLEY
BACKPACKERS BARN

Conwy Valley Backpackers is situated on a peaceful working farm with organic status in the heart of the beautiful Conwy Valley, with excellent access to Snowdonia. Centrally heated with fully equipped self-catering kitchen, log fires, hot showers and a fire alarm system. There are three separate dorms sleeping 4, 6 and 10, two of which have their own toilet facility. Secure bike/canoe storage, grazing for horses and tourist information are available. Beside the barn is a small stream and guests may picnic and BBQ on the river bank. An ideal space for restoration, relaxation and retreat. Bring a sleeping bag or hire bed linen (£3). Continental breakfast (£3.50) and packed lunch (£5) are available by arrangement. Local activities range from fishing and hiking to white water rafting and mountain biking. Surf Snowdonia is within walking distance and Zip World a short drive away. There are great pubs and eating places within walking distance. Groups and individuals are welcome. Sorry - no dogs.

DETAILS

- **Open** - All year, all day.
- **Number of beds** - 20: 1 x 4; 1 x 6; 1 x 10.
- **Booking** - Not essential but recommended
- **Price per night** - From £20pp. Sole use from £250. £3pp bed linen hire.
- **Public Transport** - Train stations and coaches at Llandudno Junction and Conwy. Local bus 19 or 19a runs every 20 minutes from Conwy and Llandudno Junction, ask driver to drop you at Pyllau Gloewon farm gate.
- **Directions** - GR 769 697. Six miles south of Conwy on the B5106, look for Backpackers sign just before entering Tal-y-Bont.

CONTACT: Claudia or Helen
Tel: 01492 660504
claudia.bryan@btconnect.com www.conwyvalleybarn.com
Pyllau Gloewon Farm, Tal-y-Bont, Conwy, Gwynedd, LL32 8YX

LLANDUDNO
HOSTEL

James and Melissa would like to invite you to their charming Victorian 4 star boutique hostel. We are a friendly hostel where individuals, families and groups (including schools) are welcome all year. Some of the guests' comments: "friendliest hostel we've ever stayed in", "Wow isn't it clean", "these bathrooms are fabulous, as good as any hotel". Come and try us, we love to meet new people and look forward to getting to know you. Set in the heart of the Victorian seaside resort town of Llandudno, an ideal place to shop or explore the many and varied local attractions. Excellent blue flag beaches, dry slope skiing, toboggan run, ten pin bowling, bronze age copper mine, traditional pier and many museums, fishing trips, etc. Llandudno is within easy travelling distance of Snowdon, Bodnant Gardens and local castles. We are able to book local attractions for groups and secure some discounts.

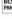

DETAILS

- **Open** - All year (telephone in winter prior to arrival). All day.
- **Number of beds** - 46: 2x8, 2x6, 4x2, 1x4, 1 x family.
- **Booking** - Essential April to July.
- **Price per night** - From £21 per person, £51 per private twin room, £55 per private twin en suite. Group and family rates on request. Special offers autumn /winter.
- **Public Transport** - Trains at Llandudno. Turn right as you exit station, cross road, turn left down Vaughan Street (towards the beach), left into Charlton Street.
- **Directions** - From the A55 take A470 and follow signs to Llandudno town centre, straight through all roundabouts, after Asda turn 3rd left into Vaughan Street (signed train station), then 1st right into Charlton Street. Hostel is No 14.

CONTACT: James
Tel: 01492 877430
info@llandudnohostel.co.uk www.llandudnohostel.co.uk
14 Charlton Street, Llandudno, LL30 2AA

TRINITY
HOUSE

Trinity House is located on the lower slopes of the Great Orme overlooking the magnificent bay of Llandudno and the mountains of Snowdonia in North Wales. Part of Trinity Language Centre, Trinity House specializes in providing full inclusive accommodation packages for groups of up to 50 children, young people or adults. With en suite bunk rooms, leaders/teachers rooms, family rooms, group dining facilities, games room and chill out area, the centre is ideal for school, sports or large family groups. Larger groups can book exclusive use of the centre at very competitive rates. Your hosts, Raquel and Lloyd, are experienced in welcoming young people to Llandudno and will support teachers and leader to ensure the safety, enjoyment and personal development of groups staying at the centre. The Victorian town of Llandudno is a safe and beautiful place to visit with many activities and attractions available locally.

DETAILS

- **Open** - Open all year, all day.
- **Number of beds** - 57: 8x4; 2x2; 1x3; 2xdbl + sgl; 2xdbl + bunk; 2xdbl
- **Booking** - Booking essential. Please call or email directly. Groups of 10+ only.
- **Price per night** - Min of 2 nights, B&B from 23pp, B&B+packed lunch from £25pp, Full Board from £28pp. Exclusive use B&B for 30 people: June to Sept £1800 for 2 nights plus £800 per extra night plus £20 per extra person. Oct to May £1400 for 2 nights plus £600 per extra night plus £18 per extra person. All meals £12 per person.
- **Public Transport** - Trains to Llandudno (half mile) or Llandudno Junction (3 miles). Air: Liverpool or Manchester pick up from airport/stations by arrangement.
- **Directions** - Through town centre to top of Mostyn Street. Turn right then left by Empire Hotel. First right into Hill Terrace. (No turning for large minibus or coaches).

CONTACT: Lloyd William or Raquel Perez-Williams
Tel: 01492 874592 (From Overseas +44 1492 874592) or 07960 118830
info@trinitylc.com www.trinitylc.com
Trinity Language Centre, Hill Terrace Llandudno, Conwy LL30 2LS

PLATTS FARM
BUNKHOUSE

Platt's Farm Camp-site and Bunkhouse is situated within a range of Victorian farm buildings dating back to 1858, in the charming village of Llanfairfechan. Ideally situated close to the A55, the Bunkhouse sits at the start/end of the 14 Welsh 3000 peaks walks in the Snowdonia National Park, within a 10 minute walk of the Wales coastal path and on the No.5 cycle route. There are 2 bedrooms to sleep a total of 10 people in bunk beds. The kitchen is equipped with a four ring cooker, microwave, kettle, fridge/freezer, toaster, TV, table to seat 10 and electric fire. Heating is by electric storage heaters and all heating and lighting are included in the price. Pans, crockery, cutlery, sheets and pillowcases are provided. Bring your own sleeping bags/duvets. Ample off road parking and adjacent covered area for BBQs. 11 camping pitches with covered picnic areas also available. Shops, pubs and cafés are within 5 minutes' walk.

DETAILS

- **Open** - All year, check out before 11am, check in after 2pm.
- **Number of beds** - 10
- **Booking** - Deposit required. Non refundable balance is payable 2 weeks before arrival. Most major credit or debit cards and PayPal accepted.
- **Price per night** - £15.00 per person per night. Exclusive use £150 per night.
- **Public Transport** - By train to Llanfairfechan station. Bus from Llandudno or Bangor stops right by the entrance. National cycle route No 5 passes the entrance
- **Directions** - A55 westbound Exit 15, remain on this road. The entrance to Platt's Farm is a sharp turn on the right just after the traffic lights and bus stop. A55 eastbound Exit 14 follow the road over the A55 then turn left on to Aber Road.

CONTACT: Sam Davies
Tel: 0(44)1248680105
sam@plattsfarm.com www.plattsfarm.com
Platts Farm Bunkhouse, Aber Road, Llanfairfechan, Conwy, LL33 0HL

TOTTERS

Totters is situated in the heart of the historic castle town of Caernarfon. Sheltered by the castle wall, it is only 30 metres from the shores of the Menai Straits and enjoys some fantastic sunsets. The town not only offers the visitor a huge selection of pubs and restaurants to choose from, but also acts as the perfect base for trips into the Snowdonia National Park. There is very good public transport in and out of the National Park. The hostel is a 200-year-old, five floored town house, which is fully heated and with all the comforts of home. Facilities include a common room with TV and games, book exchange, dining room and a secure left luggage facility. There are five bedrooms which sleep either 4 or 6 and can be arranged as mixed or single sex dorms and the Penthouse room, a huge double en suite room with views over the Straits, this can be a double or a family room. Across the road there is a self-catering town house which sleeps 6. See website for more details of all our accommodation.

DETAILS

- **Open** - All year, all day access. Book in by 10pm.
- **Number of beds** - 28 : 3 x 6, 2 x 4, 1 x 2 (en suite), 1 x 2 (twin)
- **Booking** - Booking is essential for groups in June, July, August and September.
- **Price per night** - £18.50pp in a dorm. £50 for a double/twin en suite. £44 for a twin. Discounts for groups.
- **Public Transport** - Bangor train station is 9 miles from the hostel. Catch a bus from outside the station to Caernarfon. National Express coaches drop off in Caernarfon 200m from the hostel.
- **Directions** - Coming by road: follow signs for town centre, turn right 200m after the big Celtic Royal hotel, keep going and Totters is the last house on the left.

CONTACT: Bob/Henryette
Tel: 01286 672963 Mob: 07979 830470
totters.hostel@googlemail.com www.totters.co.uk
Plas Porth Yr Aur, 2 High Street, Caernarfon, Gwynedd, LL55 1RN

The Arete Outdoor Centre in Snowdonia National Park, offers excellent access to the stunning coastline, meandering rivers, awesome mountains and large lakes of North Wales and Anglesey. With comfortable, affordable, bunkhouse style accommodation and large kitchens for easy catering this is a great base for groups of friends or family. The area is passionate about its language, music and history and is rich with magnificent castles, steam railways, heritage and festivals, so there's plenty to do. The team are happy to help with advice on how best to spend your stay and a range of exciting outdoor activities are available through the centre's well qualified and experienced staff. Catering for up to 70 people is available. Several social rooms allow space for down-time, the games room having pool and table tennis tables. Large storage for bikes, kayaks and surfboards and individual cloakrooms for outdoor kit. Car parking available. For local eating out the Glyntwrog Inn is just 200m away.

DETAILS

- **Open** - All year, all day.
- **Number of beds** - 77 in 16 rooms can be split into two blocks of 24 and 53 beds.
- **Booking** - via email: info@aretecentre.co.uk or phone 01286 672136.
- **Price per night** - Catered from £30pp, self-catering from £15 pp. Sole use deals available
- **Public Transport** - Anglesey Airport. Train to Llanfairpwll or Bangor. Buses to Caernafon and local buses from Bangor and Caernarfon,
- **Directions** - Sat navs use LL55 4AP. From A55 at jct 11 follow signs to Llanberis and then Llanrug. Turn left just before the Glyntwrog pub the Centre is 200m on your right. Pickups from Bangor station can be arranged or use taxi or local bus.

CONTACT:
Tel: 01286 672136
info@aretecentre.co.uk www.aretecentre.co.uk
Arete Outdoor Education Centre, Llanrug, Caernarfon, Gwynedd, LL55 4AP

PENTRE BACH
BUNKHOUSE

Pentre Bach Bunkhouse provides dog friendly alpine style accommodation, outdoor activities and a camp-site. The Bunkhouse is heated with electric radiators and has two floors. The ground floor has tables with benches and a cooking area with gas burners, microwaves, fridge and freezer. Upstairs are alpine sleeping platforms with mattresses for 16. Drying room and toilets with washing facilities and showers, shared with the camp-site, are just across the yard. Based between Waunfawr and Betws Garmon, Pentre Bach is surrounded by the superb scenery of Moel Eilio and Mynydd Mawr and has views towards Mount Snowdon. There are great walks from the bunkhouse or take a short car journey to the Nantlle ridge and the main footpaths up Snowdon. Bach Ventures provides guided walks, kayaking, climbing, gorge-scrambling and coasteering. Large or small groups and individuals all welcome. Local pub is CAMRA Pub of the year in the area. Great beer and good food.

DETAILS

- **Open** - All year. Enquires 9am-10pm. Arrival from 4pm until late.
- **Number of beds** - 16: 1x16.
- **Booking** - One night's deposit required with balance payable before arrival. Short notice bookings accepted by phone or email with deposit/balance payable on arrival.
- **Price per night** - £12 per person (inc gas / electric / showers). Sole use bookings negotiable according to group size.
- **Public Transport** - Train station at Bangor. S4 bus from Caernarfon to Beddgelert stops at the bottom of the drive on request.
- **Directions** - GR 531 579. At Pentre Bach just south of Waunfawr on the Caernarfon to Beddgelert road (A4085). Look for Pentre Bach Bunkhouse sign.

CONTACT: Karen Neil
Tel: 01286 650643(5-10pm) or 07798733939(9-5pm)
info@bachventures.co.uk www.pentrebachbunkhouse.co.uk
Pentre Bach, Waunfawr, Caernarfon, Gwynedd, LL54 7AJ

CWM PENNANT
HOSTEL/TRAINING CENTRE

Cwm Pennant Hostel is a 56 bed independent hostel offering relaxed accommodation for individuals, families and groups. It also offers adventure activities for groups provided by Outdoor UK Ltd and catering is available to groups and individuals. The hostel is set within stunning grounds in the Snowdonia National Park and has fantastic views of the Cwm Pennant valley and Moel Hebog. It is 5 miles from Porthmadog. Cwm Pennant Hostel has a lounge, drying room, games/training room and self-catering kitchen. Home cooked food is available on request. Guests have access to complimentary tea and coffee. A range of additional facilities are available including a power washer for mountain bikes, on-site parking and secure storage for bikes, kayaks and canoes. The area is ideal for hill walking, rock climbing and canoeing.

DETAILS

- **Open** - February to December for advanced booking, 7:30-12noon; 4.30-10pm.
- **Number of beds** - 56: 4 x 4, 1 x 6, 1 x 8, 1 x 10, 1 x 16.
- **Booking** - Advance booking recommended, a deposit of 20% is required.
- **Price per night** - £18.50 (adult), £15 (under 16), under 3's free. From £1,450 for two night weekend with sole use. Breakfast options from £4 to £7 with discounts for advanced booking. Packed lunches from £4.95. Evening meals available on request.
- **Public Transport** - Porthmadog train station is 5 miles away. Take the number 1 bus towards Caernarfon and get off at the Cwm Pennant turning on the A487. From here follow the brown hostel signs - 1 mile walk to the hostel.
- **Directions** - Porthmadog train station is 5 miles away. Take the number 1 bus towards Caernarfon and get off at the Cwm Pennant turning on the A487. From here follow the brown hostel signs - one-mile walk to the hostel.

CONTACT:
Tel: 01766 530888 or 01706 877320
info@cwmpennanthostel.com www.cwmpennanthostel.com
Golan, Garndolbenmaen, Gwynedd, LL51 9AQ

SNOWDON LODGE
GROUP HOSTEL

Stay in the birthplace of Lawrence of Arabia! Snowdon Lodge hostel provides comfortable self-catering style group accommodation in a large grade 2 listed character building. The property is located in the picturesque village of Tremadog. Snowdon Lodge is perfect for a family reunion or simply as a base for a group of friends to explore this beautiful part of Snowdonia and the nearby Lleyn Peninsula. The hostel has 10 rooms of different sizes (twins, doubles and small dormitories). Bathroom and shower facilities are shared. There is a large fully equipped self-catering kitchen, a dining room seating 38, 2 lounge/TV rooms with real log fires in winter, a drying room and a private car park leading to extensive woodland walks. Snowdon Lodge is ideally positioned just 6 miles from Mount Snowdon, yet only 2 miles from beautiful beaches such as Black Rock Sands. The famous Italianate village of Portmeirion is also only 4 miles away. Within a mile are the Ffestiniog and Welsh Highland railways and the famous Tremadog rocks for climbers. Sorry, no stag or hen parties.

DETAILS

- **Open** - January – December, all day access.
- **Number of beds** - 35: 2 x 6 (family), 1 x 5, 1 x 6 , 3 x twin, 3 x double
- **Booking** - Essential.
- **Price per night** - Sole use £550 per night. Minimum 2 nights, bank holidays minimum 3 nights. Longer stays could attract discounted prices, please ask.
- **Public Transport** - Half mile from Porthmadog train station and 250 yards from National Express coach stop.
- **Directions** -   800mtrs from Porthmadog just off the on Caernarfon road (A487).

CONTACT: Carl or Anja
Tel: 01766 515354
info@snowdonlodge.co.uk www.snowdonlodge.co.uk
Lawrence House, Church Street, Tremadog, Nr Porthmadog, Snowdonia, LL49 9PS

ABERSOCH
SGUBOR UNNOS

Croeso/Welcome! Sgubor Unnos provides luxury bunkhouse accommodation on a Welsh speaking, traditionally run, family farm in the village of Llangian, one mile from Abersoch. Abersoch is famous for its watersports and there are great surfing beaches at Hell's Mouth and Porth Ceiriad. Centrally located, the bunkhouse is the ideal base for outdoor activities including walking the newly opened Llyn Coast Path, surfing, cycling, golf, fishing and sailing. A few miles from Llangian, at the tip of the Peninsula lies Bardsey Island where 20,000 saints are buried! Why not pay them a visit? Trips around the island can be arranged. The modern bunkhouse offers three bedrooms ideal for individuals or groups. There is a fully equipped kitchen/lounge, disabled facilities, covered BBQ area, secure storage and private parking and Free WiFi. There is a traditional village shop and phone box 500m away. For details on area see website. Photos taken by Tony Jones www.llynlight.co.uk

DETAILS

- **Open** - All year, all day.
- **Number of beds** - 14: 2 x 4 : 1 x 6
- **Booking** - Not essential but recommended.
- **Price per night** - £20 (adult), £10 (under 10 years), including a light breakfast and bed linen. Discount for more than 2 nights.
- **Public Transport** - Nearest train station is Pwllheli (7 miles). Good local bus and taxi service to Llangian. Public transport details on website.
- **Directions** - GR 296 288 On entering Abersoch from Pwllheli, take the right hand turning up the hill signed to Llangian (follow brown signs). On left on leaving village.

CONTACT: Phil or Meinir
Tel: 01758 713527
enquiries@tanrallt.com www.tanrallt.com
Fferm Tanrallt Farm, Llangian, Abersoch, Gwynedd, LL53 7LN

ABERDARON FARM
BUNKHOUSE

Aberdaron Farm Bunkhouse is two miles from Aberdaron village with its white-painted fishermen's houses, sandy beach and water's edge church. The Bunkhouse has underfloor central heating and 3 bunk rooms sleeping 8, 4 (en suite) and 3 (en suite) in a bunk and camp bed. There is a large social room with dining tables, chairs, beanbags, TV, Nintendo Wii and board games. The small basic kitchen has a hob, microwave, George Foreman cooking machine, kettle and toaster. A self service breakfast of cereal, bread, tea and coffee is provided. Bring sleeping bags or hire duvet and pillow for £3. There is a drying room with washing machine & tumble dryer and toilet & shower blocks. Whistling Sands is only 1.5 miles away and Bardsey Island (Ynys Enlli) lies across The Sound two miles off the tip of the Llyn Peninsula. The Island has been a place of pilgrimage since early Christianity and a boat from Aberdaron to Bardsey is a great place to see the seals. Pets allowed (with notice). Bike hire available. Holiday cottages and camping are also available on the farm.

DETAILS

- **Open** - All year, all day (arrive after 4pm and leave by 11am).
- **Number of beds** - 15: 1x8, 1x4 (en suite), 1x3 (en suite)
- **Booking** - Deposit of 50% paid by credit or debit card, remainder to be paid 4 weeks prior to arrival. Booking held for 5 days without deposit.
- **Price per night** - £16pp, £18 pp (en suite) inc breakfast. Enquire for sole use of room or bunkhouse and family room prices. Minimum of 3 days on bank holidays.
- **Public Transport** - Arriva bus17, Pwllheli to Aberdaron, 6 times a day (not Sun).
- **Directions** - Follow signs for Anelog, the first one is just after entering Aberdaron.

CONTACT: Gillian Jones
Tel: 01758 760345 Mob: 0779 414 7195
enquiries@aberdaronfarmholidays.co.uk www.aberdaronfarmholidays.co.uk
Y Gweithdy, Anelog, Aberdaron, Pwllheli, LL53 8BT

ANGLESEY
OUTDOOR CENTRE

Anglesey Outdoor Centre is an ideal base for groups, individuals or families to explore and enjoy the outdoor playground and mild climate of Anglesey. There are opportunities for adrenalin adventures and gentle relaxation - from coasteering, sea kayaking, climbing, and windsurfing to beach activities, gentle walks and bird watching. Anglesey Outdoors is just a mile from Porthdafarach Beach and the coast path, and only 2km from Sustrans Cycle Route 8. The Centre has four self contained areas each with their own self-catering and bathroom facilities. These can be hired individually or together, ideal for all group sizes and budgets. There are dorms, private and family rooms. Bedding is provided or you can use your own sleeping bags in the Gogarth dorms. Full catering available and an on-site bar/bistro. The Centre is set in 14 acres of grounds providing plenty of space for groups and individuals. Gear store, ample parking, drying room and free WiFi. Yurts and Cabans also available.

DETAILS

- **Open** - All year, 24 hour access.
- **Number of beds** - 68; Main Centre 33:1x7,4x5,1x4,1x2. Maris Annexe 10:5x2. Ty Pen Annexe 8:1x4,2x2. Gogarth Dorms 16:1x7,1x7,1x2. Some extra beds available.
- **Booking** - Essential during the peak season and recommended at other times.
- **Price per night** - £9pp (Gogarth Dorms) to £18pp (en suite twin). Ask for sole use.
- **Public Transport** - 2km from trains and ferry at Holyhead. Regular buses ½ mile.
- **Directions** - Arriving at the last roundabout on the A55, take the third exit toward Trearddur Bay. Immediately take the first left turning onto Porthdafarch Rd. Follow for approx 1.5miles. Signed on left hand side for Anglesey Outdoors & Paddlers Return.

CONTACT: Penny Hurndall
Tel: 01407 769351
angleseyoutdoors@gmail.com   www.angleseyoutdoors.com
Porthdafarch Road, Holyhead, Anglesey, LL65 2LP

Wonderfully situated at the south end of Holy Island, Anglesey, in a 7 acre Area of Outstanding Natural Beauty, and 300m from a beach. The centre is an excellent base for so much in the outdoors and is immediately adjacent to the Anglesey Coastal Path - good walking on a varied and accessible coast. All around there are prehistoric remains, spectacular geology, a wide range of habitats and species of marine life and plants, and excellent bird watching opportunities. For kayakers there are classic sea tours, overfalls, playwaves, surf and rockhopping. Climbers have Gogarth nearby and Rhoscolyn offering all grades in an attractive setting. Divers can beach launch for wrecks and fish. The Centre has two self-contained units and camping with toilets and showers. Careful energy use is encouraged, with composting and recycling. Nearby Holyhead has rail links and ferries to Ireland. Walking distance to pub.

DETAILS

- **Open** - All year, 24 hour access.
- **Number of beds** - 20: 2x2, 1x4, 2x6. 16: 1x3, 2x4,1x5.
- **Booking** - Essential
- **Price per night** - £365 for exclusive use, £20.50 per person.
- **Public Transport** - Trains at Holyhead (10km) (London direct 4.5 hrs) or Valley (5km). National Express at Valley (6km). Bus 23/25 Holyhead - Rhoscolyn (1km) or 4/44 Holyhead - Four Mile Bridge (3km). Ferry: Holyhead - Dublin or Dun Laoghaire.
- **Directions** - GR SH 278 752. From A5 traffic lights at Y Fali/Valley take B4545 Trearddur. After 2km at Four Mile Bridge fork left at sign to Rhoscolyn 2miles. After 2km sharp left at camping symbols. After 800m fork right at large white gatepost.

CONTACT: Jacqui Short
Tel: 01407 860469
enquiries@outdooralternative.co.uk www.outdooralternative.co.uk/
Cerrig-yr-Adar, Rhoscolyn, Holyhead, Anglesey, LL65 2NQ

South Scotland

511
510
Inverness 490
SKYE
503
492
489
499
502 500
494 Aviemore
480
Newtonmore
495
497
Mallaig
EIGG 498
496 478
474,477
COLL
Fort William 472,476
469
Kinlochleven 442
462 470
TIREE
464
MULL 467,468 Oban 440 441 438
IONA 465
466 452-459 436
435
432 433
434
460 Stirling
COLONSAY
425,426
Tarbert BUTE Glasgow
431
418
ISLAY
ARRAN
430
427
428 Ayr

0   miles   50
0   kilometres   80

Stranraer Castle
Douglas
412

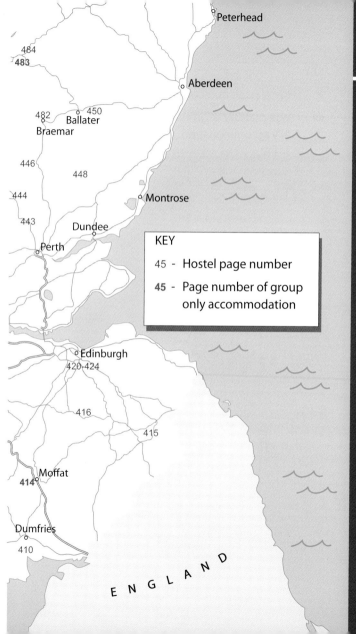

Peterhead

484
483

Aberdeen

482 o 450
o Ballater
Braemar

446

448

444

443

Montrose

Dundee

Perth

KEY

45 - Hostel page number

45 - Page number of group
         only accommodation

Edinburgh
420-424

416

415

Moffat

414o

Dumfries

410

E N G L A N D

KEY

45 - Hostel page number

45 - Page number of group only accommodation

| 0 | miles | 50 |
| 0 | kilometres | 80 |

Durness 521

507

506 Stornoway
508,509

LEWIS

515

Ullapool
513 ° 514

512

HARRIS 505

Gairloch

NORTH UIST

511

510

Portree

SKYE 503

492

SOUTH UIST

502 500 499

494

495

BARRA
504

497

Mallaig 478

498 496 474,477

EIGG Fort William 472,476

469

COLL Kinlochleven

462 470

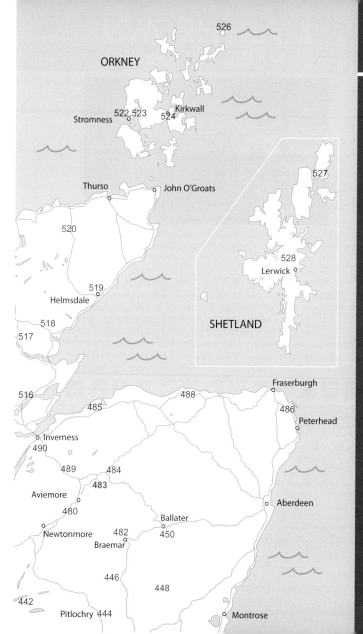

ORKNEY

526

522 523
Stromness
Kirkwall
524

Thurso
John O'Groats

527

520

528
Lerwick

519
Helmsdale

518
517

SHETLAND

516

Fraserburgh

488
485

486
Peterhead

Inverness
490

489
484

483

Aviemore

480

Ballater

Newtonmore
482
450

Braemar

Aberdeen

446
448

442

Pitlochry 444

Montrose

North Scotland

MARTHROWN
SCOTLAND OF MABIE BUNKHOUSE

Marthrown is set in the heart of Mabie Forest, about 6 miles south of Dumfries. It has a traditional sauna, a wood burning spring water hot tub, a large BBQ, garden areas, a challenge course and plenty of room for groups.

The forest has a variety mountain bike routes, ranging in length and difficulty and the 7Stanes mountain bike trails are nearby. Although we are a self-catering hostel meals are available to order. Marthrown is suitable for all age groups. Facilities include secure store for bikes and equipment and a large dining area suitable for meetings. For something a little different why not try staying in the Roundhouse or Yurt? Are you looking for a completely different type of Scottish wedding venue to tie the knot? The Bunkhouse, Round house and Yurt are also available for forest and outdoor weddings. For more info see website.

DETAILS

- **Open** - All year, 24 hours - late arrival by arrangement.
- **Number of beds** - 26: 1x8:1x7:1x6:1x5 + Roundhouse, Yurt, Tipi and camping.
- **Booking** - Telephone a few days in advance.
- **Price per night** - £16 to £19.50.
- **Public Transport** - From Dumfries (White Sands) take the Stagecoach bus service 372 to Mabie Forest. It is best to arrive in daylight. 1.5 mile walk from road.
- **Directions** - From Dumfries take A710 (west) to Mabie Forest passing through the village of Islesteps. Turn right signposted Mabie Forest and Mabie House Hotel. Follow tarmac road over speed bumps to the end of the Hotel and Forest Rangers Office, through courtyard and onto forest track, Marthown is signposted and is exactly one mile into the forest.

CONTACT: Mike or Pam Hazlehurst
Tel: 01387 247900
pamhazlehurst@hotmail.com www.marthrownofmabie.com
Mabie Forest, Dumfries, DG2 8HB

CASTLE CREAVIE
HAY BARN

Castle Creavie Haybarn has recently been converted to a comfortable family friendly independent hostel sleeping 4. Quietly set on a working farm it is surrounded by spectacularly beautiful Galloway countryside. Hugely spacious open plan design, oak floors, with 4 comfortable beds, dining area, wood burning stove, separate kitchen with basic cooking facilities, fridge, washroom and W.C. Also available on site are: hot showers, washing/drying facilities, bike wash and safe store, farmhouse breakfast (pre booked) £7.50 pp. Ideal base for walkers and cyclists with 7Stanes and NCN Route 7 (3 miles away). Guests are welcome to enjoy the farm footpaths and observe the daily life on this working sheep farm. Available seasonally: fresh baked bread, cakes and honey, home reared pork and lamb, sausage, bacon and fresh farm eggs. Castle Creavie is named after two Iron Age forts, and is 4 miles from the popular harbour town of Kirkcudbright which has a good range of pubs, cafés, and restaurants. Galloway is famed for its many castles, abbeys, first class walks and long sandy beaches.

DETAILS

- **Open** - All year, all day.
- **Number of beds** - 4: 1x4.
- **Booking** - Book by phone and online. Deposit required by post or PayPal.
- **Price per night** - £15pp with beds made up. £60.00 for sole private use.
- **Public Transport** - 4 miles from Kirkcudbright citylink services.
- **Directions** - From the A75 take the A711 to Kirkcudbright. In the town centre turn left at the Royal Hotel onto the B727 (Gelston), pass the cemetery and at the next road junction go straight on (Auchencairn / Dundrennan). Follow for approx 4 miles.

CONTACT: Charlie and Elaine Wannop
Tel: 01557 500238
elaine@castlecreavie.co.uk www.castlecreavie.co.uk
Castle Creavie, Kirkcudbright, Dumfries and Galloway, DG6 4QE

WELL ROAD CENTRE
SCOTLAND GROUP ACCOMMODATION

The Well Road Centre is a large Victorian house set in its own grounds in the charming spa town of Moffat. The centre is ideal for youth groups, adult groups, conferences, residential workshops, sports events, multiple family gatherings and outdoor activity clubs. All rooms are fully carpeted and centrally heated. The Centre has two spacious meeting rooms, a large bright self-catering kitchen fully equipped for 65, a games hall for indoor activities, a table tennis room and a snooker room. There are 13 bedrooms of various sizes, two of them with en suite facilities. Two separate toilet/shower areas for mixed groups. Bring your own sleeping bags or duvets. Ample parking for cars, minibuses and equipment trailers and the nearby park can be used for sports activities. Moffat is in the Southern Uplands, an hour from Edinburgh and Glasgow. An ideal area for golfers, bird watchers, walkers and cyclists, it is central to the "7Stanes" mountain bike venues. All groups have sole use.

DETAILS

- **Open** - All year, all day.
- **Number of beds** - 70: in 13 rooms (2 en suite).
- **Booking** - Check availability and send £100 deposit to secure booking.
- **Price per night** - From £750 for two nights for up to 30 people. £25 per person for 31 people or more.
- **Public Transport** - Trains at Lockerbie (16m). Citylink bus to Glasgow/Edinburgh.
- **Directions** - From A74 take Moffat turning and enter the High Street (town square). Turning to the right around the shops on the south side of the square, follow Holm St to the T-junction. Turn left into Burnside, following up and right into Well Rd.

CONTACT: Ben Larmour
Tel: 01683 221040
Ben8363@aol.com www.wellroadcentre.com
Well Road Centre, Well Road, Moffat, DG10 9BT

Kirk Yetholm Friends of Nature House, nestling below the picturesque village green, is a former village school that has been offering hostel style accommodation for over 70 years. Located at the start / end of the Pennine Way it is a classic stop and is also ideal for those doing the St. Cuthbert's Way and for cyclists on the Borderloop Cycle Route or Sustrans Route 84. A great base for local day hikes, particularly suited to individuals, families and small groups. Recently upgraded, the house offers a friendly and peaceful retreat after a day exploring the stunning countryside and local heritage. There is a comfortable lounge, a well equipped kitchen, seating for 18 in the dining area and secure bike storage. Evening meals and breakfast are available in adjacent Border Hotel. Well stocked village shop and other eateries 10 min's walk away. FoN is one of Europe's oldest environmental groups with 600K members and 800 houses across Europe.

Under 16's should be accompanied by an adult sharing the same dorm.

DETAILS

■ **Open** - All year (Nov-Feb incl. groups only). Reception 5pm-11pm & 8am-10am.
■ **Number of beds** - 22: 1x7, 1x5, 1x4, 2x2 (twin), 1x2 (bunk).
■ **Booking** - Book via website, email or phone. Verbal bookings held until 6pm daily.
■ **Price per night** - From £18, under 18's from £15. Discounts for IFN / SYHA/HI.
■ **Public Transport** - Kelso to Kirk Yetholm approx every 2hrs. Stops within 100m of building. Connections onwards from Kelso to all parts of country and to rail station
■ **Directions** - OS Grid Ref: NT 826 282. Geo-Coord: 55.533378 -2.277233. 7 miles from Kelso on Pennine Way. Located 100m below the village green at Kirk Yetholm.

CONTACT: Manager
Tel: 01573 420639
kirkyetholm@thefriendsofnature.org.uk www.thefriendsofnature.org.uk
Friends of Nature House,Waukford,Kirk Yetholm,Kelso,Roxburghshire,TD5 8PG

KAILZIE
BUNKHOUSE

Nestled between the River Tweed and the Cardrona Forest, part of the Tweed Valley Forest Park within easy access of Glasgow and Edinburgh, Kailzie Bunkhouse is the perfect base for walkers, cyclists and nature lovers wanting to visit this beautiful part of the Scottish Borders. Under new management from June 2015 the bunkhouse has been newly decorated. It sleeps 28 in rooms of various sizes with en-suite shower or bath rooms.

The large communal kitchen is well equipped. There a dining/sitting rooms with seating for everyone and a cosy sitting room with TV, DVD, music and a wood-burning stove. Near the back door there is a large shower room, drying room and loos where you can wash off the mud from your day's adventure. There is secure bike storage and wash down area outside and an outdoor sitting area with a barbecue. Evening meals and breakfasts available on request. Dogs permitted on request for exclusive use bookings of bunkhouse.

DETAILS

- **Open** - All year, all day.
- **Number of beds** - 28: 2x4, 1x5, 1x2, 1x6, 1x7
- **Booking** - deposit of 50% is payable by bank transfer to confirm your booking
- **Price per night** - £22 pp, rates for sole use available on application.
- **Public Transport** - X62 bus from Edinburgh stops 5 mins' walk from the hostel.
- **Directions** - From A72 east of Peebles, take turning for Cardrona, Follow signs for Tweed Valley Forest Park (B7062). Kailzie Bunkhouse is of to the right just before the left hand turn for the forest park. Sat Nav users – follow signs to Cardrona.

CONTACT: Linda Frazer
Tel: 07859 888186
linda@bunk-house.co.uk www.bunk-house.co.uk
Cardrona, Peebles EH45 9HT

WEE ROW
HOSTEL

Located in the heart of New Lanark World Heritage Site 'Wee Row' provides a unique hostel experience nestled in the spectacular South Lanarkshire Valley in southern Scotland. Only one hour drive from Glasgow and Edinburgh, Wee Row is the perfect base to explore these popular cities but you don't have to go far to find plenty to do.

The award winning New Lanark Visitor Centre is on the doorstep. Here you can step back in time and rediscover life of this working mill village. The hostel sleeps 62 guests in 18 private rooms all with en suites and has terrific views over the River Clyde and surrounding countryside.

There is a modern fully equipped self-catering kitchen; comfortable dining area and TV lounge. WiFi is complimentary throughout the public areas. Facilities include bike storage and there is a laundry and drying room. Traditional cooked breakfasts are available and an evening dinner menu is also available.

DETAILS

- **Open** - All year.
- **Number of beds** - 62: 6x2, 1x3, 3x3, 8x4 +Studio appt
- **Booking** - www.newlanarkhostel.co.uk
- **Price per night** - From £19.50 per person
- **Public Transport** - Buses and train to Lanark. 30 min walk to hostel.
- **Directions** - M75 Jct11 A70 toward Lanark. Follow brown tourist signs to New Lanark. (New Lanark Road) take sharp right on to Rosedale Street

CONTACT: Reception
Tel: 01555 666 710
weerowhostel@newlanark.org www.newlanarkhostel.co.uk
Wee Row Hostel, Wee Row, New Lanark, Lanark, Lanarkshire, ML11 9DJ

HAGGIS
HOSTELS

Occupying a recently renovated building dating from 1862, Haggis Hostels, is situated in the heart of Edinburgh just 50 metres from Princes Street. The hostel offers self-catering facilities and fully equipped rooms with privacy curtains, reading lights and international sockets. There is adjustable heating in every room. The communal kitchen is high spec and features two of every appliance, ideal for groups of up to 34. Being so centralised in the Scottish capital, Haggis Hostels has everything on its doorstep whether you're heading to the theatre, concert hall, pub or club. There is something for everyone. Friendly staff will help you plan your excursions around Edinburgh and provide you with all the information you need to make your stay enjoyable. The hostel offers free breakfast, high speed free WiFi internet access, luxury bedding and towels, a laundry service, secure storage and a communal kitchen with dining area. For more information please download our free smartphone app or visit our website

DETAILS

- **Open** - All year, 24 hour reception.
- **Number of beds** - 34.
- **Booking** - Online on our website, phone or email.
- **Price per night** - Standard mixed room from £18. Female or male only room from £22. Family room for £80. Breakfast and taxes included in all prices.
- **Public Transport** - Buses to St Andrew Square bus station. Air link shuttle service to Edinburgh's Waverley train station direct from Edinburgh Airport. Trains to Edinburgh's Waverley train station. Tram service to St Andrew's Square.
- **Directions** - At the east end of Princes Street, follow the road around to the left and you will find us on the right.

CONTACT:
Tel: 0131 557 0036
info@haggishostels.co.uk www.haggishostels.co.uk
Haggis Hostels 5/3 West Register Street, Edinburgh,EH2 2AA.

ROYAL MILE
BACKPACKERS

Royal Mile Backpackers is a small and lively hostel with its own special character! Perfectly located on the Royal Mile, the most famous street in Edinburgh, Royal Mile Backpackers is the ideal place to stay for the independent traveller.

Our comfortable beds and cosy common areas will make you feel at home and our friendly staff are always on hand to help you make the most of your time in Edinburgh.

DETAILS

- **Open** - All year, all day. Reception 7am – 3am (24hrs during August).
- **Number of beds** - 48
- **Booking** - Booking not always essential, 1st night's payment required for booking.
- **Price per night** - From £14 per person. ID required for check in.
- **Public Transport** - Only a 5/10 minute walk from both Edinburgh bus station and Waverley train station. A taxi costs between £3-£5 from each. The airport bus also stops out side the train station on the last stop so is very easy to get to the hostel.
- **Directions** - From main bus station turn left onto Princes Street then take first right onto Northbridge. At top turn left onto the High St. on the Royal Mile. From train station take the Princes Street exit (up Waverley Steps), at top go right then right again up Northbridge, then left at cross roads, hostel is on the left above the Oxfam shop. From airport take bus no.100 to city centre, get off at Waverley Bridge. Walk away from Princes St. towards the roundabout, go over roundabout onto Cockburn Street. At the top of Cockburn Street turn left onto the High St. on the Royal Mile. Cross traffic lights at Northbridge and hostel is on left above Oxfam.

CONTACT: Receptionist
Tel: 0131 557 6120
royalmile@scotlandstophostels.com www.scotlandstophostels.com
105 High Street, Edinburgh, EH1 1SG

CASTLE ROCK
HOSTEL

SCOTLAND

In a wonderful location, facing south with a sunny aspect and panoramic views over the city, Castle Rock Hostel is just steps away from the city centre with the historic Royal Mile, the busy pubs and late-late nightlife of the Grassmarket and Cowgate and of course the Castle.

Most of the rooms have no traffic noise, there are loads of great facilities, 24 hour reception and no curfew. With its beautiful and dramatic skyline Edinburgh is truly one of the world's great cities. The cobbled streets of the Old Town lead past mysterious gothic buildings up to the magnificent castle. Below the castle's rocky pinnacle lies the New Town's 200 year old Georgian splendour.

DETAILS

- **Open** - All year, all day.
- **Number of beds** - 302
- **Booking** - Booking not always essential. First night's payment needed to book.
- **Price per night** - From £14 per person. ID required for check in.
- **Public Transport** - 5/10 minute walk from Edinburgh bus stn and Waverley train stn. (taxis £3-£5). Airport bus goes to train station so it's easy to get to the hostel.
- **Directions** - 10 minutes' walk from Waverley train station – turn left out of the station and continue to small roundabout. Cross over and continue up Cockburn Street to the top. Turn right onto the Royal Mile and follow uphill towards the Castle. Take the left fork at the Hub (church) and the hostel is situated 200 yards on the left side of Johnston Terrace next to two red telephone boxes. By Car – follow signs for city centre towards the Castle turning onto Royal Mile uphill towards the castle then left fork at the Hub on to Johnston Terrace.

CONTACT: Receptionist
Tel: 0131 225 9666
castlerock@scotlandstophostels.com www.scotlandstophostels.com
15 Johnston Terrace, Edinburgh, EH1 2PW

HIGH STREET
HOSTEL

The High Street Hostel has become a hugely popular destination for world travellers since opening in 1985 and is one of Europe's best regarded and most atmospheric hostels.

Located just off the historic Royal Mile in a 400 year old building it is the perfect base for exploring all the city's attractions – and of course its wonderful nightlife.

Providing excellence in location, ambience and facilities, the hostel is highly recommended by more than ten of the world's top backpacker travel guides.

DETAILS

- **Open** - All year, all day.
- **Number of beds** - 156.
- **Booking** - Booking in advance not always crucial, 1 night's payment for booking.
- **Price per night** - From £14 per person. ID required for check in.
- **Public Transport** - Only a 5/10 minute walk from Edinburgh bus station or Waverley train station. Taxis cost between £3-£5 from each. The airport bus also stops outside the train station on the last stop so it is very easy to get to the hostel.
- **Directions** - From the bus station (St Andrews Square) turn left onto Princes Street then first right onto Northbridge. At top turn left onto the High Street on the Royal Mile and hostel is on Blackfriars St. on right. From railway station main exit turn left onto Waverley Bridge then right at the mini rounbdaout and straight ahead up the Mound, at the junction go left, then at cross roads left again going down the Royal Mile. Cross at the traffic lights at Northbridge and Blackfriars St is second on the right. From airport take bus 100 to last stop, Waverley Bridge and follow as above.

CONTACT: Reception
Tel: 0131 557 3984
highstreet@scotlandstophostels.com www.scotlandstophostels.com
8 Blackfriars Street, Edinburgh, EH1 1NE

A smarter alternative to a hotel in the city, with a prime location, five mins' walk from Glasgow Central Station, friendly staff, lively bar and clean comfortable private/shared en suite rooms. Perfect for clubbing, shopping, discovering the city's cultural heritage, vibrant nightlife and live music scene, visiting family, coast to coast cycle rides, sporting events or a good sleep to break a long journey. The hostel's stylish bar "Mint & Lime " provides an 'all you can eat' buffet breakfast and bar meals (12–9pm). It is the perfect place to sit back and relax with other guests, with teas, coffees and a Sky Sports screen also available. An ideal pre-club venue. Our 24 hour reception will help you with discounted sightseeing tickets, free nightclub tickets, room upgrades and discounted car parking. The hostel offers a self-catering kitchen, dining area and laundry. Group dinners and half board packages can be arranged. FREE WiFi and internet kiosks throughout. Five mins' drive from the new Hydro, SECC and Clyde auditorium. Five mins' walk to the arches, 02 academy & Hamden.

DETAILS

- **Open** - All year, early check in/late check outs no problem.
- **Number of beds** - 364: single, doubles, twins, 4, 8 and 14 person all en suite
- **Booking** - Book online with 10% deposit, Full balance within 28 days for groups.
- **Price per night** - From £10 B&B pp en suite. Discount available online at www.euro-hostels.co.uk. Ask about our group discounts.
- **Public Transport** - Central railway station 2 mins, Queen Street railway station 7 mins, Buchanan Bus Station 10 mins, Glasgow Airport 8 miles.
- **Directions** - The hostel is on the corner of Jamaica Street and Clyde Street.

CONTACT: Reception
Tel: 0141 222 2828
glasgow@euro-hostels.co.uk www.euro-hostels.co.uk
318 Clyde Street, Glasgow, G1 4NR

TARTAN
LODGE

The perfect location - within walking distance of Merchant City and Glasgow City Centre and also to thriving Dennistoun. Old world charm and contemporary elegance are interwoven in this hostel set within a former 19th century church and Masonic Lodge on Alexandra Parade, Glasgow. Tartan Lodge provides affordable accommodation for budget and business travellers, comprising a selection of double bedrooms and twin rooms all with en suite bathrooms and LCD Tvs. Additionally, there are shared dormitories for budget travellers and backpackers, with a choice of eight, six, four and three bed dormitories for male and female only offering bespoke bunk bed design. Dorm room facilities include a double plug socket, shelve and underneath storage for each bunk. All dorms are en suite and also have family facilities. Towels can be hired for £2 (plus £5 deposit), or purchase a padlock for your bunk for £2. A reading light for each bunk available from reception.

DETAILS

- **Open** - All year. Check in from 2pm. Check out by 11am
- **Number of beds** - 93: 5xdouble, 2xtwin, 1xtriple. Dorms: 2x3, 8x4, 1x4 female, 2x6, 1x6 female, 2x8
- **Booking** - on line. Early/late check in available for extra charge.
- **Price per night** - Dorms from £18pp, Private rooms from £50 per room
- **Public Transport** - Bus First38 from Glasgow Central and Glasgow Queen Street stations
- **Directions** - From M8 take the exit toward A803/Kirkintilloch, turn left onto Castle St , turn left at the 1st cross street onto Alexandra Parade/A8, Hostel is on the Left before the petrol station.

CONTACT: Reception
Tel: 0141 554 5970
info@tartanlodge.co.uk www.tartanlodge.co.uk
235 Alexandra Parade, Glasgow, G31 3AW

KILMORY LODGE
BUNKHOUSE
SCOTLAND

Kilmory Lodge Bunkhouse provides ideal group accommodation in a tranquil, rural setting. The Isle of Arran is one of the most accessible Scottish islands, only one hour by ferry from the mainland. It offers the visitor hill-walking, mountaineering, golf, fishing, cycling, pony trekking and a bewildering choice of extreme sports. The bunkhouse is affordable, modern, comfortable and able to sleep up to 23. All the bed linen is supplied, so there's no need to bring anything except your towels and food! There is a great, contemporary kitchen with all you'll need. Attached to the bunkhouse is the village hall which can provide extra rooms and an auditorium at extra cost. Ideal for educational groups, weddings, music workshop groups, clubs or any group needing extra facilities. Kilmory Lodge welcomes your family, club, group, school or any combination of these except stag parties! Also adjoining the bunkhouse is the 1934 Club (Social Club) which is open at the weekend. Phone or email with your queries. Registered Scottish Charity SC028200.

DETAILS

- **Open** - All year, 24 hours.
- **Number of beds** - 23: 2 x 8, 1 x 4 (en suite) 1 x 3 (en suite)
- **Booking** - Book ahead, 40% deposit. Groups - £150 security deposit on arrival.
- **Price per night** - £16 per person for groups of 15+. £21 pp for smaller groups.
- **Public Transport** - Buses stop on demand directly outside the hall and bunkhouse. These buses meet all the ferries that arrive and depart from the main ferry terminal at Brodick.
- **Directions** - Bunkhouse attached to Kilmory Public Hall located in village centre.

CONTACT: Manager
Tel: 01770 870345
kilmory.hall@btinternet.com www.kilmoryhall.com
Kilmory, Isle of Arran, KA27 8PQ

CAMPBELTOWN
BACKPACKERS

The Campbeltown Backpackers is housed in the newly refurbished Old Schoolhouse, a Grade B listed building. Offering easy access to the facilities of Campbeltown including swimming pool, gym, the "wee toon" cinema and Springbank distillery tours, it is a good final stop along the Kintyre Way which gives walkers spectacular views of the surrounding islands. The area also enjoys very good wind surfing, surfing, mountain bike routes and other major cycle trails as well as golf, horse riding along beaches or forest trails, and geocaching from the Network Centre in Carradale. Kintyre is full of cultural and historical interest being the place where St Columba came ashore from Northern Ireland bringing Christianity to Scotland. Robert the Bruce spent time in Kintyre on his way to Rathlin, whilst the beach at Saddell was the location for Paul McCartney and Wings' video for "Mull of Kintyre". For wildlife lovers the Kintyre Peninsula is a great place to see otters, seals and even golden eagles as well as red, roe and sika deer.

              BEST PRICE

DETAILS

- **Open** - All year, out by 10.30am on day of departure.
- **Number of beds** - 16 1x6, 1x10
- **Booking** - By email, only phone if you require a booking within 4 days
- **Price per night** - £18 per person
- **Public Transport** - 5 buses a day from Glasgow (926). Passenger and cycle ferry links to Northern Ireland and Troon. The islands of Gigha, Islay, Jura and Arran are all served by ferries. Two flights per day to and from Glasgow International Airport
- **Directions** - Adjacent to the Heritage Centre on the B842 towards Machrihanish

CONTACT: Alan
Tel: 01586 551188
info@campbeltownbackpackers.co.uk www.campbeltownbackpackers.co.uk
Kintyre Amenity Trust, Big Kiln, Campbeltown, Argyll, PA28 6JF

WELCOME
Campbeltown
BACKPACKERS
Tel: 01586 551188

IFFERDALE FARM
BUNKHOUSE

A warm welcome awaits you at Ifferdale, a working family farm set deep in the countryside at the head of Saddell Glen. The farm buildings have been renovated to provide a bunkhouse and three self-catering cottages with a district heating system and lots of hot water. The farm is managed sustainably producing beef and lamb, and is surrounded by ancient forests buzzing with wildlife. There is a fantastic beach at Saddell and activities available in Kintyre include golf, sailing, walking, surfing, fishing, stargazing or simply mucking about on the beaches and enjoying quality Scottish fayre. Campbeltown has a leisure centre with swimming pool and other rainy-day activities. The Bunkhouse sleeps 8 and shares its kitchen and dining accommodation with The Bothy which sleeps 2-3. The other two cottages are ideal for couples or families. Towels and linen are provided. Eggs, beef and lamb produced by the farm are available and evening meals and packed lunches can be ordered in advance.

DETAILS

- **Open** - All year round.
- **Number of beds** - 17: 8: Bunkhouse, 2-3: Bothy, 2-4: Hayloft, 2: Loosebox
- **Booking** - Full payment to secure booking. Deposit taken for longer group bookings.
- **Price per night** - From £24 per person in bunkhouse. Hayloft £80 per night, min of 2 nights. £420 a week. Loose box £60 per night, weekly rate available.
- **Public Transport** - West Coast Motors Cambeltown to Carradale Bus stops in Saddell (2 miles away), Buses connect Cambeltown to Glasgow
- **Directions** - On the B842 10 miles north of Campbeltown, North of Saddell take turning west signed Ifferdale Farm. Follow lane 1.5m to farm.

CONTACT: Monica Gemmill
Tel: 01583 431666
ifferdale@gmail.com ifferdalefarm.co.uk
Ifferdale Farm, Saddell By Campbeltown, PA28 6QZ

BUTE BACKPACKERS ⁴³¹
HOSTEL
SCOTLAND

Bute Backpackers, a friendly independent hostel with panoramic views of Rothesay seafront, has 40 beds with a mixture of single, twin, double and family rooms. The main house has a sea front sun lounge with woodburner and open fire. The self-catering kitchen is equipped to the highest standard and there is a large seafront dining room with catering facilities. Some of the rooms are en suite and there are separate male and female showers and toilets on each level. There is also a separate self-contained cottage dorm with its own fully equipped kitchen and bathroom. Other facilities include Sky TV, internet, WiFi access, drying room and laundry. There is a private car park for twelve cars and secure bike racks. There are regular live music sessions which includes open mic for any budding musos to join the fun. VisitScotland rated as 4 star.

DETAILS

- **Open** - All year 24hr access, no curfew. Reception 10am - 10pm.
- **Number of beds** - 40: Main House 32 in 14 rooms; Cottage 8.
- **Booking** - Deposit only required for group bookings.
- **Price per night** - From £20 per person.
- **Public Transport** - Take train to Wemyes Bay Station and Ferry Port (40 mins from Glasgow Central). Then ferry to Rothesay, Isle of Bute. Hostel 900m from ferry or take a taxi (taxi rank adjacent to port) which costs approximately £2.50.
- **Directions** - Turn right as you leave ferry and walk straight ahead for 200m past the discovery centre and putting green. Continue straight ahead for another 250m and Bute Backpackers is on your left. By car turn right on to main road. Continue for 300m to the mini roundabout . Head straight on for a further 300m and the hostel and access to the private car park is adjacent to the main road on your left.

CONTACT: Reception
Tel: 01700 501876
butebackpackers@hotmail.com   www.butebackpackers.co.uk
The Pier View, 36 Argyle Street, Rothesay, Isle of Bute, PA20 0AX

TORRAN BAY
HOSTEL

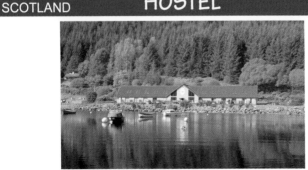

With 16 en suite rooms and great views of Loch Awe, Torran Bay Hostel is the perfect base for a fantastic Highlands holiday. Free fishing from Torran Farm land is included, or why not venture out on the loch? Boat and canoe launching is available along with a large parking area. Boat hire can be arranged through the hostel. Just 30 miles from Oban, 13 miles from Lochgilphead and close to the Crinnan canal, Torran Bay is located at the south end of Loch Awe which is 25 miles long. Excellent for fishing for brown trout, pike, arctic char, perch and roach or just a day relaxing on the loch with TBFL boat hire. Other activities include walking, on Torran Farm land and beyond, hiking, cycling, bird watching and golf. The hostel can accommodate up to 40 guests, with rooms arranged in different combinations. It has two well equipped kitchens for self-catering and the local Indian/Chinese takeaway delivers to the hostel. Prices includes continental breakfast and all rooms have TV, DVD and WiFi

DETAILS

- **Open** - All year round, all day.
- **Number of beds** - 34: 10 x 2, or double, 2 x double and single, 1 x 4 , 2 x 3
- **Booking** - booking 4 rooms or more, full payment required 14 days before arrival
- **Price per night** - from £45 to £72 per room. inc continental breakfast and parking. Group bookings welcome. Please note. prices per room not per person.
- **Public Transport** - Buses Lochgilphead to Ford, Monday, Wednesday and Saturday
- **Directions** - From Glasgow take A82 to Tarbet then take the A83 to Lochgilphead, Lochgilphead to Kilmartin A816. 1 mile past Kilmartin follow signs to Ford B840. From Ford take Dalavich road for 1 mile. Hostel on the right.

CONTACT: Joachim or Sheila Brolly
Tel: 01546 810 133 or 01546 810 270
torranbayhostel@mail.com www.torran-bay.co.uk
Torran Farm, Ford, Lochgilphead. PA31 8RH

Inveraray Hostel is a purpose-built wooden building in extensive grounds. An excellent self-catering kitchen, plus dining and sitting areas, provide a friendly ambience where the staff encourage guests to interact. Small 2 or 4 bed dorms make the hostel equally suitable for solo travellers, couples, families and small groups. Bed linen is provided and towels are available for hire. A large car park, bike shed and drying room are available.

Inveraray is a small planned town in the southern Highlands of Scotland with a range of shops, restaurants, 2 pubs and cash machines. Attractions include a magnificent C18th castle set in wooded grounds and gardens, and a jail where you can experience the lifestyle of former inmates! There are local forest walks and a modest climb to a viewpoint with a fantastic view down the loch. From Inveraray you can drive to access points for several Munros and the famous "Cobbler". Well-located for cyclists, walkers, motor bikers and those touring Scotland by car.

DETAILS

- **Open** - March to October. Sole-use October to March. Reception 4pm-9pm.
- **Number of beds** - 28: 4 x 4, 6 x 2, all bunk beds
- **Booking** - On website. Larger groups and families book by email.
- **Price per night** - From £17pp.Families please enquire. Breakfast £3.50 May-Sept.
- **Public Transport** - Bus 926 or 976 from Glasgow (about 6 per day, 7 days). Bus 976 from Oban (3 per day, 7 days). Bus 926 from Campbeltown.
- **Directions** - From A83 at Inveraray take A819, hostel 200m on left.

CONTACT: Manager
Tel: 01499 302 454
info@inverarayhostel.co.uk www.inverarayhostel.co.uk
Dalmally Road, Inveraray, Argyll, PA32 8XD

BALMAHA
BUNKHOUSE / HOSTEL

Set on the banks of Loch Lomond on the West Highland Way, Balmaha Bunkhouse offers quality assured accommodation for up to 14 at an affordable price. Continental breakfast, bedding, WiFi, tea and coffee are included and there is a self-catering kitchen. The bunkhouse is ideal for hen, stag and family get togethers, corporate away-days, meetings, conferences or as a base to explore the wider area. There is a private self-catering chalet called The Roost sleeping 4 people in a double bed and one set of bunks and bed & breakfast in the main house with en suite rooms and breathtaking views over the loch. The accommodation is situated on the shores of Loch Lomond, just 5 minutes' paddling to the first of the islands (Inchcailloch), from where you can explore other islands with ancient graveyards with the burial place of Rob Roy`s cousin and scenic landscapes. Kayaks and canadian canoes can be hired on site. Friendly dogs welcome, please visit our website for details. Welcome to the romantic, adventurous and beautiful experience of Loch Lomond.

DETAILS

- **Open** - All year subject to availability. Arrive 2pm-7pm, leave before 10am.
- **Number of beds** - Bunkhouse 14: 1x6,1x4 (family),1x2 (double/twin),1x2 (twin); The Roost 4: 1x4; B&B: 1xDbl, 1x2(bunks)
- **Booking** - phone or email for availability. Book in writing. Nov-Feb Groups 6+ only.
- **Price per night** - £20pp. Sole use of bunkhouse £280. Chalet £80. Dog (in bunkhouse only) £5, B&B £35. No credit/debit cards.
- **Public Transport** - Train from Glasgow Queen Street to Balloch then 309 Bus.
- **Directions** - Opposite the bay and the telephone box. Bus stop 100m from hostel

CONTACT: Jock and Gwen Cousin
Tel: 01360 870 218 Mob: 07921 293285
jock@balmahahouse.co.uk www.balmahahouse.co.uk
Balmaha, Loch Lomond, Stirlingshire, G63 0JQ

Now specialising in group bookings of the whole house. Trossachs Tryst has been purpose-built on its own 3 acre site, set amidst beautiful scenery (on Sustrans route 7c) just outside the bustling tourist town of Callander. The 4 star hostel, was opened in 1997. It is finished to a very high standard and has won accolades in guide books and on the web. Trossachs Tyrst has proved extremely popular with all kinds of groups from musicians and family reunions through to yoga and corporate events. The rooms are all en suite and are either 8, 6 or 4 bedded with the 4 bed rooms making ideal family or twin rooms. There is a spacious dining/common room, well equipped kitchen, drying room and a large comfortably furnished sitting room with great views to the surrounding hills. There is an on-site cycling centre.

Other activities available locally include hill walking, pony trekking, Go-ape, Segway treks, canoe hire/instruction, fishing and sailing.

DETAILS

- **Open** - All year (Sept to June, whole hostel bookings only). Reception 8am - 9pm.
- **Number of beds** - 30
- **Booking** - Groups must book with deposit.
- **Price per night** - From £17 including linen and free tea/coffee. 2 night minimum with discounts for 4 nights or longer.
- **Public Transport** - Nearest train station Stirling (15 miles). Nearest Citylink coach stop Callander (1.5 miles). Pick up from Callander can usually be arranged.
- **Directions** - GR 606 072. The hostel is situated one mile up Invertrossachs Rd from its junction with the A81 (Glasgow Rd) in Callander.

CONTACT: Mark or Janet
Tel: 01877 331200
info@scottish-hostel.com www.trossachstryst.com
Invertrossachs Road, Callander, Perthshire, FK17 8HW

CALLANDER
HOSTEL

Situated within the town of Callander at the start of the Loch Lomond and Trossachs National Park, Callander Hostel is a great location for tourists and outdoor enthusiasts alike. With outstanding views over Ben Ledi this Visit Scotland 5 star Hostel has recently been refurbished to a high standard. The comfortable beds, en suite rooms and fully equipped self-catering kitchen will ensure that you have all you need for the perfect retreat. The bunk beds have a utility board with reading lights, plug sockets and USB charging facilities. The hostel has a bright, spacious lounge with comfy sofas, WiFi and a wood burning stove. The gardens have a childrens play area, BBQ pods and seating to enjoy the stunning views. Callander is known as the Gateway to the Highlands and has walking and cycling routes, golf, fishing, sailing, horse riding and canoeing. Callander Hostel is an inspiration from the Callander Youth Project. Check out the hostels website to find out more.

DETAILS

- **Open** - All year, all day. Open 24 hours.
- **Number of beds** - 28: 2 x 8 bed dorms, 1 x 6, 1 x twin/double, 1 x family room (4)
- **Booking** - Debit/credit card secures booking
- **Price per night** - £18.50 per person in dorm, £60 per twin/double en suite room.
- **Public Transport** - There is a bus from Stirling to Callander. Easy walk from bus stop to the hostel. Exit the bus at Ancaster Square, turn left and walk down the street to the "Golf Shop", then turn left on to Bridgend.
- **Directions** - From A84 in Callander turn onto Bridgend and cross the bridge. Callander Hostel is on the right hand side just over the bridge.

CONTACT: Patricia
Tel: 01877 331465
bookings@callanderhostel.co.uk www.callanderhostel.co.uk
6 Bridgend, Callander, FK17 8AH

COMRIE
CROFT

Welcome to Scotland's hiking and mountain biking holiday destination.

Stay in the 4* homely hostel, Nordic Katas or eco camping (fires allowed too), dine in the on site cafe (seasonal) and explore the biking and hiking trails. Biking facilities on site include a bike park, graded, grin enducing, down hill tracks, family-friendly valley routes, and a bike shop for hire and repairs. For hiking there are four way-marked trails on site, a path to the village of Comrie and access to glens and mountains beyond.

Just over an hour's drive from Edinburgh or Glasgow, the Croft is great for any kind of getaway on wheels or legs. You can even get married there! Comrie Croft holds a 'Gold' award in the Green Tourism Business Scheme. Guests arriving without a car get a 10% discount.

DETAILS

- **Open** - All year. All day.
- **Number of beds** - 56 + 46 + 14 (3 units)
- **Booking** - Recommended
- **Price per night** - From £16 adults, £8 U16, U5 free.
- **Public Transport** - Train stations: Dunblane, Stirling, or Perth. Our own bus stop is served by no. 15 from Perth (approx. every hour). Summer only Citylink service to Oban and Fort William. Ring of Breadalbane hop-on hop-off service from Easter to October (see breadalbane.org)
- **Directions** - Signposted from A85 between Crieff (5miles) and Comrie (2miles).

CONTACT:
Tel: 01764 670140
info@comriecroft.com www.comriecroft.com
Comrie Croft, By Crieff/Comrie, Perthshire, PH7 4JZ

BY THE WAY
SCOTLAND HOSTEL AND CAMPSITE

By The Way Hostel and Campsite can be found in the Loch Lomond National Park halfway between Arrochar's peaks and the grandeur of Glencoe. The site is aimed primarily at outdoor enthusiasts and with great walking (the West Highland Way passes by the hostel), climbing, and white water rafting. There is lots to be enthusiastic about, Munro-baggers can find 50 Munros within 20 miles. Accommodation options range from camping (with an indoor cooking/dining area and campers' drying room), basic trekker huts/cabins (own cooking utensils required) and a purpose built four star hostel with twin and double rooms as well as dormitory accommodation, great self-catering facilities and drying room. For more comfort still there's a three bedroom chalet and two bedroom chalet. By The Way is in Tyndrum with the village pub, shops, café and Tourist Information Centre nearby. The Glasgow to Fort William road is 250m from the site (far from the madding traffic noise) and both the Glasgow Oban and Glasgow Fort William trains stop in Tyndrum.

DETAILS

- **Open** - All year. Camping from April to end September. 8am - 10am & 2pm - 8pm.
- **Number of beds** - 26 in hostel; 36 in huts; 50 camping.
- **Booking** - Always phone in advance. Deposit (Visa/Access) guarantees bed.
- **Price per night** - Hostel dorms from £18pp. Huts vary in price. Camping £8pp
- **Public Transport** - Intercity coach and rail service pick-up points in Tyndrum to Edinburgh, Glasgow, Fort William and Oban. Sleeper service to London.
- **Directions** - GR NN 327 302. Travelling on A82 follow sign in village for Tyndrum Lower Station. Hostel is immediately before station.

CONTACT: Kirsty Burnett
Tel: 01838 400333
info@TyndrumByTheWay.com www.TyndrumByTheWay.com
Lower Station Road, Tyndrum, FK20 8RY

STRATHFILLAN
WIGWAMS
SCOTLAND

On a working farm within the Loch Lomond and Trossachs National Park this is an ideal location for a single night, weekend or a week's let for families or groups. An ideal base for hill walking with Munros, the West Highland Way, canoeing, fishing, and skiing nearby. The Wigwams are comfortably equipped with mattresses, electric lights and heating etc (not metered). Large wigwam sleeps 4/5 on benches. Small wigwam sleeps 4 with mattresses on the floor. Each has own car park, picnic bench and campfire. Beaver is a deluxe wigwam sleeping 5 with kitchen, toilet, shower & TV. Also available: five self catering lodges, some with separate bedrooms, lounge, kitchen, shower and toilet; space for camping and caravans; Kirkton Farmhouse for groups up to 12; and a yurt sleeping 5. Logs,kindling and peat available in the shop, also our own sausages to cook on your camp fire. Site has toilet /shower block, hot and cold water and a fully equipped kitchen. Bedding & towels can be hired @£3/set.

DETAILS

- **Open** - All year,
- **Number of beds** - 133: Wigwams: 5x4, 18x5 Lodges: 1x8, 1x6, 1x5, 1x4
- **Booking** - Book by phone or email.
- **Price per night** - Small wigwam £40 for 2. Large wigwam £46 for 2. Yurt £70 for 2. £10/extra adult, £8/extra child. From £230 per week. Lodges from £280-500/week. Short breaks in lodges from £60/night.
- **Public Transport** - Train and buses at Tyndrum 2 miles away.
- **Directions** - Situated on Scottish Agricultural College's research farm on the A82 three miles north of Crianlarich, thirty minutes south of Glencoe Ski-Centre.

CONTACT:
Tel: 01838 400251
wigwam@sac.ac.uk   www.wigwamholidays.com/Strathfillan_Wigwam_Village
Auchtertyre, Tyndrum, Crianlarich, Perthshire FK20 8RU

RANNOCH FOREST
LODGE & CABIN
SCOTLAND

Set in two-thirds of an acre of private land, Rannoch Forest Lodge & The Log Cabin nestle on the edge of the Blackwood of Rannoch. They are ideally suited for outdoor enthusiasts with trails for mountain biking and an abundance of walks. It's a nature lovers paradise with red squirrel, pine martin, capercaillie and stags practically on the doorstep. A short walk takes you to the shores of Loch Rannoch where water activities and fishing are available. Accommodation at Forest Lodge consists of three 2 bed rooms (bunks) and one triple room, a large comfortable communal lounge with log burner, and well equipped shared kitchen. There is a bathroom and an additional toilet room. Whether you are looking to book a bed, a room, or the entire Lodge for exclusive group-use Rannoch Lodge provides a comfortable and inexpensive option. The Log Cabin sleeps five people in one triple and one twin room. There is a comfortable lounge with log burner, well equipped kitchen, and large bathroom.

DETAILS

- **Open** - All year.
- **Number of beds** - Log Cabin: 1x3, 1x twin. Forest Lodge: 1x3, 3x twin.
- **Booking** - Book via Facebook, email or phone
- **Price per night** - from £20 per person
- **Public Transport** - There is no public transport but private transfer can be arranged from Rannoch Railway Station or Pitlochry for an additional charge.
- **Directions** - At Kinloch Rannoch turn right at the Country Store onto the South Shore. After 5 miles take the first left after the Dall Estate sign. Follow track to the cul-de-sac then take the track on the right past Tigh-Na-Froach..

CONTACT: Amanda
Tel: 07971 653975
hepburnhillhouse@aol.com www.facebook.com/Rannochlodge
Dall, Rannoch, Perthshire, Scotland, PH17 2QH

In the centre of Birnam just 10 minutes' walk from Dunkeld, this refurbished Victorian manse has 7 bedrooms and offers a mix of self-catering hostel and bed & breakfast accommodation. Tucked away in the forests of Perthshire the village of Birnam is a perfect base to discover the mountains, waters, rich culture and heritage of Big Tree Country. GTBS Gold award winning Jessie Mac's has private doubles, bunk rooms and family rooms, all en suite, offering a warm welcome and a good night's rest. The ground floor double room has wheelchair access. LGBT friendly and well behaved dogs are welcome by arrangement. An hour by car from Edinburgh and Glasgow with good public transport links. A great choice whether you're looking for an affordable hostel room to share with friends or prefer a private room to yourselves.

DETAILS
- **Open** - Check in between 4 & 6.30 pm. Check out by 10.30am.
- **Number of beds** - 21: 4x2, 2x4, 1x5
- **Booking** - Book via website, email or phone
- **Price per night** - Dorm £20pp. Continental Breakfast £25, Cooked Breakfast £28. Private Double £28pp (based on 2 sharing), £33, £36. Child £9 in shared room. Infants free. Group rates available.
- **Public Transport** - Direct buses from Edinburgh/Inverness and connections from Glasgow. Direct trains from Edinburgh and Glasgow. Non car users are treated to a mug of tea/coffee, a bun and a fluffy towel on arrival!.
- **Directions** - Take Birnam/Dunkeld turning off the A9, Jessie Macs is in the centre of Birnam on the main "Perth Road"

CONTACT: Brenda Roddy
Tel: 01350 727 324
info@jessiemacs.co.uk jessiemacs.co.uk
Murthly Terrace, Birnam, Dunkeld PH8 0BG

PITLOCHRY
SCOTLAND **BACKPACKERS HOTEL**

Located right in the centre of beautiful Pitlochry, this friendly and comfortable hostel is an old Victorian hotel literally bursting with character and providing dorms and private rooms (with en suite). Comfy beds come with fitted sheets, duvets and 2 fluffy pillows and private rooms have fresh towels included. If you are visiting Pitlochry to enjoy the vast array of outdoor activities or simply want to get away from it all and relax, the hostel has everything you need to ensure you make the most of your time in this beautiful Perthshire town. Overlooking the street below, the bright spacious lounge has comfy sofas and as much free tea, coffee and hot chocolate as you can drink. It also has free WiFi, loads of local information, some games and musical instruments and a free pool table. A separate Movie Lounge has comfy sofas and loads of films to chose from. A great place to meet like minded people and although you might think you're only staying one night, you'll end up staying three or four - it's that kind of place!

DETAILS

- **Open** - March to November. Open 7.30am-1pm and 5pm-10pm (please check at reception as times may vary).
- **Number of beds** - 79.
- **Booking** - Booking in advance not always essential, first night's payment required.
- **Price per night** - From £15pp for dorms. Private rooms from £20 pp
- **Public Transport** - Buses stop on Atholl Road and the hostel is only 1 min walk. The train station exits onto Atholl Road also, only 5 mins' walk.
- **Directions** - Take the A924 Atholl road from the A9 the hostel is on the right if coming from the south and left if coming from the north as customer car park behind the building is accessed from Birnham Place (just past/before the hostel).

CONTACT: Receptionist
Tel: 01796 470044
info@pitlochrybackpackershotel.com   www.pitlochrybackpackershotel.com
134 Atholl Road, Pitlochry, PH16 5AB

GULABIN
LODGE

Gulabin Lodge is beautifully situated in the heart of Glenshee at the foot of Beinn Gulabin and is the nearest accommodation to the Glenshee ski slopes. The lodge offers excellent accommodation for individuals, families and groups, has under-floor heating throughout and two cosy lounges with log fires for those colder months. All rooms have been tastefully decorated with some rooms having mezzanine platforms which are ideal for families. Based on site at the lodge there are many activities available for all ages and abilities including a Ski School and equipment hire facility for the winter months. The lodge is an ideal base for schools groups and for activities such as climbing, walking or mountain biking. Mountain bike hire and guided trips are also available. Meals can be provided for groups and also transport to and from airports and rail stations. Registered 4 Star VisitScotland Activity Accommodation provider. AALS Registered L9768/R1801.

DETAILS

- **Open** - All year, 24 hours.
- **Number of beds** - 37: 9 rooms available.
- **Booking** - Booking advisable.
- **Price per night** - From £20pp self catering. Family rooms, twins, 4 person and 6 person rooms. Full board available. Sole use available. Separate 12 bed also available
- **Public Transport** - Train and bus stations at Pitlochry (22 miles), Blairgowrie (20 miles), Glasgow (100 miles), Edinburgh (70 miles). Post bus calls half a mile away.
- **Directions** - Gulabin Lodge is on the A93 road at Spittal of Glenshee - 20 miles north of Blairgowrie and 19 miles south of Braemar. Transport can be arranged.

CONTACT: Darren and Tereza
Tel: 01250 885255 Mobile: 07799 847014
info@gulabinlodge.co.uk www.gulabinoutdoors.co.uk
Spittal of Glenshee, By Blairgowrie, PH10 7QE

PROSEN
HOSTEL

Glenprosen is the most intimate of the Angus Glens on the southernmost edge of the Cairngorms National Park. Two Munros, the Mayar and Driesh link Glenprosen to the Cairngorms plateau. The Minister's Path leads over to Glen Clova, whilst a footbridge and path along the prettiest stretch of the river Prosen connect to Glenisla and the Cateran Trail in Perthshire. Prosen Hostel was converted from the old primary school to provide accommodation for those using the upgraded East Cairngorms footpath network. Converted to the latest and greenest specification, the living room has a wood burning stove, internet connection, and raised area for admiring the view (and red squirrels) through the school's huge windows. A drying room and laundry facilities complete the cosy welcome. It sleeps a total of 18 in 4 bunkrooms, sleeping 4, 4 and 6 and a family room sleeping 4. The nearby village hall is available to rent for ceilidhs, music sessions, parties and celebrations. STB 4 star.

DETAILS

■ **Open** - All year, all day.
■ **Number of beds** - 18:1x6, 3x4
■ **Booking** - Book by phone or email.
■ **Price per night** - £17 - £20 per person. Minimum periods & prices apply for Christmas and New Year.
■ **Public Transport** - Trains Dundee; No public transport beyond Kirriemuir .
■ **Directions** - From Kirriemuir follow B955 signed to Prosen, Clova and Cairngorms National Park. At Dykehead fork left. Carry on for 7 miles until public road ends at telephone kiosk. Turn acute right and follow tarmac 200m uphill to hostel.

CONTACT: Hector or Robert
Tel: 01575 540238/302
sih@prosenhostel.co.uk www.prosenhostel.co.uk
Prosen Hostel, Balnaboth, Kirriemuir, Angus, DD8 4SA

HABITAT
@ BALLATER

Set in the village of Ballater with a range of shops, pubs and restaurants, this is a stunning, purpose built hostel ideal for families, groups and independent travellers. Within the Cairngorms National Park it is a great position for enjoying a variety of outdoor activities.

All rooms are en suite, ranging from 8 bed dorms to 4 bed rooms suitable for families and a twin/single room. The hostel is fully accessible for wheelchair users. Bedding is included. There's a large kitchen /dining / lounge area with wood burning stove. There is an excellent drying and laundry room and secure storage for bikes.

Ballater is an ideal location for exploring the eastern Cairngorms, Royal Deeside and Aberdeenshire.

Habitat@Ballater is a VisitScotland five star hostel.

DETAILS

- **Open** - All year, (closed mid November-Xmas) all day.
- **Number of beds** - 25: 1x8, 1x6, 3 x private room (sleeping 2 to 4), 1x single.
- **Booking** - Book by phone, email or online.
- **Price per night** - Bunkrooms from £20 per person. Private rooms from £25 per person.
- **Public Transport** - From Aberdeen bus station (phone 01224 212266).
- **Directions** - On A93 just west of bridge over river in centre of Ballater.

CONTACT: Claudia Leith
Tel: 013397 53752
info@habitat-at-ballater.com   www.habitat-at-ballater.com
Bridge Square, Ballater, Aberdeenshire, AB35 5QJ

BACKPACKERS PLUS
OBAN

Many people's favourite hostel thanks to its friendly atmosphere and beautiful seaside town setting. Excellent facilities include free WiFi throughout, free breakfast, free all-day hot drinks, clean spacious rooms, secure bike storage, laundry service, cool communal areas with lots of character, strong hot showers, comfortable beds, and a well-equipped self-catering kitchen. There's a pool table and other games and lots of information from the knowledgeable staff about the area. Oban has spectacular views across to the islands and the bustle of fishing boats, ferries, yachts and seabirds make the waterfront a lovely place to be. Easy ferry access to the many beautiful Scottish Isles. Ancient standing stones, medieval castles, hairy coos and whisky distilleries are all nearby. The best fish and chips in Scotland are within 200 metres. Choose between custom made spacious bunk beds (including your own personal reading light, double power socket and locker), or a little extra privacy in one of our comfortable single, twin, double or family rooms. Experience backpacking with a Plus!

             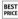

DETAILS

■ **Open** - All year, reception 7am-10pm, occasionally closed in middle of the day.
■ **Number of beds** - 50-60 dorm beds, family, double, twin rooms, some en suite.
■ **Booking** - recommended but not essential. Deposit = 1st nights board required.
■ **Price per night** - dorms from £12 pp, private rooms from £18 pp
■ **Public Transport** - From Citylink bus and train station walk along the waterfront, up George Street, past the Taj Mahal restaurant. Hostel is straight ahead on the left.
■ **Directions** - From A85 turn left at the Kings Knoll Hotel onto Deanery Brae. Sharp right onto Breadalbane Street. Hostel is at the bottom of the street on the right.

CONTACT: Receptionist
Tel: 01631 567189
info@backpackersplus.com www.backpackersplus.com
The Old Church, Breadalbane St, Oban, Argyll, PA34 5PH

JEREMY INGLIS
OBAN HOSTEL

Excellent value, warm and friendly hostel accommodation in Oban, Argyll. The Jeremy Inglis Hostel has been operating for more than 30 years and in that time has built up an excellent reputation for quality and value.

The hostel is centrally situated just off Argyll Square, Oban and is the closest hostel to all transport connections. Ferries to the Islands leave 300 metres away, trains and buses 200 metres. Three large supermarkets are close by. Cosy twin, double, single and family rooms (no bunk beds) give some privacy.

Prices include linen and towels as well as a continental breakfast with muesli, cereals and toast, vegemite and home-made jams; raspberry, damson and marmalade etc. There is a large, modern and well equipped kitchen with free tea, coffee and WiFi.

DETAILS

- **Open** - Closed until May 2016.
- **Number of beds** - 37
- **Booking** - Booking preferred. Deposit in certain circumstances.
- **Price per night** - Special dorm rate from £13.00. Double or twin from £15pp and singles from £17pp (depending on availability and season).
- **Public Transport** - Nearest train and Citylink drop off 150 metres from hostel. Ferries to islands 300 metres. For ferry enquiries phone 01631 566688.
- **Directions** - The hostel is in Airds Crescent, one of the streets off Argyll Square. The hostel is on the second floor, pink door.

CONTACT: Jeremy Inglis, Katrin or Michael
Tel: 01631 565065
jeremyinglis@mctavishs.freeserve.co.uk www.jeremyinglishostel.co.uk
21 Airds Crescent, Oban, Argyll, PA34 5SJ

OBAN
BACKPACKERS

Whether you're passing through Oban on the way to the Islands, or staying for a couple of days and exploring historic and beautiful Argyll, the original Oban Backpackers is a great place to stay, meet like minded people and probably end up staying longer than planned. Situated in the heart of the town Oban Backpackers is perfectly located to enable you to experience all Oban has to offer without burning a hole in your wallet. Completely refurbished in May 2013 the hostel offers dormitory accommodation with wide, comfortable, bunks, made up with fitted sheets, duvets and pillows. Powerful showers with loads of hot water add to the comfort and if required, towels can be hired from reception. The fully equipped kitchen has everything you will need to cook up your favourite meals and there is plenty of storage and fridge space available. The big cosy lounge with a real fire, pool table, free hot drinks, WiFi, musical instruments, games and book swap makes it a great place to stay and unwind.

DETAILS

- **Open** - March - November. 7am - 10pm.
- **Number of beds** - 54: 1x12, 1x10, 1x8, 4x6
- **Booking** - Online or by phone, first night's fee as deposit
- **Price per night** - From £15. Whole hostel bookings-email for quote
- **Public Transport** - 10 minute walk to Oban train station and Citylink buses
- **Directions** - From A85 turn left onto Deanery Brae take the sharp right onto Breadalbane Street. Oban Backpackers is on the left. From bus and train - walk along the waterfront keeping sea on left. Continue straight up George Street, bare right to Bredalbane Street. The hostel is on the right.

CONTACT: Reception
Tel: 01631 562 107
info@obanbackpackers.com www.obanbackpackers.com
Breadalbane Street, Oban, PA34 5NZ

CORRAN
HOUSE

Corran House is part of a Victorian terrace with magnificent seascapes across the bay to the Isle of Kerrera and the hills of Mull. There is a warm welcome for visitors and reasonably priced accommodation for singles, couples, families and groups. The house has a large self-catering kitchen, spacious TV lounge, comfortable, commodious, well appointed guest rooms and 4 bed dormitories with generous size beds. Most rooms have en suite facilities. Corran House is well situated for exploring Argyll and visiting the inner Hebrides. It is only a short walk along the sea front to the bus, train and ferry terminals. Downstairs is Markie Dans bar with patio and spectacular views. The pub offers great highland hospitality, tasty meals, live entertainment, widescreen TV, pool table and a late licence all year round to enable the discerning drinker to sample the best range of malt whiskies on the west coast. Pony trekking trips available with prior booking.

DETAILS

■ **Open** - All year. All year. Reception 10am-11pm. Check in after 3pm.
■ **Number of beds** - 62 in total - 26 bunks- 5x4 1x6. Plus guest rooms: 16
■ **Booking** - Advisable. Credit card secures bed. Early/late arrival with notice.
■ **Price per night** - Bunk rooms £17 standard/£19 en suite. Guest rooms from £22pp. Out of season rates available
■ **Public Transport** - Oban train, bus and ferry terminals are 900m from the house.
■ **Directions** - Corran House overlooks Oban Bay to the west of the town centre. From the Tourist Information and all the Oban transport terminals, with the sea on your left, walk along George Street past the Columba Hotel into Corran Esplanade. Follow the seafront for 300m. Corran House is on your right above Markie Dans Bar.

CONTACT:
Tel: 01631 566040
enquiries@corranhouseoban.co.uk www.corranhouseoban.co.uk
1 Victoria Crescent, Corran Esplanade, Oban, Argyll, PA34 5PN

COLONSAY
SCOTLAND BACKPACKERS LODGE

Colonsay Backpackers Lodge is located on a peaceful and idyllic Inner Hebridean island to the south of Mull which boasts magnificent sandy beaches, ancient forests and beautiful lochs. The place is teeming with wildlife which includes dolphins, seals, otters and many rare species of bird. There are ancient standing stones and a 14th century priory with exceptional carved Celtic tombstones. The famous Colonsay House gardens and café are open to visitors three times a week. The pub, café, shop and village hall, where there are regular ceilidhs, are all within three miles. Fresh lobster and crab can be bought from fishing boats in the harbour and the best oysters in the world are grown on Colonsay. Play a round of golf or treat yourself to a meal in the hotel. The lodge is a refurbished former gamekeeper's house with bothies. Centrally heated, it has 2 twin, 3 twin bunk and 2 three bedded rooms. It has a large dining/cooking/sitting area and a sitting room with log fire. Bed linen, towels and Wifi provided.

DETAILS

- **Open** - All year, 24 hours.
- **Number of beds** - 16: 5 x 2; 2 x 3
- **Booking** - Payment required 24 hours in advance.
- **Price per night** - £25pp twin, £19.50pp bothy
- **Public Transport** - Train and coach to Oban. Caledonian MacBrayne ferry to Colonsay takes 2.5 hours. Flights Hebridean Air from Connel
- **Directions** - Ferry departs Oban 6 times per week April to October; Sun, Mon, Wed, Thurs, Fri, Sat (rest of year Mon, Wed, Fri, Sat). Flights Tues, Thurs from Connel Airport, nr Oban. Transport from the harbour can be arranged if required.

CONTACT: The Manager
Tel: 01951 200312
cottages@colonsayestate.co.uk www.colonsayestate.co.uk
Colonsay Estate Cottages, Isle of Colonsay, Argyll, PA61 7YP

COLL
BUNKHOUSE

Coll Bunkhouse provides five star hostel accommodation in the Inner Hebrides. The beautiful Isle of Coll offers so much, whether you are into walking, stargazing, wildlife-spotting, diving, cycling, sailing or kayaking, you can do it all.

The bunkhouse is bright and airy, with 16 beds in two dorms of 6 and one family room for 4 which can also be booked as a twin room. Ideal for small groups or independent travellers. The building is brand new, with a fully equipped kitchen and modern facilities throughout. Whether you're looking for an island adventure or a quiet place to relax, a warm welcome awaits.

DETAILS

■ **Open** - All year, 24 hours.
■ **Number of beds** - 16: 2x6, 1x4
■ **Booking** - Not always essential but highly recommended. Full payment is required at time of booking, or a deposit for a group booking.
■ **Price per night** - £21pp (dorm). Private rooms £80 (quad), £65 (triple), £50 (twin). Discounts for group bookings (exclusive use) of two nights or more from 5% to 50%
■ **Public Transport** - Ferry from Oban takes 2.40 hours. Sailings every day in summer and five times a week in winter. Flights from Oban four times a week. Bikes are free on the ferry and can be booked onto trains to Oban. Free car parks in Oban.
■ **Directions** - Coll Bunkhouse is situated in the centre of the village of Arinagour, very close to the local shop and the hotel/bar. From the ferry walk along Main Street continuing onto Shore Street. The bunkhouse is on your left hand side, next door to An Cridhe, the new community centre. From the airport take the road to Arinagour and the bunkhouse will be on your right hand side as you enter the village.

CONTACT: George
Tel: 01879 230217
info@collbunkhouse.co.uk www.collbunkhouse.com
Arinagour, Isle of Coll, Argyll, PA78 6SY

MILLHOUSE
HOSTEL

Tiree is an idyllic Hebridean island, perfect for outdoor pursuits, wildlife enthusiasts, and those wanting to experience the tranquillity of stunning white beaches and crystal clear seas.

A warm welcome and excellent facilities await you at Millhouse. There are bikes for hire to explore the island, visit the lighthouse museum, 'ping' the ringing stone, find the standing stones, wonder at the Machair flowers or watch the seals. Watersports take place on adjacent Loch Bhasapol, and the secluded Cornaig beach is a ten minute walk away.

There is a resident RSPB warden on the island and a bird hide near the hostel. For walkers, Millhouse is on the Tiree Pilgrimage route linking the ancient chapels and monuments around the island. 4 star hostel with free WiFi.

DETAILS

■ **Open** - Mar-Oct, open in winter by arrangement. Open all day. Check in 4pm Check out 10am.
■ **Number of beds** - Hostel 16 : 2 x 2/3, 2 x 5. Farmhouse 10: 3 x 4 (limit 10)
■ **Booking** - Advisable, please check vacancies before boarding the ferry
■ **Price per night** - Dorm from £19pp. Twin from £24pp. Family room £60-£95 per room.
■ **Public Transport** - Caledonian MacBrayne ferry from Oban to Tiree or Flybe flight from Glasgow. Local ring and ride bus 01879 220419.
■ **Directions** - From end of ferry road turn right at T junction and continue for 5 miles to Millhouse Hostel.

CONTACT: David Naylor
Tel: 01879 220892
mail@tireemillhouse.co.uk www.tireemillhouse.co.uk
Cornaigmore, Isle of Tiree, Argyll, PA77 6XA

KERRERA
BUNKHOUSE

Located on the island of Kerrera off the coast from Oban, overlooking the stunning Gylen Castle and coast, Kerrera Bunkhouse can sleep up to 9, all bedding supplied. Self-cater using the small kitchen equipped with cooker/oven, sink, pots, pans and crockery, microwave and fridge with a small freezer compartment. Basics like tea, coffee, salt, pepper, washing up liquid, are supplied but please bring everything else as there are no shops on the island. Lunches available in the Kerrera Tea Garden next door. Toilet and showers are in an adjoining block (BYO towels). Larger group? Hang out in the Byre (£25pn) a converted cow shed- with wood-burning stove, sofas, comfy seats and a large dining table. No TV or phone signal. A bell tent on a purpose built platform has a comfy double bed (bedding provided), a wood burner and adjacent sheltered cooking area, commands stunning views of the Firth or Lorne with many islands dotted in the distance including Seil, Jura, Colonsay, Mull and the Garvellachs.

DETAILS

- **Open** - All year, 10am to 6pm. No curfew.
- **Number of beds** - Bunkhouse: 9, 1x4 (bunks) downstairs, 1x3 double/twin + single upstairs + sofa bed
- **Booking** - Essential due to ferry restrictions. Contact for long term booking deals.
- **Price per night** - Bunkhouse: sole use £100, £80 thereafter, or £15pp, The Byre £25 per night (inc basket of wood for the fire), bell tent is £45 (includes firewood)
- **Public Transport** - Ferries from Gallanach Road, 1.5m south of Oban http://www.kerrera-ferry.co.uk 50 min walk to Kerrera Bunkhouse (pick ups can be arranged)
- **Directions** - From the ferry terminal take the path on the left, taking you south along the coast (50 min walk). Follow the teapots!

CONTACT: Aideen and Martin
Tel: 01631 566 367
info@kerrerabunkhouse.co.uk www.kerrerabunkhouse.co.uk
Lower Gylen, Isle of Kerrera, By Oban, Argyll PA34 4SX

IONA
HOSTEL

'BEST ECO-HOSTEL IN SCOTLAND' (GTBS). Tucked into the rocky outcrops at the north end of the island, Iona Hostel has spectacular views to Staffa and the Treshnish Isles, and beyond Rhum to the Black Cuillins of Skye. The hostel is situated on the working croft of Lagandorain (the hollow of the otter).

This land has been worked for countless generations, creating the familiar Hebridean patchwork of wildflower meadow, crops and grazing land, home to an amazing variety of plants and birds. It offers quiet sanctuary for those that seek it, within easy reach of island activities.

Whether travelling on your own, with friends, or as part of one of our many visiting groups, Iona Hostel offers you a warm welcome - with the best views this side of heaven. 4 star STB. Green Tourism Gold Award. We regret no dogs.

DETAILS

- **Open** - All year, closed 11am-1pm for cleaning - no curfew.
- **Number of beds** - 21: 1x2, 2x4, 1x5, 1x6.
- **Booking** - Strongly advised
- **Price per night** - £21.00 adult / £17.50 under 10's (bedding included).
- **Public Transport** - Caledonian Macbrayne ferry service from Oban or Mull 08705 650000. For buses on Mull 01546 604695. Taxi service on Iona 0781 0325990.
- **Directions** - You cannot bring your car onto Iona, but there is free parking in Fionnphort on Mull at the Columba Centre. Iona Hostel is the last building at the north end of the island, 2 km from the pier and up beyond the abbey.

CONTACT: John MacLean
Tel: 01681 700781
info@ionahostel.co.uk www.ionahostel.co.uk
Iona Hostel, Iona, Argyll, PA76 6SW

CRAIGNURE
BUNKHOUSE

SCOTLAND

Craignure Bunkhouse is an eco-sensitive hostel in an atmospheric setting, close to Craignure Pier where the ferry arrives from Oban. Next to the bunkhouse is The Craignure Inn, a popular traditional inn offering food, drink and and a welcoming atmosphere. Craignure is the hub for the island bus services and tourist information. The bunkhouse has a biomass boiler and solar powered heating. There are two rooms of 6 beds and two rooms of 4 beds, each with an en suite shower. Each bunk has a locker, a reading light and USB port. The Convivial is a large communal room, with well equipped kitchen, ample dining space, plenty of books/games and a large Freesat television surrounded by comfortable couches and chairs. Free WiFi throughout the building. Bedlinen is provided and towels can be hired. Laundry, equipment/bike store and drying room are available. Mull has great beaches. A visit to Duart Castle, a sea trip to Staffa, ferry trip to Iona, or shopping trip toTobermory are all recommended.

DETAILS

- **Open** - All year, closed 11am-4pm for cleaning.
- **Number of beds** - 20: 2x4, 2x6
- **Booking** - Booking through website or phone.
- **Price per night** - £20 per person per night. 4 berth rooms, £75 per night. 6 berth rooms, £110 per night. Whole hostel, £350 per night, by prior arrangement.
- **Public Transport** - Ferries from Oban dock at Craignure Pier. Coaches and trains run frequently from Glasgow to Oban. Craignure is the hub for the island buses.
- **Directions** - From Craignure peir, turn left and look out for the Craignure Inn 350 metres down the road. The bunkhouse is next door.

CONTACT: Chris, James or the warden
Tel: 01680 812043 Mob:07900 692973
info@craignure-bunkhouse.co.uk www.craignure-bunkhouse.co.uk/
Craignure Bunkhouse, Craignure, Isle Of Mull, Argyll And Bute, PA65 6AY

SHIELING
HOLIDAYS

Right on the sea, with views to Ben Nevis. There are otters on site, and you may see porpoises, dolphins and eagles. Your accommodation is in shared Shielings, unique carpeted cottage tents, made on Mull, which are clean, bright and spacious, and have real beds for 2, 4, or 6 people. Or you can hire a Shieling to yourself or stay in a self catering cottage. There are super showers, and a communal Shieling with woodburning stove, TV, payphone and launderette. Free WiFi. Campfire. Bike hire.

Stroll to the ferry, pub, café, shops, and swimming pool. Walk to Duart Castle, home of the Clan Maclean. Catch the bus for Tobermory for Iona (where Columba brought Christianity to Scotland) and for Staffa (home of puffins, and inspiration for Mendelssohn's overture 'Fingal's Cave'). A perfect base for all Mull. You don't need a car.

DETAILS

- **Open** - April to October, 24 hours (reception 8am - 10pm).
- **Number of beds** - 18: 6 x 2, 1 x 6.
- **Booking** - Please email a booking enquiry from our website.
- **Price per night** - £14.00 pp. Under 15s £10. Bedding £4 pp.
- **Public Transport** - From Glasgow, rail or bus (0871 266 3333) at 12.00, ferry (01680 812343) at 16.00 from Oban, arrive Mull 16.46; back by 10.55 ferry, arrive Glasgow by 1600. Please check times before travel.
- **Directions** - Grid Ref 724 369. From ferry, left on the A849 to Iona. After 400 metres, left opposite church past old pier to reception by the sea - 800 metres in all.

CONTACT: David Gracie
Tel: 01680 812496
sales@shielingholidays.co.uk www.shielingholidays.co.uk
Craignure, Mull, Argyll, PA65 6AY

CORRAN
BUNKHOUSE

Corran Bunkhouse 4 star accommodation is situated in a stunning lochside location surrounded by mountains in the magnificent Highlands of Scotland, 8 miles south of Fort William and 7 miles north of Glencoe. The Corran Bunkhouse is made up of two fully equipped self-catering bunkhouses which between them can offer comfortable accommodation for up to 32 people. One bunkhouse sleeps 12 and the other sleeps 20 making Corran Bunkhouse an ideal base for small and large groups. Individual travellers are welcome and the room sizes make the bunkhouse ideal for family groups. All bedrooms have a TV and en suite facilities. There are fully equipped kitchen/dining areas, drying room, central heating, laundry facilities, private parking and a steam room situated in the smaller bunkhouse. Children and pets welcome. Group discounts. Come and enjoy the many outdoor activities available in the area such as climbing, walking, canoeing, kayaking, cycling and mountain biking.

DETAILS

- **Open** - All year.
- **Number of beds** - 32: 8x2 1x3 2x4 1x5
- **Booking** - Advisable but not necessary - major credit cards accepted.
- **Price per night** - £20 per person, £18 per person for group bookings. £24 for single occupancy. Prices include all bedding.
- **Public Transport** - Trains at Fort William (8 mile bus or taxi ride to hostel). Regular buses toward Fort William from the south and from Inverness stop 100m from hostel (ask for Corran Ferry). Check the Citylink web site for bus details.
- **Directions** - On the Onich side of the Corran Ferry 8 miles south of Fort William. Turn onto A861 Corran Ferry Road from A82. Bunkhouse on the left before slipway.

CONTACT: Alan Hood
Tel: 01855 821000
info@corranbunkhouse.co.uk www.corranbunkhouse.co.uk
Corran Ferry Approach Road, Onich, Fort William, PH33 6SE

GLENCOE
SCOTLAND INDEPENDENT HOSTEL

Glencoe Independent Hostel, centred around an old highland croft in the heart of Glencoe, offers great value accommodation for groups, families and individuals. It is set in secluded and peaceful woodland midway between Glencoe village and the Clachaig Inn with immediate access to world class cycling, walking, climbing and kayaking. The hostel is 20 minutes from Glencoe Ski Centre and the West Highland Way and 40 minutes from Nevis Range. The hostel has 4 rooms, a lounge with open fire, cooking and dining facilities and offers private family and couples rooms when available. The Alpine bunkhouse sleeps 16 in 3 rooms, ideal for outdoor activity and school groups. Also available are luxury and economy caravans for 2 to 4 people and a log cabin for 2 to 3 people. The site has a top class drying room, bike storage, and mountains all around. Free WiFi in reception. Go Glencoe Guided walks now available too!

DETAILS

- **Open** - All year (phone in Nov and Dec), 9am - 9 pm.
- **Number of beds** - Hostel: 26, bunkhouse: 16, 4 caravans of 2-4, log cabin: 2-3.
- **Booking** - Booking advised in summer. 30% non refundable deposit (min. £10).
- **Price per night** - From £12.50 to £22 per person.
- **Public Transport** - 1.5 miles from bus stop in Glencoe Village (crossroads). Citylink buses 914, 915 and 916 from Skye, Fort William, Glasgow. Bus 44 from Fort William and Kinlochleven. For West Highland Way take White Corries near Kingshouse Hotel to Glencoe Crossroads (20 mins) then 1.5 miles' walk.
- **Directions** - From A82 south, take right turn for Clachaig Inn, 1 mile after pub on left. From north, take left turn for Kinlochleven, then immediate right to Glencoe Village. 1 mile out of village on right.

CONTACT: Keith or Davina
Tel: 01855 811906
info@glencoehostel.co.uk www.glencoehostel.co.uk
Glencoe Independent Hostel, Glencoe, Argyll, PH49 4HX

FORT WILLIAM
BACKPACKERS

Deep in the Highlands, surrounded by spectacular mountain scenery lies Fort William, a mecca for those with a spirit of adventure. You can start (or end) the 'West Highland Way' in Fort William, hike or bike along mountain trails, go for a boat trip on the sea loch or just take it easy amidst the wonderful scenery. Even in winter Fort William stays busy with skiing, snow-boarding, mountaineering and ice-climbing. Nestling on a hillside above the town, with wonderful views, this characterful and comfy hostel provides everything you'll need after a day in the hills. In the evening put your feet up in the elegant lounge in front of a real fire or stroll down to the choice of local pubs. Ben Nevis, Britain's highest mountain, is just around the corner and below it is Glen Nevis, perhaps Scotland's prettiest glen, with wonderful waterfalls and ancient pine forest. Dramatic and eerie, Glencoe awaits a few miles away for an excellent day trip.

DETAILS

- **Open** - All year, all day. Reception 7am-noon and 5pm-10.30pm (times may vary).
- **Number of beds** - 38
- **Booking** - First night's payment required to confirm booking.
- **Price per night** - From £17 per person. ID required for check-in.
- **Public Transport** - Train and bus stations are only 5/10 minute walk from hostel.
- **Directions** - From north on the A82 go right at roundabout towards town centre. Turn left onto Victoria Road, then left at fork onto Alma Road. From south on the A82 go straight over first roundabout. At second roundabout go right onto Belford Road following Inverness signs, then turn right up Victoria Road then into Alma Road at left fork. From stations walk past supermarket, turn left before the underpass, heading onto the Belford Road. The hostel is just a bit further up, on Alma Road, on the right.

CONTACT: Receptionist
Tel: 01397 700 711
info@fortwilliambackpackers.com www.fortwilliambackpackers.com
Alma Road, Fort William, PH33 6HB

SMIDDY
BUNKHOUSE

Find a friendly welcome at this comfortable, mountain hostel with a loch-side location overlooking the Caledonian Canal. The pine clad interior has a cosy, friendly atmosphere. Stunning mountains and water on the doorstep with the meeting of the West Highland Way and Great Glen Way only yards away. Hot showers. Fully equipped kitchens available at all times (local shop open until 11pm daily). Use of 2 efficient drying / laundry rooms. All bedding provided. Fully heated for all year round use. Lockable bike & canoe stores. Ample off road parking. Outdoor information, daily weather & snow reports. Advice/ instruction/guiding available from resident mountain and water based instructors for: winter and summer walking/climbing; river, loch and sea kayaking; dinghy sailing. Hire of sea and river kayaks/open canoes, dinghy and other equipment. AALS licensed & DofE Approved Activity Provider (Assessor available). Group and family accommodation. Meeting / lecture room available by arrangement.

DETAILS

- **Open** - All year, all day (with key).
- **Number of beds** - 24: 3x4, 2x6.
- **Booking** - Book on-line or telephone / e-mail.
- **Price per night** - £15 - £ 20 (seasonal) pp (incl. bedding).
- **Public Transport** - Two minutes' walk from Corpach Railway Station-the Mallaig Line. Three miles - 2 stops out from Fort William (trains from Glasgow and London).
- **Directions** - Take A82 north out of Fort William towards Inverness. After one mile take A830 west towards Mallaig and follow for 2 miles to village of Corpach. Turn left before shops, signposted 'Snowgoose Mountain Centre'. The hostel is 30 yds on left.

CONTACT: John or Tina
Tel: 01397 772467
enquiry@highland-mountain-guides.co.uk www.accommodation-fortwilliam.co.uk/
Snowgoose Mountain Centre, Station Road, Corpach, Fort William, PH33 7JH

BANK STREET
LODGE

Bank Street Lodge is situated 100 metres from Fort William High Street which has numerous shops, pubs, restaurants and banks. There is a fully equipped kitchen with cooker, fridge, microwave, cutlery and crockery provided. The common room lounge has a TV, it also provides tables and chairs for eating self prepared meals, and a snack vending machine.

All bedding is provided. Some rooms are en suite (twins, doubles and family). WiFi is also now available in our lounge/TV room. The Stables Restaurant, at the front of the building, serves fine food for lunches and dinners (also breakfast from May to September) - treat yourself! Fort William is an ideal base from which to enjoy walking, climbing, cycling or mountain biking. The world-renowned Nevis Range Mountain Bike Trails and Ski Centre are only a short distance from the town centre. Three star STB rating.

DETAILS

- **Open** - All year (closed for 3 days at Xmas), 24 hour reception. Entry from 1.00pm, depart by 10.00am.
- **Number of beds** - 43: 6 x 4, 4 x 3, 1 x 7
- **Booking** - Booking advised. Deposit required for long stays or groups.
- **Price per night** - From £18 to £22.00 per person. Group rates available
- **Public Transport** - Train and bus stations at Fort William, 500 metres from Lodge.
- **Directions** - Head for town centre via the underpass, turn left after Tesco supermarket on Bank Street, then head up the hill for 150 metres. Hostel is above the Stables Restaurant. Car parking is available.

CONTACT: Reception
Tel: 01397 700070
bankstreetlodge@btconnect.com www.bankstreetlodge.co.uk
Bank Street, Fort William, PH33 6AY

FARR COTTAGE
LODGE
SCOTLAND

Farr Cottage is a 4 star hostel in Corpach just 4 miles from Fort William, the outdoor capital of the UK. It has a breath-taking view of Ben Nevis and views across Loch Linnhe. There is a full range of in-house facilities including freesat TV with DVD player in the lounge, free WiFi, licensed bar, self-catering facilities, drying room and a laundry service. The hostel has central heating and hot showers. Bike storage, bike hire and free on-site parking are available. Some pet friendly rooms are available please ring for details. Breakfast and picnic lunches can be provided when pre-ordered. The hostel organises many outdoor pursuits including white water rafting, canyoning, climbing, abseiling, skiing, snowboarding, fishing, and golf. Check website for special offers and details of music nights and events nights. Farr Cottage's professional team are geared to meet your needs and requirements.

DETAILS

- **Open** - All year. Reception 4:30pm - 10pm.
- **Number of beds** - Cottage 30: 2 x double, 2 x 8,1 x 10. Fully self-contained.
- **Booking** - Advance booking advised particularly in winter months.
- **Price per night** - £16.50pp in mixed dorms, From £17pp in double room. Group rates available.
- **Public Transport** - Corpach train station is 200m from the hostel. The nearest Citylink service is three miles away at Fort William. Taxi fare from Fort William centre is approximately £7.50.
- **Directions** - Follow the A82 north from Fort William centre towards Inverness for 1.5 miles. Turn left at the A830 to Mallaig. Follow this road for 1.5 miles into Corpach. We are on the right.

CONTACT: Cliff or Lyn
Tel: 01397 772315 Mob: 07534749285
mail@farrcottage.com www.farrcottage.com
Corpach, Fort William, PH33 7LR

ÀITE CRUINNICHIDH

Àite Cruinnichidh, 15 miles northeast of Fort William, occupies a unique sheltered spot adjacent to the Monessie Gorge where you can explore remote glens, mountain passes and lochs. There are numerous walks easily accessible from the hostel and seven magnificent canoeing rivers within 20 miles. The location is ideal for climbing (rock and ice), mountain biking, skiing or just relaxing. A warm, peaceful, friendly, country hostel in a converted barn, Àite Cruinnichidh has been renovated to high standards and sleeps 30 in four rooms with all bedding supplied. The hostel has a fully equipped kitchen/dining room, sitting room, excellent showers, sauna suite, seminar room and garden. There is a good selection of maps, board games, magazines, books and a small reading room. No TV and, although the hostel has WiFi, guests are encouraged to socialise and enjoy the natural environment that the hostel has to offer. Advice available on walking/cycling routes. Groups and individuals welcome. No wheelchair facilities but glad to accommodate people with disabilities.

DETAILS

- **Open** - All year, all day.
- **Number of beds** - 30: 1x6, 4x4, 1x twin, 1x double, 1x family/double en suite.
- **Booking** - Booking advised, 50% deposit.
- **Price per night** - From £16 per person.
- **Public Transport** - Roy Bridge station & bus stop (2 miles) has several connections to Fort William daily. Pick up from Roy Bridge with advanced notice
- **Directions** - From Spean Bridge take A86 miles to Roy Bridge. Go though village and continue for 2 miles. Hostel is on right 100m after Glenspean Lodge Hotel.

CONTACT: Gavin or Nicola
Tel: 01397 712315
gavin@highland-hostel.co.uk   www.highland-hostel.co.uk
1 Achluachrach, By Roy Bridge, Near Fort William, PH31 4AW

INSH HALL
LODGE

Situated between Loch Insh and the foothills of Glenfeshie, Insh Hall Lodge provides comfortable double, twin and family rooms on a room only basis. Rooms are equipped with bed linen and TVs. Facilities include large meeting room, laundry/drying room, sauna and mini gym, outdoor volleyball and basketball, as well as private car parking. Meals are available in the Boathouse Restaurant situated by the shore, 120 yds from the lodge.

Loch Insh Watersports provides a range of accessible watersports on-site. This is also the starting point for many local walks, lochside trails and cycle routes. Loch Insh is on Sustrans Route 7 Cycle Way. Anyone staying two nights or more between April and October has free use of the water sports equipment or between November and March has free use of dry ski slope - from 8.30 to 10.00 and from 4.00 to 5.30pm.

DETAILS

- **Open** - All year. All day.
- **Number of beds** - 50+: Double, twin or family rooms en suite.
- **Booking** - Booking is recommended but not always required. Deposit taken.
- **Price per night** - From £15 per room.
- **Public Transport** - Trains at Aviemore and Kingussie (7 miles from Loch Insh). Nearest airport is Inverness, approximately one hour north of Loch Insh.
- **Directions** - Situated near Kincraig, 7 miles south of Aviemore, 7 miles north of Kingussie on the B9152, follow signs for Loch Insh Watersports. Local bus routes from Aviemore to Kincraig, approx. 1 mile from the Lodge.

CONTACT: Receptionist
Tel: 01540 651272
office@lochinsh.com www.lochinsh.com
Insh Hall, Kincraig, Inverness-shire, PH21 1NU

BRAEMAR
LODGE BUNKHOUSE

Surrounded by the beauty of Deeside, Braemar Lodge Hotel and Bunkhouse is in a quiet setting only a two minute walk from the village itself. Braemar Lodge Hotel was formerly a Victorian shooting lodge and is set in extensive grounds two minutes from the centre of Braemar in the heart of Royal Deeside. The great value Bunkhouse provides comfortable accommodation for up to 12 people within the hotel grounds.

The bunkhouse is equipped with two shower rooms, one of which is suitable for wheelchair access. The bunkhouse also has good drying and laundry facilities, excellent for damp clothes and ski boots. A generous fully equipped kitchen is available for all your self-catering needs. Guests are also welcome to use the hotel's excellent dining facilities if a rest from self-catering is required. All bed linen and towels are supplied for the duration of your stay.

DETAILS

- **Open** - All year, all day.
- **Number of beds** - 12: 3x4
- **Booking** - Book by phone or email
- **Price per night** - From £15 per person
- **Public Transport** - Aberdeen airport 59 miles. Railway stations at Perth (50 miles) and Aberdeen. Buses to Braemar from Aberdeen where the bus and rail station are side by side. Two minute walk to hotel from Braemar village bus stop.
- **Directions** - The hotel is situated on the A93 on the left if you are arriving from the south. Two minutes' walk from the village centre.

CONTACT: Reception
Tel: 01339 741627
mail@braemarlodge.co.uk   www.braemarlodge.co.uk
6 Glenshee Rd, Braemar, Aberdeenshire, AB35 5YQ

ABERNETHY
BUNKHOUSE

Sharing a car park with the Speyside Way and just yards from the river, the converted Nethy Station offers all that a group of 10-26 could expect from a bunkhouse and you only pay for a maximum of 20 beds. It is well equipped, fully central heated and has two public areas. Most rooms have triple bunks and there is a 2 bunk room with unusual access: we call it Narnia, as you get there through a wardrobe! There is also 'The Shed'.

Whether you self-cater or we cook for you as a group, you will have access to the kitchen at all times. We never ask people to share the building so you may sleep, walk, ski, board, hike, ride, fish, etc. at your own convenience. The bunkhouse is only 200 yards from the centre of Nethy Bridge with its shop, butcher, pub and interpretive centre and half way between two winter sports areas. Dogs are welcome but please do not let them sleep on the beds!

DETAILS

- **Open** - All year, anytime.
- **Number of beds** - 2x9 + 3x2
- **Booking** - Essential (with deposit)
- **Price per night** - £16 per person. Minimum of 10 people.
- **Public Transport** - Take train or Citylink coach to Aviemore. Local buses are available from Aviemore to Nethy Bridge Post Office, phone 01479 811566.
- **Directions** - GR 002 207. Hostel is adjacent to the Speyside Way. From the B970, with Post Office on your right, go over the bridge and turn left immediately. Go past the butcher turn second right.

CONTACT: Patricia or Richard
Tel: 01479 8214370
info@nethy.org www.nethy.org
Station Road, Nethy Bridge, PH25 3DN

ARDENBEG
BUNKHOUSE

Part of the award-winning Craggan Outdoors activity centre, Ardenbeg offers good value self-catering accommodation across rooms of four, five, six & eight bunks, along with two well appointed kitchen / dining / common room areas, four bathrooms and a large private garden with BBQ, picnic tables & a children's play area.

The property is situated on a quiet residential street in Grantown-on-Spey, the historic capital of Strathspey. As well as the wide range of outdoor activities on offer through Craggan Outdoors (see www.cragganoutdoors.co.uk), Ardenbeg is perfectly situated - 15 minutes from Aviemore, 45 minutes from Inverness, 2 hours from Aberdeen, 3 hours from the Central Belt - to enjoy all that the Cairngorms National Park & wider central Highlands has to offer.

DETAILS

- **Open** - Year round, access 24 hours.
- **Number of beds** - 23: 1x4, 1x5, 1x6, 1x8.
- **Booking** - In advance to avoid disappointment
- **Price per night** - From £16.50 to £24 per person per night, subject to number of people & duration of stay.
- **Public Transport** - Rail: Aviemore. Bus: stop on the High Street in Grantown. Air: Inverness
- **Directions** - Once in Grantown-on-Spey, find the Co-op on the High Street, & then take the road that runs beside the Co-op (keeping it on your right), & turn left after 100 yards into Grant Road. Ardenbeg is the fifth building on the right.

CONTACT: Keith & Jill Ballam
Tel: 01479 873283 / 01479 872824
info@cragganoutdoors.co.uk www.cragganoutdoors.co.uk
Grant Road, Grantown-on-Spey, Moray PH26 3LD

FINDHORN
VILLAGE HOSTEL

SCOTLAND

Located in the heart of the coastal village of Findhorn, on the Moray Coast, an Area of Outstanding Natural Beauty, Findhorn Village Hostel is just a stone's throw from a beautiful bay. A short walk from the hostel are the dunes and the Findhorn Foundation Eco Village. Extensive sandy beaches, great wildlife sites and the Speyside distilleries are within reach of the village. The Cairngorm mountains are under an hours drive. The hostel provides newly renovated self-catering accommodation in a former village school which can be booked by groups or individuals. It has a well equipped kitchen and communal area, WiFi, TV, DVD, modern showers and central heating. Sleeping accommodation is in shared bunk-bed rooms, a two person room and a en suite family room. A new annex, available to smaller groups or families, has a small kitchenette and en suite shower room. The communal areas provide plenty of space for large groups but can be rearranged into a more intimate setting for individuals.

DETAILS

- **Open** - All year. Office hours 9am-1pm Mon to Fri.
- **Number of beds** - 6 - Annex; 2x8; 1x2; 1x4/5
- **Booking** - Booking is essential via email or phone. Groups should send a deposit and pay in full one month prior to visit. Individuals should pay in full on booking.
- **Price per night** - £17pp individuals. £14.50pp groups. Minimum group charge £116 (8 people). Groups subject to a £30 cleaning charge. Bed-linen £3.50 per bed.
- **Public Transport** - Trains and intercity buses to Forres. Bus No 31 runs hourly (except Sundays) from Forres to Findhorn (until 18.15) and stops by the church.
- **Directions** - B9011 into Findhorn. at the end of the one-way system through the village take a left turn. Findhorn Village Centre is directly ahead.

CONTACT: Karin
Tel: 01309 692339
findhornvillagecentre@gmail.com www.findhornvillagehostel.com
Church Place, Findhorn, Forres, Moray, IV36 3YR

RATTRAY HEAD
ECO-HOSTEL

Rattray Head Eco-Hostel is a former lighthouse shore station among huge dunes on an isolated 11 mile long sandy beach.

Come and relax in this gorgeous most easterly part of mainland Scotland, and enjoy one of its driest, sunniest, midge-free areas.

The 1892 granite building has been renovated to form a modern, non-smoking, dog-friendly coastal retreat. The hostel has self-catering kitchens, bunkrooms, and double and family bedrooms, and is part of the SIH network. The North Sea Cycle Route (Sustrans 1) is 17 miles inland and passes through historic Aberdeenshire with stone circles, castle ruins and golf courses.

DETAILS

- **Open** - All year, phone in winter Check in 4–8pm, check out 11am. No curfew.
- **Number of beds** - 24: 1x3, 4x4, 1x5
- **Booking** - Booking is available with first night as deposit.
- **Price per night** - Bunk £16pp. Triple £19pp. Double/Twin £24pp. Includes bedding and drinks.
- **Public Transport** - Airport, coach and train stations at Aberdeen (43 miles). Buses 60, 63 run frequently between Aberdeen and Peterhead. Bus 69 runs hourly between Peterhead and Fraserburgh. Taxi from Peterhead about £23.
- **Directions** - NK103577 Rattray is signed from the A90 Peterhead to Fraserburgh road. The hostel is at the end of the lane near the lighthouse, about 3 miles from the A90.

CONTACT: Rob and Val
Tel: 01346 532236
hostel@rattrayhead.net www.rattrayhead.net/hostel
Lighthouse Cottages, Rattray Head, Peterhead, Aberdeenshire, AB42 3HA

CULLEN HARBOUR
HOSTEL

Cullen Harbour Hostel's special location on the shores of the Moray Firth offers guests a relaxing break with the sound of the sea at night and coastal walks by day. Accommodation is spacious with wooden details, slate floors and sumptuous fabrics. The solid single beds have thick curtains around them. The kitchen has a wood burning Rayburn and comfortable seating. There is a power shower and a separate bathroom. The hostel has been awarded 4 stars by VisitScotland. Next to the hostel is a holiday cottage sleeping 4, this has a single room, an upstairs sitting room with single bed and a magnificent double bedroom with sea views. Cullen is at one end of the Speyside Way and on the National Cycle Route 1. Outdoor activity groups enjoy sea kayaking, surfing, rock climbing and wildlife watching. Dolphins are seen from the hostel. Children enjoy the sandy harbour and rock pools. Pubs and food are readily available.

DETAILS

- **Open** - All year, all day. but please check in initially by 21.00. Telephone enquiries are welcome from 07.00 to 20.00.
- **Number of beds** - 14 + 4: 2x6, 1x4 en-suite (family room) + 4 in holiday cottage.
- **Booking** - Book by e-mail or phone. Group and peak season bookings pay in advance by bacs. Other bookings pay by cash on arrival.
- **Price per night** - £20pp (£18 without bedding). Four-bed family room with en suite shower: £88 for four people, £72 for three and £52 for two. Cottage from £280/week.
- **Public Transport** - Nearest station Keith (12 miles). Taxi from Keith is economical if there are a few people, or bring a bike!
- **Directions** - The hostel is found immediately adjacent to the harbour, a 5 min walk downhill from Cullen village square.

CONTACT: Ruth or Howard
Tel: 01542 841997, Mob: 07432 591201(Ruth) 07912 079416(Howard)
ruth@cullenharbourholidays.com www.cullenharbourholidays.com
The Sailors Store, Portlong Rd, Cullen, AB56 4AG

Slochd Mhor Lodge is perfectly situated in spectacular Strathspey in the Cairngorms National Park, halfway between the villages of Carrbridge and Tomatin. The Lodge is on an 'off road' section of the No 7 Sustrans cycle route, surrounded by hills and forests. This is perfect walking country and in winter there are nordic ski trails from the doorstep. Slochd Mhor Lodge offers a genuine welcome in warm cosy surroundings with full central heating. Fully equipped kitchen and a spacious dining area together with large lounge/lecture room with woodburner, TV, WiFi, books and games. Other facilities include a drying room and laundry facilities, some en suite rooms, bedroom, shower and toilet suitable for wheel-chair users, on site cycle shop/workshop, MT bike hire and nordic ski hire. Locked bike shed. Coffee and tea. Outside seating and BBQ area. Ample parking. VisitScotland 4 star graded. Silver Green Tourism Award. Cyclists and Walkers Welcome.

DETAILS

- **Open** - All year, new arrivals 5-9pm. Checked in gets key.
- **Number of beds** - 22: 1x10, 1x6, 2x5, 1x2. Maximum 22 people.
- **Booking** - Booking recommended
- **Price per night** - £21, £20 for 2+ nights. Family rooms sleep 5 from £21 each. 2-12 yrs £15, under 2s free. Prices include bedding and linen. Towels extra. Sole use rates available for Christmas, New Year, clubs, meetings, courses etc.
- **Public Transport** - Nearest bus and train station Carrbridge (4miles). City Link London/Edinburgh and Glasgow/Inverness stop at Aviemore (11 miles).
- **Directions** - Northbound on A9, after mileage board 'Inverness 23' travel 1.5 miles, take first left marked 'Slochd', then first right after ¼ mile into large car park.

CONTACT: Liz or Ian
Tel: +44 (0)1479 841666
Slochd666@aol.com www.slochd.co.uk
Slochd, Carrbridge, Inverness-shire, PH23 3AY

INVERNESS
STUDENT HOTEL

Set amongst some of Scotland's most fascinating attractions, the bustling town centre of Inverness soon gives way to lochs, hills, forests and glens. Close to Inverness Castle, the cosy and friendly Student Hotel enjoys panoramic views of the town and the mountains beyond. After a hard day's Nessie hunting, the hostel provides the perfect place to unwind, just yards from the city's varied night-life and a few minutes' walk from bus and train stations. Relax in the fabulous lounge with real log fire and drink as much free tea, coffee & hot chocolate as you like. Knowledgeable staff can give you tips on what to see and do in the area and free WiFi is available. Visit the beautiful ancient pine forest of Glen Affric, tranquil but deeply historic Culloden Battlefield, the 4,000 year old standing stones at Clava Cairns or stroll down the riverbank to the waterfront to try to glimpse the wild dolphins in the nearby Moray Firth. Famous Loch Ness lies just a few miles upstream and of course has its own special wild animal.

DETAILS

- **Open** - All year, all day, reception 7am - 10.30pm.
- **Number of beds** - 57.
- **Booking** - First night's payment required to confirm booking.
- **Price per night** - From £15 per night. ID required for check in.
- **Public Transport** - Inverness train station and bus station are a mere 10 minute walk from the hostel. Alternatively jump in a taxi for around £5.
- **Directions** - From train/bus station left onto Academy St, take right down Inglis St. then right onto High Street, turn left onto Castle St past the castle. Continue up Culduthel Road and hostel is on right. By road take B861 over the river then follow the road round into Castle Street/Cuthuthel Road the hostel is on the right

CONTACT: Receptionist
Tel: 01463 236 556
info@invernessstudenthotel.com www.invernessstudenthotel.com
8 Culduthel Road, Inverness, IV2 4AB

LOCH NESS
SCOTLAND BACKPACKERS LODGE

Loch Ness Backpackers is a warm and friendly little hostel with a relaxed atmosphere, good music and no curfew. It has grown from an 18th century farm cottage and barn and provides a warm open fire to greet you on cold nights. The house forms the main area of the hostel with reception, bar and restaurant, lounge, dining room, kitchen and toilets/showers on the ground floor, and two dormitories and one double room in the upstairs area. A converted barn (the bunkhouse) contains four more dormitories, toilets/showers. There are two comfortable family rooms. There is also a great BBQ area, garden and car park. Loch Ness Backpackers is within easy walking distance of Loch Ness, Urquhart Castle, three pubs, restaurants, a supermarket, a fish and chip shop, post office, bank, gift shops and bus stops. A perfect location for activity or relaxation amongst spectacular scenery. Horse riding, fishing on the loch and mountain biking can all be arranged locally (great bikes available for hire).

DETAILS

- **Open** - All year. All day.
- **Number of beds** - House 16: Bunkhouse 24: (1x2, 2 x family room, 6 x dorms).
- **Booking** - Check availability on website or by phone.
- **Price per night** - From £17 per person. Discount applied to group bookings or long term stays.
- **Public Transport** - Nearest trains at Inverness. Rapsons and Citylink buses all pass close to the hostel.
- **Directions** - Near the A82 Inverness to Fort William road. Turn off is next to the stone bridge in Lewiston near the Poachers pub

CONTACT: Wendy and Neil MacIntosh
Tel: 07985 988015
info@lochness-backpackers.com www.lochness-backpackers.com
Borlum Bridge, East Lewiston, Drumnadrochit, Inverness, IV63 6UJ

MORAGS LODGE
LOCH NESS

A multi-award winning hostel with a range of rooms to meet all needs and budgets in the bustling village of Fort Augustus on the banks of Loch Ness. The perfect base to explore the Loch Ness area and an ideal stop off on the Great Glen Way. Surrounded by stunning mountain scenery and set in wooded grounds this is the perfect budget accommodation option in the hub of the Highlands! A variety of room types include dorms, doubles, twins, and family rooms; 24 hour self-catering facilitates, excellent home-made cheap meal options, a rustic bar stocked with a great selection of local beers and malts, a beer garden, free WiFi, bike hire, ample car parking, an awesome team to look after you, plus a whole lot more. FINALIST "Tourism Everyone's Business" 2015 & "Best Holiday Accommodation" 2014, WINNER 'Best Self Catering Accommodation' 2012 Highlands & Islands Tourism Awards. WINNER 'Team of the Year' Hospitality Assured Business Excellence Awards 2012. Member of Europe's Famous Hostels, 4 Star VisitScotland.

DETAILS

■ **Open** - Open all year. Check in from 4pm (earlier by arrangement).
■ **Number of beds** - 75: 1x7, 6x6, 6x4, 4x2/3
■ **Booking** - Booking recommended.
■ **Price per night** - From £22pp in dorm beds. Doubles/twins from £26pp. Family rooms from £78.
■ **Public Transport** - Bus stop for Fort William and Inverness only 200m away.
■ **Directions** - From north, arrive at Fort Augustus, turn first right up Bunoich Brae. From south through village past petrol station & car park. Next left up Bunoich Brae.

CONTACT: Claire
Tel: 01320 366289
info@moragslodge.com www.moragslodge.com
Bunoich Brae, Fort Augustus, Inverness-shire, PH32 4DG

GREAT GLEN
HOSTEL

Nestled between mountains and lochs in the heart of the "Outdoor Capital of the UK", 20 miles north of Fort William and 10 miles south of Loch Ness, the Great Glen Hostel is an ideal location whether you're touring the Highlands, bagging Munros or paddling rivers and lochs, and it is only a few minutes' walk from the Great Glen Way.

The hostel provides comfortable accommodation in twin, family and dormitory rooms. Hostel facilities include a self-catering kitchen, drying room, laundry, bike and canoe storage, free internet access, hot showers and a hostel store.

The whole hostel is available for exclusive rental for groups throughout the year.

DETAILS

- **Open** - All year, all day. Please call first Nov-March.
- **Number of beds** - 49: 3 x 2, 1 x 3, 4 x 5, 2 x 6, 1 x 8
- **Booking** - Booking recommended. Please telephone in advance or book online
- **Price per night** - Dorm beds from £18. Twin rooms from £22 per person. Whole hostel available for exclusive hire from £350 per night.
- **Public Transport** - Citylink bus services between Glasgow and the Isle of Skye, and between Fort William and Inverness will stop nearby. Nearest railway station: Spean Bridge. Nearest airport: Inverness.
- **Directions** - We are located 11 miles north of Spean Bridge and 3 miles south of Invergarry on the A82 in a small settlement called South Laggan. Citylink buses stop 100m north of the hostel on the A82. If you are walking the Great Glen Way, stay on the Way until you see signs directing you to the hostel.

CONTACT: Clem or Kirsty
Tel: 01809 501430
bookings@greatglenhostel.com www.greatglenhostel.com
South Laggan, Spean Bridge, Invernessshire, PH34 4EA

GLENFINNAN
SLEEPING CAR

Glenfinnan sleeping car provides unique, comfortable accommodation in an historic railway carriage adjacent to Glenfinnan Station. An ideal location for the mountains of Lochaber, Rough Bounds, Moidart and Ardgour.

Glenfinnan makes a great starting point for bothy expeditions and is a useful stopping-off point on the route to Skye. Why not use it also for extended stays using road or rail for trips to fishing, golf, ferries, cruises, and beach locations? The sleeping car has a fully equipped kitchen, showers, a drying room and total hydro-electric heating. The adjacent dining coach provides excellent meals to give you a break from self-catering.

Your overnight stay includes free admission to the railway museum housed in the station buildings.

DETAILS

■ **Open** - All year, 24 hours.
■ **Number of beds** - 10
■ **Booking** - Booking preferred and advisable to avoid disappointment.
■ **Price per night** - £15 pppn, £5 for hire of bedding and towels, £130 for exclusive use of whole coach.
■ **Public Transport** - Bunkhouse is adjacent to Glenfinnan Railway Station on the West Highland Line (Glasgow-Fort William-Mallaig) and is 100m from a bus stop.
■ **Directions** - On the A830, 15 miles from Fort William and 30 miles from Mallaig with ferry connections to the Small Isles and Skye.

CONTACT: John or Hege
Tel: 01397 722295
glenfinnan@btconnect.com www.glenfinnanstationmuseum.co.uk
Glenfinnan Station, Glenfinnan, nr Fort William, PH37 4LT

SHEENAS
BACKPACKERS LODGE SCOTLAND

The Backpackers Lodge, the oldest original croft house in Mallaig, offers a homely base from which you can explore the Inner Hebrides, the famous white sands of Morar and the remote peninsula of Knoydart.

Mallaig is a working fishing village with all the excitement of the boats landing. You can see the seals playing in the harbour waiting for the boats, whale and dolphin watching trips are available from the harbour. The hostel provides excellent budget accommodation with two rooms each with six beds, full central heating and fully equipped kitchen/common room with free WiFi. Scottish Tourist Board three star. All hot water and heating provided by renewable energy.

On site is the Tea Garden Café (open from 9am to 6pm March to November and 9am to 6.30pm June, July and August) serving quality meals, snacks, speciality coffee and home baking. See website for pictures of the restaurant and the beautiful countryside around.

DETAILS

- **Open** - All year, 24 hours.
- **Number of beds** - 12: 2 x 6
- **Booking** - Telephone ahead for availability and bookings.
- **Price per night** - £18 per person.
- **Public Transport** - Mallaig has a train station and services by Citylink coaches. For information on local buses phone 01967 431272.
- **Directions** - From railway station turn right, hostel is two buildings along.

CONTACT: Norman or Sheena
Tel: 01687 462764
backpackers@btinternet.com www.mallaigbackpackers.co.uk
Harbour View, Mallaig, Inverness-shire, PH41 4PU

GLEBE
BARN

Situated on the extraordinary Isle of Eigg in a charmingly converted 19th century building, the Glebe Barn offers 4 Star, homely hostel accommodation within 1 mile of the well stocked island shop and cafe/restaurant. The hostel boasts outstanding sea views, a well equipped kitchen, cozy log fire and wide range of books and games for all ages. Sleeping up to 22 in a combination of twin, triple, family and dormitory rooms, Glebe Barn is perfect for individuals, families or large groups. If you fancy more privacy an adjoining 2 person mezzanine apartment is also available. What better place than Eigg to relax or energise. A haven for nature and wildlife lovers, photographers or outdoor enthusiasts, with stunning beaches and coastal landscapes, traditional music sessions and exquisite local produce and cuisine, a magical Hebridean holiday.

DETAILS

- **Open** - Groups all year round; individuals from April to October. Open 24 hours.
- **Number of beds** - 22: 1x2, 2x3, 1x6, 1x8.
- **Booking** - Booking essential prior to boarding ferry. Deposit required.
- **Price per night** - £20(1-2 nights), £18(3+ nights). Twin room £45 (1-2 nights), £40 (3+nights), £36 (6+nights). Triple room £60 (1-2 nights), £54 (3+nights), £48 (6+ nights). Exclusive use: £330 (1-2 nights), £297 (3-5nights), £248 (6+ nights).
- **Public Transport** - Passenger ferry (1 sailing per day) from Mallaig with Caledonian MacBrayne or Arisaig (summer only). Check Caledonian Macbrayne or Arisaig Marine ferry timetables before booking beds. Eigg taxi contact 01687 482404.
- **Directions** - 1 mile from ferry pier. Take the shore road that forks right from the ferry pier. Pass a white cottage close to the road & continue uphill away from the bay. Take the track, signed Glebe Barn, on the right before reaching the church.

CONTACT: Tamsin or Stuart
Tel: 01687 315099
mccarthy@glebebarn.co.uk www.glebebarn.co.uk
Isle of Eigg, Inner Hebrides, PH42 4RL

Kintail Lodge stands at the foot of the Five Sisters of Kintail, right on the shores of Loch Duich. It is an ideal base for touring Skye and the Western Highlands or for bagging some of the 30 Munros in the area. In the grounds of the hotel there are two budget accommodation units which are especially popular with walkers, climbers and fishermen. The Wee Bunk House has a cosy room with bunks to sleep 6 people and a snack kitchen containing fridge, hot rings, kettle, microwave and basic cooking utensils. There is a shower room with a toilet and the building is wheelchair friendly. The Trekkers' Lodge sleeps 6 people in two twin rooms and two single rooms, each with their own washbasin. There are 2 shower rooms with toilets and a snack kitchen equipped as in the Wee Bunkhouse. After a long day in the hills you can unwind in the relaxed atmosphere of the traditional Kintail Bar, where good food is served, or enjoy the lochside garden and patio. Packed lunches available.

DETAILS

- **Open** - All year with winter restrictions. All day (restricted winter hours).
- **Number of beds** - Trekkers' Lodge 6: 2x2, 2x1, Wee Bunkhouse 6: 1x6.
- **Booking** - Book by phone or email with credit card details.
- **Price per night** - £17.00pp, 3+ nights £16.50pp. Sole use of Trekkers' Lodge £95, Sole use of Wee Bunkhouse £90. Duvet and towel £6.50. Full Scottish breakfast in the hotel £15.00. Continental breakfast in hotel £10.00.
- **Public Transport** - See Citylink website. Inverness to Skye or Glasgow to Skye.
- **Directions** - Kintail Lodge is situated on the A87 between Invergarry and the Isle of Skye Bridge.

CONTACT: Reception
Tel: 01599 511275
reception@kintaillodgehotel.co.uk www.kintaillodgehotel.co.uk
Kintail Lodge Hotel, Glenshiel, Kyle of Lochalsh, Ross-shire, IV40 8HL

SKYE
BACKPACKERS

Skye Backpackers sits in the picturesque fishing village of Kyleakin, skirted by mountains and sea. It's a small, cosy hostel with an open fire in the lounge and a lovely backyard garden. Whether you are coming to Skye to tackle the mighty mountains, meet the legendary faeries or simply want somewhere relaxed and comfortable to chill out, Skye Backpackers has everything you will need to ensure that you make the most of your time on this magical island.

The hostel has dorm, double and twin rooms and all beds come complete with sheets, duvets and 2 comfy pillows. There is also a fully equipped self-catering kitchen, a sunny dining area, as much free tea, coffee & hot chocolate as you can drink and free WiFi. Friendly & knowledgeable staff know all of the best places to visit and are on hand for you to ask them to help you plan your Skye adventure.

DETAILS

- **Open** - All year, all day. Reception 7am-12noon and 5pm-10pm (times may vary).
- **Number of beds** - 39
- **Booking** - Booking in advance not always essential, first night's payment required.
- **Price per night** - From £12 per night. ID required for check in.
- **Public Transport** - Trains at Kyle of Lochalsh, only a short bus ride (approx 10 mins) from the hostel. The bus drops opposite the hostel.
- **Directions** - From Kyle of Lochalsh go over the Skye Bridge then take first exit at roundabout, which takes you into Kyleakin. The hostel is on the right hand side after the Kings Arms Hotel. Park in the car park opposite hostel or in the grounds.

CONTACT: Receptionist
Tel: 01599 534510
info@skyebackpackers.com www.skyebackpackers.com
Benmhor, Kyleakin, Isle of Skye, IV41 8PH

BROADFORD
BACKPACKERS

Ideally located for enjoying the Isle of Skye, this child-friendly hostel is clean and cosy, with helpful staff for advice and information. There is a large kitchen for self-catering and a pleasant dining room overlooking the garden. The communal area has a TV and comfortable seating with plenty of board games and tea or coffee. Put in a lovely house cat and you've got yourself a home away from home. There are family rooms sleeping 4 (a double and two single beds), private double and twin rooms and small dorms sleeping 6 or 3. There is a bathroom with bath, a large garden and on-site parking. Cots and high chairs are available. Bedding and linen is provided and towels can be hired. From the hostel it is a short walk to the supermarket, shops, restaurants, beach and regular public transport, which connects Broadford with the rest of Skye and the mainland. Broadford Backpackers makes a perfect base for hiking, climbing, mountain biking and enjoying the spectacular scenery of Skye.

                BEST PRICE

DETAILS

- **Open** - All year, from 9.00 am to 10.30 pm.
- **Number of beds** - 38:1x7, 1x6, 1x4, 2x3, 2 x family, 2 x dbl, 1 x twin
- **Booking** - To book please telephone or email
- **Price per night** - Low Season: Dorm £15pp, double /Twin £40. High Season: Dorm £18.80, double /Twin £57
- **Public Transport** - Either: ferry from Mallaig to Armadale and a short bus ride; or any bus that is going to Skye will stop at Broadford (regular buses from Glasgow and Inverness); or train to Kyle of Lochalsh and then a short bus ride.
- **Directions** - From west on A87, in Broadford turn right onto High Road, then hostel is on right after 0.3 mile.

CONTACT:
Tel: 01471 820333
broadfordbackpackers@gmail.com broadfordbackpackers.blogspot.co.uk
High Road, Broadford, Isle of Skye, IV49 9AA

Raasay is considered a real 'hidden gem' for backpackers and budget travellers. Although off the beaten track there is a great ferry connection to the Isle of Skye and Raasay House itself is a mere stones' throw from the ferry terminal on the Raasay side. With a bus taking you direct to Sconser ferry terminal on the Isle of Skye there really isn't an easier way to step into a small authentic Hebridean island community before continuing your Isle of Skye itinerary. Hostel style rooms have the price tag of private and shared hostel rooms whilst having access the same facilities as the rest of the house. If you are happy climbing a couple of flights of stairs and a TV isn't top of your list of requirements then these simplistic rooms might be the option for you.

Raasay House is an out door activity centre so why not have a go at sea or loch kayaking, coasteering, climbing, sailing, abseiling or much more. Or maybe you just want to explore this idyllic, wildlife rich, island quietly on foot or bike.

DETAILS

- **Open** - All Year, 24 hour reception.
- **Number of beds** - 28: 1x2, 1x3, 1x4, 1x5, 1x6, 1x8
- **Booking** - Book online via the website
- **Price per night** - from £17 pp in dorm (not including breakfast)
- **Public Transport** - Citylink Coaches to Sconser ferry terminal. Train to Kyle of Lochalsh then city link to the ferry. Pick up from the ferry can be arranged.
- **Directions** - Ferry from Sconser on Isle of Skye. Follow road from ferry terminal, take first left then next right. Raasay House is on the left (7 min walk, 1 min drive)

CONTACT: Reception
Tel: 01478 660300
info@raasay-house.co.uk www.raasay-house.co.uk
Raasay House, Isle of Raasay, IV40 8PB

DUNARD
HOSTEL

Dunard is a warm, friendly, family-run hostel on the beautiful island of Barra in Scotland's Outer Hebrides. The hostel has a cosy living room with a lovely fire, hot showers and spacious kitchen. There are bunk, twin and family bedrooms. Situated in Castlebay, the hostel has views over the castle to beaches and islands beyond. Close to the ferry terminal, a handful of shops, and bars which often fill with live music. During the summer the island is alive for 'Feis Bharraidh' a gaelic festival of music, song and dance. Take time and explore this truly beautiful island with stunning white beaches, quiet bays where otters hunt and seals bask on rocks, dunes and meadows carpeted in flowers, and wild windswept hills home to golden eagles. Join one of our friendly guided sea kayaking trips and paddle amongst sheltered islands for really close-up wildlife encounters, hire a sit-on-top kayak, or experience the ultimate adventure of coasteering, (no experience needed). www.clearwaterpaddling.com

DETAILS

- **Open** - All year, except Christmas and New Year, all day.
- **Number of beds** - 18: 3x4 3x2
- **Booking** - Booking advised particularly in summer. Booking essential for groups.
- **Price per night** - £18 per person bunk room and twin cabin. £20 pp twin room. £60 per family room (sleeps 4). Private block booking from £295.
- **Public Transport** - The hostel is a 3 minute walk from the ferry terminal in Castlebay. If using a local bus ask to be dropped at the hostel.
- **Directions** - From ferry terminal in Castlebay head up hill, turn left and we are the third house past the old school (200m from terminal).

CONTACT: Katie or Chris
Tel: 01871 810443
info@dunardhostel.co.uk www.dunardhostel.co.uk
Dunard, Castlebay, Isle of Barra, Western Isles, HS9 5XD

N°5 Drinishader is located on the Isle of Harris, Outer Hebrides, 5 miles from Tarbert and 8 miles from the white sandy beaches. Situated above Drinishader Harbour, overlooking the beautiful East Loch Tarbert, the hostel and self-catering units provide a variety of accommodation for individuals, families and groups as well as activities.

The hostel has a cosy lounge with open fire, a well-equipped kitchen, shower, WC and comfortable beds. Pick-up services from Tarbert can be arranged for a small cost if there are no bus services. Among the activities guests enjoy are coastal/hill walking, cycling, kayaking, boat trips, sightseeing, bird/wild life watching or simply chilling out. Breakfast and packed lunches are available. Croft camping will be available from 2016. For full information on activities please visit the website.

DETAILS

- **Open** - All year, 0700-2300.
- **Number of beds** - 20
- **Booking** - Advisable to confirm beds, may require deposit.
- **Price per night** - From £20 per person. Reductions for families, groups and longer stay.
- **Public Transport** - Caledonian MacBrayne ferries (01876 500337) from Ullapool to Stornoway or from Uig (Skye) to Tarbert. Drinishader is a 10 min bus journey from Tarbert (01851 705050). Bus stop at hostel. There are 5 buses each day.
- **Directions** - From Tarbert follow the A859 south. After 3.5km turn left along the Golden Road. The hostel is located just above the small harbour in Drinishader.

CONTACT: Roddy or Alyson
Tel: 01859 511255
info@number5.biz www.number5.biz
Drinishader, Isle of Harris, HS3 3DX

OTTER
BUNKHOUSE

Otter Bunkhouse is on the shores of West Loch Roag, in Carishader on the Isle of Lewis. It offers a cosy hideaway with modern facilities for walkers, climbers, cyclists and anyone who enjoys unspoiled natural beauty and wildlife. There are two resident otters and an abundance of wildlife in the Loch including seals, divers, terns, eagles and the occasional dolphin. The bunkhouse is in a perfect position for stargazing and winter storm watching. You may be lucky enough to witness the awe-inspiring Northern Lights. The local area has many beautiful beaches ideal for surfing and kite surfing. The clear blue Atlantic waters provide a great feeding ground for marine mammals. The bunkhouse has a separate lounge with kitchenette facilities for self catering and a bedroom with 8 comfortable bunk beds with privacy partitions. Bedding is included in the price, and towels are available. There is an outside decking area, with stunning views over the Loch. Private access to the Loch for kayakers and ample car parking.

DETAILS

- **Open** - Open all year, all day access available.
- **Number of beds** - 8: 1 x 8
- **Booking** - Book by phone or email.
- **Price per night** - £20 per person. Sole hire of the bunkhouse is available.
- **Public Transport** - Flybe flights to Stornoway from Edinburgh, Glasgow and Inverness. Bus from Inverness to Ullapool connects with the Caledonian MacBrayne Ferry to Stornoway. Twice daily bus from Stornoway passes the bunkhouse.
- **Directions** - On the B8011 from Garynahine to Uig. At the far end of Carishader you will see a sign for Otter Bunkhouse on the right hand side.

CONTACT: Michele
Tel: 07942 349755
otterbunkhouse@gmail.com www.otterbunkhouse.com
Otter Bunkhouse, Carishader, Uig, Isle of Lewis, HS2 9ER

HOSTEL & BUNKHOUSE SCOTLAND

Part of the Gearrannan Black House Village, The Gearrannan Hostel was 'Taigh Dhonnchaidh' (Duncan's House) with its solid drystone walls and thatched roof. It has been newly refurbished inside to sleep 13 including a 3 bed family room.

The hostel (available to individuals) has a well equipped kitchen and cosy warmth from radiators heated with renewable energy. The bedrooms have cosy bunk-beds, and all linen is provided. There are two modern shower rooms. The bunkhouse (group only), Taigh Làta (John MacLeod's house) sleeps 14 in bunks, with heating, solid fuel stove, a kitchenette and hot showers. The perfect base for visitors to enjoy the many and varied local attractions from surfing at the local stunning beaches to country walks, archaeology, cycling, wildlife and more. Further accommodation available in Blackhouse holiday cottages. It is advisable to buy your provisions before arrival as there are no shops nearby.

DETAILS

- **Open** - All year.
- **Number of beds** - Hostel: 13: 1x10 1x3. Bunkhouse: 14: 2x6 1x2. Black houses: 1x2, 2x3-5
- **Booking** - advisable to be certain of availability, walk ins accepted if space is available. Book via website, phone or email.
- **Price per night** - From £15.00 per person. Family Room £47.00.
- **Public Transport** - Ferry service between Ullapool and Stornoway, or Uig (Isle of Skye) and Tarbert. Gearrannan is on bus route W2.
- **Directions** - Gearrannan is about 25 miles west of Stornoway, and about 45 miles north west of Tarbert. Follow signs for Càrlabhagh (Carloway) on the A858.

CONTACT: Mairi
Tel: 01851 643416
info@gearrannan.com www.gearrannan.com
5a Gearrannan Carloway Isle of Lewis HS2 9AL

HEB
HOSTEL

The Heb Hostel is a family-run backpackers' hostel in the heart of Stornoway on the enchanting Isle of Lewis. It is an ideal stop/stay for travellers visiting the Hebrides. Surfers, cyclists, walkers, families and groups are all welcome.

Clean, comfortable, friendly and relaxed, Heb Hostel aims to provide you with a quality stay at budget prices.

There are many facilities, including a common room with TV, peat fire, local guides and information.

DETAILS

- **Open** - All year, all day. New arrivals phone for access code if warden not around.
- **Number of beds** - 26: 1x8, 2x7,1x4 (family dorm).
- **Booking** - Booking is not essential but may be advisable at busier times. Deposits are only required for groups. Payment is due on arrival by cash or cheque.
- **Price per night** - £18 per person per night. Family dorm £72 for a family, £80 for adults only
- **Public Transport** - By plane: from Glasgow, Edinburgh or Inverness (Flybe), Aberdeen (Eastern Airways), Inverness & Benbecula (Highland Airways). By ferry (Caledonian McBrayne) Ullapool to Stornoway (Lewis), Uig (Skye) to Tarbert (Harris) or Berneray (Uists) to Leverburgh (Harris)
- **Directions** - From bus station: exit front door, cross South Beach St and walk up Kenneth St. Pass 1st intersection and we are 2nd on the right. From ferry terminal come out main exit, turn left, follow pedestrian walk-way to the bus station. From airport take bus to Stornoway bus station.

CONTACT: Christine Macintosh
Tel: 01851 709889
christine@hebhostel.com www.hebhostel.com
25 Kenneth St, Stornoway, Isle of Lewis, HS1 2DR

LAXDALE
BUNKHOUSE
SCOTLAND

Laxdale Bunkhouse is contained within Laxdale Holiday Park which is a small family-run park set in peaceful tree-lined surroundings. Located 1.5 miles away from the town of Stornoway this is an ideal centre from which to tour the islands of Lewis and Harris. Built in 1998, the bunkhouse has four bedrooms with four bunks in each room and caters for backpackers, families or groups looking for convenient, low cost accommodation. There is a drying room, a spacious fully equipped dining kitchen which provides two cookers, fridge and microwave and a comfortable TV lounge in which to relax. Toilets and showers are located within the building and are suitable for the disabled. Outside there is a covered veranda, picnic table and BBQ area. Sole use booking of the bunkhouse is available or you can book a room for your own use or book by the bed. Wigwams were a new addition in 2014.

DETAILS

■ **Open** - March to November 9am - 10pm.
■ **Number of beds** - 16: 4x4.
■ **Booking** - July and August booking advisable one week in advance.
■ **Price per night** - £18 adult, £16 child, £65 room (3 or less people) £250 sole use.
■ **Public Transport** - Buses every 30 mins stop close to hostel. Taxi fare from town centre approximately £5.00.
■ **Directions** - From Stornoway ferry terminal take the A857. Take the second turning on the left past the hospital. Follow camping signs for one mile out of town. The bunkhouse is located inside the holiday park. From Tarbert or Leverburgh take A859 for 40 miles to Stornoway. Turn left at the roundabout and 2nd left after hospital then as above.

CONTACT: Gordon Macleod
Tel: 01851 706966 / 01851 703234
info@laxdaleholidaypark.com www.laxdaleholidaypark.com
Laxdale Holiday Park, 6 Laxdale Lane, Stornoway, Isle of Lewis, HS2 0DR

LEDGOWAN LODGE
HOTEL & BUNKHOUSE

Ledgowan Lodge is a traditional country house hotel with cosy log fires, original features and friendly bar open to residents and non-residents. The bunkhouse is adjacent to the hotel and bunkhouse guests have full use of the hotel's facilities. Ledgowan Lodge is perfectly situated for the hill walker, climber or anyone wanting low cost basic overnight accommodation. It is within easy driving distance of the Torridon and Fannich Mountain ranges and Fionn Bheinn Mountain is on the doorstep. The bunkhouse sleeps ten adults in five separate rooms, each with a set of bunk beds, hand basin, chest of drawers and thermostatically controlled heating. There is a one off charge for providing pillow, 2 sheets and blankets. There is a bathroom with shower and a toilet. There are cooking facilities and a refrigerator for self catering, but it is recommended that guests socialise within the hotel where the welcome provides a restaurant, bar meals, real fires and lively conversation. There is ample car parking in the grounds and an excellent drying room within the hotel. Camping available.

              BEST PRICE

DETAILS

- **Open** - All year, all day.
- **Number of beds** - 10: 5 x 2
- **Booking** - Book by phone or email.
- **Price per night** - £17pp. £34 for sole use of 2 bed bunkroom. Linen £7 (one off charge). Camper vans and tents £6pp
- **Public Transport** - Achnasheen Station is one mile from the hotel/ bunkhouse.
- **Directions** - On the A890, 1 mile south of Achnasheen

CONTACT: Reception
Tel: 01445 720252
info@ledgowanlodge.co.uk www.ledgowanlodge.co.uk
Ledgowan Lodge Hotel, Achnasheen, Ross-shire, Scottish Highlands, IV22 2EJ

KINLOCHEWE
BUNKHOUSE
SCOTLAND

Walkers, climbers and mountain bikers enjoying the Torridon Mountains and wilderness areas will be delighted to find the Kinlochewe Hotel with its warm, welcoming bar and bunkhouse accommodation. There are over 20 Munros within 20 miles of Kinlochewe and the hotel provides a great base from which to explore them. The hotel bar is open all the year round, and serves excellent home-made food, a selection of real ales and over 70 malt whiskies. The bunkhouse is ideal for outdoor enthusiasts with a well-equipped self-catering kitchen, an efficient drying room, toilets and hot showers. There is one dormitory with 12 bunks (this makes it unsuitable for children). Each bunk has an individual locker and a pillow with pillowcase is provided (please bring your own sleeping bags, towels and padlock for the locker).

DETAILS

- **Open** - All year, 8am - midnight.
- **Number of beds** - 12.
- **Booking** - Essential for groups. Advisable for individuals.
- **Price per night** - £16.50 per person. Special offer: reduction for group bookings with sole occupancy for 2 nights or more
- **Public Transport** - Nearest train station is in Achnasheen (10 miles away). In summer trains run four times a day (twice a day on Sundays) from Inverness and the lunchtime train can be met by the local Dial-a-Bus which comes to Kinlochewe. Phone 01520 722205 for further details. On Tuesdays, Thursdays and Fridays the 5pm Westerbus from Inverness to Gairloch stops outside the bunkhouse at 6.45pm.
- **Directions** - Kinlochewe is situated at the junction of the A832 Garve to Gairloch road and the A896 north from Torridon.

CONTACT: Andrew and Gail Staddon
Tel: 01445 760253
bookings@kinlochewehotel.co.uk www.kinlochewehotel.co.uk
Kinlochewe by Achnasheen, Wester Ross, IV22 2PA

SAIL MHOR
CROFT

Sail Mhor Croft is a small rural hostel which is situated at Dundonnell on the shores of Little Loch Broom. The mountain range of An Teallach, which has the reputation of being one of the finest ridge walks in Great Britain, is right on the doorstep and the area is a haven for walkers of all experience as well as for photographers. Whether you wish to climb the summits, walk along the loch side, visit a beautiful sandy beach or just soak up the tranquillity of the area, you know the scenery cannot be beaten anywhere in the country.

The hostel offers accommodation for up to 16 persons in three dorms which are fitted with anti-midge screens during the summer. Bedding is provided (just need personal towel). It is advisable to ring in advance in order to book yourself a bed.

DETAILS

■ **Open** - All year except Xmas, New Year and January, flexible hours.
■ **Number of beds** - 16: 2 x 4: 1 x 8
■ **Booking** - Always phone in advance. Groups should book as soon as possible.
■ **Price per night** - £17.00 per person self-catering only. £215.00 per night sole occupancy.
■ **Public Transport** - Nearest train station is Inverness (60 miles). Nearest City Link bus drop off is Braemore Junction (15 miles). Wester bus passes the hostel 3 times a week; Mon, Wed and Sat. It also provides a service between Gairloch and Ullapool on Thursday afternoon.
■ **Directions** - GR 064 893 (sheet 19) 1.5 miles west of Dundonnell Hotel on A832.

CONTACT: Dave or Lynda
Tel: 01854 633224
dave.lynda@sailmhor.co.uk www.sailmhor.co.uk
Camusnagaul, Dundonnell, Ross-shire, IV23 2QT

BADRALLACH
BOTHY AND CAMPSITE SCOTLAND

On the tranquil shores of Little Loch Broom overlooking An Teallach, one of Scotland's finest mountain ranges, Badrallach Bothy and Camp Site, with its welcoming traditional buildings, offers a fine base for walking and climbing in the hills of Wester Ross, Caithness and Sutherland. You can fish in the rivers, hill lochs and sea, or simply watch the flora and fauna including many orchids, golden eagles, otters, porpoises, pine martens, deer and wild goats. Guests often sit around the peat stove in the gas light (there is now electric here too) and discuss life over a dram or two. Hot showers, spotless sanitary accommodation (STB graded 4 star excellent), an unbelievable price (thanks to S.N.H), and the total peace makes the Bothy and camp site (12 tents only) one that visitors return to year after year.

There is also a 4 star cottage and B&B, with breakfast/dinner served in our new eco-crofthouse. Hire canoes, kites, bikes, boats and blokarts.

              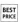

DETAILS

- **Open** - April-September, Access all day.
- **Number of beds** - 12 plus bedspaces (Alpine style platforms). We have had 20 at a squeeze, mats & sleeping bags required.
- **Booking** - Recommended.
- **Price per night** - £8pp, £2 per vehicle. £100 sole use.
- **Public Transport** - Westerbus (01445 712255) operate Mon/Wed/Sat between Inverness/Gairloch and drops at road end Dundonnell, 7 miles from hostel. Pick-up can be arranged.
- **Directions** - GR 065 915 Located on the shore of Little Loch Broom 7 miles along a single track road off the A832, one mile east of the Dundonnell Hotel.

CONTACT: Mr / Mrs Stott,
Tel: 01854 633281
mail@badrallach.com www.badrallach.com
Croft No 9, Badrallach, Dundonnell, Ross-shire, IV23 2QP

THE CEILIDH PLACE
BUNKHOUSE

The Ceilidh Place is a small complex consisting of a music venue/performance space, restaurant, hotel, bar, bookshop, coffee room, gallery and bunkhouse. There are regular ceilidhs and concerts (sometimes jazzy/classical) at the Ceilidh Place with visits from folk musicians and small touring theatre companies occuring regularly. The bunkhouse (group only) does not have self-catering facilities but the coffee shop is open from 8.30am to late evening, 7 days a week. It serves hot food, soups, salads, great coffee and cakes and is a super place to relax, read and write cards or memoirs. Rooms for individuals are also available in the hotel where there is a social living room area and balcony. The village of Ullapool is a small exciting port and fishing town, with ferries from the Outer Hebrides. The Ceilidh Place is in the centre of the village of Ullapool. It is also next to the camp site. The bunkhouse is much favoured by hill walkers and families as an ideal base for touring.

DETAILS

- **Open** - All year.
- **Number of beds** - Bunkhouse: 32
- **Booking** - Booking is advisable in summer.
- **Price per night** - Get in touch for prices.
- **Public Transport** - Nearest train station Garve (33 miles). Citylink coaches from Inverness stop at Ullapool pier a short walk from the Hostel. Phone (0990 505050) for details. Also leaving from the pier are ferries to Stornoway on the Isle of Lewis.
- **Directions** - Turn right after the pier and first left. Check in at Ceilidh Place reception.

CONTACT: Effie
Tel: (01854) 612103
stay@theceilidhplace.com www.theceilidhplace.com
14 West Argyle Street, Ullapool, IV26 2TY

INCHNADAMPH
LODGE
SCOTLAND

Situated at the heart of the dramatic Assynt mountains, Inchnadamph Lodge has been tastefully converted to provide luxury hostel accommodation at a budget price. Twin, family and dormitory (4-8 people) rooms are available and a continental-style breakfast is included. There is a large self-catering kitchen, a games room, a lounge and a dining room (both with real fires). Bar meals are usually available at the Inchnadamph Hotel just across the river. Based at the foot of Ben More Assynt, and overlooking Loch Assynt, visitors are free to explore one of the wildest areas in the Highlands. Mountains can be climbed from the door, there are caves and other exciting geological features in the Traligill river valley, and a wide diversity of birds, plants, animals can be found. Nearby lochs are popular for trout fly fishing. Details and photos are on the website.

DETAILS

- **Open** - Mid March to Mid November. 24 hours.
- **Number of beds** - 38: 8x2: 7x2: 4x2 (dormitory) 12 (twin/double).
- **Booking** - Strongly advised. No vacancies June 2016. From Nov-March booking is required as the hostel may be closed.
- **Price per night** - £19-£21(dormitory), £27-£32 (twin room) incl. continental breakfast and linen. Group discounts.
- **Public Transport** - Transport is available to the door from Inverness 6 days a week, by coach to Ullapool and minibus to Inchnadamph. Times vary - please call for details.
- **Directions** - Inchnadamph is 25 miles north of Ullapool on the Lochinver/Durness road. The lodge is the big white building across the river from the hotel.

CONTACT: Chris
Tel: 01571 822218
info@inch-lodge.co.uk   www.inch-lodge.co.uk
Inchnadamph, Assynt, Nr Lochinver, Sutherland, IV27 4HL

BLACK ROCK
BUNKHOUSE

Situated in beautiful Glenglass and sheltered by Ben Wyvis, this comfortable bunkhouse is named after the breathtaking Black Rock Gorge. It is an ideal base for touring the Highlands and seeing wildlife, including seals in the Cromarty Firth and dolphins at Cromarty. The bunkhouse is at the eastern end of a hikers' route across Scotland and on the Lands End to John O'Groats route for walkers and cyclists. The Highland Games are held throughout the area. The village has a general shop, Post Office, bus service and an inn (serving good bar meals and breakfasts) 250m away. Available to groups or individuals, accommodation is in four rooms of four. Sheets and duvets are provided free of charge. There is a self-catering kitchen and dining area with TV. Showers and launderette facilities are available on site. There is also a camping ground. All areas of the bunkhouse are easily accessible by wheelchair and suitable for the disabled.

DETAILS

■ **Open** - April 1st to October 31st, 24hr access. New arrivals 12noon - 9pm.
■ **Number of beds** - 16 : 4 x 4,
■ **Booking** - Not always essential. Deposit of 1 night's fee to secure booking.
■ **Price per night** - £13 - £15 per person. 10% off for groups of 8+.
■ **Public Transport** - Nearest train station Dingwall (6 miles). Nearest Citylink drop off Inverness (15 miles). There are local buses hourly.
■ **Directions** - Follow A9 north from Inverness, 2 miles north of Cromarty Firth bridge take left turn for Evanton. Follow camping signs.

CONTACT: Lillian
Tel: 01349 830917
janemacpherson@btconnect.com www.blackrockscotland.com/backpackers-bunkhouse
Evanton, Dingwall, Ross-shire, IV16 9UN

BUNKHOUSE
@ INVERSHIN HOTEL

A small hotel in the north Highlands run by a young family. The bunkhouse is situated within the hotel and consists of 4 rooms which share a shower room and toilet. Guests can use the large, comfortable, reception area and the cosy wee bar where the fire is always lit, and enjoy an evening meal and a real cask ale. Situated on the main route north if wanting to avoid the A9, and ideally placed to reach the far north, as well as both east and west coasts. Cyclists, walkers, bikers, fishers, munro baggers, families, groups, and lone travellers are all welcome. Breakfast: tea/coffee, cereal, toast, homemade jam/marmalade,(£5) or fully cooked (£10), is served in the conservatory with views overlooking the Kyle of Sutherland. Bed linen is included but not towels. There are no self-catering facilities available, however breakfast and a small selection of home cooked meals in the evening are available. Discount for parties of 6 or more, please enquire when booking. Some spots at the back of the hotel for campers. Free WiFi within the hotel public areas.

DETAILS

- **Open** - April - end October. Check in from 4pm.
- **Number of beds** - 10 1x double, 1x twin, 2x triple (bunkbeds)
- **Booking** - Please call for any booking enquiries or questions.
- **Price per night** - £20pp. Breakfast: £5 or £10. Discount for groups 6 or more.
- **Public Transport** - Train daily to Inverness from Invershin station (30 secs walk from hotel). The local bus to Tain stops outside the hotel. Connecting buses to Inverness from Tain. Approx 1 hour 20 minutes drive from Inverness Airport.
- **Directions** - on the A836 from Bonar Bridge to Lairg beside the railway bridge.

CONTACT: Angus or Cheryl
Tel: 01549 421 202
enquiries@invershin.com www.invershin.com
Invershin Hotel, Lairg, Sutherland, IV27 4ET

SLEEPERZZZ.COM

Stay on a first class train in Rogart in the heart of the Highlands, halfway between Inverness and John O'Groats. The three railway carriages have been tastefully converted, with many original features. One sleeps 8, one sleeps 6 and one is subdivided to sleep 4 and 2. There are two beds per room, and a kitchen, dining room, sitting room, showers and toilets. The carriages are heated and non-smoking. All bedding is included. There is also a cosy showman's wagon which sleeps 2. Four trains per day in each direction serve this small crofting community which has a shop, post office and pub with restaurant. Glenmorangie and Clynelish distilleries, Dunrobin Castle and Helmsdale's Heritage Centre are easy to reach by train or car.

See the silver salmon leap at Lairg and the seabirds and seals in Loch Fleet. Or just enjoy the peace of Rogart. The climate is good and the midges are less prevalent than in the west! Families welcome. Free use of bikes for guests.

DETAILS

■ **Open** - March to September inclusive, 24 hours.
■ **Number of beds** - 22: 1x8, 1x6, 1x4, 2x2
■ **Booking** - Booking is advisable
■ **Price per night** - From £17 per person, 12yrs and under £12 per person. (10% discount if you arrive by cycle or train).
■ **Public Transport** - Wick to Inverness trains stop at the door.
■ **Directions** - We are at the railway station, 4 miles from the A9 trunk road, 54 miles north of Inverness.

CONTACT: Kate
Tel: 01408 641343   Mobile/Text: 07833 641226
kate@sleeperzzz.com www.sleeperzzz.com
Rogart Station, Pittentrail, Sutherland, Highlands, IV28 3XA

HELMSDALE
HOSTEL
SCOTLAND

Helmsdale Hostel is temporarily closed for refurbishment. It will be reopening in 2017 and is taking bookings. Set in the scenic coastal village of Helmsdale (halfway between Inverness and John O'Groats), the hostel offers spacious en suite accommodation including fully equipped kitchen and comfortable lounge area with log burning stove plus a large garden area. On the main Land's End to John O'Groats route, the hostel is popular with 'end to enders' and walkers exploring the Far North Marilyn hills such as Morven and Scaraben. An ideal stop when travelling to and from Orkney and great location for beach walks, archaeology, geology, mountain biking, horse riding, fishing, bird and wildlife watching. Dogs welcome on request (private rooms only). Groups welcome any time. Discount for sole use of the hostel during the months of April and October.

DETAILS

■ **Open** - Closed for refurbishment. Re-opening in 2017.
■ **Number of beds** - 24: 2x8, 2x4
■ **Booking** - Advance booking not essential - book on line, by email or phone.
■ **Price per night** - Adults from £19. Children from £12. En suite rooms from £50. During April & October sole use of the hostel is available for groups for £350 per night with a minimum of 3 nights booking.
■ **Public Transport** - Helmsdale is served by the City Link bus service and is on the railway line from Inverness to Thurso.
■ **Directions** - The hostel is situated on the corner of the A9 and Old Caithness Road. From bus: walk up the slope for 100 metres. The Hostel is after the old church on your left. (200 metres). From train: Cross over the old bridge, turn right along Dunrobin Street, then left up Stafford Street. Hostel is 200m up the slope on the left.

CONTACT: Irene
Tel: 07971 516287 or 07778 377078
info@helmsdalehostel.co.uk www.helmsdalehostel.co.uk
Helmsdale Hostel, Stafford Street, Helmsdale, Sutherland, KW8 6JR

CORNMILL
BUNKHOUSE

Cornmill Bunkhouse is situated on a traditional croft which has been in the family for many generations. The croft runs ewes, spring-calving cows, and grows winter feed and woodland. The mill was built in the early 1800s and was active until around 1926. It has been converted into 4 star affordable and comfortable accommodation for individuals or groups. The bunkhouse can sleep up to 14 people. It has a large self-catering kitchen and open-plan sitting room on the first floor, in which the old grinding wheel now serves as a coffee table. There is level access to the first floor at the rear of the building, with an easy going stair down to the ground floor, which has two bunk rooms, a disabled access toilet/wetroom and a toilet with a shower. The first bunk room sleeps 8. The second sleeps 6 and has a patio door looking onto the workings of the old mill with its large wooden cog driving wheels. Activities can be organised for groups including Laser Tagging, Shooting and Clippage. Hen and Stag parties welcome. Come and enjoy this historic setting. 4 star tourist board graded.

DETAILS

- **Open** - All year, advanced notice required 1st Oct - 1st April. all day.
- **Number of beds** - 14: 1x8,1x6
- **Booking** - Please enquire for availability by phone or email.
- **Price per night** - £15 per person. Discounts available for group bookings.
- **Public Transport** - Forsinard railway station is only 10 miles away. The line runs from Inverness to Wick, stopping at Forsinard three times a day.
- **Directions** - The Cornmill Bunkhouse is located on the A897, 6 miles from Melvich, 20 miles to Thurso, 42 miles to John O'Groats and 34 miles to Helmsdale.

CONTACT: Sandy Murray
Tel: 01641 571219   Mob: 07808 197350
sandy.murray2@btinternet.com www.achumore.co.uk
Cornmill Bunkhouse, Achumore, Strathhalladale, Sutherland, KW13 6YT

KYLE OF TONGUE
HOSTEL & HOLIDAY PARK SCOTLAND

Kyle of Tongue Hostel is a stone lodge, magnificently situated on the romantic shores of the Kyle of Tongue on the north coast of Scotland. It has supreme panoramic views of Castle Varich, Ben Hope and the queen of Scottish mountains - Ben Loyal.

The hostel is relaxed and welcoming with irresistible home baking on offer. Beautifully furnished, like a boutique hotel, but with all the friendliness of a hostel. There are comfortable private bedrooms, roomy shared dormitories and relaxing communal areas. Relax in the lounge, well equipped dining area or the spacious self-catering kitchen. There is a drying room and bike shed for your outdoor gear and an onsite well stocked mini shop. Camping also available.

The atmosphere of this remote area is quite special. To truly leave the hustle and bustle of life behind, you must escape to the very edge of Scotland.

DETAILS

- **Open** - Open all year, check in from 4pm.
- **Number of beds** - 36:
- **Booking** - Book via e-mail or telephone.
- **Price per night** - Dormitory beds from £17, Private rooms from £39.
- **Public Transport** - Train station - 37 miles. Public bus routes through Tongue, Ferry terminal (Scrabster) - 45 miles
- **Directions** - Situated on the A838 road in the village of Tongue, in the north of Scotland within the Scottish Highlands

CONTACT: Richard Mackay
Tel: 01847 611789
kothostelandhp@btinternet.com www.tonguehostelandholidaypark.co.uk
Kyle of Tongue Hostel & Holiday Park, Tongue, By Lairg, Sutherland, IV27 4XH

HAMNAVOE
HOSTEL

On the Stromness waterfront, a short distance from the ferry terminal, Hamnavoe Hostel makes an ideal base for your visit to Orkney. It has single, twin, twin en suite and family rooms. The rooms have easy access to the shower, bathroom and toilet on each floor. All bedrooms are fitted with hand basins, pine bunk beds and have stunning views out across Hamnavoe. The light and airy kitchen is well appointed with two cookers, microwave, double fridge, fridge freezer and a large dining table allowing you to enjoy your meals whilst taking in the fantastic views of the Stromness harbour and marina. The lounge has comfortable seating, freeview TV, DVD's and a stock of books. The laundry room has a coin operated washing machine and tumble drier. The hostel has WiFi internet connection throughout. Entry to the hostel is by a coded door lock and individual rooms have keys. Free long stay car park is available in front of the hostel. Come and visit the nearby islands of Graemsay and Hoy, check out the World Heritage Sites or just relax in the tranquillity of island life.

DETAILS

- **Open** - All year, all day. No curfew, check in from 2pm and check out by 10am. Reconfirm your booking by 7pm on the scheduled date of arrival.
- **Number of beds** - 13: 1x4, 1x1, 4x2.
- **Booking** - Book with deposit of first night, re-confirm by 7pm on the arrival day.
- **Price per night** - From £20pp. Private rooms £22.
- **Public Transport** - Orkney Ferries run to Stromness ferry terminal. There is a regular bus service to and from the town of Stronmness from the terminal.
- **Directions** - On the waterfront a short walk from Stromness ferry terminal.

CONTACT: Mr George Argo
Tel: 01856 851202
info@hamnavoehostel.co.uk www.hamnavoehostel.co.uk
10a North End Road, Stromness, Orkney, KW16 3AG

BROWNS
HOSTEL AND HOUSES SCOTLAND

Brown's Hostel and Houses make ideal bases for your stay in Orkney, situated close to all amenities and just 3-5 minutes' walk from the bus and ferry terminal. Stromness is a small friendly town full of character, has a museum, art centre, scuba diving, free fishing, golf, festivals etc. The hostel is within walking/cycling distance of the historical sites at Maeshowe, Standing Stones, Ring of Brodgar, Skara Brae etc.

Self catering accommodation is offered nightly or weekly. Facilities include fully equipped kitchens and sitting rooms and accommodation is in single, double, twin, triple and family rooms from the smaller to the very comfortable en suite bedrooms, all with bed linen and towels provided. All properties have computer/ internet access and WiFi. There is a shed for cycle storage and free car parking up the lane.

DETAILS

- **Open** - All year, all day. No curfew, keys provided.
- **Number of beds** - 28: 3x1; 4x2; 3x3; 2x4
- **Booking** - Booking advisable especially if wanting private rooms.
- **Price per night** - From £20.
- **Public Transport** - Train or bus to Thurso, bus 2 miles to Scrabster then boat to Stromness. Alternatively from Gills Bay to St Margarets Hope by boat or John O'Groats by boat to Burwick then bus to Stromness via Kirkwall.
- **Directions** - Brown's accommodation is just three minutes' walk along the street from the Stromness ferry terminal and bus stop.

CONTACT: Sylvia Brown
Tel: 01856 850661
info@brownsorkney.co.uk www.brownsorkney.co.uk
45/47 Victoria Street, Stromness, Orkney, KW16 3BS

ORCADES
HOSTEL

Welcome to Orcades Hostel in Kirkwall. A warm and friendly welcome awaits you at this modern, comfortable 4 star hostel which makes an excellent base for exploring the beautiful Orkney isles.

The family who run the hostel have carefully considered the guest's comfort to create a homely feel. Accommodation is in doubles, twins, 4 and 6 bedded rooms (mixed or single sex). All of the bedrooms have en suite toilet/shower rooms, TVs and all bedding is provided. There is a stylish kitchen fully equipped, including oils and spices for cooking. The lounge has a DVD player, XBOX 360, lots of board games and books and free internet access. There is WiFi throughout the building. Welcome to Orcades Hostel in Kirkwall.

DETAILS

■ **Open** - All year. Check in after 2pm. Check out by 10.30am on day of departure.
■ **Number of beds** - 34: doubles, twin, 4,and 6 bed
■ **Booking** - Book by email or phone. Credit or debit card details must be given to secure bookings.
■ **Price per night** - £20 pppn in a shared room, £26 pp in a double or twin room (£52 for the room), £40 for single occupancy of a double/twin room. Winter rates available
■ **Public Transport** - Kirkwall is the centre for buses on mainland Orkney and the harbour is the hub for ferries to the Northern Isles.
■ **Directions** - Take Pickaquoy Rd from roundabout at the west side of the waterfront. Proceed for 300m, turn left onto Muddisdale Rd and hostel is after 500m.

CONTACT: Erik or Sandra
Tel: 01856 873745
orcadeshostel@hotmail.co.uk www.orcadeshostel.com
Muddisdale Road, Kirkwall, KW15 1RS

OBSERVATORY
HOSTEL

The North Ronaldsay Bird Observatory is situated at the south west corner of the island with outstanding views and an adjacent shell sand beach. Seals and the unique seaweed-eating sheep are abundant along the coast which skirts the 34 acres of croft managed by the observatory. The observatory sees spectacular bird migration through the island in spring and autumn. It offers a special attraction for those interested in wildlife, but welcomes all visitors. The Observatory Hostel consists of three dormitories and a self-catering kitchen in a converted barn and byre of the croft. The Byre sleeps four in two bunks and has en suite washing, shower and toilet facilities, great for family use. The Barn also sleeps four and shares facilities with the Bøl which has a single bunk sleeping two. Adjacent is the Observatory Guest House (3 star) which has a lounge bar and meals which are available to hostellers. Camping and grocery shop on site.

DETAILS

- **Open** - All year, 24 hours, open all day, no curfews.
- **Number of beds** - 10: 2x4, 1x2; guest house: en-suite rooms.
- **Booking** - Advance booking essential.
- **Price per night** - Hostel £17.50-£18.50. Half board in hostel from £37. Guest house private rooms £55 - £72.50 half board.
- **Public Transport** - Loganair flights from Kirkwall (Orkney) leave daily. Ferry from Kirkwall on Fridays and between May-Sept also on Tuesdays (subject to tides and weather). Small boats may be chartered. Orkney can be reached by vehicle ferries from Aberdeen, Thurso (Scrabster) and Gill's Bay, and a passenger summer service from John O'Groats.
- **Directions** - Situated at the south west corner of the island

CONTACT: Duty Warden
Tel: 01857 633200
bookings@nrbo.prestel.co.uk www.nrbo.co.uk
NRBO, North Ronaldsay, Orkney Islands, KW17 2BE

Gardiesfauld Hostel is on Unst, the most northerly of the Shetland Isles. The island has spectacular cliffs sculpted by the Atlantic Ocean on the west and secluded, sandy beaches on the east with rocky outcrops where seals and otters appear. The Gulf Stream provides a moderate climate and offers an invigorating chance to relax in a community where crime is unknown. During the summer enjoy long hours of daylight and the twilight of the "simmer dim" while in winter the long nights provide the backdrop for a vibrant cultural life. Situated on the picturesque shore at Uyeasound, this refurbished hostel combines superb facilities with a relaxed atmosphere. There is a kitchen, dining room, lounge, conservatory, coin operated laundry, showers (coin operated) and rooms with en suite facilities. A 5 berth caravan site is a busy addition as well as a large garden to pitch your tent.

DETAILS

- **Open** - April to October. Open in winter for pre-bookings, open all day.
- **Number of beds** - 35: 1x11, 2x6, 2x5, 1x2
- **Booking** - Book by phone or email
- **Price per night** - Adults £15pp, children £8pp. Camping from £6. Hook ups £15
- **Public Transport** - Ferry from Aberdeen to Shetland (Northlink Ferries). The bus meets the ferry and continues to Unst. Ask for Uyeasound. Flights to Lerwick (BA). From Fetlar catch 7:55am ferry from Oddsta (Bus meets ferry)
- **Directions** - Take the A970 north from Lerwick to Voe then the A968 north to Toft . Take the ferry from Toft to Ulsta in Yell. Take the A968 north to Gutcher. Take the ferry from Gutcher to Belmont. Follow the A968 north and head into Uyeasound (B9084). Follow the road to the pier and look out for the hostel sign board.

CONTACT: Warden
Tel: 01957 755279
enquiries@gardiesfauld.shetland.co.uk www.gardiesfauld.shetland.co.uk
Uyeasound, Unst, Shetland, ZE2 9DW

The Shetland camping böd network offers low cost accommodation in nine historic buildings with fantastic scenery - giving the opportunity to tour these beautiful islands, staying in böds en route. Due to the böd's historic nature, no two buildings are the same and facilities vary. The smallest böd sleeps four and the largest sixteen. Electricity, hot water and showers are available in six of the nine buildings and solid fuel stoves and mains water in all. Each böd has a story to tell, for example Voe Sail Loft was once a knitwear workshop, where the jumpers for Sir Edmund Hillary's expedition to reach the peak of Mount Everest in 1953 were produced. Seven out of nine have local meals available within two miles and seven out of nine have (variable) facilities for less able people. Under 16s must be accompanied by an adult. No pets allowed. Explore Shetland on a budget - bed down in a böd. For further info log onto: www.camping-bods.co.uk.

DETAILS

■ **Open** - 1st March – 31st October. Böds are unmanned. Contact custodian up to 9pm on day of entry.
■ **Number of beds** - 4 to 16 (depending on böd).
■ **Booking** - Booking is not essential however, as böds are unmanned it is best to book in advance to ensure the custodian is available before arrival.
■ **Price per night** - £8 to £10 pp. Group discounts are also available.
■ **Public Transport** - Information on public transport within Shetland: www.shetland.gov.uk/transport/. Information on cycle and car hire: http://visit.shetland.org/car-and-bike-hire
■ **Directions** - Ferry from Aberdeen to Shetland (NorthLink). Flights to Shetland from Orkney, Inverness, Aberdeen, Edinburgh and Glasgow (Flybe).

CONTACT: Reception
Tel: 01595 694688
info@shetlandamenity.org www.camping-bods.co.uk
For info: Shetland Amenity Trust, Garthspool, Lerwick, Shetland, ZE1 0NY

Lakeland Camping Barns

www.lakelandcampingbarns.co.uk

Dry camping in prime locations around the English Lake District. Camping barns offer the opportunity to stay in restored farm buildings at affordable prices. Experience Cumbria's stunning lakes and lofty peaks literally from your doorstep. All the barns are unique and offer differing facilities. Visit our website to take our virtual tours.

We look forward to welcoming you and your families and friends in 2016.

Barn	Facilities	Page
St John's-in-the-Vale Camping Barn	OPEN 6 PUB 2 🚿 🐾 💡 🚰 🔥 BBQ	247
Bents Camping Barn	OPEN 6 PUB 2 💡 ⚡ 🍳 BBQ 🔥	204
Catbells Camping Barn	🍴 OPEN 2 PUB 1 🚿 💡 🚽 🚰 ⚡ 🔥	252
Swallow Barn Camping Barn	OPEN 3 PUB 1 🚿 🐾 💡 🚽 🚰 BBQ 🔥	256
Murt Barn Camping Barn	OPEN 4 PUB 2 🚿 💡 🚰 ⚡ BBQ 🔥	
Cragg Barn Camping Barn	OPEN 5 PUB 2 🚿 💡 🚰 🔥	
Dinah Hoggus Camping Barn	OPEN PUB 2 🚿 🐾 💡 🚽 🚰 🔥 ⚡ BBQ 🍳	
Fell End Camping Barn	OPEN 3 PUB 2 🔥 🔥 BBQ 🔥	
Hudscales Camping Barn	OPEN 2 PUB 2 🚿 🚰 ⚡ 🔥 BBQ 🍳	
Wythmoor Farm Camping Barn	🚿 🐾 💡 🚰 ⚡ ♿ BBQ 🍳 💡	205

SYMBOLS

🍴 Breakfast bookable in advance

OPEN Shop (miles)

PUB Pub (miles)

🚿 Shower

🐾 Pets by arrangement

💡 Electric lighting

🚽 Toilets not in main building

🚰 Hot water

🔥 Campfire

⚡ Powerpoints

♿ Disabled facilities

🔥 Wood burning stove

BBQ BBQ aea

🍳 Cooking facilites

🔥 Heating

COME AND STAY DIFFERENT IN SWISS HOSTELS!

Quality independent Hostels and low budget hotels in Switzerland. We offer accommodation for individual travellers, families and groups. Checking-in at one of over 30 Swiss Hostels, we will make

OVER 30 HOSTELS IN SWITZERLAND

7050	Arosa, Mountain Lodge Arosa, info@arosamountainlodge.ch	0041 81 378 84 23
6677	Aurigeno, Baracca Backpacker, info@baracca-backpacker.ch	0041 79 207 15 54
3011	Bern, Backpackers Hotel Glocke, info@bernbackpackers.ch	0041 31 311 37 71
2560	Biel/Nidau, Lago Lodge, sleep@lagolodge.ch	0041 32 331 37 32
8784	Braunwald, Adrenalin Backpackers Hostel, info@adrenalin.gl	0041 79 347 29 05
1874	Champéry, Le Petit Baroudeur Backpacker, info@lebaroudeur.ch	0041 24 479 14 07
7002	Chur, JBN Just be Nice Hostel, info@justbenice.ch	0041 81 284 10 10
1202	Geneva, City Hostel Geneva, info@cityhostel.ch	0041 22 901 15 00
1202	Geneva, Geneva Hostel, info@genevahostel.ch	0041 22 732 62 60
3826	Gimmelwald, Mountain Hostel, mountainhostel@tcnet.ch	0041 33 855 17 04
3818	Grindelwald, Mountain Hostel Grindelwald, info@mountainhostel.ch	0041 33 854 38 38
6086	Hasliberg-Reuti, C'est la Vie Hostel, info@cestlavie.ch	0041 79 765 02 53
3800	Interlaken, Backpackers Villa Sonnenhof, mail@villa.ch	0041 33 826 71 71
3800	Interlaken, Happy Inn Lodge, info@happy-inn.com	0041 33 822 32 25
3800	Interlaken, River Lodge, welcome@riverlodge.ch	0041 33 822 44 24
3800	Interlaken/Matten, Balmer's Herberge, mail@balmers.com	0041 33 822 19 61
3807	Iseltwald, Lake Lodge Iseltwald, lakelodge.iseltwald@gmail.com	0041 33 845 11 20

you feel home with our friendly and helpful staff.
People of all ages welcome. No membership required.

60 TOP QUALITY
INDEPENDENT HOSTELS
THROUGHOUT GERMANY

CASTLE NEUSCHWANSTEIN, FÜSSEN

INDEPENDENT
HOSTELS
OF GERMANY

BOOK WITH BEST
PRICE GUARANTEE HERE:

WWW.GERMAN-HOSTELS.DE

BENEFITS
FOR IHUK MEMBERS

Members are listed on our website, in this guidebook and on the Long Distance Walkers website.

We actively promote members accommodation on Twitter, Facebook, YouTube, Pinterest and Instagram.

Our group booking service promotes members' accommodation to group leaders and the IHUK stand tours the UK's leading consumer shows.

Active message boards host conversations between members and our emails keep them in touch with industry news.

IHUK signs let guests know that accommodation is in the IHUK network.

Official **(IH)** Member

Independent Hostels UK
The largest network of hostels,
bunkhouses & group accommodation
in England, Scotland and Wales

Independent Hostels UK is the largest network of bunkhouses, hostels and group accommodation centres in the UK.

The network's website is viewed by 140,000 individuals each year. The guidebook, is distributed by bookshops, Tourist Information Centres, hostels and at events.

To join IHUK visit:-
www.independenthostels.co.uk/advertise-your-hostel
or phone 01629 580427

INDEX

INDEX